Indian and Western Philosophies: Unity in Diversity

Indian and Western Philosophies: Unity in Diversity

FERNANDO TOLA
CARMEN DRAGONETTI

MOTILAL BANARSIDASS
SINCE 1903 IN INDOLOGY

MOTILAL BANARSIDASS PUBLISHERS
PRIVATE LIMITED • DELHI

2nd Reprint : Delhi, 2017
First Edition : Delhi, 2013

Earlier published as **On the Myth of the Opposition between Indian Thought and Western Philosophy** by Georg Olms Verlag AG, *Hildesheim 2004, Germany*

ISBN: 978-81-208-3509-2

MOTILAL BANARSIDASS
41 U.A. Bungalow Road, Jawahar Nagar, Delhi 110 007
8 Mahalaxmi Chamber, 22 Bhulabhai Desai Road, Mumbai 400 026
203 Royapettah High Road, Mylapore, Chennai 600 004
236, 9th Main III Block, Jayanagar, Bengaluru 560 011
8 Camac Street, Kolkata 700 017
Ashok Rajpath, Patna 800 004
Chowk, Varanasi 221 001

MLBD Cataloging-in-Publication Data
Indian and Western Philosophies: Unity in Diversity
by FERNANDO TOLA, CARMEN DRAGONETTI
ISBN: 978-81-208-3509-2
Includes, Introduction, References, Index
I. Philosophy, II. Tola, Fernando, and Dragonetti, Carmen

Printed in India
by RP Jain at NAB Printing Unit,
A-44, Naraina Industrial Area, Phase I, New Delhi–110028
and published by JP Jain for Motilal Banarsidass Publishers (P) Ltd,
41 U.A. Bungalow Road, Jawahar Nagar, Delhi-110007

DR. TSUGUNARI KUBO
Director of the *Zaike Bukkyo Kokoro no Kenkyūjo,* Tokyo,
with our respect, gratitude and friendship,
and with our admiration for what he has done
for the spread of the knowledge
of the noble teachings of the Buddha.

Preface to the Indian Edition

This book was published for the first time by Georg Olms Verlag of Hildesheim, Germany, in 2004. It bore the title *On the Myth of the Opposition between Indian Thought and Western Philosophy*. Its conclusion was that the opposition between both, "thought" for India and "philosophy" for the West, constitutes a fallacy grounded in an ethnocentric prejudice introduced by Hegel and followed by many European philosophers and books on Philosophy. It is our opinion that this is only "a myth" that deserves to be rejected, and that this rejection can open a new path for Philosophy as such leaving aside old, strong and too optimistic false ideas on it.

We avail of this opportunity of an Indian edition, given to us by the kind permission of Olms Verlag and the generous offer of N.P. Jain of Motilal Banarsidass, for referring to the positive opinion on "our task in rejecting the myth" expressed by one of the most important European Indologists today, Professor Ernst Steinkellner, in his review on that first German edition, published in *Wiener Zeitschrift für die Kunde*

Südasiens, Austria, in 2005, in which we kindly ask the reader of this book to rely.

We are perfectly aware that Indologists – as Professor Anand Amaladass says in his review on the book, published in *Journal of Intercultural Philosophy*, No. 6, August 2004 – could think that we are "labouring to prove the obvious". Let us say in this respect that in Western philosophical tradition this task we have proposed ourselves is not at all useless. Whosoever has studied Philosophy in a Western country knows that even now there are people and books *who still pass judgements on Indian thought without making the effort to examine the extensive literature available* (as Prof. Amaladass himself affirms in his review), and thus are still maintaining Hegel's opinion denying the existence of an Indian Philosophy as such considering that only European mind can create it. But our book has a larger intention: not only *to reject the absurd myth* which had its origin in Hegel, but also to make evident that for a better understanding of any Philosophy it is necessary to confront it with other philosophical traditions. This task does not mean at all to reduce one to the other, but on the contrary to have a more profound insight in both of them – insight derived precisely from that confrontation.

For many Westerners the "discovery" of what Indian philosophical thought in fact is, via the study of its texts and the prodigious labour carried out by Indology and Buddhology, could produce many good effects we point out in Chapter I of this book, i.e. in short: the elimination of a prejudice, the increase and enrichment of knowledge, and also the self-questioning of Western philosophy with regard to its own value, not in the limited context of a sole continent but in a much more extensive and universal. For many Indian scholars on Indology as well as on Philosophy this confrontation of their traditional philosophical ideas with other similar in the Western philosophical tradition could also help them understanding of their own traditions in a larger context. Let us insist here in the wise advice of the great philosopher Bhartṛhari we admire so much:

> *prajñā vivekaṃ labhate bhinnair āgamadarśanaiḥ/*
> *kiyad vā śakyam unnetuṃ svatarkam anudhāvatā//*

> "Intelligence acquires the faculty of distinguishing and classifying things according to their real properties through the study of different systems of thought transmitted by tradition. How can a man, limiting himself to his own reasoning, make it progress?"

Now we would like to extend here the expression of our deep thanks to the following persons and institutions for their varied support: first and foremost to the John Simon Guggenheim Memorial Foundation of United States of America that granted Carmen Dragonetti a Fellowship Award, 2004 for continuing our Project of the comparative study of both, Indian and Western Philosophies (what we are actually doing with other systems of Indian Philosophy), and to our friend Professor Dr. Mario Bunge, who confided in our project; again to Carlos Arturo Salamanca, our son-in-law and in heart, for his technical help in the preparation of the manuscript, and as always to our daughters: Eleonora and Florencia, and last but not least to our little and luminous granddaughter Lua, all of whom have in one way or another given us the necessary strength, energy and optimism to perform this task.

FERNANDO TOLA
CARMEN DRAGONETTI
Buenos Aires, January 2006
cldragon@retina.ar

Contents

Preface to the first edition

This book offers a few conclusions we have reached after many years dedicated to the study of Indian philosophy in which we asserted the possibility of the existence of Indian Philosophy in opposition to those scholars or professors of Western Philosophy who have negated it. This volume is an initial result of the broader research on Indian Philosophy, which we are carrying out using the criteria applied in this book.

We would like at this point to express our deep thanks to the following persons and bodies for their constant and varied support: first and foremost the National Agency for the Promotion of Science and Technology in Argentina; institutions such as the National Council for Scientific and Technological Research in Argentina; the Reiyukai in Tokyo and Mexico, The International Institute for Buddhist Studies, Tokyo, which made it possible for us to visit Japan and Mexico in order to give lectures and do research work; the Institute for Advanced Studies of World Religions of New York

University at Stony Brook, the Nyingma Institute at Berkeley, the Yin Shun Foundation in New Jersey, which invited us and allowed us to work at the University of New York, Berkeley University, Columbia University, The University of Michigan and Harvard University; the members and friends of Institute of Buddhist Studies Foundation in Argentina; our students, friends and colleagues in Latin America and abroad; Carlos Arturo Salamanca for his valuable technical help in the preparation of the manuscript of this book for printing; and finally our daughters, all of whom have in one way or another given us the necessary strength, energy and optimism to perform this task, which had its difficult moments.

FERNANDO TOLA
CARMEN DRAGONETTI
Buenos Aires, April 2003
cldragon@retina.ar

Introduction

... da der menschliche Verstand über unzählige Gegenstände viele Jahrhunderte hindurch auf mancherlei Weise geschwärmt hat, so kann es nicht leicht fehlen dass nicht zu jedem Neuen etwas altes gefunden werden sollte was damit einige Ähnlichkeit hätte.

E. KANT, Prolegomena, p. 1

The Four Theses: The question as to the existence of philosophy in India

The question as to the existence of Indian philosophy has not lost any of its validity. As J. Bronkhorst says in his article "Why is there philosophy in India?":

> "Many indologists are deeply concerned to show that there is such a thing as Indian philosophy. They are upset by the fact that most people in the modern Western world, including philosophers, do not expect to find such a thing in ancient India. India, common knowledge teaches, is a land of spirituality and wisdom, but not of hard-headed analysis and serious debate. This common knowledge dates to before the beginning of our era, and it is unlikely that it will disappear any time soon".

We agree with Bronkhorst's opinion but we would like to add here that there are some manifestations of a different way of thinking regarding that question. It seems that some scholars versed in Western philosophy are now beginning to consider that there was in fact such a thing as philosophical thinking in ancient India. We shall restrict ourselves here to mentioning seven great modern encyclopaedias of philosophy, which include articles on various notions proper to Indian systems of thought considered as philosophical systems by scholars of Indology. These encyclopaedias are:

1. José Ferrater Mora, *Diccionario de Filosofía*, Barcelona: Editorial Ariel, 1994.
2. Joachim Ritter *et al.* (edd.), *Historisches Wörterbuch der Philosophie*, Darmstadt: Wissenschaftliche Buchgesellschaft, 1971 ff.
3. Jürgen Mittelstrass *et al.* (ed.), *Enzyklopädie Philosophie und Wissenschaftstheorie*, Stuttgart-Weimar: Verlag J.B. Metzler, 1995 ff.
4. Edward Craig *et al.* (ed.), *Routledge Encyclopedia of Philosophy*, London and New York: Routledge, 1998.
5. Miguel Cruz Hernández (ed.), *Enciclopedia Iberoamericana de Filosofía*, Vol. 19, Madrid: Editorial Trotta / Consejo Superior de Investigaciones Cientīficas, 1999.
6. Denis Huisman, *Dictionnaire des Philosophes*, Deuxième édition, revue et augmentée, Paris: Presses Universitaires de France, 1993.
7. Franco Volpi (ed.), *Großes Werklexikon der Philosophie*, Stuttgart: Alfred Kröner Verlag, 1999.

Many of the articles on Indian philosophical notions included in these encyclopaedias were written by well-known Indologists.

Nevertheless, like Bronkhorst we are of the opinion that the general trend is to deny the existence of philosophy in ancient India.

A very odd element of the question as to the existence of Indian philosophy is that the great majority of persons who deny the existence of Indian philosophy do not know anything, or at most know only very little, about Indian thought as it was in the many centuries during which Indian culture existed. Serious knowledge of what was thought in ancient India is indispensable in order to answer this question; without that knowledge, an answer to it deserves no respect, cannot be taken into consideration and has no value – be it negative or affirmative. Nevertheless, as we have said, in the majority of cases ignorance with regard to Indian thought is a characteristic of those who deny the existence of Indian philosophy. We remember a well-known Italian professor of philosophy who, at an international congress of philosophy held in Buenos Aires some years ago, emphatically said that there was no such thing as Indian philosophy. We asked him which Indian texts he knew which could support his thesis. With some pride he answered that he knew none.

This fact is not surprising. Hegel, who dogmatically denied the existence of Indian philosophy and has inspired, and still inspires, many scholars to adopt a similar position, knew very little, if at all, about Indian philosophical thought. Besides his ignorance, his opinion was strongly influenced by his ethnocentric European prejudices and his fascination for all things Hellenistic. We shall deal at length with Hegel's opinion with regard to the existence of Indian philosophy in Chapter I of this book.[1]

If it is possible to say in favour of Hegel that, in his epoch, very little was known about Indian thought, whereas now our knowledge of Indian thought has increased enormously, thanks to the Indological work done during the last two centuries, and a very good bibliography is now available with which one can acquire a thorough and solid knowledge of what and how Indians thought – knowledge which, as we have said, is one of the principal requirements for answering the question as to the existence of Indian philosophy.

---

[1] Cf. F. Tola and C. Dragonetti, "What Indian philosophy owes Hegel", in *Annals of the Bhandarkar Oriental Research Institute,* Poona, India, 2003, and in Spanish in *Pensamiento,* Madrid, Spain, Vol. 58, núm. 222, 2002, pp. 353-385.

First, second and third theses maintained in this book

After a good number of years doing research work in what is considered by Indologists to be Indian philosophy, i.e. the systems of thought described by Haribhadra Sūri in his *Ṣaḍdarśanasamuccaya* and Mādhavācārya in his *Sarvadarśanasaṃgraha* or in any modern treatise on the history of Indian philosophy such as those by S. Radhakrishnan, S. Dasgupta, M. Hiriyanna, J. Sinha, P. Masson-Oursel, E. Frauwallner, H. von Glasenapp, etc. and on the basis of what we know about Greek and Western philosophies, we came to the conclusion that, up to the 17th century at least, in India on the one hand and in Greece and Europe on the other, there was frequent reflection on the same philosophical subjects, and it was carried out in the same way (**first thesis**). Until that epoch at least, we can find similar or identical philosophical problems, similar or identical approaches and similar or identical solutions to these problems in India, Greece and Europe.

Also, as a consequence of our study of Indian thought and due to our acquaintance with Greek, European and Indian philosophies, we also reached the conclusion that, in the history of Greek and European philosophies, we can find what is usually (correctly or incorrectly) called "manifestations of irrationality" in many forms (one of which is fanciful mental creation or imagination), and these are as numerous as they are in the history of Indian thought (**second thesis**), not only in the centuries corresponding to the ancient (Greek) and mediaeval (European) periods, but also in the centuries that came after. Greece and Europe have never been characterized by rationality only and India has never wholly submitted to irrationality. In both regions of the world, we can find the same mixture of dominant irrationality and limited rationality, which manifested itself only timidly and was not a predominant or excluding factor at all. The birth of Pallas Athena from the head of Zeus has never been an easy or rapid process.

Similar assertions can be made regarding freedom of thought and the search for truth for its own sake. Let us not forget that rationality, intellectual freedom and the search of truth for its own sake are considered to be the principal attributes of philosophical thinking. In India and in the West, there has been a similar submission to authority (tradition, religion) and a similar tendency to put philosophical reflection at the service of other interests, and in conjunction with these tendencies there have been various manifestations of intellectual freedom and efforts to search for the truth for its own sake.

If, in the history of Indian thought and of Greek and European philosophies, we can find similar subjects, approaches and solutions as well as a similar coexistence of irrationality, submission to authority and subordination of philosophical thinking to other aims in conjunction with the opposed attitudes, we are authorized to affirm that such a thing as Indian philosophy did exist in India (**third thesis**).

Comparison between Indian and Western doctrines

The exposition of the first two theses, which we have developed, implies a comparative activity, a confrontation of Indian and Western thought. With regard to this point, we must now make a few remarks on the limits of this activity.

Our intention is not to carry out a detailed comparative study of Indian doctrines and Greek or Western doctrines, which are apparently similar. This would require a deep and broad knowledge of Greek and Western thoughts on our part, which we do not claim to possess. Without going into details, we merely wish to point out some of the Greek or Western doctrines, which present similarities to Indian doctrines without taking into account the systems to which they belong.

In addition, we think that it is not possible to compare an Indian philosophical system as a whole with a Western system as a whole. In general, Indian and Western systems start from different postulates (such as re-existences and *anāditva* or beginninglessness on the Indian side as opposed to a unique existence and a first beginning in the Western systems), and this fact makes a comparison of both an impossible task. However, we think that it is possible to point out Greek or European doctrines, which constitute elements of Greek or European systems and present similarities to Indian doctrines, which are in turn elements of certain Indian systems.

Helmuth von Glasenapp used to say that systems of thought are like large mosaic paintings each one of which represents a different scene: all of them have many small pieces of material (glass, tiles, etc.) of similar or identical colour and form in common. It is impossible to compare a mosaic painting as a whole with another as a whole, but it is possible to discover identical or similar pieces in each of them. The same thing happens with philosophical systems: as wholes they may be utterly diverse, but it is possible to find doctrines that can rightly be compared in each of them. This is the sort of comparison which we think is necessary when we examine whether there was such a thing as philosophy in India or not.

A comparison, no matter how superficial, between Indian and Western doctrines, besides being necessary with regard to the problem of the existence of Indian philosophy, can help us to understand, accept and evaluate Indian thought under better conditions. This comparative procedure allows us to discover that Indian thought is not as remote from Western thought as is generally believed, since many things that were thought in India and may appear strange, exotic or even absurd to us were also thought in the West and enjoyed a profound acceptance for a long time. We recall the case of a professor of Western philosophy in Buenos Aires in this context. When he came to learn that the Indian Sāṃkhya philosophical system postulated the existence of two absolute principles – Spirit and Matter – he stated that this philosophical position was unacceptable a priori, but he finally accepted the possibility of such a thesis when he remembered that Manichaeism maintained a similar one.

There is no doubt that, without a thorough knowledge of what has been thought in India, how it has been thought, and which points of contact there are between philosophical Indian thought and philosophical Western thought, it is impossible to give a serious answer to the question as to the existence of philosophy in India. Without that knowledge, whatever is said on this question can only be the product of ignorance and prejudice. Unfortunately, this is generally the case with those persons who emphatically declare that philosophy only existed in Greece and in the West.

Chronological limits of the comparison: fourth thesis

With regard to the comparison between Indian and Western doctrines, there is one most important point which must always be kept in mind: the comparison between Indian and Western thought must limit itself to confronting both as they manifested themselves before the 17th century, or even in the centuries that followed, but in this case only when and if they maintained certain forms in extension of the philosophies found previous to that date (**fourth thesis**).

From the 16th century onwards, a series of factors appeared in the West, including the coming forth of modern science and the modern scientific mind, the discovery of the New World, the increase of European economic and military power, the weakening of ecclesiastical authority and the limitations it imposed on thinking, and the consciousness of the equality of individual rights and liberties. These factors gave a new course to universal history and led to modern culture. From the 16th century onwards, Western culture in all its expressions began to adopt a wholly novel form, which was different from all previously known forms and succeeded in imposing itself worldwide to differing degrees.

India has only taken part in this transformation in a profound way since the middle of the 20th century, when she got her independence from the British Empire. To compare Indian thought before the 16th or 17th centuries with Western thought following that date would be to compare two things, which belong to two completely incomensurable epochs as a result of the intrusion of the factors indicated.

We can compare Indian and Western thoughts under the chronological conditions indicated. In this way we can inquire as to what they have in common, what they have which differs and in which respect one of them stands out in relation to the other; we can inquire whether India anticipated certain theories (for instance in the field of epistemology and of idealism) and was able to adopt attitudes (for instance, with regard to freedom of thought and tolerance) which did not appear in the West until much later. This way of going about things will allow us to give a fairer and wiser answer to the question as to whether there is such a thing as Indian philosophy.

The achievements of the European Culture are indeed worthy of great admiration, but they must not make us forget, as it generally happens, the negative elements, which also characterized the history of Europe: fanaticism and intolerance, greed and ambition, abstruse and odd beliefs that with great frequency had recourse to actions of violence and aggressivity to impose themselves – and all this not only against foreign people but also against its own people, provoking thus cruel sufferings and deaths.

Let us point out – as examples and not intending to be exhaustive at all – among the negative aspects of the European Culture in its relation with the rest of the world: the violent appropriation of territories in the world, the boundless exploitation of the conquered or colonized people in the benefit of the European domains, the sadism manifested by the conquistadors, the carnage Europe produced by its conquest wars, famines and illnesses in the indigenous America, the extermination of redskins in North America, the transformation of India into a prey for the merchants of the East India Company, as if India's sole destiny was to be impoverished and plundered, the abandonment of Africa to its own fate once its coasts had been shamelessly exploited, and the scourge of slavery, which was defended by many jurists and theologians brandishing texts from Aristotle (*Politics* I, 2, 1253 b-1255 b) and Saint Thomas (*Summa Theologiae* II, II, 57, 2 and 58, 3, and *Summa contra gentiles* III, 81), and which in the inhuman traffic of slaves wrenched from their native land more than nine millions persons.[2] And, in short, almost all the world converted into an annex subordinated to European interests.

Europe was not less hard with its own children, as is demonstrated by the vast communities submerged in poverty, the exaltation of some members of the society, the only ones with right to enjoy the good and noble things of life, the bloody persecutions, caused by the difference of ideas and beliefs, carried out under the pretext of defending the most elevate values, and in fact concealing the lowest and most censurable feelings of greed and hatred, the constant fratricidal wars that emulated in ferocity the acts of violence by Assyrians and Mongols.

---

[2] Cf. Jean Meyer, *L'Europe et la conquête du monde*, specially pp. 192-218, and 343-347; and on the subject of European slavery: the article by E. Flaig, "Sklaverei", in *Historisches Wörterbuch der Philosophie*, Band 9, col. 976-985; N.S.H. Linguet, *Théorie des lois civiles*; Aimé Césaire, *Victor Schoelcher et l'abolition de l'esclavage*; Abbé Grégoire, *De la traite et de l'esclavage des noirs*; P. Gravatt, *L'Église et l'esclavage*; F. Renault et S. Daget, *Les traites negriéres en Afrique*; and P. Pluchon et P. Suteau, "L'exception coloniale", in *État et société en France aux XVII et XVIII siécles, sous la direction de J.P. Bardet, etc.* pp. 437-455; Olivier Pétré-Grenouilleau, *Les traits négriéres, Essai d'histoire globale*; Thierry Lentz, Pierre Branda avec la participation de Chantal Lheureux-Prévot, *Napoléon, l'esclavage et les colonies*, Paris: Fayar, 2006; Françoise, Vergés, *La mémoire enchaînée. Questions sur l'esclavage*; Christiane Taubira, *L'esclavage raconté á ma fille*; *Esclaves des Îles françaises*; Julia Ferloni, *Marchands d'esclaves. De la traite á l'abolition. Entretien avec Aimê Césaire par Jean Loiseau.* See also in the editions of Dalloz, 2006 and of Éditions Sépia, 2006, the execrable *Codes Noirs* (Black Codes) dictated by the French kings in the years 1685 and 1723, which make manifest the awful treatment the slaves received. Let us indicate that there is a bibliography by Joseph C. Miller, *Slavery and Slaving in World History. A Bibliography*, Millwood, New York: Kraus International Publishers, 1999, which is updated each year in the journal *Slavery and Abolition.*

On the structure of this book

It may seem paradoxical, but we shall begin this book (Chapter I) with a study of Hegel's opinion concerning the existence of philosophy in India. This study is included in the book because, as we have said, many Western philosophers are only repeating Hegel's opinion when they deny the existence of philosophy in India.

We think that, once we have eliminated the support on which this negative opinion is based, the reader will enjoy more freedom to form his or her own personal idea as to the question indicated, taking into account the information on some aspects of Indian and Western thought and the astonishing similarities between them which we shall give in Chapters II, III and IV of the book.

In order to support the four theses indicated, in Chapter II (The dawn of Indian philosophy) we shall go on to indicate some points of contact between Western doctrines and Vedic doctrines, which we consider to be the first step of Indian philosophy; in Chapter III (The blooming of Indian philosophy), we shall show some points of contact between Western doctrines and Upanishadic doctrines, in which we already find the powerful metaphysical impulse so characteristic of Indian thought as well as bold intuitions in conjunction with the overcoming of mythical forms of thinking; and in Chapter IV (A pinnacle of Indian rationalism), we shall point out some similarities between Western doctrines and Sāṃkhya doctrines, which will impress the reader with its modern and audacious theories as well as with its strict use of reason.

As we have said, in our exposition of Indian thought we do not intend to give a detailed and complete account of the theories and doctrines concerned. We shall restrict our attention to a few subjects, which are interesting in themselves from a philosophical point of view, and give occasion to a comparison with Western thought. The Western theories and doctrines to which we shall compare the corresponding

Indian ones are included in the sections we have entitled Remarks on the previous subject.

In the case of both Indian and Western thoughts, we shall rely on original texts in which the theories are clearly expounded, and we shall include them in their original language accompanied by our own English translation for the convenience of the reader.

We have made frequent references to a few important modern Western encyclopaedias of philosophy, only in order to point out the presence in them of many philosophical Western notions, which were in fact also current in Indian philosophical systems.

With regard to the transcription of Sanskrit sounds, let us indicate the following only: lingual vowel ṛ (ri); palatal sibilant ś (sh); lingual sibilant ṣ (sh); nasal guttural ṅ; lingual consonants ṭ, ṭh, ḍ, ḍh, ṇ ; the nasal-sign anusvāra ṃ ; and the surd breathing visarga ḥ.

Chapter I
Hegel: The origin of the Myth

I.1 Introduction

At the beginning of 19th century, Hegel proclaimed that philosophy could only be born in Greece, and was therefore born there, and that it could not exist in India, and was consequently not born there. After him, this opinion was subscribed to and transmitted by professors and manuals, histories and encyclopaedias of philosophy.[1]

I.2 Hegel's positive opinion with regard to Indian philosophy

In some passages of his *Vorlesungen über die Geschichte der Philosophie,* Hegel speaks in a way which seems to indicate

[1] On the general subject of the relation of Hegel to India and specially of Hegel to Indian philosophy see Wilhelm Halbfass, "Hegel on the philosophy of the Hindus", in *German Scholars on India,* pp.107-122; Helmuth von Glasenapp, *Das Indienbild deutscher Denker,* Part I, Chapter 5; Wilhelm Halbfass, *Indien und Europa. Perspektiven ihrer geistigen Begegnung,* Part I, Chapter VI; Michel Hulin, *Hegel et l'Orient*; and Roger-Pol Droit, *L'Oubli de l'Inde. Une amnésie philosophique,* specially pp. 185-197.

his acceptation of the existence of Indian philosophy and even his positive appraisal of it. Here are some examples:

1. In the lessons of 1825/26, p. 375, Felix Meiner Verlag edition, Hamburg, 1993 (M in what follows) = volume I, p. 149, Suhrkamp Verlag edition, Frankfurt am Main, 1986 (S):

> *Die indische Philosophie steht also so innerhalb der Religion, wie die scholastische Philosophie im Mittelalter innerhalb der christlichen Dogmatik ... Erst vor kurzem haben wir bestimmte Kenntnis von der indischen Philosophie erhalten; im ganzen verstand man darunter die religiösen Vorstellungen; in neuerer Zeit hat man aber eigene philosophische Werke der Inder kennengelernt; besonders hat uns Colebrooke, Präsident der Asiatischen Gesellschaft in London, in [den] >Transactions of the Asiatic Society I< aus zwei indischen philosophischen Werken Auszüge mitgeteilt, und das ist das eigentlich erste, was wird über indische Philosophie haben.*
>
> "Indian philosophy thus stands within religion, just as scholastic philosophy in the middle-age [stands] within Christian dogmatics ... It is quite recently that we obtained a definite knowledge of Indian philosophy; in general one understood by this expression religious representations; but only very recently one has come to know specific philosophical works (eigene philosophische Werke, M's reading) [really philosophical works: wirklich philosophische Werke, S's reading] of the Indians. Colebrooke, President of the Asiatic Society in London, in particular has transmitted to us, in Transactions of the Asiatic Society I, abstracts from two Indian philosophical works; and this is the properly first [information] we have about Indian philosophy".

In Hegel's essay "Über die unter dem Namen Bhagavad-Gita bekannte Episode des Mahabharata von Wilhelm von Humboldt", in *Berliner Schriften 1818-1831*, p. 143 S (Volume 11 of *G.W.F. Hegel Werke*), a similar idea is expressed.

2. In the lessons of 1827/28, according to J. Gibelin's French translation, p. 103, which he made using J. Hoffmeister's edition, Leipzig, 1940 and 1944:

> *Il est bon de remarquer en général tout de suite que nous trouvons aussi chez les hindous des philosophies abstraites et une logique très formelle dèveloppèe:*
>
> "It is convenient to remark at once in a general way that we find abstract philosophies and a developed formal logic among Hindus too".

Cf. the next quotation.

3. In the lessons of 1829/30, pp. 346-347 M:

Die orientalische Philosophie begegnet uns also zuerst. Wir können sie als den ersten Teil, also als wirkliche Philosophie ansehen, können sie aber auch als vorausgeschickt, als Voraussetzung der Philosophie ansehen, und machen den Anfang erst mit der griechischen Philosophie. Der andere Teil ist dann die germanische Philosophie ...Bei der Ausbildung der orientalischen Welt finden wie wohl auch Denken und Philosophieren, ja das tiefste Philosophieren. Wir finden das Denken in seiner äussersten Abstraktion sich bewegen und seine Figuren ziehen.

"Oriental philosophy thus meets us in the first place. We can consider it as the first part [of the history of philosophy] and consequently as real philosophy, but we can also consider it as anticipation, as presupposition of philosophy, and begin [that history] with Greek philosophy before anything else. The other part is then the German philosophy ... In the development of the Eastern world we certainly also find thinking and philosophizing, even the most profound philosophizing. We find that thinking in its extreme abstraction moves and draws its representations".

In the following, the part of this text which comes next is to be found among Hegel's quoted texts, which negate the possibility of Oriental philosophy.

4. In his quoted essay "Über die unter dem Namen Bhagavad-Gita bekannte Episode des Mahabharata", p. 144 S, after affirming that "from the highest Indian point of view, also expressed in Canto V, stanza 5 of the Bhagavad-Gita" *(auf dem höchsten indischen Standpunkte, wie dies auch im Bhagavad-Gita in der 5. Lekt., 5. sl., ausgesprochen ist)*, both Sāṃkhya and Yoga have a single aim, Hegel adds that:

Andererseits kann erinnert werden, dass, sosehr in diesem letzten Ziel indische Religion und Philosophie übereinkommen, doch die Ausbildung dieses einen Zieles und wesentlich des Weges zu diesem Ziele, wie sie durch und für den Gedanken zustande gebracht worden, so zu dem Unterschied von der religiösen Gestalt gediehen ist, dass sie sehr wohl den Namen der Philosophie verdient. Vollends zeigt sich der Weg, den die Philosophie vorzeichnet, eigentümlich und würdig, wenn man ihn mit dem Wege vergleicht, welchen die indische Religion teils vorschreibt, teils, wenn sie selbst den höheren Schwung zu dem Joga-Sinne nimmt, noch gleichsam vermengungsweise zulässt. So würde man der indischen Philosophie, welche Sankhja-Lehre ist, höchst unrecht tun, wenn man sich ein Urteil über sie und ihre Weise aus dem, was nach obigem in dem Bhagavad-Gita Sankhja-Lehre heisst und was über die gemeinen popular-religiösem Vorstellungen nicht hinausgeht, machen würde.

"On the other side it can be recalled that, however much Indian religion [= Yoga] and philosophy [= Sāṃkhya] may agree with regard to this last aim, anyhow the [theoretical] construction of this single aim and essentially of the path that leads to that aim, as it has been accomplished by means of and for thinking, has had such a success in its differentiation from the religious form, that it deserves very well the name of philosophy. The path that philosophy draws reveals itself completely peculiar and worthy, when one compares it with the path that Indian religion in part prescribes and in part however admits when it takes the higher impulse towards the sense of the Joga [= Yoga] – in a way that creates confusion. A great injustice would be made to that Indian philosophy which is the teaching of the Sankhja [= Sāṃkhya] [system], if one forms a judgment about it and its nature starting from what, according to what has been previously expressed, is called the teaching of the Sankhja in the Bhagavad Gita, [teaching] which does not go beyond common and popular representations".

In the texts quoted above, let us point out the comparison of Indian philosophy with scholastic Christian philosophy, which forces us, if the former is eliminated from the realm of philosophy, to also eliminate the latter (Text 1); the following expressions are applied to Indian thought: "specific philosophical works" or "really philosophical works" (according to each edition) (Text 1), "the properly first [information] we have about Indian philosophy" (Text 1), "abstract philosophies" (Text 2), "a developed formal logic" (Text 2), and the rejection of the *Bhagavad-Gītā* (syncretistic and devotional episode of the great epic poem *Mahābhārata*) as a criterion for judging the value of the Sāṃkhya system (Text 4).

Let us also point out that the Sāṃkhya system can be considered as one of the most important creations of Indian rationalism.

J.M. Bocheński, *Formale Logik*, p. 481, affirms in the same way as Hegel does that a formal logic was developed in India. Cf. K. Bhattacharya, "A Note on Formalism in Indian Logic", in *Journal of Indian Philosophy*, 29, 2001, pp. 17-23.

I.3 H.T. Colebrooke

This positive attitude of Hegel can be said to be a result of the fact that he knew Parts I and II (which refer to the Indian systems – Sāṃkhya, Nyāya and Vaiśeṣika) of the celebrated essay by H.T. Colebrooke "On the Philosophy of the Hindus",[2] which Hegel utilized for his lessons of 1825/26.

Hegel quotes Colebrooke several times, for instance in *Vorlesungen über die Geschichte der Philosophie I*, pp. 375-377, 388, 392 M, and he sums up in detail the contents of Parts I and II of the essay mentioned, exalting and extolling the work of its author.

In his quoted essay on the *Bhagavad-Gītā*, p. 143 S, Hegel says with regard to the extracts of Indian philosophical texts provided by Colebrooke that "they belong to the most valuable enrichments that our knowledge in this field could have received": *zu den schätzenswertesten Bereicherungen gehören, welche unsere Kenntnis auf diesem Felde erhalten konnte.*

Hegel did not know, or at least did not utilize, Parts III-V of Colebrooke's essay dedicated to the Mīmāṃsā and Vedānta systems and to the "heretics" (heretical): Jainism, Buddhism, materialism etc.

The two parts known by Hegel total only 44 pages of the above mentioned 1858 edition of *Essays on the Religion and Philosophy of the Hindus* by Colebrooke.

---

[2] Parts I and II of the essay were read by Colebrooke himself in public meetings of the Royal Asiatic Society on the 21st. June 1823 and the 21st. February 1824; Parts III, IV and V were read respectively on the 4th March 1826, the 7th April 1827 and the 3rd February 1827. The essay was published in the *Transactions of the Royal Asiatic Society*, Volumes I (Parts I and II) and II (Parts III-V), 1824 and 1829 respectively. An edition of this Essay was included in *Essays on the Religion and Philosophy of the Hindus*, London-Edinburgh: Williams and Norgate, Paris: B. Duprat, 1858. This last edition is the edition utilized by us.

I.4 Hegel's negative opinion with regard to Indian philosophy

Besides the texts of Hegel which show a positive attitude towards the existence and value of Indian philosophy, there are others which, while negating in an absolute way the possibility of philosophy in the Oriental world (by "Orient" or "Oriental world", he means China and India), also negate Indian philosophy, affirming that philosophy began in Greece and could only exist there. Let us now quote a few of these texts in detail in order to show the requirements and conditions which, according to Hegel, must be given in a people if philosophy is to arise, as well as the type of reasoning which allowed Hegel to draw the conclusion that philosophy did not exist in India.

Here are some examples from *Vorlesungen über die Geschichte der Philosophie*:

1. Lessons of 1823/24, p. 190 M, cf. Volume I, pp. 116-117 S:

> *... so findet es sich, dass da der Anfang der Geschichte der Philosophie ist, wo ein Volk eine konkrete Gestalt hat, dessen Prinzip das Bewusstsein der Freiheit ausmacht. Ein Volk das dieses Bewusstsein hat der Freiheit, ein solches Volk gründet sein Dasein auf dieses Prinzip; die Verfassung, das ganze Dasein gründet sich auf die Kategorie, unter welcher der Geist von sich selbst weiss.*
>
> *Wenn wir also sagen, zum Hervortreten der Philosophie gehört das Bewusstsein geistiger Freiheit, so erfordert sie ein Volk, dessen Existenz dies Prinzip zur Grundlage habe. Zur Freiheit des Geistes verlangten wir, dass sich der Geist von dem Natürlichen losgerissen habe, dass das Denken bei sich sei - also die Trennung des Geistes von seinem Versenktsein in den Stoff, in die Anschauung, in die Natürlichkeit des Wollens. Die Gestalt, die dieser Stufe der Trennung vorangeht, bestimmt sich aus dem Gesagten so, dass sie ein Standpunkt sei der Einheit des Geistes mit der Natur. Diese Einheit ist als erste, anfangende, keine wahrhafte; es irren also viele, wenn sie diese Einheit des Geistes mit der Natur für die vortrefflichste Weise des Bewusstsein annehmen; diese Stufe ist nicht durch den Geist selbst hervorgebracht; es ist das orientalische Leben, die orientalische Welt überhaupt, während die Gestalt des geistigen, freien Selbstbewusstseins die griechische ist.*

"... so it is found that the beginning of the history of philosophy is where a people has a concrete form whose directive principle is constituted by consciousness of freedom. A people which has this consciousness of freedom, such a people bases its existence on that principle; the [political] Constitution, the whole existence [of that people] is based on the category under which the Spirit knows about himself.

Thus, if we say that consciousness of spiritual freedom is necessary for the appearance of philosophy, then it requires a people whose existence has that principle as its basis. For the freedom of the Spirit we demanded that the Spirit had separated itself from the natural [condition], that thinking be in itself - consequently the separation of the Spirit from its immersion in matter, in intuition, in the naturality of will. The form that is previous to this stage of separation is defined, according to what has been said before, so that it is a viewpoint of the unity of Spirit with Nature. This unity, as the first, initial one, is not a true [unity]; thus many are mistaken when they assume that this unity of the Spirit with Nature is the most excellent form of consciousness; this stage is not produced by the Spirit itself; this is the Oriental life, the Oriental world in general, while the form of the spiritual and free self-consciousness is the Greek [world]".

2. Lessons of 1823/24, pp. 195-196 M, cf. I, p. 122 S:

... daraus folgt, dass ich nur insofern frei bin, als ich die Freiheit anderer setze, und dass ich nur insofern frei bin, als ich durch andere als frei anerkannt bin. Freiheit ist nur unter mehreren wirkliche, existierende Freiheit. Damit ist das Verhältnis von Freien zu Freien gesetzt – Gesetze der Sittlichkeit, vernünftige Rechte ... Diesen Begriff der Freiheit finden wir zuerst im griechischen Volk austreten, und darum fängt hier die Philosophie an. Übrigens aber ist in Griechenland die reale Freiheit mit einer Einschränkung. Nämlich, wie wir wissen, finden sich in Griechenland Sklaven. Das bürgerliche Leben selbst konnte nicht ohne Sklaven bestehen. Die Freiheit also ist noch beschränkt. Und dies gibt den Unterschied zwischen dem Orient, Griechenland und Germanien. Im Orient ist nur einer frei, einige in Griechenland, alle in der modernen Welt. In ihr ist der Mensch als Mensch frei.

"... therefrom it follows that I am free only insofar as I establish the freedom of the others, and that I am free only insofar as I am recognized as free by the others. Only among many freedom is real, existent freedom. Therewith the relation of free beings with free beings is established - laws of morality, rational rights ... We find this concept of freedom arising for the first time in the Greek people, and because of this philosophy begins there. But in fact in Greece true freedom is given with a limitation: as we know there are slaves in Greece. Bourgeois life could not maintain itself without slaves. Freedom thus is still limited. And this makes the difference among Orient, Greece and Germany. In the Orient only one is free [the despot, according to I, p. 122 S], some in Greece, all in the modern world. In it man as man is free".

3. Lessons of 1825/26, p. 266 M, cf. I, pp. 119-120 S:

Dies ist der allgemeine Zusammenhang der politischen Freiheit mit dem Hervortreten der Freiheit des Gedankens; in der Geschichte tritt daher die Philosophie also nur da auf, wo und insofern freie Verfassungen sich bilden.

Die orientalische Welt fällt uns zuerst in der Geschichte auf. Da aber kann keine eigentliche Philosophie vorhanden sein. Denn um den Charakter dieser Welt kurz anzugeben, so geht der Geist wohl im Orient auf, aber das Verhältnis ist noch so, dass das Subjekt, die Individualität - ich für mich - nicht als Person ist, sondern nur untergeht, nur bestimmt ist als negativ, untergehend in dem Objektiven überhaupt. In dem orientalischen Charakter ist das substantielle Verhältnis das Herrschende; die Substanz wird als übersinnlich vorgestellt, als Gedanke, oder auch wohl mehr sinnlich, und das Verhätnis des Individuellen, des Besonderen ist dann, dass dieses nur ein Negatives ist gegen das Substantielle, und das Höchste, wozu die Individualität kommen könnte, sei die ewige Seligkeit als ein Versenktsein in diese Substanz und ein Vergehen des Bewusstseins und so des Unterschieds zwischen Substanz und Individualität - Untergehen in der Substanz mithin Vernichtung. Sofern ist das Verhältnis geistlos, wo die Substanz das an und für sich Seiende ist; also das Höchste des Verhältnisses ist Bewusstlosigkeit.

"This is the general connection between political freedom and the arising of freedom of thought; thus, philosophy appears in history only where, and as far as, free [political] Constitutions are built.

The Oriental world presents itself to us first in history. But no true philosophy can be given in it. In order to describe briefly the character of that world, [we have to say that] of course the Spirit comes forth in the Orient, but the relation [of the individual with substance] is still such that the subject, the individuality - I for myself - does not exist as person, but only disappears, it is only determined as [something] negative, generally disappearing in the objective. In the Oriental character the substantial relation is the predominant one; the substance is represented as supersensible, as idea, or also perhaps as more sensible; and the relation of the individual, of the particular [with substance] consists then in that this [the individual] is only something negative in face of the substantial; and the highest which the individuality could reach would be the eternal bliss [considered] as sinking into this substance and as an extinction of consciousness and thus of [any] difference between substance and individuality - extinction in substance, consequently annihilation. The relation is consciousnessless in which substance is what exists in and for itself; thus the highest of the relation is the lack of consciousness".

4. Lessons of 1825/26, p. 268 M, cf. I, pp. 120-121 S:

Als Folge ist anzusehen, dass hier kein philosophisches Erkennen stattfinden kann, denn dazu gehört das Wissen von der Substanz und dem Allgemeinen, das gegenständlich ist und so bleibt, das, sofern ich es weiss und indem ich es denke, es in mir entwickle, es bestimme [gegenständlich I, p. 120 S] für sich bleibt, so dass ich in der Substanz zugleich meine Bestimmung habe und darin affirmativ erhalten bin, so dass es nicht nur meine subjektiven Bestimmungen, Gedanken, mithin Meinungen sind, sondern dass ebenso als es meine Gedanken sind, es auch Gedanken des Objektiven, also Substantiellen – objective Gedanken sind.

Das orientalische ist also im ganzen aus der Geschichte der Philosophie auszuschliessen.

"As a consequence [of what has been said] it has to be admitted that here [in the Orient] no philosophic knowledge can take place, since for that is required the knowledge of substance and of the universal which is objective and remains as such, which inasmuch as I know it and so long as I think it, and I develop it in myself, and I determine it, it [objectively I, p. 120 S] maintains itself for itself, so that at the same time I have in the substance my [own] determination and there I keep myself affirmatively; so that my subjective determinations not only are [mere] ideas, consequently [mere] opinions, but, just as they are my ideas, they also are ideas of the objective, then of the substantial - objective ideas.

Therefore **the Oriental [thinking] must as a whole be excluded from the history of philosophy**". [the bold type is ours]

5. Lessons of 1825/26, p. 269 M, cf. I, pp. 121-122 S:

Die eigentliche Philosophie geht in Okzident erst hervor; da geht der Geist auf, geht in sich dort unter, vertieft sich in sich, setzt sich dort als frei, ist für sich; so ist es erst möglich, dass Philosophie existiert. Damit ist im Zusammenhang, dass im Okzident freie Verfassungen sind, denn es gehört dazu, dass Philosophie sei, dass das Subjekt ausharre in dem Substantiellen, dass es sich nicht herabwürdige, dass das Absolute gegeständlich sei, aber dass ich mich nicht nur als Knecht, als abhängig, der Vernichtung geweiht, dazu verhalte, um einzig mit dem Absoluten mich ganz aufzugeben, sondern die okzidentalische Seligkeit ist so bestimmt, dass darin das Subjekt als solches ausdauere und beharre im Substantiellen.

Im Okzident sind wir auf dem eigentlichen Boden der Philosophie...

"Philosophy proper emerges for the first time in the West; there the Spirit arises, penetrates into itself, submerges in itself, establishes itself there as free, is for itself; in this way it is for the first time possible that philosophy exist. With this is related that in the West free Constitutions exist, since for the existence of philosophy it is necessary that the subject endure in the substantial, that it do not humiliate itself, that the Absolute be objective, but that I do not behave only as a slave, as a subordinate, destined to annihilation, in order that I, one with the Absolute, completely surrender myself, being it so that Western bliss is determined in such a way that the subject as such may remain and persevere in the substantial.

In the West we are on the true field of philosophy... ." [the bold type is ours]

6. Lessons of 1827/28, p. 309 M, cf. I, pp. 115-116 S:

Die erste Frage ist, wo wir mit der Geschichte der Philosophie anzufangen haben. Sie fängt da an, wo der Gedanke rein hervortritt, wo er allgemein ist und wo dieses Reine, dies Allgemeine das Wesentliche, Wahrhafte, Absolute ist, das Wesen von allem. Die Wissenschaft, wo wir den reinen, allgemeinen Gedanken zum Gegestand haben, ist die Logik. Gewöhnlich pflecht man zwar nur das subjektive Denken, den Gedanken in der Form des bewussten Denkens in der Logik zu betrachten; der Wert des Gedankens, glaubt man, liege auf der Seite des Subjekts. In der Philosophie aber hat man zwar auch den Gedanken zum Gegestand, aber nich bloss als etwas Subjektives, als eine innere Tätigkeit in uns, sondern den Gedanken in dem Sinn, dass er objektiv allgemein ist; also abstracter Gedanke und Allgemeines ist eins. Wollen wir wissen, wie etwas beschaffen, wie es in Wahrheit sei, so denken wir darüber nach, produzieren Gedanken darüber, erkennen das Wesen, erkennen etwas Allgemeines. Das Produzieren des Gedankens ist eben Erkennen des Wesens; es ist allgemeine denkende Betrachtung, die das Wesen zum Ziel hat. In der Philosophie nun gelten die Gedanken selbst als das Wesen. Also fängt die Philosophie erst da an, wo das Wesen der Dinge in der Form des reinen Gedankens zum Bewusstsein kommt; und dies ist in der griechischen Welt der Fall.

"The first question is where we have to start the history of philosophy. It begins there where the idea arises pure, where it is universal and where this purity, this universality is the essential, the true, the Absolute, the essence of everything. The science, in which we have as its object the pure, universal idea, is logic. Usually it is common to consider in logic only the subjective thinking, the idea in the form of conscious thinking; the value of the idea - it is believed - stands on the side of the subject. But in philosophy one certainly also has the idea as its object but not only as something merely subjective, as a [mere] inner activity within us; but [one has] the idea in the sense that it is something objectively universal; thus abstract idea and universal is the same. If we want to know how something is constituted, how it is in truth, then we think upon it, we produce ideas in relation to it, we come to know the essence, we come to know something universal. To produce the idea is in fact knowledge of the essence; it is a universal thinking reflection, which has essence as its aim. In philosophy then the ideas themselves are equivalent to the essence. Thus **philosophy begins for the first time where the essence of things reaches consciousness under the form of pure idea; and this is the case in the Greek world"**. [the bold type is ours]

7. Lessons of 1829/30, pp. 346-347 M:

Im Orientalischen haben wir ungeheure Gestaltungen von Staaten und Religionen, Wissenschaften und Kenntnissen ausgearbeitet vor uns. Aber in dem orientalischen Staat ist das Allgemeine, das gediegene Substantielle so sehr das Herrschende, Überwiegende, dass das freie Denken, die Subjektivität, die subjective Freiheit, die Freiheit des Individuums ein Züruckgesetztes ist. Im Orient steht die Substantialität auf der einen Seite, und auf der anderen Seite steht allerdings auch hier die Subjektivität, aber als ausgelassene Willkür des Einzelnen, des Despoten, der Wille des Individuums; aber diese Seite, die das Konkrete ausmacht, ist dann wesentlich in der Form der Äusserlichkeit, in der Form der Zufälligkeit, in der Akzidentalität gegen die Substanz.

"In the Oriental [world] we have before us, elaborated, enormous formations of States and religions, sciences and knowledges. But in the Oriental State the universal, the genuine substantial is in such a way the dominant, the prevalent, that free thinking, subjectivity, subjective freedom, freedom of the individual is something postponed. In the Orient the substantiality stays on one side and on the other side stays of course also here the subjectivity, but as the ungoverned arbitrariness of a single [man], the despot, the will of one individual; but this side, which constitutes the concrete, is essentially in the form of exteriority, in the form of casualty, in the accidental in face of substance".

8. Lessons of 1829/30, pp. 347-348 M:

Die eigentliche Philosophie beginnt für uns in Griechenland. Da beginnt Mass und Klarheit – das sich selbst bestimmende Allgemeine, wodurch es eben zum Begriff wird. Dieser Begriff, der vereinigt sich nun mit dem Dasein, zeicht sich so als sich vereinigend mit dem Konkreten der geistigen und natürlichen Welt, als durch Begriffe begreifend. Die Welt in ihrem Dasein, die Gestaltungen der Welt sind da nicht blosser Schmuck für das Substantielle; es ist nicht bloss ein Akzidentelles an demselben, nicht bloss ein Fliehendes, noch auch weiter nichts als ein Nichtiges. Sondern dem Griechen ist wohl in seiner Welt; er fühlt sich einheimisch in derselben, und der Begriff ist einheimisch in der Gegenwart, der Begriff ist identisch mit ihr. Die griechische Philosophie ist eben deswegen plastisch, sie bildet sich zu einem Ganzen aus. Der Gedanke zieht sich nicht züruck von dem, was konkret ist. Hier haben wir den Gedanken als den Begriff. In dem freien griechischen Leben zeigt sich der Begriff als frei und denkt sich.

"**Philosophy proper begins for us in Greece.** [the bold type is ours] There begin measure and clearness - the universal that determines itself, wherewith in fact it becomes a concept. This concept, which unites itself with the existence, shows itself as uniting itself with the concrete of the spiritual and natural world, as grasping through concepts. The world in its existence, the formations of the world are not there a mere ornament for the substantial; it is not merely something accidental on it or merely something fugacious or, even more, nothing else than a nothingness. On the contrary the Greek is at ease in his world; in it [= world] he feels at home, and the concept is at home in the immediate reality, the concept is identical with it. Greek philosophy is therefore plastic; it constructs itself as a whole. Thinking does not separate itself from what is concrete. Here we have thinking as the concept. In the free Greek life the concept shows itself as free, and thinks itself".

It can be said that the idea that philosophy arose in Greece, that there is no philosophy in the Orient and that there is no such thing as Indian philosophy, expressed in such a decisive way in his cited lessons, is considered to be Hegel's authentic and definitive opinion. This opinion persisted, is today repeated by many Western professors and students of philosophy and is also to be found in many histories of Western philosophy.

I.5 Hegel's way of acting

Let us now see in which way Hegel founds his negative thesis on the existence of Indian philosophy.

In the *Einleitung* to his *Vorlesungen über die Geschichte der Philosophie I*, pp. 11-123 S, and in *Anhang III*, pp. 465-519 S, Hegel develops his ideas on the notions of "philosophy" and "history of philosophy".[3]

Hegel also establishes the requirements which must be given and the conditions which a people must have in order for philosophy to arise in it. Among these requirements and conditions are:

"consciousness of freedom; consciousness of spiritual freedom" "that the Spirit separate itself from the natural [condition]"; "that thinking be in itself"; "the separation of the Spirit from its immersion in matter, in intuition, in the naturality of will" (Text 1);

"political freedom, freedom of thought, free [political] Constitutions" (Text 3);

"the knowledge of substance and of the universal" (Text 4);

"that the Spirit arise, penetrate into itself, submerge in itself, establish itself as free, be for itself"; "the existence of

[3] Cf. the article of O. Marquard on Hegel's concept of philosophy, "Von Kant bis zum Beginn des 20. Jh.", in *Historisches Wörterbuch der Philosophie*, Vol. 7, col. 718.

free Constitutions"; "that the subject endure in the substantial, do not humiliate itself, that it do not behave only as a slave, as a subordinate, destined to annihilation, in order to completely surrender itself to the Absolute"; "that the subject as such remain and persevere in the substantial" (Text 5);

"that the idea arise pure, and be universal, that purity and universality be the essential, the truth, the Absolute, the essence of everything";

"that the essence of things reach consciousness under the form of pure idea" (Text 6);

"that there be measure and clearness, the universal that determines itself and becomes a concept, that unites with the existence, with the concrete of the spiritual and natural world, and grasps through concepts"; "that the world be not conceived as a mere ornament of the substantial, as something merely accidental on it or as something fugacious or as something that is nothing else than a nothingness"; "that thinking does not separate itself from what is concrete"; "that thinking be taken as the concept"; that the concept show itself as free, and think itself" (Text 8).

Finally, in a very general way Hegel describes the character, way of being and psychology of Greek and Oriental people, and among them especially the Indian people, and points out how Greeks and Indians were and how they behaved in relation to each of the requirements and conditions which he established.

Hegel concludes that philosophy could originate in Greece *only* because it is in Greece that the requirements and conditions that make it possible were given, whilst there could be no philosophy in India as these requirements and conditions were in his opinion not given.

We shall deal neither with Hegel's notion of philosophy nor with the requirements and conditions which he established for the development of philosophy. We shall only carry out some reflections concerning what he said about

Greece and India, the idea he had of these two countries and the knowledge he possesses of the culture of both.

I.6 Hegel's opinion with regard to Greece

According to Hegel, the requirements and conditions which are enumerated above and which are necessary if philosophy is to arise can be found in Greece.

We must in the first place remark that all of these requirements and conditions are in general expressed with an intrinsic obscurity, ambiguity and confusion; much could be said in this respect in order to clarify them, precisely pin down their meaning and determine the degree to which they can be applied to Greece. As a remarkable example of confusion, let us quote the last sentence of Text 2 here: "In the Orient only one is free [the despot, according to I, p. 122 S], some in Greece, all in the modern world. In it man as man is free." For Hegel, all men were free in the Europe of the early 19th century! Is this naïveté or incapacity to see reality?

Also, Hegel's judgment is a generalization, since he deduces a general exclusive affirmation from a few individual cases. Greece has had a long and complex history reaching from the epoch in which the Indo-Europeans (who would later be known as the "Greeks") invaded the lands that would later be called "Greece" in the third millennium B.C. up to several centuries after the birth of Christ. In this period, Greece was divided into a multiplicity of city-states such as Athens, Sparta, Corinth, Thebes etc. to which Macedonia was added in the middle of the 4th century B.C. All of these states had distinct histories, different forms of government, diverse political positions and even divergent cultures and values. Though all of these city-states constitute what is called "Greece", it is not legitimate to attribute to all of the states what was proper to one of them in a certain epoch only, or to attribute to all Greeks something which only characterized a certain group of them in a certain place at a certain moment. *Greece* is a name which has included heterogeneous elements during its history, and Hegel's generalizations are not applicable to some of them.

Finally, let us point out that Hegel had an exaggerated fascination for Greece. This was a common attitude in his days, and it co-existed with an equally exaggerated fascination for India in other German authors contemporary with Hegel. The fascination which Hegel felt for Greece made him idealize it. In Text 8. Hegel gives expression to this idealization, affirming that in Greece "begin measure and clearness" (*Da beginnt Mass und Klarheit*). Thus, for Hegel, Greece is the native soil and the home of reason and the place where rationality was born and then existed.[4]

I.7 Irrationalism in Greece

Our greater, more profound and more objective present knowledge of the multiple manifestations of Greek culture, our stronger consciousness of the complexity of human communities and of their creations, the now quite diffuse knowledge of Greek history, art, philosophy and literature which effaced the youthful enthusiasm proper to discoverers with which Germans encountered the Greek classics around the middle of the 17th century, as shown by H. Trevelgyan, *Goethe and the Greeks* – all of these facts and other similar ones ensure that no-one is now unaware of the fact that countless irrational attitudes in fact existed in Greece. As P.M. Schuhl says on page 27 of his *Essai sur la formation de la pensée grecque*:

> "the atmosphere of Greece was not always so limpid as it was desired to believe".[5]

---

[4] See D. Janicaud, *Hegel et le destin de la Grèce* on Hegel's attitude to Greece.

[5] In the following works a corroboration of the affirmation of Schuhl can be seen: E.R. Dodds, *The Greeks and the Irrational*; R. Flaceliéres, *Divins et oracles grecs*; G. Lanata, *Medicina magica e religione popolare in Grecia*; M. Ninck, *Die Bedeutung des Wassers im Kult und Leben der Alten*; E. Rohde, *Psyché*, F. Schwenn, *Die Menschenopfer bei den Griechen und Römern*; R. Graves, *The Greek Myths*; R. Bloch, *Les prodiges dans l'Antiquité Classique*, the article "Magic (Greek and Roman)", pp. 269-289, in the *Encyclopaedia of Religion and Ethics*,

On the other hand, the Greeks believed in their Gods, though many find it difficult to admit this fact because these Gods present a type of divinity which is different to that found in other religions, and in spite of the elements to be found in the traditions concerning these Gods which could seem disgusting, elements which were criticized by ancient thinkers and which the ancient Christian authors took great care to point out.[6] For the Greeks, what is today called "Greek mythology" and is considered as an aggregate of beautiful or interesting legends to which no religious value is attributed was a part of the religious beliefs in which they put their faith.[7] And irrational elements abounded in Greek religion and mythology to a considerable extent.

It is hard to believe that Greek thinkers kept themselves totally apart from irrationality, some of whose manifestations are revealed to us by the books quoted and affected the consciousness of the society of which these thinkers were a part. It is enough to think of the attitude of the Greek thinkers towards *mantiké* or *divinatio.*[8]

Vol. 8; Fritz Graf, *La magie dans l'Antiquité Gréco-Romaine. Idéologie et pratique*; and the excellent articles on "Astrologia", "Mantik", "Orakel", "Prodigium", in *Paulys Realencyclopädie der classischen Altertums-wissenschaft* and in *Der kleine Pauly Lexicon der Antike* in five volumes; A. Bouché-Leclerq, *Histoire de la divination dans l'Antiquité*, E. Suárez de la Torre, "Oráculos de Apolo en la Grecia Antigua (Bibliografía)", in *'Ilu, revista de ciencias de las religiones*, No. 4, 1999, pp. 371-386; W. Burkert, "Tragedie grecque et rite sacrificiel", in *Sauvages origines*, pp. 11-69. It is interesting to remark that G. Leopardi, the great Italian poet, wrote in 1815 his celebrated essay *Saggio sopra gli errori popolari degli antichi*, where he deals with many "errors" (superstitions) current in Greece and Rome.

[6] Cf. P. Decharme, *La critique des traditions religieuses chez les Grecs*; and among Christian authors, Theodoret de Cyrrhus, *Thérapeutique des Maladies Hellèniques*; Athenagoras of Athens, *Supplique au sujet des Chrétiens et sur la Résurrection des morts*; Athanase d'Alexandrie, *Contre les païens.*

[7] See the works of Walter Otto, *Theophania*; *Die Götter Griechenlands*; and *Der Dichter und die alten Götter.*

[8] See the information given by Cicero in his *De Divinatione* I, 5 and 6, Arthur Stanley Pease ed.; Clemens of Alexandria, *Stromata* I, 21, O. Stählin ed.; (Plutarch), *De placitis philosophorum* in The Loeb Classical Library, Vol. IX, in *Doxographi Graeci*, H. Diels ed., and in Les Belles Lettres ed. Vol. XII2;

If the archaic and classical epochs of Greece were not entirely immune to irrationality, the latter became even more manifest in the Hellenistic era. There is no reason to exclude the Hellenistic era from Greek history if we want to characterize the Greek culture of which it was a part.[9]

In all of the authors quoted by us in note 9 of this part, fancy, credulity, mysticism, appraisal of asceticism, complacency with regard to rites and ceremonies, the exaggerated value attributed to the latter, the coexistence of doctrinaire philosophical and religious elements of various origins and of a contradictory nature, respect for "authorities", etc. coexist to differing degrees,[10] just as they do in many manifestations of Indian thought which Westerners enjoy criticizing.

The preceding remarks show that Greek culture had many points of contact with Indian culture with regard to irrationality.

---

and the works quoted in note 5 of this Part I on these subjects, and specially A. Bouché-Leclercq, *Histoire de la divination dans l'Antiquité*, Introduction III. *La divination et la philosophie*, pp. 45-84, where the author studies the position of the Greek philosophers in face of divination.

[9] In order to prove such a thing, it is sufficient to read the following works: *Porphyrii Philosophi Platonici Opuscula Selecta*, iterum recognovit Augustus Nauck; *Corpus Hermeticum*; Proclus, *The Elements of Theology*; Plotin, *Ennéades*; Numénius, *Fragments*; Jamblique, *Les Mystères d'Égipte*; Saloustios, *Des Dieux et du Monde*; Philostratus, *The Life of Apollonius of Tyana*; Apulée, *Opuscules philosophiques et Fragments*; Apulée, *Apologie. Florides*; Clément d'Alexandrie, *Le Protreptique*; *Oracles Chaldaïques*; Synesii Cyrenensis *Opuscula*, specially the treatise *De Insomniis*.

[10] On the irrational elements in the Hellenistic Epoch can be seen the following works that confirm the testimony of the texts we have mentioned before: R. Reitzenstein, *Die hellenistischen Mysterien-religionen*; F. Cumont, *Astrology and Religion*; F. Cumont, *Les Religions Orientales dans le Paganisme Romain*; F. Cumont, *The Mysteries of Mithra*; A.J.F. Festugiére, *La Révélation d'Hermés Trismégiste*, Volumes I-IV; Peter Green, *Alexander to Actium. The Hellenistic Age*, Chapter 33: "Foreign and Mystery Cults, Oracles, Astrology, Magic".

I.8 Other points of contact between Greek Culture and other cultures

There exist many other points of contact between Greek culture and other ancient cultures, which are alien to philosophy and religion and are of a negative nature.

Let us for example mention the point of contact provided by the cruelty, violence and inhumanity exerted by Greeks on prisoners of war recorded in Pierre Ducrey's book *Le traitement des prisonniers de guerre dans la Grèce antique des origines à la conquête romaine.* The sinister aspects of this treatment of prisoners of war in ancient Greece are the same as those found among the Assyrians, the Romans and the Moghuls.

Another point of contact between Greek Culture and other cultures is found in the peculiar institution of slavery, blemish of mankind, which existed in Greece as well as in other cultures, Eastern (including India) and Western.[11]

Moreover, any old or modern History of Greece[12] gives information on the violence, instigated by ambition, greediness, will of power, which prevailed in the Greek world: wars among cities, bloody political conflicts inside the cities, tyrannical and oligarchic régimes, exploitation of poor and helpless classes by the powerful and rich classes - e

vils that have afflicted humanity in every epoch, in all regions of the world, and which seems to us today a manifestation of the powerful irrational forces which have dominated mankind since many centuries ago.

---

[11] See G. Glotz, *La cité grecque,* and the articles by several authors in *Encyclopaedia of Religion and Ethics,* Vol. XI, pp. 595-631 under the title "*Slavery*"; E. Werner and J. Heinrichs (ed.), *Sklaven und Freigelassene in der Gesellschaft der römischen Kaiserzeit;* H. Wallon, *Historie de l'esclavage dans l'antiquité;* article by E. Flaig: "Sklaverei", in *Historisches Wörterbuch der Philosophie,* Vol. 9, col. 976-985; Marguerite Garrido-Hory (ed.), *Routes et marchés d'esclaves. 26e colloque du GIREA;* Peter Garnsey, *Conceptions de l'esclavage d'Aristote á saint Augustin;* Joseph Vogt, *Sklaverei und Humanität im klassischen Griechentum;* Marco Melluso, *La schiavitù nell'etá giustinianea, Disciplina giuridica e rilevanza sociale.*

[12] For instance J.B. Bury, *History of Greece,* in its multiple editions, and K.J. Beloch, *Griechische Geschichte,* 4 volumes.

Art provides us with another example of coincidence between Greek Culture and the other cultures. The idea of the Greek world as characterized by clarity (*Klarheit*), as Hegel claimed (cf. Text 8 previously quoted), or of the Greek art as it was conceived by J.J. Winckelmann (1717-1768), luminous, ideal, abstract, have their origin, in part at least in the damages caused by the passing of time and by the rains in the Greek statues, which have reached us. The whiteness of the Greek statues, which we admire in the museums, is due to fact that, owing to the indicated causes of the passing of time and the inclemencies of nature, the shining and bright colours, which covered these statues disappeared from them.

P.M. Schuhl in the first chapter, p. 1, of his well documented book, *Platon el l'art de son temps*, refers to this subject:

> "It is firstly a passage of the Republic [IV, 420 c-d] which puts us face to face with the Greek statuary under a most disturbing aspect for moderns, accustomed as they are to the white figures of our museums: the polychromy".

Plato, in the quoted passage of his work, refers to the colours that were applied to the diverse parts of the body represented by the statues. Immediately after Schuhl mentions the statues of the *Korés* in the Acropolis of Athens, discovered in 1885:

> "with their red lips and hairs, their clothes decorated with red and blue embroideries ... a dark line marked the arch of the eyebrows, and indicated the eyelashes in the border of the eyelids; the iris was red, the pupil black".

In p. 2, note 3 Schuhl also points out other remains of polychromy in the Greek statues, and in p. 3, notes 1 and 2, he refers to the techniques utilized for the application of colours in statues, even in those parts of the body that were not covered by the clothes.

The polychromy was a characteristic of the "white" Greek statues that we admire today as refined and abstract products of a free rationality, as well as the sculptures that India shows even today in the famous temple of Madurai in the South for instance.

The previous remarks do not mean of course that we do not acknowledge the greatness of Greek culture or that we do not admire its magnificent achievements in many fields of intellectual and artistic endeavours.

I.9 Hegel's opinion with regard to India

According to Hegel, the requirements and conditions necessary for the arising of philosophy in any people were given in Greece and not in India, and consequently philosophy did not arise in India.

We have already referred to the lack of clarity and precision of these requirements and conditions.

Also, as in the case of Greece, Hegel makes a series of generalizations about India, which are *a priori* as dangerous as all generalizations and cannot serve as a basis for correct reasoning. The history of Indian thought embraces a long period of time from around 1500 B.C., when Indo-Europeans invaded India, up till now. In these approximately three thousand years, Indian thought experienced an intense evolution, giving rise to doctrines based on a variety of tendencies.

In the following we shall indicate in a nutshell the principal texts and/or schools of philosophical thinking in India, pointing out some of their doctrines with the sole purpose of demonstrating the weakness of Hegel's generalizations. Many of these doctrines are common to several schools and came forth in a period which extended from 1500 B.C. to the first centuries of present era:

1. The *Vedas* (the One as the origin of all, *Ṛg Veda* X, 129; the Cosmic Order).
2. The *Upaniṣads* (the substantialist position; the notion of *Brahman* as an abstract, transcendent, heterogeneous absolute).

3. The Masters of Error (materialists, amoralists, atomists, sceptics, determinists).
4. Jainism (*anekāntavāda* or theory of non-unilaterality or multi-laterality or the possibility of several simultaneous affirmations, each of them valid, though contradictory with regard to each other).
5. Buddhism (the phenomenalist position, universal contingency; negation of substance, God and the soul; inexistence of a beginning or first cause), whose principal schools (or systems) are as follows:
    i. The Abhidharmika school (Hīnayāna) (theory of the *dharmas* or factors or elements of existence; their classification; their characteristics, of which we shall name instantaneousness and conditionality here; theory of causality).
    ii. Nāgārjuna's school (Mahāyāna) (theory of universal contingency carried to extremes; extreme deconstructionism).
    iii. Yogācāra school (Mahāyāna) (idealist position: only mind exists, all is mental creation; theory of mind; subliminal impressions; the unconscious aspect of mind; the peculiar concept of the object of knowledge).
    iv. The school of logic and epistemology (the study of the *pramāṇas* or means of correct knowledge and of fallacies of reasoning, etc.).
6. Materialism (existence of matter only; negation of the validity of the means of knowledge; rejection of any religious tradition).
7. Brahmanism and Hinduism (substantialism) whose principal schools (or systems) are:
    i. The Mīmāṃsā school (theory of hermeneutics; eternity of the world; supremacy of the *Veda* = *Logos*).
    ii. The Vedānta school (acceptance of a supreme principle, *Brahman*, an abstract or personalized

Absolute). It was divided into several schools of which we shall indicate only three here:

a. The non-dualist school (only the abstract principle *Brahman* exists; the world is unreal, the Īśvara (God) and the empirical ego are illusory creations; the individual soul (*ātman*), is identical with *Brahman*).

b. The qualified non-dualist school (a personal God; the world is real; the souls are parts, modes or the body of God and are different from Him).

c. The dualist school (a personal God; the world is real; insurmountable differences between God, the material products and the soul; predestination).

iii. The Sāṃkhya school (dualist system: Matter-Spirit; materialist monism; evolutionism; atheism).

iv. The Yoga school (metaphysics similar to that of the Sāṃkhya; precarious acceptation of God; basically a technique of Yogic or mystic trance).

v. The Nyāya school (logic, epistemology).

vi. The Vaiśeṣika school (theory of categories; atomism).

8. The philosophy of language that has Bhartṛhari as its principal representative (theory of language; sentences conceived of as the basic semantic unities of language; the theory of *pratibhā*, intuitive knowledge; the philosophical notions which serve as a basis for the grammatical categories, etc.).[13]

In view of such a picture of Indian thought with its diversity and richness, it is very difficult to give a definition

---

[13] Cf. The histories of Indian Philosophy by H. von Glasenapp, P. Masson-Oursel, E. Frauwallner, S. Dasgupta, Chandradhar Sharma, M. Hiriyanna, J. Sinha, etc.; and F. Tola, "Filosofía de la India I. Vedismo, Brahmanismo, Hinduismo", in the volume *Filosofías no occidentales* in the *Enciclopedia Iberoamericana de Filosofía,* Miguel Cruz Hernández ed., Madrid: Editorial Trotta/Consejo Superior de Investigaciones Científicas, 1999, pp. 97-135, and C. Dragonetti, "Filosofía de la India II. Budismo", *ibidem,* pp. 137-177.

which encompasses and unifies all of this diversity or to apply a qualification to it which could be valid for it as a whole.

Finally, Hegel reveals a very incomplete and superficial knowledge of Indian philosophical thought, whose principal texts and/or schools we have just summed up in brief for the indicated purpose only.

I.10 Hegel's lack of knowledge with regard to Indian thought

1. In the previous section, we pointed out two interesting subjects as being proper to the *Vedas*: the One as the origin of all, and the Cosmic Order. In the second article of his essay on the *Bhagavad-Gītā*, pp.197-198 S, Hegel refers to the Hymn of Creation (*Ṛg Veda* X 129) translated by Colebrooke in his article "On the Vedas, or Sacred Writings of the Hindus", p.17 (which is a part of his *Essays on the Religion and Philosophy of the Hindus* which we have already quoted). This hymn presents the idea of the One from which everything arises. However, Hegel was unable to understand the meaning or grasp the greatness of this magnificent hymn composed ten to fifteen centuries B.C. Neither does Hegel refer to the Vedic idea of a Cosmic Order.

2. Hegel does not mention the Latin translation of the *Upaniṣads* made by A.H. Anquetil Duperron (1731-1805) from a Persian translation and published in 1801-1802 under the title *Oupnek'hat id est Secretum tegendum* ... This translation was the only one in Hegel's time to provide comprehensive knowledge of these important texts. Hegel quotes only two short passages from two *Upaniṣads* in the second article of his essay on the *Bhagavad-Gītā*. On page 193 S he mentions "Oupnekat, which is a late and sectarian *Upaniṣad* dedicated to Śiva-Rudra, the important Hindu God, entitled *Atharvaśiras-Upaniṣad*". If Hegel did not know Anquetil Duperron's translation, he could at least know of the existence of this *Upaniṣad* through the work of Th. A. Rixner, *Versuch einer neuen Darstellung der uralten All-Eins-Lehre*, Nürnberg, 1808, which presents the German translation of

some extracts of Anquetil Duperron's book. In page 197 S of the same essay, Hegel refers to "the first Upanischad of the 4⁰ Weda (= Atharva Veda)" following a quotation of Colebrooke in "On the Vedas, or Sacred Writings of the Hindus," pp. 56-57, which we have already mentioned. This passage quoted by Colebrooke and then by Hegel is from the *Muṇḍaka-Upaniṣad* I, 8-9, and even if it is not as modern as the previous one, it is not found among the oldest *Upaniṣad* in which Upanishadic thought manifests itself in all of its originality and richness.

3. Hegel does not deal with the Masters of Error.

4. Hegel does not mention Jainism. Colebrooke gives some information on Jainism in Part V of his essay.

5. Hegel does not say anything regarding the great philosophical systems of Buddhism, which is one of the most important intellectual movements, not only in India, but in the whole world. We shall refer to Buddhism later.

6. Neither does Hegel say anything about Materialism, a topic to which Colebrooke dedicates two and a half pages of Part V of his essay.

7., 8. and 9. As we have already mentioned and as is well known, there are six "orthodox" systems of Hinduism: Mīmāṃsā, Vedānta, Sāṃkhya, Yoga, Nyāya and Vaiśeṣika. Hegel only makes a detailed exposition of three of these six systems in his *Vorlesungen über die Geschichte der Philosophie* I, pp. 150-170 S = pp. 377-395 M: Sāṃkhya, Nyāya and Vaiśeṣika. It is a correct exposition since it is based on Colebrooke's essay *On the Philosophy of the Hindus,* Parts I and II, to which we have already referred. And Colebrooke can be considered as the founder of Sanskrit philology. He had a profound and comprehensive knowledge of Indian texts and his expositions are characterized by the trustworthiness of the information they provide as well by their conciseness and clarity.[14]

---

[14] On Colebrooke see E. Windisch, *Geschichte der Sanskrit-Philologie und indischen Altertumskunde,* pp. 26-36.

In relation to Mīmāṃsā and Vedānta systems, the situation is different. Colebrooke deals with them in Parts III and IV of his essay, which Hegel does not mention and which he probably did not know. In Part I, Colebrooke refers to these systems in a very succinct way only.

10. Hegel knew the existence of the Mīmāṃsā via the references, which Colebrooke made to it in Part I, but in his work we do not find an exposition of this system, no matter how brief, with the exception of some slight references which follow Colebrooke.

11. With the Vedānta, the situation is more complex. We would like to point out the following facts in this context:

i. As in the case of the Mīmāṃsā, in his *Vorlesungen über die Geschichte der Philosophie* Hegel mentions this system, relying on the brief references which Colebrooke made to it in Part I of his essay, but he does not offer an exposition of it.

ii. As we have said, Hegel does not mention the *Upaniṣads,* although they are some of the most ancient works of India and constitute the doctrinaire foundation of the Vedānta. As we mentioned above, the Upaniṣads were translated from the Persian to the Latin by Anquetil-Duperron as early as 1801-1802.

iii. Hegel does not refer to Śaṅkara, the most important author of the non-dualist school of Vedānta. In Part IV of his essay, Colebrooke gives a detailed exposition of Śaṅkara's system.

iv. He does not mention the other schools of the Vedānta system.

v. Hegel knew the *Bhagavad-Gītā* especially through the English translation by Charles Wilkins (London, 1785) and the Latin translation by A.W. Schlegel (Bonn, 1823) as well as the article by Wilhelm von Humboldt on the *Bhagavad-Gītā* (Berlin, 1827) to which Hegel dedicates his well-known essay. The *Bhagavad-Gītā* now has about seven hundred stanzas.

In all probability, other stanzas were added to a small original central nucleus with a limited number of stanzas until the poem acquired its present form. The *Bhagavad-Gītā* is a "*syncretistic*" work from a doctrinal point of view. It combines elements of very different origins: notions from the Sāṃkhya, Yoga, the non-dualist Vedānta, polytheistic and monotheistic beliefs, the concept of a transcendent and heterogeneous Absolute, faith in a personal God, devotional and pietistic inspiration, etc. It is in fact the only text related in part to Vedānta, which Hegel dealt with.

The *Bhagavad-Gītā* is not a philosophical treatise, and much less is it a technical work; it is rather a magnificent episode of the great epic poem of India, the *Mahābhārata,* intended for popular recitation and the edification of minds. In his essay on the Bhagavad-Gītā, p. 144 S, Hegel expresses that the *Bhagavad-Gītā* "does not go beyond the common popular religious representations": *über die gemeinen populär-religiösen Vorstellüngen nicht hinausgeht.* The "common, popular-religious" information which the *Bhagavad-Gītā* gives from its peculiar syncretistic and devotional perspective on subjects proper to the Vedānta cannot be considered as adequate information for providing "*technical*" and "*philosophical*" knowledge of the Vedānta system. The same can be said concerning the information given by the reports of the missionaries and travellers to which Hegel had access.

12. With regard to the Yoga system, let us remark here that Colebrooke does not dedicate a special study to it, instead only making brief references to it in Part I. Hegel also makes some references to Yoga in his *Vorlesungen über die Geschichte der Philosophie* as well as in his essay on the *Bhagavad-Gītā,* but Hegel knows only very little of this system, and for this reason he has incorrect ideas about it which cause him to utter erroneous opinions.

13. Hegel is completely ignorant of the important accomplishments of Bhartṛhari's system of the philosophy of language.

I.11 Hegel's errors with regard to the Yoga system

Before pointing out the errors, committed by Hegel in relation to Yoga, it would be convenient here to say something about what Yoga is. Yoga is a technique aiming at providing a method by means of which one can reach a 'trance' which grants the kind of extraordinary and *sui generis* knowledge - non-discursive and intuitive - described by the ancient Indian commentators of Yoga (7th-12th centuries) in terms similar to those utilized by Leibniz, Descartes and St. Thomas to describe intuition, as shown in our commentary on the aphorism I, 48 by Patañjali in our book *The Yogasūtras of Patañjali.*[15]

Yoga is and was a technique known and practised in India in the most diverse environments and from very early times. Between the beginning of the 4th century and the beginning of the 6th century A.D., the great theoretician Patañjali systematized the Yoga teachings in his celebrated treatise *Yogasūtras,* which has been the object of innumerable and very remarkable commentaries showing the most diverse tendencies. Yoga is closely related to the dualist Sāṃkhya system (which affirms the existence of two Absolutes - Spirit and Matter) which provides it with a metaphysical foundation; Yoga in turn provides Sāṃkhya with the method for reaching the goal of separation of the Spirit from Matter.

1. At the beginning of the second article of his essay on the *Bhagavad-Gītā* (p. 145 S), Hegel says that its explanations

> sich vornehmlich mit der Joga-Lehre, dem Innersten der Religion dieses Volkes, beschäftigen, worin ebensosehr die Natur seiner Religiosität als seines höchsten Begriffes von Gott enthalten ist.

[15] Cf. on the Yoga system, J. H. Woods, *The Yoga-system of Patañjali. On the Ancient Hindu Doctrine of Concentration of Mind*; Hariharānanda Āranya, *Yoga Philosophy of Patañjali*; F. Tola and C. Dragonetti, *The Yogasūtras of Patañjali on Concentration of Mind*; M. Eliade, *Yoga, Immortality and Freedom*; J.W. Hauer, *Der Yoga. Ein indischer Weg zum Selbst*; G. Feuerstein, *The Yoga-Sūtra of Patañjali. An Exercise in the Methodology of Textual Analysis*; G. Feuerstein, *The philosophy of Classical Yoga.*

> "... deal especially with the doctrine of the Joga [= Yoga], the essence of the religion of this people [= the Indian people], in which is contained the nature of its religiosity as well as its more elevated concept of God".

Never was Yoga "the essence of the religion of the Indian people" nor was it even a "religion" of India. As we have already said, Yoga is and was only an Indian trance technique which always has been, and continues to be, at the service of a large number of different religious movements and/or philosophical systems. There is Yoga in Hinduism; there is Yoga in Buddhism too, as there is in Jainism. Yoga can be used in any mystical context in any form of religion, even non-Indian. Many Indians practise their religion without having recourse to Yoga and many persons can practise Yoga without adhering to any of the Indian religions.[16]

2. In relation to the "more elevated concept of God" of the Indian people, Yoga is precisely the place where it cannot be found, since Yoga was initially an atheistic system. This is logical considering its doctrinaire subordination to the Sāṃkhya system, which supports a dualism in which the idea of God has no place. The notion of "Lord" (*Īśvara*) is a late inclusion into the Yoga system, which thus became theistic. In any case, *Īśvara* does not have an important function in the Yoga system: it can be the object, it can be a support for the concentration of mind (like a luminous point etc.) or it can be an accelerator or helper of the process (like the fervour and energy which the adept puts into his practices). Cf. our commentary on the aphorisms I, 23-26, and especially pp. 84-85, in *The Yogasūtras of Patañjali.* The treatises of some Vedānta schools like those of Rāmānuja and Mādhava and the Nyāya system are the places where we can find a lofty and largely developed idea of God as a Supreme Being endowed with the most excellent qualities imaginable.

---

[16] Cf. F. Tola and C. Dragonetti, "Misticismo y Yoga", in *Revista Latinoamericana de Filosofia,* Vol. I, No 1, March, 1975, pp. 61-63, and *The Yogasūtras of Patañjali On Concentration of Mind,* already cited, pp. XVI-XVII.

3. Although he had such scanty information on Yoga, Hegel on p. 145 S of his essay on the Bhagavad-Gītā affirms:

> *Der Ausdruck Joga-Lehre nicht das Missverständnis veranlassen darf, als ob Joga eine Wissenschaft, ein entwickeltes System sei. Es ist damit nur eine Lehre in den Sinne gemeint, wie man etwa von der mystischen Lehre spricht, um einen Standpunkt zu bezeichnen, der, als Lehre betrachtet, nur etliche wenige Behauptungen und Versicherungen enthält und vornehmlich erbauend, zur geforderten Erhebung ermahnend und aufregend ist.*
>
> "The expression doctrine of the Joga [= Yoga] must not lead to a misunderstanding, as if Joga were a science, a developed system. With this expression is only meant a doctrine in the sense in which one speaks for instance of a mystical doctrine to designate a point of view which, considered as a doctrine, contains only some few affirmations and assertions, and is specially edifying, exhorting and inciting to a propounded [spiritual] elevation".

It seems opportune here to reproduce the words with which we finished our article "On the Yogasūtras of Patañjali" published in *Annals of the Bhandarkar Oriental Research Institute* of Pune (Poona), India, Vols. LXXII and LXXIII, 1991-1992, pp. 437-462, referring to the analysis which Patañjali gave of the concentration of mind, which constitutes the central nucleus of his system:

> "What we most admire in Patañjali - true or fake name of the author, compilator or interpolator of the First Book of the *Yogasūtras* - is his scientific attitude. He elected for his study a most subtle, complex and recondite phenomenon of mental life: the Yogic or mystic trance. He approached it not as a *mysterium* or *secretum tremendum,* but as a human fact that can be produced by human factors. He had to extract the material for his study from the Indian Yogic tradition and (probably) from his own Yogic experience and from the experience of other yogins, requiring all this a great knowledge of that tradition, a gift for introspection and a great power of observation. He analyzed the Yogic phenomenon in a most dispassionate and cool way - as Pāṇini does with regard to Sanskrit language. And he described this subtle, complex and recondite phenomenon in 51 short and concise sentences, achieving a high degree of precision and clearness that is not usual in this kind of studies. He impressed

on the material he had gathered from diverse sources the mark of an organic unity, which follows step by step the evolution of the Yogic process. He offered with his study *On Concentration of Mind* a model of insight into, and exposition of, a human experience so much enshrined not only in Indian culture but in the history of Mankind".

The analysis of the concentration of mind (*samādhi*) given by Patañjali is the subject of the first book of his treatise. The second book basically offers a lucid exposition of the method (*sādhana*) for attaining the aim of the most profound mental concentration. The third book refers to the extraordinary powers (*ṛddhi*) or "miraculous" powers, which gradually appeared in the course of Yogic practice according to Indian tradition, many of which correspond to some paranormal states of consciousness, which are an effect of the same Yogic practice. The fourth book is the philosophical analysis of the notion of "isolation" (*kaivalya*) of the Spirit (*puruṣa*) in the face of Matter (*prakṛti*). The four books, which thus constitute the *Yogasūtras* of Patañjali are structured in an orderly and systematic way, to such a degree that they constitute a model of a "system" and of a "scientific" procedure - both concepts rejected by Hegel in relation to Yoga, of whose key book he was totally ignorant.

4. Also in his essay on the *Bhagavad-Gītā*, pp. 146-147 S, Hegel points out:

> *Dass Colebrooke von den special topics der Patandschali-Lehre nichts Näheres anführt, während er von den anderen Lehren sehr ausführliche und bestimmte Auszüge gibt, hat wohl seinen guten Grund; es is nicht zu vermuten, vielmehr scheint es der Natur der Sache nach eher unmöglich, dass viele andere als uns fremdartige, wilde, abergläubische Dinge, die mit Wissenschaft-lichkeit nichts zu tun habe, zu berichten gewesen wären.*

"The fact that Colebrooke does not give more detailed information in relation to the *special topics* [in English in the text of Hegel] of the doctrine of Patandschali [= Patañjali], while he gives in relation to the other doctrines very extensive and precise summaries has certainly a very good reason: it is not necessary to have recourse to suppositions [to know why Colebrooke acted in

> this way]; rather it seems impossible, according to the nature of things, that [in Yoga] could have existed many other things to be informed that were not for us strange, savage, products of superstition, that have nothing to do with the scientific character".

The "*special topics*" with which Colebrooke did not deal for example include the excellent analysis of the process of mental concentration which we have just mentioned.

Let us quote, with reference to special topics concerning Yoga which Colebrooke could have dealt with, some opinions of a well-known Western scientist like Prof. Dr. h.c. J.H. Schultz of Berlin in his book *Das autogene Training. (Konzentrative Selbsentspannung). Versuche einer klinisch-praktischen Darstellung*, Chapter XI:

> "...it is surprising the profundity and fineness of the [Yoga] system";
>
> "It provoques admiration the fact that Hindu mind created four millennia ago so strange practices ... that only now begin to be the object of a scientific explanation from the most diverse points of view";
>
> "What we are interested to point out is that the method of the 'autogenous training' on a physiological and rational basis, exhibits a structuration in stages analogous to that exposed in the ancient Yogic traditions, as well as an appreciation of the posture factors, that possess so much importance also in these traditions. It is to be expected that ... we may be able to extract from this very ancient Yogic tradition all the elements that can be assimilated and utilized by Western people".

It was thus a mistake for Hegel to think that, among the points not dealt with by Colebrooke, there were only "strange..., savage, products of superstition, that have nothing to do with the scientific character".

It is evident that the error made by Hegel is due to an attitude inspired by prejudice: the conclusion which he draws from Colebrooke's silence is a judgment contrary to the "doctrine of Patañjali", which he did not in fact know. Hegel's procedure, not at all rigorous, contrasts with that of Wilhelm von Humboldt who, (according to Hegel himself, ibidem, p. 146 S) in view of the scarcity of information on the Yoga of Patañjali provided by Colebrooke, abstains from voicing an opinion on "in which extent what Krischna [Kri ṣṇa] expounds on the Bhagavad-Gita agrees with it [= with the Yoga of Patañjali]": *inwiefern das, was Krischna in the Bhagavad-Gita vorträgt, damit übereinstimme.*

5. On pages 146-151 S of his essay on the *Bhagavad-Gītā*, Hegel comments on the opinions of Wilhelm von Humboldt, A.W. von Schlegel, Alexandre Langlois and Charles Wilkins on Yoga. In none of these pages do we find the definition of Yoga given by Patañjali himself in the second aphorism of the first book of his Yogasūtras: "The Yoga is the repression of the processes of mind (*cittavṛttinirodha*)", and in the third aphorism of the same Book: "Then [in the moment of the total repression of the processes of mind] the establishment of the Spirit in its own nature [i.e. isolation, *kaivalya,* of the Spirit in face of Matter, *prakṛti*] is produced." That these authors as well as Hegel were ignorant of these two aphorisms, which provide the precise notion of what Yoga is, indicates the lack of knowledge, which existed in that epoch with regard to what Yoga in fact is. Another negative consequence of this ignorance is that it allows these authors as well as Hegel to apply to the Yoga system what the *Bhagavad-Gītā* expresses with regard to Yoga according to its own practical finality as a syncretistic and devotional work in which the concept of God has a preponderant role. And so these authors and Hegel erroneously consider that the aim of Yoga *is always* union with God (p. 148 S), neglecting to take into account that its aim depends on the philosophical or religious presuppositions of the system, which has recourse to it.

I.12 Hegel's errors with regard to Buddhism

Let us add a few points with regard to Buddhism as presented by Hegel. Hegel refers to Buddhism as a religion in his *Vorlesungen über die Philosophie der Geschichte* and *Vorlesungen über die Philosophie der Religion.* His utterances on Buddhism are very serious errors, which also have to do with Buddhist philosophy. Let us point out some of them here.

1. Hegel has a very confused idea of the different forms into which Buddhism is divided. In his *Vorlesungen über die Philosophie der Religion* I, p. 376 S, he says:

> *Geschichtlich ist diese Religion vorhanden als die des* Fo; *sie ist die Religion der Mongolen, Tibetaner im Norden und im Westen Chinas, ferner der Birmanen und Ceylonesen, wo jedoch das, was sonst* Fo *heisst,* Buddha *genannt wird. Es ist überhaupt die Religion, die wir unter dem Namen der* Lamaischen *kennen.*
>
> "From a historical point of view, this religion [that of being or abiding within oneself: *Insichsein*] manifests itself as the [religion] of *Fo*; this is the religion of the Mongols, Tibetans in the North and West of China, also of the Burmese and Ceylonese, where [i.e. in Burma and Ceylon] nevertheless, what elsewhere is called *Fo*, is named *Buddha*. It is especially the religion that we know under the name of *Lamaism*".

As was already well known in Hegel's time, Buddhism was divided into two great branches: Hīnayāna Buddhism or Buddhism of the South, which spread through Ceylon (Sri Lanka) and Southeast Asia (Burma, Thailand, Laos and Cambodia) and Mahāyāna Buddhism or Buddhism of the North, which spread through Tibet, China, Mongolia, Korea and Japan. If Hīnayāna Buddhism presented a great homogeneity in all places it reached, the same did not happen with Mahāyāna Buddhism. Mahāyāna Buddhism had assumed peculiar characteristics in China, Korea, Japan and Tibet, so that it can be referred to as "Chinese" Buddhism, "Korean" Buddhism, "Japanese" Buddhism and "Tibetan" Buddhism. The term "Lamaism" which Hegel uses can be applied to Tibetan Buddhism *only*. The word *Fo* is the pronunciation of the Chinese character by which the Pāli and Sanskrit word *Buddha* is translated.

2. Hegel presents Lamaism, which is for him equivalent to Buddhism, as a religion of the "Insichsein", of the "being or abiding within oneself". In his *Vorlesungen über die Philosophie der Religion* I, pp. 374-376 S, Hegel explains what

he understands by *Religion des Insichseins.* Here, too, we find a great deal of vagueness.

Hegel begins (I, p. 374 S) by pointing out that the general foundation of this religion of being or abiding within oneself is the same as that of the "Indian" religion (a term with which he refers to Hinduism), but that this religion implies progress consisting in that:

> ... *die Bestimmungen der indischen Religion aus ihrem wilden, ungebändigten Auseinenderfallen und aus ihrer natlrlichen Zerfahrenheit* zusammengebracht, *in ihr* inneres Verhältnis *versetzt werden und ihr haltungsloser Taumel* beruhigt *wird. Diese Religion des Insichseins ist die Sammlung und Beschwichtigung des Geistes, der aus der wüsten Unordnung der indischen Religion* in sich *und in die wesentliche Einheit züruckkehrt.*

> "...the determinations of the Indian religion, *brought together* out of their wild, untamed dispersion and out of their natural confusion, are established in their *inner relationship,* and their uncontrollable frenzy is *stilled.* This religion of being within oneself is the concentration and the pacification of the Spirit, which out of the chaotic disorder of the Indian religion returns *into itself* and into the essential unity".

It is not our aim here to analyse the most disputable, exaggerated and generalizing affirmations of Hegel on "Indian religion" (= Hinduism), in which he commits the error of not distinguishing between popular manifestations of Hindu religiosity and those lofty manifestations inspired by the severe teachings of great masters such as Śaṅkara and Rāmānuja. It can be admitted that, in all of its aspects, Hīnayāna Buddhism manifests a characteristic measuredness, moderation and austerity in thought, imagination, and emotion, but Mahāyāna Buddhism (to which Hegel incorrectly refers under the name of "Lamaism") frequently reveals a total absence of these characteristics in its religious aspect (as in the Tantric school). Nevertheless, the imaginative and emotional exuberance, which Mahāyāna Buddhism manifests in some of its aspects, did not prevent the magnificent achievements of its philosophical thought, which for instance developed with a rigorous rationality in Nāgārjuna's school and the idealistic school. Let us also indicate here that much of what Hegel expresses with regard to the religion of being in oneself at the end of the quoted passage, in I, p. 374 S (last paragraph: *Als dieses Insichsein ...*) and in I, p. 376 S (last paragraph: *Die absolute Grundlage...*), could easily apply in its entirety to non-dualist Vedānta, one of the most important forms of the "Indian religion".

3. On several occasions, Hegel relates Buddhism to the idea of God. He for example does this in I, p. 375 S, of his *Vorlesungen über die Philosophie der Religion.* Hegel states that, although the religion of being within oneself is extremely unsatisfactory, "nevertheless, here it is a firm basis, a genuine determination of God, what constitutes the foundation": ... *so ist hier doch fester Boden, wahrhafte Bestimmung Gottes, die die Grundlage ausmacht*; in I, p. 377 S (beginning of the second paragraph), he considers it an extravagance that Buddhism should identify God with Nothingness, which, according to Hegel, is the supreme principle of Buddhism, as we shall see later (cf. a similar affirmation in the last paragraph of the same page).

To think that Buddhism believes in God as Creator and Governor of the universe is a serious error, since Buddhism from its very beginning did not admit, and in fact rejected, the existence of God in an absolute way.

4. For Buddhism, according to Hegel I, p. 377 S (beginning of the page):

> ... das Nichts *und das Nichtsein ist das Letzte und Höchste. Nur das Nichts hat wahrhafte Selbständigkeit, alle andere Wirklichkeit, alles Besondere hat keine. Aus Nichts ist alles hervorgegangen, in Nichts geht alles zurück. Das Nichts ist das Eine, der Anfang und das Ende von allem. So verschiedenartig die Menschen und Dinge sind, so ist nur das eine Prinzip, das Nichts, voraus sie hervorgehen.*
>
> "... *Nothingness* and Not-being is the ultimate and highest. Only Nothingness has a true autonomy; any other reality, any particular thing has none. From Nothingness all has emerged, into Nothingness all returns. Nothingness is the One, the beginning

and the end of all. However different men and things are, nevertheless only the unique Principle, Nothingness, is that from which they [all] emerge."

At no time did Buddhism raise "Nothingness", which in Sanskrit is *asat,* to the category of a Supreme Principle or Absolute which possesses autonomy and could be the beginning and end of everything, of the One. Notwithstanding, let us indicate that Hegel's error was a very common error among Westerners during the 19th century. On this fact see the learned book of Roger-Pol Droit, *Le culte du néant,* in which pages 91 to 108 are dedicated to Hegel.

5. In I, p. 377 S (end of the page), Hegel states in a really extravagant way:

> *Gott, obzwar als Nichts, als Wesen überhaupt gefasst, ist doch gewusst als* dieser unmittelbare Mensch, *als* Fo, Buddha, Dalai-Lama. *Dieser Vereinbarung kann uns am wiederwärtigsten, empörendsten, unglaublichsten erscheinen, dass ein Mensch mit allen sinnlichen Bedürfnissen als Gott angesehen wird, als der, welcher die Welt ewig erschaffe, erhalte, hervorbringe.*
>
> "God, although conceived as Nothingness, generally as essence, is nevertheless known as *this immediate human being,* as *Fo, Buddha, Dalai-Lama.* This identification may appear to us the most repugnant, the most shocking, the most unbelievable thing – that a human being with all the physical deficiencies be regarded as God, as the one who eternally creates, maintains, produces the world".

Hegel equates God, Nothingness, Fo, Buddha and the Dalai Lama, thus attributing to Buddhism ideas, which Buddhism has never sustained.

6. In I, p. 390 S, Hegel expresses:

> *Das Dogma der Seelenwanderung ist auch der Punkt, wo die einfache Kultus des Insichseins in die mannigfachste Idolatrie umschlägt. In diesem Dogma liegt der Grund und Ursprung der unendlichen Menge von Idolen, Bildern, die überall verehrt werden, wo Fo herrscht. Vierfüssige Tiere, Vögel, kriechende Tiere, mit einem Worte: die niedrigsten Tiergestaltungen haben Tempel und werden verehrt, weil der Gott in seinen Wiedergeburten jedes bewohnt und jeder tierische Körper von der Seele des Menschen bewohnt sein kann.*

"The dogma of transmigration of souls is also the point at which the simple cult of being within oneself transforms itself into the most manifold idolatry. In this dogma are found the basis and the origin of the unlimited multitude of idols, images, which are worshipped wherever Fo prevails. Four-footed animals, birds, reptiles, in a word: the lowest forms of animals have temples and are worshipped, since God [!] in his reincarnations inhabits everywhere and each animal body can be inhabited by the soul [!] of man".

It is an error to attribute to Buddhism, which denies the existence of the soul, a belief in the dogma of "transmigration of soul". Buddhism explains transmigration without recourse to the notion of a soul, by means of a theory of the "series of consciousnesses" which is not to be developed here.[17] It is absurd to think that the belief in transmigration is the origin of idolatry, since idolatry has existed in religions, which did not have this belief. Buddhists did not worship an "unlimited multitude of idols and images"; they presented their homage and veneration to the Buddhas and Bodhisattvas, considered as the master's that imparted the teachings and represented the great ideals and values of Buddhist moral perfection. The Buddhist temples do not shelter any more images of Buddhas and Bodhisattvas than the sacred images of Christ, saints, and angels worshipped in the Catholic churches. Buddhism never erected temples in honour of animals.

7. Another example of coarse confusion in relation to Buddhism is given by Hegel in I, pp. 384-385 S:

Da das Eine als das Substantielle gefasst wird, so liegt darin unmittelbar die Erhebung über die Begierde, *den einzelnen Willen, die Wildheit, – das Versenken in diese Innerlichkeit, Einheit. Das Bild des Buddha ist in dieser denkenden Stellung, Füsse und Arme übereinandergelegt, so dass*

[17] On this important Buddhist theory see F. Tola and C. Dragonetti, "Āryabhavasaṃkrāntināmamahāyānasūtra: The Noble Sūtra on the Passage through Existences", in *Buddhist Studies Review*, London, Vol. 3, No. 1, 1986, pp. 3-18, and *Cinco Sūtras del Mahāyāna. El Budismo Mahāyāna en sus textos más antiguos*, Florham Park, New Jersey (USA): Primordia Media, Inc., 2002.

ein Zehe in den Mund geht, – dies Zurückgehen in sich, dies An-sich-selbst-saugen.

"Since the One is conceived as the substantial, so there is found, in an immediate way, the *elevation above desire,* individual will, savagery - the sinking in this inwardness, Unity. The image of the Buddha is in this meditative position, feet and arms placed across each other in such a way that one big toe goes into the mouth - this returning into oneself, this sucking of one's own self".

Buddha is never represented in meditation sucking his big toe. Indeed, Hegel most probably mistook the image of the Hindu God Kṛṣṇa, who is sometimes painted as a child in that posture in some popular images, for an image of the founder of Buddhism. This serious error gives Hegel the opportunity to build a fantastic metaphysical lucubration in relation to Buddhism.

In his *Vorlesungen über die Philosophie der Geschichte* (pp. 209-214 S, *Der Buddhismus*; Band II-IV, pp. 336-342, *Anhang: Das mongolische Prinzip* in F. Meiner edition, Hamburg, 1988, and Band II-IV, pp. 411-413, *Anhang: Der Buddhismus,* in F. Meiner edition), Hegel again commits many of these errors.

Hegel expresses his indignation about Buddhism (*Vorlesungen über die Philosophie der Religion* I, p. 377 S) because of doctrines which Buddhism never maintained. What is really deplorable is the large amount of errors, which Hegel put into circulation due to his intellectual authority and the great harm his conclusions caused to Indian philosophy and to those who adhered to his ideas.

I.13 Three modern opinions concerning Hegel's knowledge of India

There were thus great deficiencies in Hegel's knowledge of Indian thought: basically, his knowledge is limited to the only 44 pages of correct information of a scientific nature on *merely* three systems of Indian philosophy with which Colebrooke provided him.

The three opinions, which we shall paraphrase in the following, will corroborate what we have affirmed in relation to the insufficiency of the knowledge which Hegel had on India.

Helmuth von Glasenapp, who studied at the Universities of Munich, Berlin and Bonn with the illustrious Indologists Richard Simon, Ernst Kuhn, Heinrich Lüders and Hermann Jacobi, and who taught at the Universities of Bonn, Berlin, Königsberg and Tübingen, after referring to the scarce information which Hegel possessed on India and to the latter's lack of open-mindedness, says in his book *Das Indienbild deutscher Denker*, pp. 39-40:

> "Because of that, what he [= Hegel] could say about the Indian world was very insufficient (*unzulänglich*), so that a caricature (*Zerrbild*) comes forth, which notwithstanding many details correctly perceived, shows as a whole that he dared to face a task for whose accomplishment he lacked the necessary requirements".

In his trailblazing work entitled *Indien und Europa*, p. 104, Wilhelm Halbfass, who studied at Göttingen and Vienna and taught at the University of Münster and the University of Pennsylvania (Philadelphia USA), affirms the following with reference to Hegel:

> "Hegel's remarks on India and on Indian philosophy are in fact from many points of view 'insufficient', and it would be a vain effort to try to demonstrate that they possess a historical and philological correctness and objectivity".

Finally, Henri de Lubac, professor of the history of religion at the University of Lyon, France, in *La rencontre du Buddhisme et de l'Occident*, p. 128, after studying in detail the scarce knowledge which Europe had on Buddhism at the end of the 18th century, and pointing out some errors of Hegel in relation to Buddhism, asserts:

> "In these conditions, it was unavoidable that the expositions dedicated to Buddhism by Hegel in his courses on the philosophy of history and the philosophy of religion were still insufficient".

The term "insufficient" does not seem to be unjust if we consider the fact that the history of Indian thought extends from around 1500 B.C., the date at which the Indo-European tribes invaded India, to around 1500 A.D., when creative Indian thought began to decline - 30 uninterrupted centuries of reflection; neither does it seem unjust considering the extent and variety with which Indian thought manifested itself, as we have shown before.

I.14 Increase of knowledge related to India from the end of the 18th century

It is not surprising that Hegel knew so little about Indian thought, since it is only in the late 18th and early 19th centuries that the scientific study of India was begun in India and Bengal by the illustrious English scholars William Jones (1746-1794), Charles Wilkins (1750-1813), Horace Hayman Wilson (1784-1860) and Henry Thomas Colebrooke (1765-1837), to whom we have already referred. With the exception of Colebrooke, who dealt with the systems of Indian thought, the English scholars mentioned were interested more in Indian literature and religion.

They were followed in Europe and the United States of America by many others who endeavoured to master Sanskrit and other languages of India, dedicated themselves to the editing, translating and studying of texts written in those languages and thoroughly studied the many different aspects of Indian culture, submitting themselves in their research work to the rigorous norms of historical and philological methods, which they transferred from the field of Greco-Latin antiquity to that of Indian antiquity.

Of course, knowledge increased only gradually, and so did the scientific quality of the work that was being done.

In time, the accomplishments reached in India and in the West by Indology, which also includes Buddhology, did not in any way lag behind those reached by Greco-Latin classical studies, and they represent a brilliant intellectual achievement of which the world can be proud.[18]

[18] See E. Windisch's already quoted work, *Geschichte der Sanskrit-Philologie und indischen Altertumskunde*, that deals in a detailed way with the accumulated

I.15 The ethnocentric prejudice

Hegel not only did not know much about India, for which reason he committed numerous errors; he was also dominated by a strong ethnocentric prejudice. The ethnocentric prejudice induces us to think that our own culture is unique and superior to all others, to only see the good in one's own culture and the bad in others and to judge everything from the point of view of one's own culture. These prejudices take away any validity that the judgment accompanying them may have had, preventing the construction of a rational, solid and valid reasoning and standing in the way of the acquisition of new knowledge.

A case, which has nothing to do with religion or philosophy but with linguistics, indicates the magnitude of the danger of being blinded by ethnocentrism. In the 19th century, the existence of the Indo-European family of languages was established, especially through the work, carried out with absolute scientific rigor, of the German linguist Franz Bopp, who was born in 1791 and published his revolutionary *Über das Conjugationssystem der Sanskritsprache in Vergleichung mit jenem der griechischen, lateinischen, persischen und germanischen Sprache* in 1816. The languages belonging to this family include Sanskrit, Latin, Greek, Persian as well as the Germanic and the Slavic languages.

This discovery was of enormous importance and caused angry protests among the great European scholars, most of whom belonged to Western classical studies, like Gottfried Hermann, Haupt, Westermann, Stallbaum and others: they could not tolerate the idea that *their* Latin and Greek were languages cognate to the languages spoken by the "*the so-called Niggers of India*" (p. 26 of Max Müller's book quoted below), and they laughed at the studies of Bopp, to such a degree that Dugald Stewart (1753-1828), a well-known Scot philosopher, dared to claim - in order to ensure the rejection

knowledge in Europe and in United States of America about Indian Culture from the indicated date.

of any relationship whatsoever between Hindus and Scots - that the whole Sanskrit language and the whole Sanskrit literature (a literature extending over three thousand years and larger than the ancient literature of either Greece or Rome) was "*a forgery of those wily priests, the Brahmans*", according to the words of the great German Indologist Max Müller, who came to be an eminent Professor of Oxford University, in his book *India What can it teach us* ?, pp. 26-27.

I.16 Hegel's ethnocentric prejudice

For Hegel, dominated as he is by the ethnocentric prejudice, India and the Indians are only a mass of defects and imperfections. This opinion is probably at least partly due to the influence of reports by English persons writing on India. It would not be the first time that conquerors diminished the peoples they conquered in order to justify the violence they employed against them and the subjugation they imposed on them. A first example is given by the Indo-Europeans that invaded India and subdued the aboriginal inhabitants that in some aspects were more culturally developed than the invaders.[19] Recent examples are provided by European colonizers and conquerors, who appropriated vast regions of the world.

Hegel's position can also be explained as a reaction against the childish Romantic enthusiasm with which many German intellectuals of his epoch extolled India in an exaggerated way: Like ethnocentrism, the fascination for other cultures is a form of prejudice too. Well-known European intellectuals were dominated to a greater or lesser degree by the prejudice of fascination for India, for example the German Romantics J.G. Herder (1744-1803), F. Majer (1772-1818), J. Görres (1776-1848), N. Müller (1770-1851), G. Ph.F. von Hardenberg = Novalis (1772-1801), F. Schlegel (1772-1829), F.W.J. Schelling (1775-1854) and A.W.

---

[19] Cf. F. Tola and C. Dragonetti, "Buddhism and Justification of Violence", in *Hokke Bunka Kenkyu*, Tokyo, No. 27, March, 2001, pp. 63-100.

Schlegel (1767-1845).[20] The idealizing interpretation of India is manifest even at the end of the 19th century, for instance in the celebrated work of H. Zimmer (1851-1910) *Altindisches Leben*, which was published in 1879. Of course, now there are no Indologists who adhere to this idealizing interpretation of ancient India. India has suffered from both types of prejudice, which have both presented distorted and impoverished images of its rich and complex culture.

Hegel's idea of India could also have been influenced by the fascination he felt for the culture of Greece, a fascination which could easily induce him to diminish the value of other cultures.[21]

Finally, another factor explaining Hegel's attitude must have been the conviction that Europe was superior to all other nations in the world, an idea produced by the progress, which Europe was in fact acquiring from the 16th century onwards. Hegel was a son of his epoch and had to react as such.

I.17 Two texts on India by Hegel

We shall now present two paragraphs written by Hegel himself in *Vorlesungen über die Philosophie der Geschichte*, which clearly manifest the prejudiced and uncritical attitude of the author and whose exaggeration, aggressiveness and unilateral nature are very good reasons for rejecting them.

> *Bei den Indern gibt es insofern keinen solchen Aberglauben, als dieser der Gegensatz gegen den Verstand ist; sondern vielmehr ihr ganzes Leben und Vorstellen ist nur ein Aberglauben, weil alles bei ihnen Träumerei und Sklaverei derselben ist. Die Vernichtung, Wegwerfung aller Vernunft, Moralität und Subjektivität kann nur zu einem positiven Gefühle und Bewusstsein ihrer selbst kommen, indem sie masslos in wilder Einbildungskraft ausschweift, darin als ein wüster Geist keine Ruhe findet und sich nicht fassen kann, aber nur auf diese Weise Genüsse findet – wie ein an Körper und Geist ganz heruntergekommener Mensch seine Existenz verdumpft und*

[20] Cf. A. Leslie Willson, *A Mythical Image: The Ideal of India in German Romanticism.*

[21] Cf. D. Janicaud, *Hegel et le destin de la Grèce*, already quoted.

unleidlich findet und nur durch Opium sich eine träumende Welt und ein Glück des Wahnsinns verschaft.

"Among the Indians there is not any superstition of that kind [as the one that according to Hegel exists in China], since it [= superstition] is the opposite to reason [and among Indians there is not such opposition, because in India reason does not exist], but rather their whole life and thought are only a superstition, because among them all is dreamery and submission to it. The annihilation, the elimination of all reason, morality and subjectivity, can reach a positive feeling and self-consciousness only when it abandons itself beyond measure to the force of a wild imagination; there [= in that situation] as a confused spirit it does not find peace and cannot take possession of itself, but it finds satisfaction only in this form [of existence] - as a man fallen to the lowest [state] in body and spirit finds his existence apathetic and intolerable, and only with the help of opium gets a world made of dreams and a bliss of madness".

... List und Verschlagenheit ist der Grundcharakter des Inders; Betrügen, Stehlen, Rauben, Morden liegt in seinen Sitten; demütig kriechend und niederträchtig zeigt er sich dem Sieger und Herrn, vollkommen rücksichtslos und grausam dem Überwundenen und Untergebenen ... Besonders unsittlich sind die Brahmanen. Sie essen und schlafen nur, erzählen die Engländer. Wenn ihnen etwas nicht durch ihre Gebräuche verboten ist, so lassen sie sich ganz durch ihre Triebe leiten; wo sie ins öffentliche Leben eingreifen, zeigen sie sich habsüchtig, betrügerisch, wollüstig; sie behandeln die mit Demut, welche sie zu fürchten haben, und lassen es ihre Untergebenen entgelten. Ein rechtschaffener Mann, sagt ein Engländer, ist mir unter ihnen nicht bekannt. Die Kinder haben vor den Eltern keine Achtung, der Sohn misshandelt die Mutter.

"... cunning and roguery is the fundamental character of the Indian; to cheat, to steal, to rob, to murder are in his habits; he shows himself humbly crouching and abject before the victor and lord, completely heedless and cruel to the vanquished and subordinate ... Especially immoral are the Brahmans. They only eat and sleep - the Englishmen tell. When something is not forbidden to them by their customs, they let themselves be entirely drawn by their impulses; when they partake of common life, they show themselves covetous, deceitful, lustful; they treat with humility those whom they have to fear, and let their subordinates repay for it. An Englishman says: I do not know an honest man among them. Children have no respect for their parents, the son ill-treats his mother".

If Indians were like that because "the Englishmen" and "an Englishman" say so, this imposed one consequence:

> ... *Es ist das notwendige Schicksal der asiatischen Reiche, den Europäern unterworfen zu sein, und China wird auch einmal diesem Schicksale sich fügen müssen* (Vorlesungen über die Philosophie der Geschichte, p. 179 S).
>
> "... It is the unavoidable destiny of the Asiatic kingdoms to be submitted to Europeans, and China will be forced also some day to conform to that destiny".

– this last remark is more than disagreeable due to its imperialistic nature, the exploitations and robberies of which are revealed by history, while making us smile in view of the present political situation in the world.

How could it be agreeable to Hegel that philosophy he extolled so vehemently should not be a part of the exclusive patrimony of Europe and that Indians, who according to the mean and slandering reports of his British informants were so destitute of moral qualities, had also cultivated it?

I.18 In favour of Hegel

Nevertheless, we should be fair on Hegel and acknowledge that he tried to gather information on India as best he could on the basis of the information which was available in his time and which had more to do with the literature, religion and customs of the Indian subcontinent than with philosophical thought. It was also extremely scarce and relatively untrustworthy. In this respect, Hegel differs from those who now still think as he did and emit judgments on Indian thought without making the effort of examining the ever more extensive and trustworthy bibliography, which is at their disposal today, on what and how the Indians thought.

I.19 Conclusion: Harm done by Hegel

An idea such as that maintained by Hegel, i.e. that there was no philosophy in India, which was based on confused notions, generalizations, fascinations, ethnocentric prejudices, scanty knowledge and the resulting errors, cannot *a priori* have great validity. Also, it is regrettable that an idea originating in these conditions should have gained ground in a community of persons such as those dedicated to the study of philosophy, whose mission it is to think objectively on a solid basis. Another, more negative consequence of a psychological and moral nature is the attitude of pride and arrogance which this idea caused in Westerners dedicated to philosophy, feeling, as they did, that they were the unique possessors of something as valuable as philosophy. Another negative consequence is that this kind of idea prevented many philosophers working within the Western tradition from becoming interested in the study of Indian thought, which was underestimated simply because it came from the outside. Paradoxically, they were acting against the admirable Greek tradition of which they considered themselves the heirs, and in a general manner against the Western tradition, which has always been open to all manifestations of other cultures, whether history, literature, religion, sociology or art, etc. and was always eager to deepen its knowledge of those fields.

Thus, the Western world lost an opportunity to establish a fruitful dialogue with the philosophy of ancient India which could have unsuspected consequences, not only with the aim of finding similarities and parallelisms, but also with the intention – much more important in our opinion – of showing the divergences and differences which would reveal the variety of possible ways of thinking which the human spirit can adopt. This philosophical dialogue, if realized, could allow Western philosophers and historians of philosophy to gain access to knowledge of concepts and attitudes judged to be immensely valuable, worth studying and capable of attracting a profound and enriching interest by scholars with excellent intellectual skills and possessing all of the necessary instruments for scientific investigation in the fields of Indology and Buddhology.

The "discovery" of what Indian thought in fact is via the study of its texts and the prodigious labour carried out by Indology and Buddhology could have the following effects: the elimination of a prejudice that goes back to Hegel; the increase and enrichment of knowledge; also, the self-questioning of Western philosophy with regard to its own value, not in the limited context of a sole continent but in a much more extensive and universal. The study of the Indian philosophical systems, which start from premises so different to the Western ones, present many unique points of view proper to a highly developed culture and in general manifest a high degree of technicality, abstraction and ingenuity, could serve as a stimulus for discriminative skill and clarity of thinking according to the wise advice of the great Indian philosopher of language Bhartṛhari (5th century A.D.), *Vākyapadīya* II, 489, W. Rau ed.:

> *prajñā vivekaṃ labhate bhinnair āgamadarśanaiḥ/*
> *kiyad vā śakyam unnetuṃ svatarkam anudhāvatā//*
>
> "Intelligence acquires the faculty of distinguishing
> and classifying things according to their real properties
> through the study of different systems of thought
> transmitted by tradition.
> How can a man,
> limiting himself to his own reasoning,
> make it progress?"

It is also possible that the discovery of Indian philosophy could bring new issues into Western philosophy as a result of its contact with the creations and achievements of a remote people to which the Occident is united through a common past: the mysterious Indo-European people in whose culture the Occident and India are rooted.

Chapter II
The *Vedas*: The dawn of Indian philosophy

II.1 The *Vedas*

The texts which give the first period of the history of India are the four *Vedas*. They are *Ṛg Veda, Sāma Veda, Yajur Veda* and *Atharva Veda*. Of the four *Vedas*, the oldest is the *Ṛg Veda*, which can be located at the beginning of this '*Vedic Period*' (around 1500 B.C.).

These constitute the *Śruti*, literally "what has been heard"; it corresponds to the Western term "Revelation". They are considered as sacred literature and as such they are believed to be the criterion of truth. Their function is thus similar to that of the Bible in the Western-Judeo-Christian world.

The *Vedas* profess a polytheistic religion constituted by almighty Gods divided into three groups according to their functions: sovereigns, warriors, those related to production and fertility, according to G. Dumézil's theory, which was for example developed in *Mythe et Épopée*.

Many of these Vedic Gods have their counterparts in Gods belonging to the religions of other Indo-European peoples such as the Persians, the Greeks, the Latins, the Germans, the Scandinavians, etc.

However, the *Vedas* not only constitute a text which contains the religious beliefs of the epoch; they also provide information on historical facts, cosmogonical concepts and ritual practices and offer some remarkable philosophical intuitions.

Two ideas found in the *Vedas* are especially interesting for our purpose: the idea that the origin of all was the One (*ekam*) and the idea of a Cosmic Order that regulates everything (*ṛta*). The former has to do with creation and the latter with the functioning of the world.

II.2 Myths of creation

In the *Ṛg Veda*, we find a series of hymns which refer in a more or less extensive form to the subject of the creation of the world.[1] In them, creation is presented as the result of various processes.

Sometimes creation is conceived of as a project of the kind used to build a house. For this reason, the hymns refer to the (spatial) dimensions, the materials employed (wood), the columns (which support the sky and the earth), the doors (the East from which light comes), chains (to fix the earth) etc. The makers are the Gods in general, several Gods together or some individual God. The *Ṛg Veda* knows a God: *Tvaṣṭṛ*, the divine carpenter.

At other times, the *Ṛg Veda* presents creation as an act of pro-creation. *Soma* is the father of the plants and *Sarasvatī* the mother of the rivers. However, the more general and common belief is that which declares *Dyaus* (the heaven)

---

[1] See A.A. Macdonell, *The Vedic Mythology*, pp. 11-15; W. Norman Brown, "The Creation Myth of the Ṛg Veda", and "Theories of Creation in the Ṛg Veda", in *India and Indology*, pp. 20-33 and pp. 40-52 respectively; and Thomas Oberlies, *Die Religion des Ṛgveda I -Das Religiöse System des Ṛgveda-*, pp. 363-90.

and *Pṛthivī* (the earth) to be the father and the mother of everything.

The *Ṛg Veda* (X, 90) includes a hymn of priestly and ritualistic inspiration, which relates that the world was created from the body of a primordial giant (*puruṣa*) in an act of sacrifice in which the Gods participated. The various parts of his body became heaven, air, earth, etc. In one of the verses of this hymn (probably an interpolation from a later epoch), it is said that parts of the body of the victim became the four castes: the mouth became the *Brāhmaṇa* (the priest, the expert in the rites), the arms the *rājanya* (the warrior), the thighs the *vaiśya* (the merchant), and the feet the *śūdra* (the servant). This last verse contains the only reference to the castes in the *Ṛg Veda* and served as a basis for later speculation on this social institution *peculiar* to India.

II.3 Remarks on the previous subject: Myths of creation in Greece

In Greece we also find a series of myths of creation with various protagonists, which are in general no less fanciful than Indian creational myths. It seems to us interesting to reproduce the opinion of the German historian of ancient Greek philosophy E. Zeller, *Die Philosophie der Griechen* I, 1, p. 136, with regard to the ancient Greek cosmogonies previous to Thales:

> "Taken all that into account it seems that the benefit that the most ancient cosmologies could provide to philosophy is not so important as it was wished to believe, because the concepts which support them are in part so simple that thinking, even without their precedence, easily would have been able to go so far [as they did], as soon as it would have begun to deal with scientific investigation of things, and in part they are so ambiguous in their mythic-symbolic form of expression and so covered with so many fantastic component elements that they offer to rational reflection only a very uncertain basis".

In spite of this severe judgment of Zeller, the pre-Socratic cosmogonies had a great influence on Greek culture, as can be seen by the numerous references made to them in the Greek authors.[2]

In all of these myths, the idea of *creation* as *procreation* is predominant. Many of them present common elements. Let us now refer to a few examples of these myths.

1. In Homer, the oldest Greek author, there is only very little cosmogonic information. In *Iliad* XIV, 200 and 201, repeated in XIV, 301 and 302, Homer briefly refers to the *Ocean* (Ὠκεανός) as the progenitor of the Gods, and to *Tethys* (Τηθύς) as the mother, and in XIV, 244-248, he mentions *Ocean* as the progenitor of all of the Gods. Plato in the dialogues *Theaetetus* 152 e, and *Cratylus* 402 b and Aristotle in *Metaphysica* A, Chapter III, p. 983 b lines 27-34, refer to the myth of Homer related to *Ocean* and *Tethys*.

The same Homer in *Iliad* XIV, 258, refers to *Night* (Νύξ) as a respectable figure of whom Zeus himself is afraid. *Night* was to take on special importance in other cosmogonic accounts.

2. Hesiod presents a more developed cosmogony. In verses 106 and 107 of his *Theogonia*, he mentions *Earth*, *Heaven* and *Night* as the origin of the Gods, but then in verses 116-136 he relates that the first things to come into being (γένετο) were *Chaos* (Χάος) and then *Gaia* (Γαῖα), *Earth*, and the *Tartars* or the *Underground World* (Τάρταρα) as well as *Eros* (Ἔρος = Ἔρως), *Love*; from *Chaos* was born *Erebos* (Ἔρεβος) and *Night* (Νύξ); from *Night* and *Erebos* were born *Ether* (Αἰθήρ) and *Day* (Ἡμέρη); *Gaia* produced *Uranos* (Οὐρανός), *Sky*, and the mountains and the sea, *Ponto*, and finally, after having intercourse with *Uranos*, his son and spouse, created *Ocean* and the *Titans* (Τίτανες).

---

[2] Cf. Otto Kern, *Orphicorum Fragmenta*. Now we have for the knowledge of Orphic cosmogonies the excellent edition of Albertus Bernabé, *Poetae epici graeci. Testimonia et Fragmenta*, Part II, *Orphicorum et orphicis similium testimonia et fragmenta, Fasciculus I and Fasciculus 2*, with a rich bibliography. It is easy to find in this new edition, in sections which contain fragments 19-27 and 69-89, and in pages 119, 122, 128 and 141, the fragments we have quoted according to Kern's edition.

Let us point out in Homer's and Hesiod's myths previously mentioned the *anthropomorfization, personification* and *divinization* of elements of nature and even of human feelings, as night, ocean, earth, love, etc. This procedure also appears in the Orphic cosmogonic myths that we shall mention in what follows.

3. There is a great deal of information on the Orphic cosmogonic theories, especially in the quoted book by Otto Kern. In his work *Doubts and solutions on the primary principles*, the Neoplatonist Damascius (5th century A.D.), who directed the Platonic Academy in Athens, is perhaps the principal informant on this subject.[3]

Our information on the Orphic cosmogonies comes from the Orphic work *Sacred Discourses in 24 Rhapsodies*, better known under the name of *Orphic Rhapsodies* (Fragments 60-235, pp. 140-248 Otto Kern ed.). The *Orphic Rhapsodies* gradually acquired their present form in a long process stretching from the 6th century B.C. to the 1st or 2nd centuries A.D.

Damascius presents these Orphic cosmogonic theories and interprets them symbolically from the point of view of the Neoplatonic notions of his time, and this only causes more confusion, as it is difficult to determine which elements are of Orphic origin and which are later additions. Damascius and the Neoplatonics generally take the matter of the fanciful Orphic cosmogonical speculations seriously; they consider them to be the depository of arcane wisdom and make them the object of detailed reflections in order to adjust them to their own theories. In Volume III, p. 159, Damascius, after studying the *Chaldean Oracles* on the preceding pages, analyzes the "other theologies" (i.e. the Orphic ones)

ἔι τι καὶ ἀπὸ τούτων δυνάμεθα σέβας ἀναλαβεῖν ἔτι μεῖζον καὶ ὡς ἔνι μέγιστον τῆς ὑπερβαλλούσης ἐκείνης ἐνώσεως

[3] This work of Damascius has been edited by Leendert Gerrit Westerink and translated into French by Joseph Combès, Paris: Les Belles Lettres, 1989-1991, under the title *Damascius, Traité des premiers principes.*

> "in order to see if we can get from them a reverential fear even greater [than that he got from the *Chaldean Oracles*], and the greatest possible for that transcendental union".

This attitude is understandable, since, as I.M. Linforth in The *Arts of Orpheus*, p. 306, says:

> "... through all the change and variety [that the Greek religious feeling experienced] Orpheus held tenaciously to his primacy as a prophet of religion. In the end, when paganism was engaged in its death struggle with Christianity, the particular manifestation of the religious spirit which was inherent in the things that bore his name seemed to the Neoplatonists at once so vital and so comprehensive that he was proclaimed by them as the founder of Greek polytheism itself".

We shall now sum up the principal Orphic cosmogonies in brief.

The first version (Damascius III, pp. 162-163), attributed to Orpheus and recorded by Eudemus [a Peripatetic and a disciple of Aristotle, 4th century B.C.], expresses that Orpheus located the origin of all in the *Night*, which is one of the principal protagonists of the Orphic theologies. Cf. fragment 28 in *Fragmenta veteriora* in O. Kern, *Orphicorum Fragmenta*, pp. 97-98.

Damascius himself, III, pp. 159-160, gives another version of the Orphic theology contained in the *Orphic Rhapsodies*. This theology puts *Chronos* (Χρόνος) or *Time* at the beginning of the world, and this in turn gives rise to *Ether* ('Aἰθήρ) and *Chaos* (Χάος), cf. fragment 66 of *Hieroí Lógoi*, p. 147 (quotation from Proclus) of the cited work of O. Kern. *Chronos* produces a silver egg, cf. fragment 70 of *Hieroí Lógoi*, pp. 149-150 (quotation from Damascius) of Kern's work. *Phanes* (Φάνης) then arises from the silver egg. *Phanes* is also called *Protogonos* (Προτόγονος), i.e. the *first-born*, cf. fragment 86 of *Hieroí Lógoi*, pp. 158-159 (quotation from Hermias) of Kern's work, and fragment 87 of *Hieroí Lógoi*, pp. 159-160 (quotation from the Orphic Hymn VI) of Kern's work. Other figures appear in conjunction with *Phanes*: *Metis* (Μῆτις) as the personification of *mind* (νοῦς) and *Erikepaios*

('Ηρικεπαῖος) as the personification of *force* (δύναμις) (in Damascius, p. 160, lines 6-7).

It is also Damascius, III, pp. 160-162, who describes the third Orphic theology according to the unknown authors Hieronymus and Hellanicus, cf. Kern, fragments 54-59, pp. 130-140. In their opinion, *Water* (ὕδωρ) and *Matter* (ὕλη) existed at the beginning, and these took on the shape of *Earth* (γῆ). From the two principles mentioned was born a dragon or serpent with bull's and lion's heads and the face of God between them; it also had wings on its shoulders. It was called *Chronos* (Χρόνος) and also *Heracles* ('Ηρακλέης). With *Chronos* lived *Ananke* ('Ανάγκη), also called *Adrasteia* ('Αδράστεια), *Necessity* or *Destiny*, who was incorporeal and nevertheless of cosmic proportions. The dragon *Chronos* procreates *Ether* (Αθήρ), *Chaos* (Χάος) and *Erebos* ("Ερεβος), and then it begets an egg in them. From this egg arose an incorporeal God [or one with a double body (?)], who nevertheless had golden wings on his shoulders, bull's heads on his flanks and an enormous dragon representing various kinds of animals on his head. The God born is *Phanes* (Φάνης), i.e. *the first-born,* cf. fragment 87, which we have already quoted.

According to Damascius, Vol. III, p. 162, lines 15-17, this theology extols *Protogonos* (*Phanes*) and calls him *Zeus,* the organizer of the whole cosmos, explaining that *Zeus* is for this reason also known as *Pan* (Πάν), i.e. *All. Phanes* became God the Creator.

Athenagoras in his *Pro Christianis* XVIII, 4, Sources Chrétiennes edition, presents another Orphic theology, which has certain elements in common with the previous ones. It narrates that *Water* (ὕδωρ) existed in the beginning and gave rise to *Slime* (ἰλύς); from the two of them, a living creature was generated, a dragon or serpent with a lion's head and a bull's head, and in the middle of both heads the face of a God, *Heracles* ('Ηρακλέης) and *Chronos* (Χρόνος) by name. *Heracles* generated a huge egg, which, filled by the force of his begetter, burst into two. The top part became

Heaven (Οὐρανός) and the lower part *Earth* (Γῆ). The egg also gave rise to a God with two bodies called *Phanes. Uranos* (*Heaven*) united with *Earth* to engender female beings, the three *Parcae* or Fates, and also male beings, the Cyclops. *Uranos* flung the Cyclops into the *Tartaros* when he found out that his sons would take his power from him. *Earth* was furious and gave birth to the *Titans* in order to take revenge on *Uranos.*[4]

II.4 The One. Hymn of the *Ṛg Veda* X, 129

To return to India, let us point out that, of all the myths concerning creation, which we have already mentioned, be they Indian or Greek, the one which stands out is Hymn X, 129 of the *Ṛg Veda,* which postulates the One (*ekam* in neuter) as the origin of all. Although the hymn includes a few concrete anthropomorphic elements ("it breathed airless", *ānīd avātam*; "[ascetic] heat", *tapas*; "desire", *kāma*), what is nevertheless evident is its tendency to abstract thinking, since it locates an entity of an abstract nature, the One, at the origin of everything. The concrete and mythical explanations of the cosmogonic ideas expounded in all of the other texts on creation which we have already mentioned, be they Indian or Greek, are superseded in the hymn.[5]

The One, which this hymn postulates as the origin of everything, is a prefiguration of the notion of *Brahman* (the Absolute). Śaṅkara, in his commentary of *Brahmasūtras* II, 4, 8, line 5, states that the subject matter of the hymn of the *Ṛg Veda* X, 129, is *Brahman* (*nāsadāsīye hi brahmapradhāne*

---

[4] For a more detailed exposition of the predecessors of the pre-Socratic cosmogonies, see H. Diels / W. Kranz, *Die Fragmente der Vorsokratiker,* Vol. I, pp. 1-60; G.S. Kirk & J.E. Raven, *The Presocratic Philosophers. A Critical History with a Selection of Texts,* pp. 8-72; Damascius, *ob. cit.*, Vol. III, pp. 159-165, and the corresponding notes with bibliography in the quoted edition; E. Zeller, *Die Philosophie der Griechen* I, 1, pp. 95-148, on the Orphics in special pp. 122-148; and W. Jaeger, *The Theology of the Early Greek Philosophers,* Chapter IV.

[5] Other references to the idea of the One as origin of the world are found in the same *Ṛg Veda* I, 164, 6 y 46; III, 54, 8; VIII, 58, 2; X, 82, 6.

sūkte); and Sāyaṇa, in his commentary of this hymn ad stanza 2, identifies the *ekam* of the hymn with *Brahman*: *sakalavedāntaprasiddhaṃ brahmatattvam ānīt prānīvat*: "*Brahman* well-known in all the *Vedānta* breathed", and *tad brahmaikam avibhāgāpannam āsīt*: "That Brahman One = without parts was". *Brahman* has an important position in the *Upaniṣads*, and in the schools of the *Vedānta*. It constitutes the central subject matter of the speculation made in their vast literature.

The opposition between an initial unity and a later multiplicity was to be another idea, which the philosophical schools of the following centuries would develop. In the non-dualist *Vedānta* (Advaita Vedānta), *Brahman*, the One and Only, is opposed to the plurality of the empirical world; in the *Sāṃkhya* school, *Prakṛti* (Primordial Matter) in its *avyakta* or unmanifested aspect is devoid of all empirical determination and consequently the One which leads to the multiplicity of our reality via a process of evolution.

It is interesting to point out in the hymn, verses 2 and 3, the reference to the idea that nothing existed before creation. This idea is expressed more forcibly in a passage of the *Ṛg Veda*, Hymn X, 72, 2 and 3 (the existent [*sat*] was born from the inexistent [*asat*]); in the *Atharva Veda* X, 7, 25 (Gods were born from the non-existent); in the *Śatapatha Brāhmaṇa* (a text belonging to an epoch posterior to that of the *Vedas*) VI, 1, 1, 1 ("In the beginning this [= the world] was inexistent": *asad vā'idam agra'āsīt*), and in the *Upaniṣads* (texts posterior to the *Brāhmaṇas*), there are references to persons who maintained this idea, as in the *Taittirīya* II, 7, 1 ("In the begining there was the non-existent; from this one was born the existent": *asad vā idam agra āsit / tato vai sad ajāyata*), cf. *Chāndogya* VI, 2, 1. See also, in the Fourth Chapter of this book, the section entitled *The principle* ex nihilo nihil, *the foundation of Sāṃkhya causality*.

It is surprising to find a proclamation of scepticism at the end of the hymn: it could be that even the Supreme

Surveyor of the universe does not know from what the Creation arose.

This is not the only hymn, which manifests a sceptical attitude, frequently in conjunction with atheistic affirmations. Verse 5 of Hymn II, 12 mentions a few persons (sceptics) who, referring to Indra, the principal God of the Vedic Pantheon, ask "Where is he?": *kuha seti*, and others (atheists) who say: "He does not exist": *naiṣo asti*. Hymn VIII, 100, verse 3, expresses a similar idea:

pra su stomaṃ bharata vājayanta
indrāya satyaṃ yadi satyam asti /
nendro astīti nema u tva āha
ka īṃ dadarśa kam abhi ṣṭavāma //.

"Wishing for success,
offer to Indra a truthful praise,
if it is true [that he exists].
Many say 'Indra does not exist'.
Who has seen him?
Whom should we praise?"

This sceptical position was to continue in the centuries that followed. It was present in Sañjaya Belaṭṭhaputta (6th century B.C.), one of the so-called "Masters of Error" and a contemporary of Gautama Buddha (6th century B.C.), the founder of Buddhism; in the Materialists; and in authors such as Jayarāśi Bhaṭṭa (8th century A.D.) and Śrīharṣa (12th century A.D.), who denied the validity of all of the traditionally accepted means of knowledge (perception, inference, etc.).[6]

---

[6] On the Hymn of *Ṛg Veda* X, 129, see Karl F. Geldner, *Der Rigveda in Auswahl, II, Kommentar*, pp. 207-214. On the Masters of Error see Claus Vogel, *The Teachings of the Six Heretics*; and C. Dragonetti, "Los seis Maestros del Error", in F. Tola and C. Dragonetti, *Yoga y Mística de la India*, pp. 129-153. On the Materialists see F. Tola, "Tres concepciones del hombre en la filosofía de la India", in *Pensamiento*, Madrid, pp. 29-46. On Jayarāśi Bhaṭṭa see Eli Franco, *Perception, Knowledge and Disbelief. A Study of Jayarāśi's Scepticism*. On Śriharṣa, *The Khaṇḍanakhaṇḍakhādya of Shri Harṣa*, Ganganath Jha edition.

II.5 Hymn of the *Ṛg Veda* X, 129: Sanskrit text and English translation

Due to its importance, we considered it useful to include the original text and our English translation of the *Ṛg Veda* Hymn X, 129 here, which was composed many centuries before the appearance of pre-Socratic thought in Greece which marks the beginning of philosophy in the West.

This hymn is one of the reasons, which caused us to think that the first steps in Indian philosophy are found as early as in Vedic times.

Ṛg Veda X, 129:
Sanskrit text

Nāsadāsīyasūktam

1. *nāsad āsīn no sad āsīt tadānīṃ*
nāsīd rajo no vyomā paro yat/
kim āvarīvaḥ kuha kasya śarmann
ambhaḥ kim āsīd gahanaṃ gabhīram//

2. *na mṛtyur āsīd amṛtaṃ na tarhi*
na rātryā ahna āsīt praketaḥ/
ānīd avātaṃ svadhayā tad ekaṃ
tasmād dhānyan na paraḥ kiṃ canāsa//

3. *tama āsīt tamasā gūḷham agre*
'praketaṃ salilaṃ sarvam ā idam/
tuchyenābhvapihitaṃ yad āsīt
tapasas tan mahinājāyataikam//

4. *kāmas tad agre sam avartatādhi*
manaso retaḥ prathamaṃ yad āsīt/
sato bandhum asati nir avindan
hṛdi pratīṣyā kavayo manīṣā //

5. *tiraścīno vitato raśmir eṣām*
adhaḥ svid āsīd upari svid āsīt/
rethodhā āsan mahimāna āsan
svadhā avastāt prayatiḥ parastāt//

6. *ko addhā veda ka iha pra vocat*
kuta ājātā kuta iyaṃ visṛṣṭiḥ/
arvāg devā asya visarjanenā-
thā ko veda yata ābabhūva//

7. *iyaṃ visṛṣṭir yata ābabhūva*
yadi vā dadhe yadi vā na/
yo asyādhyakṣaḥ parame vyoman
so aṅga veda yadi vā na veda//

Ṛg Veda X, 129:
Translation

Hymn of Creation

1. *"Then[7] there was not*
the non-existent nor the existent,
there was not the realm of air,
nor the heaven beyond it.
What did it cover?
Where?
In whose protection?
Was there water, bottomless, profound?

2. *Then there was not death nor aught immortal,*
there was not appearance of night, of day.
That One breathed airless,
by its own nature.
Apart from it nothing else existed.

3. *In the beginning*
there was darkness covered by darkness.
Undifferentiated water was all this.
That One,
which being on the point of becoming,
was [still] covered by the void,
was born
through the greatness of its [ascetic] heat.

---

[7] In the origin, before Creation.

4. *In the beginning*
came upon that [One] desire,[8]
that was the first seed of mind.
Sages seeking in their hearts,
thanks to their wisdom
found out in the non-existent,[9]
the link with the existent.

5. *Their measure cord was transversely extended.*[10]
Was there 'below'? Was there 'above'? [11]
There were [male] begetters;
there were [female] powers.
Below, [female] nature;
above, [male] impulse.[12]

6. *Who verily knows? Who could here declare*
whence it was born, whence this Creation?
The Gods came afterwards
thanks to the creation of this [universe].[13]
Who then knows whence it came into being?

7. *Whence this Creation came into being,*
whether He established it or did not,
He who controls this [universe]
in the highest heaven[14]
- only He knows,
or perhaps He knows not".

---

[8] The desire that came upon the One was the desire of creating.
[9] The existent came out of the non-existent.
[10] The Sages made a study of the whole reality.
[11] Relativity of the location in the space.
[12] References to the masculine active and feminine passive principles.
[13] The verse points out the secondary role of the Gods.
[14] Reference to a Supreme Being above the Gods.

II.6 Remarks on the previous subject: The doctrine of the One in Plotinus

The idea expressed in this Vedic Hymn, i.e. that the One is the origin of everything, brings to mind the similar thesis of Plotinus, which is for example to be found in the *Enneads* V, 2, 1, p. 33, line 1, É. Bréhier ed., where it is said that:

τὸ ἕν πάντα καὶ οὐδέ ἕν· ἀρχὴ γὰρ πάντων οὐ πάντα

"the One is all the things and none of them; because it is the origin (*arche*) of all things [but] it is not all the things".

Cf. V, 1, 7, p. 24, line 22 y V, 4, 1, p. 80, lines 22-23.

Plotinus constructs a complete metaphysics based on the notion of the One. This does not happen with the *Veda*, where the idea of the One as the origin of everything is merely expressed but not developed further. Later, the Non-dualist Vedānta was to be founded on the basis of this same notion, identified with *Brahman*, the Absolute. This is a remarkably sophisticated, complete metaphysical system which declares the sole existence of *Brahman*, while attributing to all the rest, i.e. the world, the personal God and the empirical ego, a merely illusory existence, a product of man's congenital error.[15]

II.7 The Cosmic Order *(ṛta)*

The second interesting idea to be found in the *Veda* is the notion expressed by the Sanskrit word *ṛta*, which has been translated by (*Cosmic) Order* and which manifests the regularity of the processes which take place in our reality, the inevitable sequence of different facts, *order* as opposed to irregularity, arbitrariness and the unpredictability of consequences and effects.

---

[15] See F. Tola and C. Dragonetti, "El sistema de Shaṅkara. Realidad, ilusión, perspectivismo", in *'Ilu, Revista de Ciencias de las Religiones*, Vol. 7 (2002), pp. 141-169, English version in *Indologica Taurinensia*, Vol. XXVI, 2000, pp. 161-186.

One manifestation of *ṛta* is the orderly succession of days and nights, seasons, sowing and harvest, the union of the parents and the procreation of the son, etc., facts which are easy to observe.

The Order also manifests itself in the desired sequence of the good act and the reward and of the evil act and the punishment. In this case the Order is conceived of as acting as a moral law of universal validity.

The *Vedas* proclaims the existence of Heaven or Yama's world, a place of happiness and pleasant living, and of Hell, a place of sorrow and suffering. Heaven was not for everybody.

A series of passages from the *Ṛg Veda* and the *Atharva Veda* indicates that the general belief was that Heaven was reserved for a certain class of the dead: those who behaved well (*sukṛt*: *Atharva Veda* VI, 120, 3) those of good heart (*suhārd*: *Atharva Veda* VI, 120, 3), those who love the Gods (*devayu*: *Ṛg Veda* I, 154, 5); those who know the divine law (*ṛtajña*: *Ṛg Veda* X, 15, 1); the truthful ones (*satya*), those who eat the oblation (*havirad*), those who drink the oblation (*haviṣpā*: *Ṛg Veda* X, 15, 10); those who give *dakṣiṇa* (fees) to the priests who intervene in the rites (*dakṣiṇāvat*: *Ṛg Veda* X, 107, 2); those who were invincible due to their asceticism (*tapasā ye anādhṛṣyās*), those who fought as heroes in the battles and lost their life (*ye yudhyante pra- dhaneṣu śūrāso ye tanūtyajaḥ*) and generously distributed *dakṣiṇa* (*sahasradakṣiṇās*) and the seers who had thousands of paths before them (*sahasraṇīthāḥ kavayo*) (*Ṛg Veda* X, 154, 2, 3, 5).

One series of texts states for which persons Hell was reserved: those who do not sacrifice (*ayajyu*: *Ṛg Veda* I, 121, 13); the evil ones, the false ones, the liars (*pāpāsaḥ santo anṛitā asatyā*: *Ṛg Veda* IV, 4, 5); the evil-doers, without further determinations (*duṣkṛt*: *Ṛg Veda* VII, 104, 3); and finally the enemies, by the mere fact of being enemies (*Atharva Veda* IX, 2, 10 and 17; X, 3, 9; XIII, 1, 32), etc.[16]

---

[16] See A.B. Keith, *The Religion and philosophy of the Veda and Upanishads* II, pp. 406-415; H. Oldenberg, *Die Religion des Veda*, pp. 530-542; W. Norman

Finally *ṛta* is also connected with ritualistic action. In the *Brāhmaṇas*, texts which come after the *Vedas*, the principal importance is attached to the idea that the rite, correctly performed, and under strict observance of the norms which regulate it, has necessary and unavoidable effects, and not even the intervention of the Gods is necessary. The rite is conceived of as an autonomous force with unavoidable consequences. This idea, whose presence is very strong in the magical context, also existed in the *Vedas*, and it probably even existed before them.[17]

Ṛta is sometimes conceived of as a law established and imposed by a God, especially *Varuṇa* and *Mitra*; at other times, *ṛta* appears as being endowed with an authority of its own, independent of the Gods, who are even subordinated to it.[18]

It is not surprising to find, in Vedic society, the conviction that a natural, moral and ritualistic order exists, because that conviction is the necessary basis for many activities proper to human communities, such as agricultural activities, and because many manifestations of the regularity of numerous natural processes are facts which can be observed easily; because man has the tendency to think that, in this life or in another, the good are rewarded and the evil punished; and because, if the conviction that ritual acts are followed by the effects attributed to them did not exist, the cult of the Gods would have no adepts. This conviction required a word to express the regularity of those natural processes and the inevitable sequence of various acts.

In many of its manifestations, especially those which take place on the levels of human conduct and ritual action, the notion of *ṛta* is linked to that of causality: all acts have certain

Brown, "The Rigvedic equivalent for Hell", in *India and Indology*, pp. 14-20; F. Tola, "Muerte e inmortalidad en el Rig Veda y en el Atharva Veda", in F. Tola and C. Dragonetti, *Yoga y Mística de la India*, pp. 75-90.

[17] See S. Lévi, *La doctrine du sacrifice dans les Brâhmanas*, and H. Oldenberg, *Vorwissenschaftliche Wissenschaft*.

[18] Cf. A.B. Keith, *The Religion and philosophy of the Veda and Upanishads* I, p. 84.

consequences. The rite, an ensemble of actions submitted to an order, is supposed to necessarily produce certain effects, and the same thing is believed to happen with the good or evil actions which man performs: they will be rewarded or punished.

It is very possible that the idea of a Universal Order, which appears in the *Veda* was of Indo-European origin, since a similar concept is found in the Avesta, where the word *aśa* is used with values similar to those of the Sanskrit term ṛta. *Ṛta* is linked not only to the Avestic term *aśa* but also to the Hittite *arta*, the Old Persian *arta* (cf. *Arta-xerxes*), the Greek *arariskô* (ἀραρίσκω), whose basic meaning is "to join", "to fit together", and the Latin word *ritus*, "order", "rite". All these words are related to the Indo-European root *AR-*, which means: "to unite", "to order", "to fit", "to join", and "to assemble".[19]

II.8 Hymn of the *Ṛg Veda* I, 113: Sanskrit text and English translation

Ṛg Veda I, 113, dedicated to the Goddess Dawn (*Uṣas*), includes the idea of a "Cosmic Order", which regulates everything.

The strong and deep impression, which the orderly sequence of heavenly phenomena caused in the Vedic poet, is present in this hymn.

The stanzas of this hymn, which expressly refer to this notion, will be given in Sanskrit and in an English translation here below.

---

[19] On *ṛta*, see A.B. Keith, *The Religion and philosophy of the Veda and Upanishads* I, pp. 83-85; H. Oldenberg, *Die Religion des Veda*, pp. 195-202, and *Vorwissenschaftliche Wissenschaft Die Weltanschauung der Brāhmana-Texte*, pp. 124-126; H. Lüders, *Varuṇa, II Varuṇa und das Ṛita*; Paul Thieme's review of Heinrich Lüders *Varuṇa. Aus dem Nachlass herausgegeben von Ludwig Alsdorf II. Varuṇa und das Ṛita*, in P. Thieme, *Kleine Schriften*, Teil 2, pp. 777-788; Thomas Oberlies, *Die Religion des Ṛgveda Erster Teil –Das Religiöse System des Ṛgveda–*, pp. 346-347. On the etymology of *Ṛta* cf. M. Mayrhofer, *Kurzgefasstes etymologisches Wörterbuch des Altindischen*, Vol. 1, *sub voce;* and É. Benveniste, *Le vocabulaire des institutions indo-européennes* II, pp. 99-101.

Ṛg Veda I, 113

Sanskrit text

Uṣasūktam

1. *idaṃ śreṣṭhaṃ jyotiṣāṃ jyotir āgāc*
citraḥ praketo ajaniṣṭa vibhvā/
yathā prasūtā savituḥ savāyañ
evā rātryuṣase yonim āraik//

2. *ruśadvatsā ruśatī śvetyāgād*
āraig u kṛṣṇā sadanānyasyāḥ/
samānabandhū amṛte anūcī
dyāvā varṇaṃ carata āminānе//

3. *samāno adhvā svasror anantas*
tam anyānyā carato devaśiṣṭe/
na methete na tasthatuḥ sumeke
naktoṣāsā samanasā virūpe//

...

8. *parāyatīnām anveti pātha*
āyatīnāṃ prathamā śaśvatīnām/
vyucchantī jīvam udīrayanty
uṣā mṛtaṃ kaṃ ca na bodhayantī//

...

12. *yāvayad dveṣā ṛtapā ṛtejāḥ*
sumnāvarī sūnṛtā īrayantī /
sumaṅgalīr bibhratī devavītim
ihādyoṣaḥ śreṣṭhatamā vyuccha//

13. *śaśvat puroṣā vyuvāsa devy*
atho adyedaṃ vyāvo maghonī/
atho vyucchād uttarāñ anu dyūn
ajarāmṛtā carati svadhābhiḥ//

...

15. ...
īyuṣīṇām upamā śaśvatīṇāṃ
vibhātīnāṃ prathamoṣā vyaśvait//

Translation

Hymn to the Dawn

1. *"This light has come,*
the most beautiful of the lights;
born is the radiant apparition
diffusing everywhere.
As the Dawn impelled
yielded up the place
to the impulse of the Impeller,[20]
so the Night yielded up the place to the Dawn.

2. *The White* [21] *has come,*
brilliant, with her brilliant calf;
the Dark to her yielded up her domains.
Of the same lineage, immortal,
following each other,
the Day and the Night move onward
alternating their colors.

3. *Identical and endless is the path of the two sisters.*
In alternated march
both follow it,
instructed by the Gods.
Maintaining between them the correct distance,
they do not clash neither do they tarry,
the Night and the Dawn
of the same spirit, of different colors.

...

8. *This Dawn follows the path*
of those who already passed,
the first of those who are coming
in eternal succession,

---

[20] *Savitṛ* in Sanskrit, is the Sun in its aspect of the great stimulator of the Universe.

[21] The White is the Dawn; the Dark is the Night, and both words are feminine in Sanskrit.

diffusing her splendor,
animating the living,
not awakening him who is dead.

...

12. *O Dawn,*
shine here and now,
you, the most beautiful of all,
chasing our enemies,
protectress of the Order (ṛta),
born in the Order (ṛta),
joy-giver,
arouser of liberalities,[22]
auspicious,
bringing with you the feast of the Gods!

13. *From immemorial time*
shone the Divine Dawn,
now and here the Generous has shone
and so she will shine on days to come.
Eternally young, immortal,
she moves on,
according to her own laws.

...

15. ...
The Dawn has shone,
the last of the already passed
in eternal succession,
the first of all that will shine".

II.9 *Karman* substitutes *ṛta*

In the course of time, the use of the term *ṛta* meaning "order" disappeared from the Sanskrit language, but the idea of an Order immanent in nature, rites and moral human conduct remained, although it was expressed by other words in Brahmanism, Hinduism and Buddhism.

[22] The Dawn is guide of liberalities, since thanks to her are initiated the religious rites, which mean gifts for the priests that take part in them.

In Brahmanism and Hinduism, the function of *ṛta* is assumed by the *karman*. This term initially and etymologically means "action", but its meaning was later expanded to express the doctrine that good or bad actions performed by men in this life or in previous lives determine his destiny in its various positive or negative aspects with the inevitable rigor of the physical laws. Man is thus the product of his past actions, i.e. of his *karman*. The same doctrine then expands its field of action and determines that the totality of the individual *karmans* gives origin to creation, conformation, development and the way of the universe in which men have to receive the good or evil "fruit", i.e. the rewards or punishments for their actions. *Karman* is thus given unlimited power, a fact which is constantly extolled in the Indian texts. An inevitable Order thus regulates everything: the destiny of men and the destiny of the universe. The world in which we live is not the "best possible world", as Leibniz thought, but it is the sole possible world due to the good and evil actions of men.

In Buddhism too, the same order function with regard to the moral order is attributed to *karman*, and Buddhism is completely aware of the rigorous way in which the laws regulating reality function.

In fact, belief in *karman* is also the belief in an Order - an Order whose moral character is emphasized since its principal effect is that good actions do not remain without reward or evil actions without punishment. It is also an Order whose anthropocentric inspiration is remarkable inasmuch as it is human action, be it in agreement with morals or not, which constitutes the predominant factor in its functioning. The Order is placed at the center of the anthropological perspective, which becomes a characteristic of Indian thought, and is transferred from the external range of nature to the internal human individual sphere of action.

The awareness of causality manifested in the doctrine of *ṛta* has a strong presence in the theory of *karman* since, according to it, all that happens in the individual sphere and in the cosmic sphere is only an effect of that cause, ultimate and supreme, without a beginning, necessary and unavoidable, which is *karman,* i.e. action. Nothing remains outside of causality. Buddhism was to give a masterly expression to this intuition, assuming as the basic principles of its philosophy that "all has a cause" (*sahetu*) and that "given this, occurs that" (*asmin sati idaṃ bhavati*).[23]

Thus, in *ṛta* we have another case, in conjunction with the notion of the One, of a doctrine formulated in the Vedic Period which was to lose none of its validity in the centuries to follow, in various forms and expressed in other words, and which was to be a component of great relevance in the systems of thought to be found in India.

II.10 Remarks on the previous subject: Exaltation of action in the West

In the West, we can also find instances of the exaltation of action similar to the exaltation of *karman* in India.

Let us begin by mentioning a literary work. In Goethe's *Faust* I, in the first *Studierzimmer* scene, Faust decides to translate John's version of the *New Testament* into his "beloved German". The first sentence of the text reads: ἐν ἀρχῇ ἦν ὁ λόγος·. "In the beginning was the Logos". Faust has doubts about the translation of the word *Logos.* After discarding the translation of *Logos* as "*Wort*" (word), "*Sinn*" (intelligence) or "*Kraft*" (force), he translates it as "*Tat*" (act), which corresponds to the Sanskrit word *karman.* Faust's translation

[23] See F. Tola and C. Dragonetti, "Buddhist Conception of Reality", in *Journal of Indian Council of Philosophical Research,* Delhi, 1996, Vol. XIV, No. 1, pp. 35-64 (Spanish version: "La concepción budista de la realidad", in *Anales de la Sociedad Científica Argentina,* Año 1999; Vol. 229, No. 1, pp. 65-88); Wendy Doniger O'Flaherty ed., *Karma and Rebirth in Indian Classical Traditions*; Wilhem Halbfass, *Karma und Wiedergeburt im indischen Denken*; Koshelya Walli, *Theory of karman in Indian Thought*; and for a contemporary criticism of the theory of *karman,* Vibha Chaturvedi, "Causality of Karmic Justice", in *Journal of Indian Council of Philosophical Research,* Delhi, 2001,Vol. XVIII , No. 3, pp. 129-156.

of the sentence is thus: *Im Anfang war die Tat*: "In the beginning was the act". The act thus became the first cause of existence.

Passing on to the doctrinaire field, we find that it was an act, a sin, committed by Adam and Eve, which caused their wretchedness and converted their descendants, humanity, into a *massa perditionis* ("mass of perdition"), condemned for ever to suffering and death, and which was the origin of the drama whose protagonist was Christ. An *act* committed by the first man and woman was the cause of all these terrible effects.

That sinful act of Adam also had important consequences for speculative activity in the West. Theologians and philosophers dealt with the theoretical problems to which that sinful act gave rise. These problems include those related to the participation of God in that act, the transmission of culpability, predestination and the contradiction between the lofty attributes of God and the occurrence of such an action and its consequences. Important works of Western thinkers such as St. Augustine's anti-Pelagian treatises, the Théodicée of Leibniz and all the immense and controversial literature related to this subject are dedicated to these and related problems.

Thus, infinite acts (in India) and one act (in the West) are conceived of as the ultimate cause of human destiny.[24]

II.11 *Ṛta* as truth

The interpretation of *ṛta* as "order" is based on texts such as Ṛg Veda I, 113 (quoted above) which suggest *prima facie* this meaning for the word *ṛta*. The etymological analysis, which we have already referred to, supports the interpretation of *ṛta* as "order".

In his work *Varuṇa* posthumously edited by Ludwig Alsdorf in 1959, Heinrich Lüders extensively expounded

[24] Cf. the article by O. Schwemmer, "Tathandlung", in *Enzyklopädie Philosophie und Wissenschaftstheorie*, Vol. 4, pp. 208-209.

an idea which he had already expressed in 1910 (*Sitzungsberichte der Preussischen Akademie der Wissenschaften*, p. 931). He rejected the idea that *ṛta* means "order", as was generally accepted, and affirmed that in fact *ṛta* means "truth", *satya* in Sanskrit, basing his thesis on a careful and masterful analysis of the pertinent texts. *Ṛta* and *satya* thus became synonyms; their common meaning was to become "truth".

Since the formulation by Lüders of this novel thesis, the opinions of Indologists have been divided into two groups, each including prestigious scholars, depending on whether they give preference to the one or the other.

However it is possible that the distance separating *ṛta* and *satya* is small. *Satya*, (truth) comes from the root *AS-*, which in some forms derived from it presents itself in the reduced form *S-*. *AS-/S-* means "to be", "to exist". *Satya* is related to the participle formed from *AS-/S-*: *sant-*, *sat-*, *satī* (existent). Etymologically, *satya* means "that which is", "that which exists", "that which is given", "that which is there" or "reality". *Satya* also signifies "the truth" in its basic meaning of 'congruence' (correspondence, coincidence, concordance) between two things: thought and word on the one hand and that to which thought and word refer on the other. The essential feature of the truth (*satya*) is thus "congruence" (etc.). The truthful (*satya*) word is congruent (*ṛta*, as adjective). If we examine the term *ṛta*, we can see that, as in the case of truth (*satya*), its essential feature is the "congruence" (correspondence, coincidence, concordance) between two things: the cause and its effect, a fact and its inevitable effect, an event and what follows it. The presence of the element of congruence in *ṛta* and *satya* brings both terms closer and allows them to be interchanged in discourse in certain contexts, as with the use of different adjectives, which can be used indiscriminately because they have a common semantic component.

Also, *ṛta* designated the Order which governs the reality in which we live and also ourselves too. Following the Vedic tendency to substantialize and materialize everything, it was possible to substantialize and materialize *ṛta*. According to another Vedic tendency, that of identification, it is also possible for Order (*ṛta*) to be identified with the reality which it orders and regulates. Given its presence in all of the aspects of existence, *ṛta* is thus par excellence what is, what exists, what is given and what is there. *Ṛta* could thus at the same time suggest the Order which governs everything as well as the whole submitted to that Order, and at the same time it could mean Order and reality. Let us remember here that the Greek term *kósmos* (κόσμος) means "order", but it also means "world".

II.12 Remarks on the previous subject: The concept of Order in the West

From a very early epoch, the idea that a certain Order reigns supreme over the world was expressed in Greece in a more or less explicit, direct and universal way. To express this idea of Order, the term *kósmos* (κόσμος) with its synonyms *eutaxía* (εὐταξία) *and táxis* (τάξις) were used. The idea that the universe is subject to an Order known as *kósmos* was to persist in the history of ideas in the West.[25]

We shall refer to three cases in the history of this long process here: the Stoic theory of the ειμαρμένη, *fatum*, "destiny", the Roman poet Manilius and a few mediaeval Latin authors quoted by M.D. Chenu.

1. The theory of the *heimarménē* (ειμαρμένη), *fatum*, "destiny", "fatality", had an extensive development in the Hellenistic and Roman periods, especially among the Stoics. It can be said to be one of their fundamental doctrines.[26] The fragments of the Stoics compiled by J. von Arnim in *Stoicorum Veterum Fragmenta*, Volume II, referring to this theory, go from page 264 to page 298.

---

[25] See in the articles "Kosmos" and "Ordnung" by diverse authors, in *Historisches Wörterbuch der Philosophie*, Vol. IV, col. 1167-1176, and Vol. VI, col. 1249-1309, a detailed study of the concept of Order in the West from Greek Antiquity through middle-age up to the modern epoch.

[26] Cf. E. Zeller, *Die Philosophie der Griechen* III, 1, pp. 160-161.

The notion of εἱμαρμένη does not bring us into the field of superstition. The εἱμαρμένη is not a mysterious and indefinable force. It belongs to the field of physics and is a notion of a rationalist nature. This fact was correctly pointed out by Cicero in *De divinatione* I, 126. From the definitions preserved in the fragments gathered by J. von Arnim, we can deduce that the εἱμαρμένη is the natural and unalterable connection of causes and effects according to which everything in the human and the cosmic sphere occurs. Basically, the εἱμαρμένη is the law of unalterable causality and an unavoidably predetermined Order, i.e. of a *ṛta* in Vedic terms. We shall now quote some of these fragments:

[Plutarch], *De fato*, Chapter XI, p. 574 d [912 von Arnim]:

> μηδὲν ἀναιτίως γίγνεσθαι, ἀλλὰ κατὰ προηγουμένας αἰτίας.
> "Nothing occurs without cause, but according to precedent causes".

Stobaeus, Anthologium I, 79, 1, K. Wachsmuth and O. Hense edd. [913 von Arnim], quoting a treatise of Chrysippus:

> εἱμαρμένη ἐστὶν ὁ τοῦ κόσμου λόγος ... λόγος καθ ὃν τὰ μὲν γεγονότα γέγονε, τὰ δὲ γινόμενα γίνεται, τὰ δὲ γενησόμενα γενήσεται.
> "The εἱμαρμένη is the *logos* of the cosmos ... *logos* according to which occurred the things that occurred, occur the things that occur, and will occur the things that will occur".

Diogenes Laertius, *Lives and Opinions of Eminent Philosophers*, VII, p. 149 [915 von Arnim], presents the opinion of several Stoic philosophers:

> ἔστι δὲ εἱμαρμένη αἰτία τῶν ὄντων εἰρομένη ἢ λόγος καθ ὃν ὁ κόσμος διεξάγεται.
> "The εἱμαρμένη is the concatenated cause of existing things or the *logos* according to which the cosmos functions".

Aëtius, *Placita* I, 28, 4 [917 von Arnim], giving a definition of the notion of εἱμαρμένη, says:

> οἱ Στωϊκοὶ εἱρμὸν αἰτιῶν, τουτέστι τάξιν καὶ ἐπισύνδεσιν ἀπαράβατον.

"The Stoïcs [say that it is] the concatenation of causes, i.e. an order and an unavoidable connection [of causes]".

Nemesius, *De natura hominis,* cp. 37, p. 299, Ch. F. Matthae ed. [918 von Arnim] has as a Stoic definition:

εἰ δὲ ἡ εἱμαρμένη εἱρμός τις οὖσα αἰτιῶν ἀπαράβατος ...

"If the εἱμαρμένη is an unavoidable concatenation of causes ..."

In his *Commentary of Virgil's Aeneid* I, 257 [923 von Arnim], Servius refers to the following "dogma" of the Stoics:

nulla ratione posse fata mutari.

"The destinies cannot be changed by any reason".

Commenta Lucani Lib. II, 306, p. 69, Usener ed. [924 von Arnim]:

et hoc secundum Stoicos qui omnia dicunt fato regi et semel constituta nec a numinibus posse mutari.

"And this according to the Stoics who say that all things are governed by destiny and constituted once and for all, and that they cannot be modified by the Gods".

2. One of the ideas which are expounded very frequently by the great Latin poet Manilius (1st century A.D.) in his unjustly neglected poem *Astronomica* (excellently edited by G.P. Goold) is that of the Cosmic Order. Manilius expresses his admiration for the rational and unalterable Order which regulates the movement of the planets and the life of the universe in well-chiseled verses such as those which we shall quote in the following:

I, 28-33
Quis foret humano conatus pectore tantum
invitis ut dis cuperet deus ipse videri
sublimis aperire vias imumque sub orbem
et per inane suis parentia finibus astra?

"Who with a human heart
would have dared so much:
to wish against the will of God
to appear himself as a God,

to uncover the paths of heaven
and, below the celestial vault
and through the space,
the stars which obey their own limits?"

I, 63-64

...deprendit tacitis dominantia legibus astra
et totum aeterna mundum ratione moveri..
"... [Experience] discovered that the stars
which dominate with silent laws
and the whole world
is moved by an eternal reason ..."

I, 139-144

et mundi struxere globum prohibentque requiri
ultra se quicquam, cum per se cuncta crearint,
frigida nec calidis desint aut humida siccis,
spiritus aut solidis, sitque haec discordia concors
quae nexus habilis et opus generabile fingit
atque omnis partus elementa capacia reddit ...
"[Earth, fire, air and water]
built the sphere of the world
and they forbid
that something beyond them be looked for,
because they alone created everything,
and the cold elements are together with the hot
and the humid with the dry
and the ethereal with the solid
and this discord maintains itself in accord,
[discord] which gives rise to efficient nexus
and to a work destined to create,
and makes the elements able to give birth to all..."

I, 182-188

nam neque fortuitos ortus surgentibus astris
nec totiens possum nascentem credere mundum
solisve assiduos partus et fata diurna,

cum facies eadem signis per saecula constet,
idem Phoebus eat caeli de partibus isdem
lunaque per totidem luces mutetur et orbes
et natura vias servet, quas fecerat ipsa ...
"I cannot believe that the stars
arise from fortuitous Orients
or that once and again the world is born,
that the sun has recurrent births,
and that their destinies last only one day,
when we see that through centuries
the stars maintain the same face
and the same Phoebus comes out
from the same regions of the sky
and the moon passes
through the same changes of splendor and form,
and nature keeps the paths
that it itself has marked out ..."
I, 475-479
non varios obitus norunt variosque recursus
certa sed in propias oriuntur singula luces
natalesque suos occasumque ordine servant.
nec quicquam in tanta magis est mirabile mole
quam ratio et certis quod legibus omnia parent.
"[The stars] do not know
diverse settings and diverse returns,
all of them arise, at fixed places,
for diffusing their own lights
and with order they keep
their birth days and their settings.
And nothing is more admirable
in such an immense mass
than the Order
and that all the heavenly bodies
obey rigorous laws".
I, 495-500
at cur dispositis vicibus consurgere signa
et velut imperio praescriptos reddere cursus

cernimus ac nullis properantibus ulla relinqui?
cur eadem aestivas exornant sidera noctes
semper et hibernas eadem, certamque figuram
quisque dies reddit mundo certamque relinquit?
"But why do we see the stars rise up
in well arranged alternances
and respect their courses
as if by an authority prescribed,
and that, because no one hurries,
no one remains behind?
Why the same stars ornate the nights of summer
and always the same those of winter,
and each day [, on being born,]
its fixed aspect gives back to the world
and [on declining]
with its fixed aspect leaves it behind?"

III, 64-65
his regimen natura dedit propriasque sacravit
unicuique vices sanxitque per omnia summam...
"[To the stars] nature gave their laws
and consecrated for each one
their own alternances
and sanctioned all
throughout the whole universe..."

3. In his book entitled *La théologie au douziéme siécle*, pp. 23-25, M.D. Chenu states the following:

> "Of this universe, and because its being a whole, the harmony is extraordinary, through the diversity itself of the beings that compose it".

He quotes a few texts by mediaeval authors related to this subject and also gives their respective bibliographical references:

Guillaume de Conches, *Glossa in Timaeum:*
Est mundus ordinata collectio creaturarum.

"The world is an ordained collection of creatures";

Honorius d'Autun, *Liber XII quaestionum*:

...omnia concorditer consonant, dum legem sibi insitam...servant...

"All things sound together harmoniously, while observing each one its innate law";

Arnaud de Bonneval, De operibus sex diarum:

...Cujus [Dei] moderamine diversa et contraria in unitatem pacis conveniunt, et immobilia et errantia ad certum ordinem revocantur...

"Because of the government of God the diverse and contrary things come together in the unity of peace, and the immobile and errant things are brought back to a fixed order".

From the 17th century onwards, the word *cosmos* designates the *world* in its integrity, which is the object of study of the natural sciences - the *world* understood as an *ordained whole* and subject to certain laws.[27]

II.13 Conclusion

The words of José Ferrater Mora, *Diccionario de Filosofía*, Vol. I (A-D), p. 705, could be applied to the Cosmic Order to which we have referred:

> "It is easy to see that all these theories [the modern cosmological ones], although grounded on astronomical observations and employing mathematical instrumental, pose problems that were already dealt with by the ancient cosmologies and that even some of their solutions are extraordinarily similar to some of those of the ancient cosmologies. It is the case of the concept of a 'primordial matter', or of an eternal expansion and concentration of the universe, or of a continuous creation of matter. Thus, as the theory of knowledge, cosmology shows very much points of intersection between the scientific and the philosophical languages".

We can also find, as we try to establish in this book, that there is a remarkable concordance between Indian thought

---

[27] Cf. the article "Kosmos" already quoted in the beginning of this section, in *Historisches Wörterbuch der Philosophie*, Vol. IV, col. 1174.

and Western thought with regard to many subjects of philosophical reflection – even in the incipient reflection which came into being as early as the most ancient Vedic Era.

Chapter III
The *Upaniṣads*: The blooming of Indian philosophy

III.1 Introduction

The *Vedic Period*, which extends from approximately 1500 B.C. to around 800 B.C. and whose representative texts are the four *Vedas Ṛg Veda, Sāma Veda, Yajur Veda* and *Atharva Veda*, is followed by what we can call the Brahmanic Period, which extends from approximately 800 B.C. to around 500 B.C. The basic texts of this second period are the *Brāhmaṇas* and the *Upaniṣads*, which are also part of the Śruti or "Revelation". For the purposes of this book, the *Upaniṣads* are the most interesting testimonies of this second period because they include numerous texts of a speculative and metaphysical character. An essential characteristic of the *Upaniṣads* is the heterogeneity of their contents due to the fact that they are works of a compilatory nature which bring together doctrines of different origin and inspiration and from different epochs. They are often divergent and even contradictory and reveal the intensity of the speculative activity of that epoch.

The most important *Upaniṣads* are as follows: *Bṛhadāraṇyaka, Chāndogya, Aitareya, Taittirīya, Kauṣītakī, Kena* (the oldest) and the *Kāṭhaka, Īśa, Śvetāśvatara, Muṇḍaka, Mahānārāyaṇa, Praśna, Maitrāyaṇa, Māṇḍūkya* which follow them.

Let us remark here that many Western scholars on Indian philosophy such as Paul Deussen, *The Philosophy of the Upanishads*, Helmuth von Glasenapp, *Die Philosophie der Inder*, Paul Masson-Oursel, *Esquisse d'une Histoire de la Philosophie Indienne*, Erich Frauwallner, *Geschichte der indischen Philosophie*, Walter Ruben, *Die Philosophen der Upanishaden*, as well as all Indian scholars on Indian philosophy, consider the Upaniṣads as containing the first manifestations of Indian philosophy.

In this period, the Gods of the Vedic era move on to second place and are deprived of their privileged status. Two new notions then occupy the highest position: *Brahman* and *Ātman*.[1]

III.2 *Brahman* and *Ātman*: Semantic evolution of both terms

Brahman is a Sanskrit grammatically neuter term. The original meaning of Brahman has been very much discussed. According to the analysis made by Paul Thieme in his article "*Bráhman*", in *Zeitschrift der Deuschen Morgenländischen Gesellschaft* 102, 1952, pp. 91-129, included in his *Kleine Schriften* Teil I, pp. 100-138, it can be considered that the original meaning of this term was "formulation" (*Formulierung*), "configuration" (*Gestaltung*), "formation" (*Formung*) (the act of formulating as well as the product of that act). *Brahman* designates thus the action of the priest in a rite, action which consists in formulating, configurating, forming something in the verbal level. But, as Thieme remarks page 112, the nouns ending in *–man* are *nomina actionis* which express the activity (*Tätigkeit*) in itself as well

---

[1] On *Brahman* and *Ātman* see *sub voce* the two articles by L. Schmithausen, in *Historisches Wörterbuch der Philosophie*, Vol. 1, col. 954-956 and col. 601-603 respectively.

as its results (*Ergebnis*). So *Brahman* expresses also what the priest formulates, configurates, forms, as a hymn for instance.[2] Afterwards it was used in the *Upaniṣads* to designate the Supreme Principle or the Absolute.

Ātman, a Sanskrit masculine word, originally meant "the breath" or "the vital breath". In the *Ṛg Veda,* the word *ātman* is used with the value of "breath" and also of "vital breath" as the principle of life.[3]

In some passages of the *Ṛg Veda,* a distinct relation is established between *ātman* and wind (*vāta* and *vāyu*). For instance, in *Ṛg Veda* I, 34, 7 d; VII, 87, 2 a; X, 168, 4 a, *Vāta* (the wind God) to whom these hymns are dedicated is called *ātmā devānāṁ,* i.e. "breath of the Gods"; in X, 16, 3 a, where it is prayed that 'the (vital) breath' (*ātman,* glossed by the great commentator Sāyaṇa with the word *prāṇa,* which also means "breath") of the dying man go to the wind (*vāta*) in the moment of death.

The word *ātman* is etymologically related to the German words *Atem, Odem,* which mean "breath".

Similar beliefs are common to many peoples in the initial stages of their cultural evolution.[4]

Afterwards, starting from this modest and primitive origin ("breath") and thanks mainly to priestly speculation, the meaning of the word *ātman* is enriched and transformed and comes to designate the individual Spiritual Principle (the soul), identical in essence and attributes to the Supreme Principle or Absolute known as *Brahman.*

---

[2] Cf. M. Mayrhofer, *Kurzgefasstes etymologisches Wörterbuch des Altindischen, sub Brahman.*

[3] See H. Grassmann, *Wörterbuch zum Rig-Veda, sub ātman.*

[4] Cf. the article by H.B. Alexander, "Soul (Primitive)", in *Encyclopaedia of Religion and Ethics,* Vol. XI, pp. 725-731; and E. Windisch, *Kleine Schriften,* pp. 403-451.

III.3 Remarks on the previous subject: Semantic evolution of the Greek words ψυχή (*psyche*), πνεῦμα (*pneuma*), and the Latin words *spiritus, animus, anima*

The terms *psyche, pneuma, spiritus, animus, anima* had a similar semantic evolution in the West. These terms started by meaning "breath" and then passed on to designate notions of higher hierarchical value: "soul", "spirit", provided with a lofty status, and to which sublime qualities are attributed, among them that of being a *res cogitans*, "a thinking thing", as Descartes says.

1. Ψυχή (*psyche*) in Greek is related to the verb ψύχω (*psychō*): "to breathe", "to blow".

Homer conceived of the ψυχή as that principle whose presence in the body gives it life and consciousness and which, on leaving the body at the moment of death and escaping through the mouth or through a wound, transforms itself into a mere shadow which, physically and intellectually, is a pale image of the man to whom it belonged and which is condemned to lead a life of sadness in Hades.[5]

2. This concept of ψυχή related to the breath was maintained for many centuries after Homer.

The ψυχή was also later designated by the word πνεῦμα (*pneuma*), whose original meaning was "wind", "breath" and is connected with the verb πνέω (pnéō),.which means "to breathe" and "to expire".[6]

3. The Stoics retained the Homeric concept with a few modifications. We shall now quote several opinions of the Stoic school as reported by J. von Arnim in his *Stoicorum veterum fragmenta*, in which this archaic concept of the soul is present.

---

[5] Cf. E. Rohde, *Psyche, Seelencult und Unsterblichkeitsglaube der Griechen* I, pp. 2-5.

[6] Cf. H. Frisk, *Griechisches etymologisches Wörterbuch, sub* πνεῦμα. According to Diogenes Laërtius IX, 19, Xenophanes was the first to use the word πνεῦμα as a synonym of ψυχή.

According to Diogenes Laërtius VII, 157 [von Arnim I, 135], Zeno, the Stoic philosopher, considered that:

πνεῦμα ἔνθερμον εἶναι τὴν ψυχήν. τούτῳ γὰρ ἡμᾶς εἶναι ἐμπνόους καὶ ὑπὸ τούτου κινεῖσθαι.

"ψυχή is a hot πνεῦμα, for it is thanks to it that we are alive and move".

Galenus, *De Placitis Hippocratis et Platonis* II, 8 [von Arnim I, 140], attributes to the Stoics Cleanthes, Chrysippus and Zeno the opinion that:

τρέφεσθαι μὲν ἐξ αἵματος... τὴν ψυχήν, οὐσίαν δ' αὐτῆς ὑπάρχειν τὸ πνεῦμα.

"the ψυχή nourishes itself with blood, and that its essence is the πνεῦμα".

Epiphanius, *Adversus haeresies* III, 2, 26 [von Arnim I, 146], tells us that Zeno, the Stoic, maintained that God is immortal while he

ἐκάλει τὴν ψυχὴν πολυχρόνιον πνεῦμα, οὐ μὴν δέ ἄφθαρτον δι' ὅλου ἔλεγεν αὐτὴν εἶναι.ἐκδαπανᾶται γὰρ ὑπὸ τοῦ πολλοῦ χρόνου εἰς τὸ ἀφανές.

"called the ψυχή 'a lasting πνεῦμα', but he said that it is not totally imperishable, for it is wasted away by long time up to its disappearance".

Nemesius, *De natura hominis* II, p. 38, Ch. F. Matthae ed., [von Arnim II, 773], informs us that:

οἱ μὲν γὰρ Στωϊκοὶ πνεῦμα λέγουσιν αὐτὴν ἔνθερμον καὶ διάπυρον

"the Stoics say that it [the ψυχή] is a hot and igneous πνεῦμα".

Sextus Empiricus, *Adversus mathematicos* I, 71-73, reports on a Stoic doctrine according to which the souls (ψυχή) do not go downwards on leaving the body since they are made of subtle particles; being of an igneous (πυρώδεις) and ethereal nature (πνευματώδεις), they ascend towards the higher regions and remain there for a long period of time, using as food the exhalations which come up from earth, and nothing exists which could destroy them.

4. The Greek word ψύχω, as indicated, means "to breathe" and "to blow", and in this sense it is related to

ψυχή and πνεῦμα in the Greek conceptions of the soul previously referred to. But ψύχω can also mean "to make cool or cold" and in passive voice "to grow cool or cold". This second meaning has also been utilized with etymologizing aims.

Aristotle, *De anima,* 405 B, lines 24-29, mentions some thinkers who linked soul with cold (τὸ ψυχρόν) and considered that the name of ψυχή (for the soul in Greek) was due "to respiration and becoming cold": διὰ τὴν ἀναπνοὴν καὶ τὴν κατάψυξιν καλεῖσθαι ψυχήν.

Origen, in his *De Principiis,* II, 8, 3, p. 392 H. Görgemanns and H. Karpp ed. = p. 158 Koetschau ed., thought that the soul was called ψυχή

> *ab eo quod refrixerit a fervore iustorum et divini ignis participatione*
>
> "because it cooled down [going away] from the fervour of the righteous before God and from the participation of the divine fire".

The Stoics went further and constructed a theory about how did fire intervene in the coming forth of the soul in the child already formed in his mother's womb. Quoted below from: Plutarch, *De Stoicorum repugnantiis,* Chapter 41, p. 1052f

> ψυχόμενον ὑπὸ τοῦ ἀέρος καὶ στομούμενον τὸ πνεῦμα μεταβάλλειν καὶ γίνεσθαι ζῷον· ὅθεν οὐκ ἀπὸ τρόπου τὴν ψυχὴν ὠνομάσθαι παρὰ τὴν ψῦξιν
>
> "The vital breath cooled by the air and hardened transforms itself and becomes alive, whence it rightly receives the name of ψυχή due to the cooling [it suffered]".

This text of Plutarch is quoted by J. von Arnim in *Stoicorum veterum fragmenta,* Vol. II, fragments 804-808 (*Anima refrigeratione orta*), together with other texts of similar contents by Plotinus, *Enneads* IV Lib. VII 11 [= IV, 8[3]; Vol. IV, p. 201 Bréhier ed.]; Tertulian, *De anima,* Chapter 25; Plutarch, *op. cit.,* p. 1053d, and *De primo frigore,* Chapter 2; Porphyrius, *De anima, apud Eusebium, Praep. evang.,* XV, p. 813c; Plutarch, *De communibus notionibus adversus Stoicos,* Chapter 46, p. 1084e; Hippolytus, Philos. 21 [= *Refutatio omnium haeresium* I, 21, p.

83, Marcovich ed.; and Origen, *De Principiis* II Chap. VIII, p. 96, ed. [= p. 392, Görgemanns and Karpp ed.].

5. With regard to the Latin words we have mentioned, let us only point out here that *spiritus* originally meant "breath" and is related to the verb *spiro*, "to breathe"; *animus* is related to the Greek word ἄνεμος, "wind", and to the Sanskrit words *aṇitum* (from the root *AṆ-*), "to breathe", *anila* (from the root *AN-*), "wind"; *anima* originally signified "current of air", "wind", "breath". The words *animus* and anima are also related to the Latin words *halare*, "to blow", "to exhale", "to breathe"; *an(h)elare*, "to breathe with difficulty", and *animal*, "animal" ("a being that breathes").[7]

6. It is interesting to remark that, many centuries after the Stoics, Descartes in his *Second Meditation, Oeuvres de Descartes*, Vol. VII, p. 26, says the following on the nature of the soul:

> *Sed quid esset haec anima, vel non advertebam, vel exiguum nescio quid imaginabam, instar venti, vel ignis, vel aetheris, quod crassioribus meî partibus esset infusum.*

In its French version, Vol. IX, quoted edition of Descartes, p. 20:

> *Mais ie ne m'arrestois point à penser ce que c'estoit que cette ame, ou bien, si ie m'y arrestois, i'imaginois que'elle estoit quelque chose extremement rare & subtile, comme vn vent, vne flame ou vn air tres-delié, qui estoit insinué & repandu dans mes plus grossieres parties.*

"But what is this soul - either I did not stop to think about, or I imagined that it was something subtle, as a wind, a flame of fire, or an air, which was diffused in my coarser parts".[8]

---

[7] Cf. Alois Walde, *Lateinisches etymologisches Wörterbuch, sub vocibus.*

[8] On the concept of "soul" in the West, its relation to breath and its evolution, see the articles: "Soul" by diverse authors, in *Encyclopaedia of Religion and Ethics*, Vol. 11, pp. 725-755; "Geist" and "Seele" by diverse authors, in *Historisches Wörterbuch der Philosophie*, Vol. 3, col. 154-204, and Vol. 9, col. 1-89; "Geist" by S. Blasche, in *Enzyclopädie Philosophie und Wissenschaftstheorie*, Vol. I, pp. 719-722, and "Seele" by J. Mittelstrass, *ibidem*, Vol. III, pp. 745-747; and "Alma", in José Ferrater Mora, *Diccionario de Filosofia*, Vol. I, pp. 109-118.

It seems to us interesting to point out, as a commentary to the idea of the semantic evolution of some words, which from very modest notions come to designate other notions of a more complex nature and of a higher level, a curious information provided by Leibniz in *Nouveaux essais sur l'entendement humain, Livre III: Des mots,* Chapitre I, § 5.

Leibniz begins saying that:

> *Le mot* Esprit *dans sa premiere signification c'est le souffle, et celuy d'*Ange *signifie messager ... dans le* credo *des Hottentots, on a nommé le saint Esprit par un mot, qui signifie chez eux un soufflé de vent benin et doux.*
>
> "The word *Spirit* in its first meaning is the 'blow' [of air] and that of *Angel* means 'messenger'... , in the *credo* of the Hottentots the Saint Spirit has been designated with a words that means among them 'a gentle and mild blow of wind' ";

and in what follows Leibniz tells that:

> *Un certain hollandois peu affectionné á la religion, avoit abusé de cette verité (que les termes de Theologie, de Morale et de Metaphysique sont pris originairement des coses grossieres) pour tourner en ridicule la Theologie et la foy chretienne dans un petit dictionnaire Flamand, où il donnoit aux termes des definitions où explications non pas telles que l'usage demande, mais telles que sembloit porter la force originaire des mots et les tournoit malignement; et comme d'ailleurs il avoit donné des marques d'impieté, on dit qu'il en fut puni dans le Raspelhuys.*
>
> "A certain Dutch, not very much affectionate to religion, had abused of that truth (that the terms of Theology, Moral and Metaphysics are originally taken from vulgar things) in order to ridicule Theology and the Christian faith in a small Flemish dictionary, in which he gave to the [technical] terms [of the Theology] those definitions or explanations that are not the ones that the ordinary use [of language] requires, but those which the originary force of the words seemed to carry with, and he maliciously distorted them; and as he had already given proofs of impiety, it is said that he was punished in the Raspelhuys ['prison', in Dutch in the original]".

Undoubtedly, the "Flemish" mentioned by Leibniz was wrong attributing to technical words of Theology, Moral and Metaphysics, the original or etymological meaning that those words have had long ago, because with the course of time and the evolution of thought that original and etymological meaning is lost and is replaced by other, as it has been shown by the examples we have examined. What has to be admitted is that the original or etymological meaning of the words reveals many times how, in remote epochs of each society, was conceived the entity, which these words designated. The "Spirit" or the *Ātman* that for Descartes or the *Upaniṣads* are sublime entities (*res cogitans* in Descartes, the Absolute in the *Upaniṣads*) originally were only faint blows of air, which on getting away from the human body, vanished in the space, putting an end to life.

III.4 *Brahman* as "arche" (ἀρχή)· Origin, foundation and end of everything

Brahman, the Supreme Principle or the Absolute with which *Ātman* is often identified, is presented in some Upanishadic texts as an abstract and impersonal entity which should be designated by the word "It" whereas other texts present it as a concrete and personal being which should be designated by the word "He"

Brahman is the "origin", the "foundation" and the "end" of all that exists. In *Taittirīya-Upaniṣad* III, 1 we find the following expression:

> *yato vā imāni bhūtāni jāyante yena jātāni jīvanti yat prayantyabhisaṃviśanti tad vijijñāsasva tad brahmeti.*
>
> "That wherefrom beings are born, thanks to which once born they live, and wherein when they die they penetrate – That you must desire to know. That is *Brahman*".

The idea that *Brahman / Ātman* is the origin of everything appears in the following texts of the *Muṇḍaka-Upaniṣad,* I, 1, 7 and II, 1, 1 (cf. *Bṛhadāraṇyaka-Upaniṣad* II, 4, 10), which are obviously characterized by a pantheistic inspiration:

> *yathorṇanābhiḥ sṛjate gṛhṇate ca yathā pṛthivyām oṣadhayaḥ sambhavanti /yathā sataḥ puruṣāt keśalomāni tathākṣarāt sambhavatīha viśvam //*

"As a spider emits and draws in [its thread], as herbs arise on the earth, as the hair of the head and the body from a living person, so from the Imperishable [*Brahman*] everything arises here".

yathā sudīptāt pāvakād visphuliṅgāḥ sahasraśaḥ prabhavante sarūpāḥ/ tathākṣarād vividhāḥ somya bhāvāḥ prajāyante tatra caivāpi yanti.

"As from a well-blazing fire sparks of the same nature by the thousands arise, so, O friend, from the Imperishable [*Brahman*] the diverse beings arise, and they return thither".

III.5 Remarks on the previous subject: The concept of "arche" (ἀρχή) in Aristotle, Marcus Aurelius and Scotus Erigena

The notion of *Brahman* / *Ātman* presents a remarkable analogy with that of ἀρχή such as Aristotle conceives of it in *Metaphysica* I, 3, p. 983 b, lines 8-9, in *Aristotelis Opera*, I., I. Bekker ed., when dealing with the pre-Socratic theories:

ἐξ οὗ γὰρ ἔστιν ἅπαντα τὰ ὄντα, καὶ ἐξ οὗ γίγνεται πρώτου καὶ εἰς ὃ φθείρεται τελευταῖον.

"That of which all is constituted, from which, as [its] first [origin], all arises, and into which, as [its] ultimate [destiny], all is dissolved".

Marcus Aurelius (2nd century A.D.) in his *Thoughts*, Book IV, Paragraph 23, addresses the Cosmos with an expression similar to the Aristotele's definition:

ἐκ σοῦ πάντα, ἐν σοὶ πάντα, εἰς σὲ πάντα.

"From you all, in you all, to you all".[9]

A notion similar to that of the *Upaniṣads* and of Aristotle surfaces some centuries later in Scotus Erigena, *De divisione naturae* I, 11, col. 451 d, ed. Migne:

[Deus] est igitur principium, medium et finis. Principium, quia ex se sunt omnia, quae essentiam participant; medium autem, quia in ipso, et per ipsum subsistunt atque moventur; finis vero, quia ad ipsum moventur quietem motus sui suaeque perfectionis stabilitatem quaerentia.

---

[9] For other uses of the same formula see E. Norden, *Agnostos Theos*, pp. 240-244.

"[God] is consequently beginning, middle and end. Beginning, because all things, which participate of [His] essence, come to being out of Him; middle, because all things subsist and move in Him and by Him; and end, because [all things] move towards Him, looking for the stillness of their movement, and the stability of their perfection".

III.6 *Brahman* as a substance: The notion of substance in the West

1. *Brahman* is a substance in the sense which is commonly given to this term: something which exists *ab se*, is the reason or cause of itself (*causa sui*) and does not receive its existence *ab alio*; something which exists *in se*, does not require any place, abode or receptacle in which to exist; something which exists *per se*, and is not in need of anything or anybody in order to subsist.[10]

2. Descartes, *Principia philosophiae*, Vol. VIII, 1, p. 24, § LI (Latin text); Vol. IX, p. 47, § 51 (French translation), *Oeuvres de Descartes*, Ch. Adam and P. Tannery ed., gives a definition of substance:

> *Per* substantiam *nihil aliud intelligere possumus, quàm rem quae ita existit, ut nullâ aliâ re indigeat ad existendum;*

in its French version:

> *Lors que nous conceuons la substance, nous conceuons seulement vne chose qui existe en telle façon, qu'elle n'a besoin que de soy-mesme pour exister.*

We give an English translation of the Latin version:

> "By *substance* we cannot understand anything else than a thing which exists in such a way that it does not need another thing for existing".

Baruch de Spinoza, *Ethica, Pars Prima. Definitiones* III, in *Spinoza Opera* II, p. 45, Carl Gebhardt ed., defines the substance in similar terms:

[10] On the concept of substance see the articles: "Substanz / Akzidens" by diverse authors, in *Historisches Wörterbuch der Philosophie*, Vol. 10, col. 495-553; "Substanz" by J. Mittelstrass, in *Enzyclopädie Philosophie und Wissenschaftstheorie*, Vol. IV, pp. 133-136; and "Substancia", in J. Ferrater Mora, *Diccionario de Filosofia*, Vol. IV, pp. 3397-3407.

> *Per substantiam intelligo id, quod in se est, et per se concipitur: hoc est id, cujus conceptus non indiget conceptu alterius rei, à quo formari debeat.*
>
> "By substance I understand that which exists in itself, and is conceived by itself: i.e. that whose concept does not need the concept of another thing, by help of which it has to be formed".

In fact, the concept of substance can only be applied to God in the West, as is rightly noted by Descartes in his *Principia philosophiae,* Vol. VIII, 1, p. 24, § LI:

> *Et quidem substantia quae nullâ plané re indigeat, unica tantùm potest intelligi, nempe Deus,*

and Spinoza, *Ethica* I, *Propositio* XIV:

> *Praeter Deum nulla dari, neque concipi potest substantia,*

since God is the only being who is beyond causes and conditions.

3. The same concept of substance applies to *Brahman. Brahman* is also beyond causes and conditions, space and time, and the concept of substance can only be applied to It / Him, as is shown by the texts that follow.

In the *Bṛhadāraṇyaka-Upaniṣad* II, 5, 19, we read:

> *tad etad Brahmāpūrvam anaparam anantaram abāhyam.*
>
> "This *Brahman* is without an earlier, without a later, without an inside, without an outside".

The *Bṛhadāraṇyaka-Upaniṣad* III, 6 graphically expresses the unconditioned character of *Brahman,* the end and limit of all, for which there is no foundation, support or basis. P. Deussen makes the following comment in his translation of the *Upaniṣads, Sechzig Upanishads des Veda,* p. 437, in relation to the mentioned passage from the *Bṛhadāraṇyaka-Upaniṣad:*

> "When we gradually ascend from the conditioned to the in each case conditioning, we finally reach the Unconditioned beyond which it is an offence [Frebel] to ask".

The *Maitrāyaṇa-Upaniṣad* VI, 17, emphatically affirms:

> *na hyasya prācyādidiśaḥ kalpante 'tha tiryag vā 'vāṅ vordhvaṃ vā.*
>
> "For It / Him [= for *Brahman*] East and the other directions of the space do not exist, neither 'across' nor 'below' nor 'above'".

The *Bṛhadāraṇyaka-Upaniṣad* II, 6, 3; IV, 6, 1 and VI, 5, 4, refers to *Brahma svayambhu* (self-existing *Brahman*).

4. In the centuries that followed, the acceptance of the existence of a "*substance*" would characterize Brahmanism / Hinduism, one of the strongest currents of thought in India, in the same way as it characterizes the majority of Western philosophies, which adhere to the notion of God. In the 6th century B.C., Buddhism was to oppose that acceptance, adopting a phenomenalist position which absolutely rejects the notion of substance and only admits the existence of *dharmas,* which are the sole factors of what exists - they are conditioned, unsubstantial and impermanent, they disappear as soon as they come forth and they are truly nothing other than "what appears", i.e. they are mere "*phenomena*".

The Buddhist position has its counterpart in the phenomenalist doctrines that have been maintained in the West, for instance by Hobbes, Berkeley, Hume, Stuart Mill, Condillac, Renouvier, Mach and Avenarius.

As in the West, the confrontation of these two great currents of thought, the *substantialist one* and the *phenomenalist one,* were to become one of the characteristic features of the history of philosophy in India. This fact is another instance of Indian thought and Western thought coinciding.

III.7 Spiritual nature of *Brahman*: Consciousness as Its / His essence

Brahman conceived of as *arche* (ἀρχή) in the sense already mentioned and as a substance possesses a *spiritual* nature. Its/His essence is knowledge or consciousness in opposition to matter, which is unconscious and inert.

The *Aitareya-Upaniṣad* III, 1, 2, enumerates diverse manifestations or aspects of consciousness which the *Upaniṣad* designates as its "names":

> *saṃjñānam ājñānaṃ vijñānaṃ prajñānaṃ medhā dṛṣṭir dhṛtir matir manīṣā jūtiḥ smṛtiḥ saṃkalpaḥ kratur asuḥ kāmo vaśa iti sarvāṇyevaitāni prajñānasya nāmadheyāni bhavanti.*

"Understanding, perception, discernment, awareness, wisdom, insight, resolution, thinking, reflection, impulse, memory, imagination, decision, life, desire, will - they are all of them names of consciousness".

Many of the translations of the terms enumerated in the Sanskrit text are only approximate, but the idea of the text is clear: it wants to indicate all of the possible aspects of consciousness.[11]

The *Aitareya-Upaniṣad* III, 3, 3, refers to consciousness as the foundation of all, as being all, and identifies it with *Brahman*:

> *eṣa brahmaiṣa indra eṣa prajāpatir ete sarve devā imāni ca pañca mahābhūtāni pṛthivī vāyur ākāśa āpo jyotīṃṣītyetānīmāni ca kṣudramiśrāṇīva bījānītarāṇi cetarāṇi cāṇḍajāni ca jārujāni ca svedajāni codbhijjāni cāśvā gāvaḥ puruṣā hastino yat kiṃcedaṃ prāṇi jaṅgamaṃ ca patatri ca yac ca sthāvaraṃ sarvaṃ tat prajñānetraṃ prajñāne pratiṣṭhitaṃ prajñānetro lokaḥ prajñā pratiṣṭhā prajñānaṃ brahma.*
>
> "It [= consciousness] is Brahmā, it is Indra, it is Prajāpati, it is all these Gods; it is these five great elements, namely earth, wind, space, water, light; it is these things and those, which are mingled of the fine as it were; the seeds of one sort and another; those born from an egg, and those born from a womb, and those born from sweat, and those born from a sprout; horses, cows, persons, elephants, whatever breathing thing there is here, whether moving or flying and what is stationary. All this is guided by consciousness, is established in consciousness; the world is guided by consciousness; consciousness is the foundation, consciousness is *Brahman*".

The *Bṛhadāraṇyaka-Upaniṣad* III, 9, 28, stanza 7, states: *vijñānam ānandaṃ Brahma: "Brahman* is consciousness, bliss"; in ibidem IV, 3, 7, it is said that the *Ātman* [= *Brahman*] is "made of consciousness": *vijñānamaya*; *ibidem* III, 8, 11,

---

[11] See the text of Descartes *Meditationes de prima philosophia*, Vol. VII (Latin text), Vol. IX (French translation), quoted in the beginning of the next section, specially *Meditatio Secunda*, p. 28, where several mental functions of a *res cogitans* are enumerated.

maintains that the Imperishable [= *Brahman*] is the only conscious entity which exists in reality; and *ibidem* II, 4, 12, the Great Being (*mahad bhūta*) [= *Brahman*] is called a "compact mass of consciousness": *vijñānaghana*.

The essence of *Brahman* as consciousness and knowledge is not subordinated to the existence of a knowable object – it even subsists in the absence of any object of cognition or contents of knowledge, as established by *Bṛhadāraṇyaka-Upaniṣad* IV, 3, 30:

> *yad vai tan na vijānāti vijānan vai tan na vijānāti na hi vijñātur vijñāter viparilopo vidyate 'vināśitvāt.*
>
> "While It [= *Brahman*] does not know, knowing indeed It does not know, for there is no cessation of the knowledge of the knower, because of the imperishability [of knowledge]".

This text thus affirms the possibility of *pure* knowledge in the sense of "devoid of an object".

Brahman is thus the *opposite to matter,* whose characteristic feature is precisely the lack of the capacity to *know* or *be conscious.*

The *spirit / matter dichotomy* was to continue in the history of Indian thought, the spirit being characterized by knowledge and consciousness and matter by their absence. The same happened in the West. It would be interesting to establish how the notions of matter and spirit arose, i.e. whether there was an evolution similar to that of *ātman* and soul and whether there are also similarities between Indian and Western thought with regard to this point.

III.8 A marginal remark: The conception of consciousness in Vasubandhu, Dharmakīrti, Fichte and Husserl

1. In contrast, several centuries later Buddhism was to maintain the impossibility of a "consciousness" which is not a "consciousness of"; the impossibility of a "knowledge" which is not a "knowledge of", as asserted by Vasubandhu, II, 23 a:

> *cittacaittāḥ sahāvaśyam.*

"Mind [or consciousness] and mental contents are necessarily together",

glossed by Vasubandhu himself:

na hyete vinā 'nyonyaṃ bhavitum utsahante,

"because they cannot come into being one without the other",

and by Yaśomitra:

na cittaṃ caittair vinā utpadyate nāpi caittā vinā cittena.

"Mind [or consciousness] does not arise without the mental contents, neither the mental contents without mind".

2. Later, certain important logical and epistemological consequences were to be derived from this postulate, for example the Buddhist theory called *sahopalambha* of the Idealistic philosophical School, which maintains that the simultaneity of the perception of the object by the sense-organs and its representation (in the mind) demonstrates the identity of the subject and the object of knowledge, i.e. proves that the object and the subject are not different, that the object of knowledge does not exist outside and has its origin in the mind. Cf. Takashi Iwata, *Sahopalambhaniyama* (2 volumes).

In Volume I, p. 259, lines 10-18 (Tibetan text) and p. 275 (German translation), *op. cit.*, Jitāri, the author of the treatise edited by Iwata and preserved only in Tibetan, clearly expresses the idealistic Buddhist thesis, and in support of his thesis he quotes Dharmakīrti, *Pramāṇavārttika* III (*Pratyakṣa*), 388.

The mentioned Sanskrit text by Dharmakīrti, R. Ch. Pandeya ed., poses the rhetoric question:

sakṛt saṃvedyamānasya niyamena dhiyā saha/
viṣayasya tato 'nyatvaṃ kenākāreṇa siddhyati//

"How is established the difference
between the object, which is [always] simultaneously perceived together with mental representation,
and that representation?"

His answer is: "in no way". There is no difference between the perceived object and its simultaneous representation in the mind. In stanza 390 he expresses:

> *nārtho 'saṃvedanaḥ kaścid anārthaṃ vāpi vedanam/*
> *dṛṣṭaṃ saṃvedyamānaṃ tat tayor nāsti vivekitā//*

> "There is no object of knowledge without perception;
> neither a perception without object;
> [only] what is seen is perceived,
> therefore there is no distinction of both".

And in the stanza 391 a-b-c, he concludes:

> ***tasmāt arthasya durvāraṃ jñānakālāvabhāsinaḥ/***
> ***jñānād avyatirekitvam*** [glossed by the commentator
> Manoratha-nandin by ***abhinnatvam***: "the fact of not
> being different "]...

> "Therefore the identity
> of the object which is manifested
> in the moment of knowledge
> and the knowledge itself
> is irrefutable".

3. Eleven centuries after Dharmakīrti, in the West, Johann Gottlieb Fichte (1762-1814) would express similar ideas in relation to the simultaneity of the sensory perception of the object and its representation in the mind. In his treatise *Die Anweisung zum seligen Leben*, Third Lesson, p. 44, Meiner Verlag ed., Fichte affirms:

> *Hoffentlich wird auch keiner, der nur der allergewöhnlichsten Besinnung mächtig ist, behaupten wollen: er könne einen Gegenstand sehen, hören, fühlen, ohne zugleich auch desselben Gegenstandes, und seines Sehens, Hörens, oder Fühlens desselben Gegenstandes, innerlich sich bewusst zu werden; er könne bewusstlos etwas bestimmtes sehen, usf.:*

> "As it is to be expected, nobody, who possesses only the most common intelligence, would like to affirm that he could see, hear, feel an object without being innerly also simultaneouly conscious of that object and of his own seeing, hearing, feeling of that same object; that he could without intervention of the consciousness see, etc. something particular".

Fichte himself explains what is the simultaneity to which he refers:

> *Dieses Zugleichsein, - Zugleichsein, sage ich, und diese Unabtrennlichkeit der äuserrn Sinneswahrnehmung, und des innern Denkens, voneinander, - dieses, und nicht mehr, liegt in der faktischen Selbstbeobachtung, der Tatsache des Bewusstseins ...:*
>
> "This simultaneity - I say *simultaneity*, and this mutual inseparability between the external sensory perception and the internal thinking, – this [simultaneity], and nothing else, lies in the actual self-observation, in the fact of consciousness..."

This Buddhist concept of mind and its object reminds us of Edmund Husserl's assertion (*Ideen zu einer reinen Phänomenologie und phänomenologische Philosophie,* I, 84) concerning what is called "intentionality of consciousness":

> "The peculiarity of any experience (*Erlebnis*) is to be conscious of something", and "a perception is perception of something".

III.9 Remarks on the previous subject of consciousness: The relation between the spirit and mental functions in the West

The relation between the *spirit* and *mental functions,* which we find in the *Upaniṣads* is also to be found in the history of ideas in the West.

For instance, Descartes in *Meditationes de prima philosophia,* Vol. VII (Latin text); Vol. IX (French translation), says categorically:

> *sum igitur praecise tantùm res cogitans, id est, mens, sive animus sive intellectus, sive ratio* (*Meditatio Secunda,* p. 27),

which in the French version (*Meditation Seconde,* p. 21): published by Descartes himself corresponds to:

> *... ie ne suis donc, precisement parlant, qu'vne chose qui pense, c'est á dire vn esprit, vn entendement ou vne raison ...*
>
> "... consequently, speaking with precision, I am only a thinking thing, i. e. a spirit, or a soul [lacking in his French version], or an intellect, or a reason".

And further Descartes in *Meditatio Secunda,* p. 28 asks himself:

> *Sed quid igitur sum? Res cogitans. Quid est hoc? Nempe dubitans, intelligens, affirmans, negans, volens, nolens, imaginans quoque, & sentiens,*

which in his French version (*Meditation Seconde,* p. 22). reads:

> *Mais qu'est-ce donc que ie suis? Vne chose qui pense. Qu'est-ce qu'vne chose qui pense? C'est á dire vne chose qui doute, qui conçoit, qui affirme, qui nie, qui veut, qui ne veut pas, qui imagine aussi, & qui sent.*
>
> "But what then am I? A thinking thing. And what is that [= a thinking thing]? It is a thing that doubts, understands, affirms, denies, wishes, does not wish, imagines also, and feels".

Similarly, in *Ethica* II, *Propositio* I, p. 86, Baruch de Spinoza states in reference to God, who is the Spirit *par excellence*:

> *Cogitatio attributum Dei est, sive Deus est res cogitans.*
>
> "Thinking is an attribute of God, or God is a thinking thing".

III.10 *Brahman* as Universal Spirit

Brahman is also considered as the *Universal Spirit* or *Universal Soul*. This is the cosmic aspect of the well-known archaic animistic concept.

This doctrine is presented by the Upanishadic thinker Yājñavalkya in *Bṛhadāraṇyaka-Upaniṣad* III, 7, 3-23, where he adopts three points of view: that of the elements of nature (*adhidaivatam*), that of beings (*adhibhūtam*) and that of the individual (*adhyātman*). Yājñavalkya begins by saying:

> *yaḥ pṛthivyāṃ tiṣṭhan pṛthivyā antaro yaṃ pṛthivī na veda yasya pṛthivī śarīraṃ yaḥ pṛthivīm antaro yamayatyeṣa ta ātmāntaryāmyamṛtaḥ.*
>
> "He who staying in the earth is other than the earth, whom the earth does not know, whose body is the earth, and who controls the earth from within – He is your Ātman, the Internal Governor, immortal".

Then Yājñavalkya repeats the same formula, substituting the word "earth" (*pṛthivī*) by the words "waters" (*āpas*), "fire" (*agni*), "intermediate space" (*antarikṣa*), "wind" (*vāyu*), "sky" (*div*), "sun" (*āditya*), "regions of the space" (*diś*), "moon and stars" (*candratāraka*), "ether" (*ākāśa*), "darkness" (*tamas*), and "light" (*tejas*) (III, 7, 4-14). Then he repeats the same formula again, changing the word "earth" to "all beings" (III, 7, 15). Finally, Yājñavalkya repeats the same formula again, changing the word "earth" to "breath" (*prāṇa*), "voice" (*vāc*), "eye" (*cakṣus*), "ear" (*śrotra*), "mind" (*manas*), "skin" (*tvac*), "consciousness" (*vijñāna*), and "semen" (*retas*) (III, 7, 16-23). With this enumeration, the text intends to encompass the whole of nature, in which the *Ātman* or *Brahman*, as a "*Universal Spirit*" or "*Universal Soul*", dwells in all beings and all things and rules them from the inside.

The *Chāndogya-Upaniṣad* VI, 8, 7, in a formula repeated in VI, 9, 4; VI, 10, 3; VI, 11, 3; VI, 12, 3; VI, 13, 3; VI, 14, 3; VI, 15, 3; VI, 16, 3, states that

> *sa ya eṣo 'ṇimaitatātmyam idaṃ sarvaṃ tat satyaṃ sa ātmā tat tvam asi śvetaketo iti.*
>
> "All this is constituted by that subtle element, it is the reality, it is the *Ātman*, and you are that, O Śvetaketu".

The *Bṛhadāraṇyaka-Upaniṣad* II, 4, 12, develops, in relation to *Brahman / Ātman*, which as the universal essence underlies and pervades all, the following comparison:

> *sa yathā saindhavakhilya udake prāsta udakam evānuvilīyeta na hāsyodgrahāṇāyeva syāt / yato yatas tvādadīta lavaṇam evaivaṃ vā ara idaṃ mahadbhūtam anantam apāraṃ vijñānaghana eva.*
>
> "In the same way as a lump of salt thrown into the water would dissolve in it, and it would not be possible to find it any more, and wherever one may take [water], it is salty, so also the Great Being, infinite, unlimited, is just a compact mass of consciousness".

There is a passage in the *Bṛhadāraṇyaka-Upaniṣad* III, 8, 9 which describes how the Supreme Principle, designated by the word "Imperishable", governs the world imposing order on it:

etasya vā akṣarasya praśāsane gārgi sūryācandramasau vidhṛtau tiṣṭhata etasya vā akṣarasya praśāsane gārgi dyāvāpṛthivyau vidhṛte tiṣṭhata etasya vā akṣarasya praśāsane gārgi nimeṣā muhūrtā ahorātrāṇyardhamāsā māsā ṛtavaḥ saṃvatsarā iti vidhṛtās tiṣṭhantyetasya vā akṣarasya praśāsane gārgi prācyo 'nyā nadyaḥ syandante śvetebhyaḥ parvatebhyaḥ pratīcyo 'nyā yāṃ yāṃ ca diśam anvetasya vā akṣarasya praśāsane gārgi dadato manuṣyāḥ praśaṃsanti yajamānaṃ devā darvīṃ pitaro 'nvāyattāḥ.

"At the command of that Imperishable, O Gārgī, the sun and the moon stand apart; at the command of that Imperishable, O Gārgī, the earth and the sky stand apart; at the command of that Imperishable, O Gārgī, the minutes, the hours, the days, the nights, the fortnights, the months, the seasons and the years stand apart; at the command of that Imperishable, O Gārgī, some rivers flow from the snowy mountains, some to the East, others to the West, in whatever direction each flows; at the command of that Imperishable, O Gārgī, men praise those who give, the Gods him who sacrifices, and the Fathers the funerary oblation - in accordance [with that command]".

In one of the following sections, *The unity of the world in the* Upaniṣads, we shall see how the Universal Soul gives unity to the world.

III. 11 Remarks on the previous subject: The Universal Soul (*anima mundi*) in the West

The animistic idea of a Universal Soul or Spirit (*anima mundi*) was very well known in the West. Many thinkers adopted it. This *Universal Spirit* was often identified with *God* or the *Holy Spirit*. We shall now refer to a few of these thinkers.

1. Plato was probably the first Greek philosopher to introduce the idea of the existence of a "Soul (ψυχή) of the World". In *Timaeus* 34 a-b, *Oeuvres Complètes* X, p. 147, A. Rivaud ed., he affirms that the Soul was placed at the center of the universe by God (Demiurge) and that it pervades everything and surrounds the universe:

ψυχὴν δὲ εἰς τὸ μέσον αὐτοῦ θεὶς διὰ παντός τε ἔτεινεν καὶ ἔτι ἔξωθεν τὸ σῶμα αὐτῇ περιεκάλυψεν.

Cf. *ibidem*, 30 b-c (= p. 143). For Plato, there is no identity between the 'Soul of the World' and the Creator.

2. Aristotle in *De anima* 411 a, lines 7-8 points out that some thinkers have maintained that the soul (ψυχή) is mixed with the universe, linking to this thesis the opinion of Thales that all is full of Gods:

> καὶ ἐν τῷ ὅλῳ δέ τινες αὐτὴν μεμῖχθαί φασιν, ὅθεν ἴσως καὶ Θαλῆς ᾠήθη πάντα πλήρη θεῶν εἶναι.[12]

3. Plotinus deals with the *Universal Spirit* or *Soul* in a much more extensive way than Plato and characterizes it in a detailed way. Let us mention some of these characteristics here: the universe has one unique Soul which pervades it completely (*Ennead* I, 1, 8, p. 44, lines 14-15, É. Bréhier ed.: κἀν τῷ παντὶ ὅλῳ οὖσα μία); the Soul of the World (ἡ τοῦ κόσμου ψυχὴ) is a God (θεός) which possesses admirable (θαυμαστή) wisdom (φρόνησις) (I, 2, 1, p. 51, lines 1-8); it arose from God (ἐκ θεοῦ ὡρμημένην) and is the cause that maintains all things united (αἰτίας τῆς συνεχούσης τὰ πάντα) (II, 1, 4, p. 10, lines 17-19); it governs all according to reason (ψυχῆς δὴ τὸ πᾶν τόδε διοικούσης κατὰ λόγον) (II, 3, 13, p. 38, lines 3-4); it created all (IV, 3, 6 *passim*); it is the principle of life (IV, 3, 4, p. 69, lines 26-27, where the 'Soul of the World' is compared to the soul of a great tree which it animates) etc.[13]

4. Under the influence of Stoicism, the great Latin poet Manilius also adheres to the doctrine of the *Spiritus Mundi*. This doctrine is referred to or expounded in many verses of his poem *Astronomica*, G.P. Goold ed.:

I, 109-111

attribuitque suas formas, sua nomina signis,
quasque vices agerent certa sub sorte notavit
omniaque ad numen mundi faciemque moveri,
sideribus vario mutantibus ordine fata.

---

[12] Cf. J. Moreau, *L'âme du monde de Platon aux Stoiciens.*

[13] For other attributes of the *Soul of the World* in Plotinus cf. É. Bréhier, Plotin, *Ennéades*, Vol. VI, 2nd part, Index, pp. 248-249. On the theory of the

"He [the creátor of Ástronomy and Astrology]
attributed to the stars their forms, their names,
and noted down the changes
that with a rigid fate they undergo,
and also that all moves
according to the divine will
[of the Spirit] of the World
and [the gestures of] His face,
while the stars with [their] diverse disposition
alter the destinies [of men]".

I, 246-254
Hoc opus immensi constructum corpore mundi
membraque naturae diversa condita forma
aeris atque ignis, terrae pelagique iacentis
vis animae divina regit, sacroque meatu
conspirat deus et tacita ratione gubernat

"The divine force of the Soul
rules this fabric of the world
constructed with an enormous body
and its members
built with the diverse forms of nature:
air, fire, earth, and the lying sea;
and with sacred motion it tends to the same aim,
and God governs it with silent reason".

I, 483-485
Ac mihi tam praesens ratio non ulla videtur,
qua pateat mundum divino numine verti
atque ipsum esse deum...

"And no other reason seems to me so evident
[as the order that rules the stars, cf. verses 474 and 482]
to make clear that the world functions
moved by a divine will,
and that the world itself is a God".

Soul of the World in other Platonists as Albinus, Atticus, Plutarch, see Clemens Zintzen (ed.), *Der Mittelplatonismus.* Atticus, in his fragment 8, deals with the *Soul of the World* according to Plato. Cf. Atticus, *Fragments,* ed. des Places S.J.

II, 60-66
namque canam tacita naturae mente potentem
infusumque deum caelo terrisque fretoque
ingentem aequali moderantem foedere molem
totumque alterno consensu vivere mundum
et rationis agi motu, cum spiritus unus
per cunctas habitet partes atque irriget orbem
omnia pervolitans ...

"Because I shall sing that a God
who dominates nature with silent mind
and infused in the sky, the earth and the sea
governs with unchangeable statutes
the enormous mass [of the world],
and that the whole world lives with mutual consent
and is impelled by the movement of reason,
since a unique Spirit dwells throughout all its parts
and animates the orb, overflying it everywhere..."

5. The theory of the *Soul of the World* did not enjoy general and lasting acceptance during the Middle Ages. As M.D. Chenu, *La théologie au douziéme siècle*, p. 122, says that the *anima mundi* is "one of the pagan subjects more difficult to conciliate with the biblical mentality". Nevertheless, there were a few mediaeval Christian thinkers who adhered to this theory.

It was adopted by Petrus Abelardus (1079-1142) and his disciples and by all of the masters of the Chartres School. One of the errors of Abelardus condemned in the *Concilium Senonense* of 1140/1141 was precisely *quod Spiritus Sanctus sit anima mundi* "that the Holy Spirit is the Soul of the World."[14]

In 1105-06, Adelard of Bath, composed a treatise entitled *De eodem et diverso,* in which he dedicates a long paragraph (H. Willner ed., pp. 15-16, cf. pp. 77-78) to the *anima mundi,* following Plato's *Timaeus.*

Previously, St. Augustine did not reject that theory, and St. Basil had accepted the identification of the "Soul of the

---

[14] Cf. Chenu, *op. cit.*, p. 121; and H. Denzinger, *Enchiridion Symbolorum. Definitionum et declarationum de rebus fidei et morum,* 370.

World" with the "Holy Spirit" (Chenu, *op. cit.*, pp. 121-122).

The success of this theory was due to the seductive influence of Plato on mediaeval Christian thought.[15]

6. However, if we pass on to the philosophy of the Renaissance, the situation is very different. Many thinkers adopted the doctrine of the *anima mundi.* Let us point out here that, in his important treatise *De occulta philosophia,* Cornelius Agrippa (1486-1535), who was influenced by Neoplatonist and Hermetic sources, dedicates several chapters to the *anima mundi* and the souls of celestial bodies.[16] The titles of those chapters which reveal the range of ideas spanned by this doctrine are:

Book I. Chapter XIV, *De spiritu mundi quis sit et quod sit vinculum occultarum virtutum*: "On the Soul of the World, who is it, and that it is the link of secret virtues".

Book II. Chapter LV, *De anima mundi et coelestium iuxta traditiones poëtarum et philosophorum*: "On the Soul of the World and of the celestial bodies according to the traditions of poets and philosophers", where the author quotes passages by Manilius (*Astronomica* I, 247-251), Lucan (*De bello civili* V, 94-95), Boethius (*De consolatione philosophiae* III, 9) and Virgil (*Aenaeis* VI, 724-31) in support of his thesis and ends up adducing the authority of numerous philosophers: *Hoc Platonici omnes, hoc Pythagorici, hoc Orpheus, hoc Trismegistus, hoc Aristoteles, Theophrastus, Avicenna, Algazeles omnesque Peripatetici fatentur atque confirmant*: "This is expressed and confirmed by all the Platonists, Pythagorists, Orpheus, Trismegistus, Aristotle, Theophrast, Avicenna, Alghazali, and all the Peripatetics".

Book II. Chapter LVI, *Idem confirmatur ratione*: "The same thing is confirmed by reason". The reasons which Agrippa presents in support of his thesis on pp. 384-385 include the

---

[15] Cf. T. Gregory, *Anima mundi. La filosofia di Guglielmo di Conches e la Scuola di Chartres*, pp. 126-154, on the acceptance and rejection of this concept in the middle-age.

[16] On Cornelius Agrippa, see Hanna-Barbara Gerl, *Einführung in die Philosophie der Renaissance*.

following: it would be absurd that "vile small animals, as flies and worms": *vilissima animalcula, muscae et vermiculi,* should have life and soul whereas "the whole world itself, the most perfect body, complete and noblest, do not live and do not have a soul": *mundum ipsum integrum, perfectissimum, totale ac nobilissimum corpus neque vivere neque animam habere.*

Book II. Chapter LVII, *Quod anima mundi et coelestes animae sint rationales ac mentem participantes divinam*: "That the Soul of the World and the celestial souls are rational and partake of the divine mind", concluding from the universal order that things "are ruled not by chance, but by reason": *non casu, sed ratione regantur.*

Book II. Chapter LVIII, *De nominibus animarum coelestium earumdemque dominio in hunc inferiorem mundum, videlicet hominem*: "On the names of the celestial souls and on their sway over this inferior world, i.e. man". In this chapter, Agrippa deals with the Greek and Latin names, which correspond to the souls of the celestial bodies, and he indicates that these superior beings rule all human beings and activities.

7. One of the principal theses of Giordano Bruno (1548-1600) is that of the *Universal Spirit or Soul* (*l'anima de l'universo*). This thesis is expounded in many passages of his work. We shall only quote a few of them here. In *De la causa, principio et uno*, p. 13, *Les Belles Lettres* ed. (*Proemiale Epistola, Ottavo*), he states:

> ... *che la prima e principal forma naturale, principio formale e natura efficiente, é l'anima de l'universo: la quale é principio di vita, vegetazione e senso in tutte le cose, che vivono, vegetano e senteno. E si ha per modo di conclusione, cheè cosa indegna di razional suggetto posser credere che l'universo et altri suoi corpi principali sieno inanimate.*
>
> "... that the first and principal natural form, formal principle and efficient nature is the soul of the universe: which is vital, vegetative and sensitive principle in all things that live, vegetate and feel. And as a conclusion we have that it is unworthy of a rational being to be able to believe that the universe and others of its principal bodies are inanimate".

Then he develops this idea on pages 133 ff. of the same dialogue.[17]

One of the theses of Giordano Bruno condemned in his trial (which had such a tragic end) by the Inquisition was the thesis:

> *terram esse animatam nedum anima sensitiva, verum etiam rationali:*
>
> "The earth is animated not only by a sensitive but also rational soul".[18]

8. We shall now refer to a small treatise by G.W. Leibniz dated 1702 (pp. 529-538): *Considérations sur la doctrine d'un Esprit Universel Unique.* In this treatise, Leibniz expounds a doctrine which was widely accepted in his time:

> *Plusieurs personnes ingénieuses ont crû et croient encor aujourd'hui qu'il n'y a qu' un seul Esprit, qui est Universel, et qui anime tout l'univers et toutes ses parties, chacune suivant sa structure et suivant les organes qu' il trouve, comme un même souffle de vent fait sonner différemment divers tuyaux d' orgue.*
>
> "Some clever persons have believed and believe even today that there exists a single Spirit, that is universal, and that animates the whole universe and all its parts, each one according to its structure and according to the organs It finds, as the same blow of air makes diverse pipes of an organ sound in different forms".

According to this belief, the *Spirit* is the "ocean" to which souls return (p. 529); it is "eternal" (p. 529); it is *l'âme immortelle universelle* (p. 530); it is *Dieu même* or created by God (p. 531); it is *une âme du monde* (p. 531); it is *un esprit commun à tous les hommes* (p. 531); it is different from matter (p. 537). Some maintain that this Spirit is *cet Esprit du Seigneur qui se remuait sur les eaux, dont parle le Commencement de la Genése* (p. 531): "The Spirit of the Lord that flew upon the waters in the beginning of the Genesis". As we have already said, this latter idea found some acceptance in the Middle Ages.

---

[17] Cf. also *La cena de le ceneri*, pp. 168-169, and *De l'infinito universo e mondi*, p. 143; and Hanna-Barbara Gerl, *op. cit.*, pp. 195-198.

[18] Cf. Giordano Bruno, *Oeuvres Complètes, Documents, I Le Procès*, p. 391, paragraph 258.

Leibniz mentions a number of thinkers who adhered entirely or partially to this doctrine, which he of course rejected.

Leibniz also deals with the belief in the "Universal Soul" in his *Essais de Théodicée sur la bonté de Dieu, la liberté de l'homme et l'origine du mal, Préface*, in *Philosophische Schriften*, Band II, 1, *Discours*, sections 8-9. He indicates the antiquity of this belief; he considers it *une mauvaise doctrine ... fort capable d'éblouir le vulgaire* (8): "an evil doctrine ... capable to dazzle common people"; he quotes verses of Virgil, *Aeneis* VI, 724-728, and *Georgica* IV, 221-225; he refers to the *Soul of the World* of Plato and to its acceptance by the Stoics, and also to its diffusion in Persia and in the states of the Great Moghul; and he mentions a few authors of his own time or predecessors of his who accepted the doctrine. He remarks that "the deification of the mystics" (... *généralement la déification des mystiques*) could in general be taken in "the bad sense" (*mauvais sens*) of the belief in the *Universal Soul* (9).

In his treatise *De la nature en elle-même, ou de la force inhérente aux choses créées et de leurs actions*, in Leibniz. *Opuscules philosophiques choisis*, P. Schrecker, ed., p. 194, Leibniz affirms that he agrees with J. Ch. Sturm in his denial of a 'Universal Soul' (*nullam dari animam universi*).

9. F.W.J. Schelling also makes a reference to the "Soul of the World (*Weltseele*)" in his treatise *Von der Weltseele*. We quote from the third edition of 1809 here.

In the Preface [*Vorrede*] of the first edition of the treatise, Schelling begins by affirming:

> *Die Betrachtung der allgemeinen Naturverändrungen sowohl, als des Fortgangs und Bestands der organischen Welt führt zwar den Naturforscher auf ein* gemeinschaftliches Princip, *das zwischen anorgischen und organischer Natur fluctuirend die erste Ursache aller Verändrungen in jener, und den letzten Grund aller Thätigkeit in dieser enthält, das, weil es* überall *gegenwärtig ist,* nirgends *ist, und weil es* Alles *ist, nichts* Bestimmtes *oder* Besondres *sein kann, für welches die Sprache ebendesswegen keine eigentliche Bezeichnung hat, und dessen Idee die älteste Philosophie, (zu welcher, nachdem sie ihren Kreislauf vollendet hat, die unsrige allmählig zurückkehrt), nur in dichterischen Vorstellungen uns überliefert hat.*

"The observation of the universal changes of Nature as well as of the development and permanence of the organic world leads the investigator of Nature to a *general principle* that fluctuating between the inorganic and the organic Nature contains the first cause of all changes in the former, and the last ground of all activity in the latter, and that because it is present everywhere, it is *nowhere*, and that because it is *all*, it cannot be something *determinate* or *particular*, and for which, consequently, language has no special designation, and whose idea has been transmitted to us by the most ancient philosophy (to which ours, after it has completed its course, has gradually returned) only in poetical representations."

In the first page of the treatise (p. 3 of the original edition), Schelling, after mentioning the two forces (*Kraft*) which cause nature to function, states that these two forces lead to "... the idea of an organizing principle, which makes the world a system": *...die Idee eines* organisirenden, *die Welt zum* System *bildenden* Princips; and considers that it is "Perhaps such [a Principle] what the Ancients wanted to mean with the expression 'Soul of the World' ": *Ein solches wollten vielleicht die Alten durch die* Weltseele *andeuten.*

Finally, in the last paragraph of the treatise (p. 305 of the original edition), Schelling says:

Da nun dieses Princip die Continuität der anorgischen und der organischen Welt unterhält, und die ganze Natur zu einem allgemeinen Organismus verknüpft, so erkennen wir aufs Neue in ihm jenes Wesen, das die älteste Philosophie als die gemeinschaftliche Seele der Natur *ahnend begrüsste ...*

"Since this Principle maintains the continuity of the inorganic and organic world, and it connects the whole Nature so as to constitute a common organism, we discover in it again that Being that the most ancient philosophy greeted, considering it the common Soul of Nature ..."

The testimonies of Leibniz and Schelling make it clear that, even in the 18th and 19th centuries, the animistic belief in an *anima mundi* was still influential in the West, being discarded by some, for example Leibniz, and accepted by others such as Schelling.[19]

III.12 *Brahman / Ātman* as a concrete-personal and as an abstract-impersonal Supreme Principle in the *Upaniṣads*

The characteristics, which we have pointed out (*arche*, substance, spirituality, Universal Spirit) present *Brahman* as a Supreme Principle, above all that exists. But, as we have already said, in some texts the *Upaniṣads* conceive of *Brahman* as a concrete-personal Supreme Principle which could be considered as a personal God (He), and in other texts as an abstract-impersonal Supreme Principle which could be considered as an Absolute (It). In some texts, both concepts appear together. Thus, due to this fact, ambivalence is present in Upanishadic thought.

The *Maitrāyaṇa-Upaniṣad* VII, 7 contains an exalted homage to *Ātman* (whose identification with *Brahman* is, as we have already said, very frequent in the *Upaniṣads*) in the following terms, in which the positive and concrete-personal formulations predominate:

> *eṣa hi khalvātmā 'ntarhṛdaye 'ṇīyān iddho 'gnir iva viśvarūpo 'syaivānnam idaṃ sarvam asminn otā imāḥ prajāḥ / eṣa ātmā 'pahatapāpmā vijaro vimṛtyur viśoko 'vicikitso 'vipāśaḥ satyasaṃkalpaḥ satyakāma eṣa parameśvara eṣa bhūtādhipatir eṣa bhūtapāla eṣa setur vidharaṇa eṣa hi khalvātmeśānaḥ śaṃbhur bhavo rudraḥ prajāpatir*

[19] On the subjects of the *Soul of the World*, animism in general, their relation to archaic culture, and their presence in European philosophy, see the articles: "Alma del Mundo" and "Animismo", in J. Ferrater Mora, *Diccionario de Filosofia*, Vol. I, pp. 122-123 and pp. 176-177 respectively; "Weltseele" by Matthias Gatzemeier and "Animismus" by Jürgen Mittelstrass, in *Enzyclopädie Philosophie und Wissenschafstheorie*, Vol. 4, p. 658, and Vol. I, p. 117, respectively; "Animismus" by K.E. Müller, in *Historisches Wörterbuch der Philosophie*, Vol. I, col. 315-319; and "Animism" by Goblet d'Alviella, in *Encyclopaedia of Religion and Ethics*, Vol. 1, pp. 535-537; and also G. Bachelard, *La formation de l'esprit scientifique*, Chapter VIII; R. Bouveresse, *Spinoza et Leibniz. L'Idée d'animisme universel*.

viśvasṛg hiraṇyagarbhaḥ satyaṃ prāṇo haṃsaḥ śāstā 'cyuto viṣṇur nārāyaṇaḥ.

"He truly, indeed, is the *Ātman* within the heart, extremely subtle, as a kindled fire, provided of all forms. The whole universe is His food. All beings are woven on Him. He is the *Ātman,* free from evil, beyond old age, beyond death, beyond sorrow, devoid of doubt, devoid of fetters, whose thought is Truth, whose will is Truth. He is the Supreme Lord, He is the Sovereign of beings, He is the Protector of beings. He is the limit that separates. He truly, indeed, is the *Ātman,* the Lord, *Śambhu* the Benefactor, *Bhava* the Existent, *Rudra* the Awful, *Prajāpati* the Lord of Creation, Creator of all, the Golden Germ, Truth, Life, the Spirit, the Governor, the Unshaken, *Viṣṇu, Nārāyaṇa*".

Brahman as a concrete-personal notion or personal principle is depicted in a general way, with the well-known features which are usually assigned to the notion of a personal God.[20]

Other texts describe *Brahman* / *Ātman* as having resort to the *via negationis*; they manifest the *abstract-impersonal trend* in the concept of *Brahman* as the Supreme Principle. Although the first aim of descriptions using negations is to show the *absolutely transcendental and heterogeneous nature* (i.e. different from everything that belongs to empirical reality and within the reach of knowledge and language) *of the principle* to which the description refers, the description using negations nevertheless has the same *extolling* effect as a description which accumulates positive epithets, and it *removes* the principle from all connections to the concrete-personal domain. Let us quote the following Upanishadic texts as examples here:

---

[20] This personal concept of God / Absolute appears not only in the *Upaniṣads* but also in an important number of philosophical thinkers belonging to different systems of Indian thought. Cf. C. Bulcke, S.J., *The Theism of Nyaya-Vaisesika. Its Origin and Early Development*; F. Tola and C. Dragonetti, "The system of Śaṅkara: Reality, Illusion, Perpectivism", in *Indologica Taurinensia,* Vol. XXVI, 2000, Torino, Italy, pp. 161-186; and F. Tola and C. Dragonetti, "Rāmānuja. No-dualidad calificada. Realismo, teísmo, panteísmo", in *Boletín de la Asociación Española de Orientalistas,* Vol. XXXVIII, Año 2002, Madrid, pp. 271-288.

Kena-Upaniṣad I, 3-4:

na tatra cakṣur gacchati na vāg gacchati no manaḥ / na vidmo na vijānīmo yathaitad anuśiṣyāt / anyad eva tad viditād atho aviditād adhi / iti śuśruma pūrveṣāṃ ye nas tad vyācacakṣire.

"There [to *Brahman*] the eye does not go, speech does not go, nor the mind. We do not know, we do not understand how one could teach It. It is different from the known and from the unknown - thus have we heard from the Ancients who taught It to us".

Taittirīya-Upaniṣad II, 4, 1:

... vāco nivartante aprāpya manasā saha:

"... words together with the mind, without attaining it, come back".

In the *Bṛhadāraṇyaka-Upaniṣad* III, 8, 8, the following description of *Brahman* is found:

asthūlam anaṇvahrasvam adīrgham alohitam asneham acchāyam atamo 'vāyvanākāśam asaṅgam arasam agandham acakṣuṣkam aśrotram avāg amano 'tejaskam aprāṇam amukham amātram anantaram abāhyaṃ.

"It is not coarse not fine, not short not long, not red [like fire], not fluid [like water]; without shadow, without darkness, without wind, without space, without adherence; without taste, without smell, without eyes, without ears, without voice, without mind; without energy, without breath, without mouth, without measure, without inside, without outside..."

In *ibidem* II, 3, 6, we find the apex of the *via negativa*, when it is proclaimed that there is no better definition of *Brahman* than the forthright negation ("No"), and, at the same time, the subsidiary positive effect of the negative formulation, when *Brahman* is proclaimed as the *ens realissimum*, the most real entity:

athāta ādeśo neti neti na hyetasmād iti netyanyat param astyatha nāmadheyaṃ satyasya satyam iti.

"Hence now the definition [of *Brahman*]: 'No', 'No', since there is nothing superior to this: 'No'. Now the designation: 'the Reality of the Reality'".

As the most lucid and clear explanation of the preceding Upanishadic text, we shall now give the well-known commentary by Śaṅkara:

> *nanu katham ābhyāṃ 'neti neti' iti śabdābhyāṃ satyasya satyaṃ nirdidikṣitam? ityucyate – sarvopādhiviśeṣāpohena / yasmin na kaścid viśeṣo 'sti – nāma vā rūpaṃ vā karma vā bhedo vā jātir vā guṇo vā; taddvāreṇa hi śābdapravṛttir bhavati / na caiṣāṃ kaścid viśeṣo brahmaṇyasti; ato na nirdeṣṭuṃ śakyate – idaṃ tad iti gaur asau spandate śuklo viṣānīti yathā loke nirdiśyate, tathā /*
>
> *adhyāropitanāmarūpakarmadvāreṇa brahma nirdiśyate 'vijñānam ānandaṃ brahma' (III, 9, 27-7) 'vijñānaghana eva brahmātmā' (II, 4, 12) ityevamādiśabdaiḥ/*
>
> *yadā punaḥ svarūpam eva nirdidikṣitaṃ bhavati nirastasarvopādhiviśeṣam, tadā na śakyate kenacid api prakāreṇa nirdeṣṭum; tadā ayam evābhyupāyaḥ – yad uta prāptanirdeśaprati ṣdha-dvāreṇa 'neti neti' iti nirdeśaḥ.*

"[If it is asked:] In what manner is it wished to define the Reality of the Reality [*satyasya satyam*] by means of these two words: 'No', 'No'? We answer: 'By the exclusion of all particular characteristics [*viśeṣa*] that constitute a limitation [*upādhi*].' [It is necessary to proceed thus] in relation to something in which there is no particular characteristic as name, form, action, difference, class, quality, since it is through these [characteristics] that the use of words is possible. And no one of these particular characteristics exists in *Brahman.* Consequently it cannot be described [in such terms as]: 'This is that', in the same way as in the common usage a cow is defined: 'It moves, it is white, it has horns.'

Brahman is [inaccurately] defined by means of the name, the form and the action, which are [erroneously] super-imposed [*adhyāropita*] on It by the use of expressions [as]: '*Brahman* is consciousness and bliss', '*Brahman-Ātman* is only a compact mass of consciousness', etc.

But when it is wished to [truly] define the own nature [of *Brahman*], devoid of all particular characteristics which constitute a limitation, then it is not possible to define It in any way. Then there is only this means, to wit: the definition:'No','No' with its rejection of all the usual definitions".

III.13 Remarks on the previous subject: The abstract-impersonal notion of God in Spinoza

In the West, Baruch de Spinoza (1632-1677) developed a concept of God which offers remarkable similarities to the abstract-impersonal notion of Brahman, the Supreme Principle, in the *Upaniṣads.* In both cases, we can find the same desire, the same will and the same effort to abandon the anthropomorphic traditional ideas, and even the concrete-personal concepts, of the Supreme Principle (*Brahman* or God) and to adopt an abstract-impersonal concept characterized by its "purified rationality".

In both cases, Spinoza and the *Upaniṣads,* this concept is very different from traditional beliefs. The *Kena-Upaniṣad* I, 6, opposes the true knowledge of the Supreme Being, which the *Upaniṣhad* reveals, to the erroneous concept which people generally have of it: *nedaṃ yad idam upāsate*: "It is not what they venerate". Spinoza opposes "the true knowledge of God": *vera Dei cognitio* (*Ethica, Pars Prima, Propositio* XV, *Scholium in initio*), to the idea which "the common people have of God": *vulgus ... intelligit (Ethica, Pars Secunda, Propositio* III, *Scholium*).

The *Upaniṣads*' Supreme Principle, *Brahman,* and Spinoza's Supreme Principle, God, are both "philosophical" entities, abstract creations.[21]

However, we must remark that, just as we find the coexistence of texts leaning to a concrete-personal concept of *Brahman* and texts leaning to an abstract-impersonal concept in the *Upaniṣads,* in Spinoza, in conjunction with the abstract-impersonal features of God, we find a few concrete-personal traits such as His *perfectissima natura*: "most perfect nature", and His *infinita potentia*: "infinite power"[22], *divina natura*: divine nature (*Pars Prima, Propositio* XV,

[21] On the God of the philosophers see Joseph Moreau, *Le Dieu des philosophes.*

[22] Cf. P. Macherey, *Introduction á l'Éthique de Spinoza,* p. 10, note 1.

Scholium), *actuosa essentia*: "acting essence" (*Pars Secunda, Propositio* III, *Scholium*).

In the *Definitio* VI, *Pars Prima* (whose title is *De Deo*) of the *Ethica*, C. Gebhardt ed., Spinoza defines God using the following words:

> *Per Deum intelligo ens absolutè infinitum, hoc est, substantiam constantem infinitis attributis, quorum unumquodque aeternam, & infinitam essentiam exprimit.*
>
> "I understand by God a being absolutely infinite, i.e. a substance constituted by infinite attributes, each of which expresses an eternal and infinite essence".

In the next pages of this same *Pars Prima* of his treatise, Spinoza completes and clarifies this definition:

"God has from himself an absolutely infinite power to exist": *Deum infinitam absolutè potentiam existendi à se habere*, "therefore He absolutely exists": *propterea absolutè existit* (*Propositio* XI, *Scholium*, p. 54, lines 7-9).

He, being an absolutely infinite substance, is indivisible (*substantia absolutè infinita est indivisibilis*) (*Propositio* XIII).

"In addition to God no substance can exist or be conceived": *Praeter Deum nulla dari, neque concipi potest substantia* (*Propositio* XIV).

"God is unique": *Deum esse unicum* (*Propositio* XIV, *Corollarium* I, p. 56, line 17).

"All that exists is in God and without God nothing can exist or be conceived": *Quidquid est, in Deo est, & nihil sine Deo esse, neque concipi potest* (*Propositio* XV). In the *Demonstratio* of this *Propositio*, Spinoza uses the expression *divina natura* with reference to God, and at the beginning of the *Scholium* of this same *Propositio* he uses again the same expression and considers that those persons are mistaken "who imagine that God like a man has a body and a mind, and is exposed to passions, ... since all who in some way have contemplated the divine nature negate that God is corporeal": ... *qui Deum instar hominis corpore, & mente constantem, atque passionibus obnoxium fingunt; sed, quàm longè hi à verâ Dei cognitione aberrent, satis ex jam demonstratis constat ... nam omnes, qui naturam divinam aliquo modo contemplati sunt, Deum esse corporeum, negant.*

"God is the efficient cause of all things": *Deum omnium rerum ... esse causam efficientem* (*Propositio* XVI, *Corollarium* I).

"God is in an absolute way the first cause": *Deum esse absolutè causam primam* (*Propositio* XVI, *Corollarium* III).

"God acts by the sole laws of His nature, and not forced by anybody": *Deus ex solis suae naturae legibus, & a nemine coactus agit* (*Propositio* XVII).

"All is in God, whereby outside Him there can be nothing that could determine or force Him to act": ... *omnia in Deo esse; quare nihil extra ipsum esse potest, à quo ad agendum determinetur vel cogatur* (*Propositio* XVII, *Demonstratio*). In *Pars Secunda, Propositio* III, *Scholium,* p. 87, lines 26-28, Spinoza attributes to God an *actuosa essentia*: an "acting essence", "and so it is impossible for us to conceive that God does not act, as well as that God does not exist": *adeóque tam nobis impossibile est concipere, Deum non agere, quàm Deum non esse.*

"To God's nature do not belong intellect or will": *ad Dei naturam neque intellectum, neque voluntatem pertinere* (*Propositio* XVII, *Scholium,* p. 62, lines 2-3).

"God is the immanent and not transitory cause of all things": *Deus est omnium rerum causa immanens, non verò transiens* (*Propositio* XVIII).

"God, i.e. all His attributes are eternal": *Deus, sive omnia Dei attributa sunt aeterna* (*Propositio* XIX).

"God's existence, as well as His essence are an eternal truth": *Dei existentiam, sicut ejus essentiam, aeternam esse veritatem* (*Propositio* XIX, *Scholium*).

"God is not only the cause of things for their beginning to exist, but also for their persevering in the existence, i.e. (for using a Scholastic term) God is the *causa essendi* ['cause of being'] of things": *Deum non tantùm esse causam, ut res incipiant existere; sed etiam, ut in existendo perseverent, sive* (*ut termino Scholastico utar*) *Deum esse causa essendi rerum* (*Propositio* XXIV, *Corollarium*).

"God is not only the efficient cause of the existence of things, but also of their essence": *Deus non tantùm est causa efficiens rerum existentiae, sed etiam essentiae* (*Propositio* XXV).

"All things are determined by the necessity of the divine nature to exist and act in a certain way": ... *omnia ex necessitate divinae naturae determinata sunt ad certo modo existendum, et operandum* (*Propositio* XXIX).

"Things have been produced by God provided with a supreme perfection, because they have necessarily derived from a most perfect given nature ... God's perfection compels to affirm this": ... *sequitur, res summâ perfectione à Deo fuisse productas: quandoquidem ex datâ perfectissimâ naturâ necessariò secutae sunt ... ipsius enim perfectio hoc nos affirmare coëgit* (*Propositio* XXXIII, *Scholium* II *in initio*).

"God's power is His own essence": *Dei potentia est ipsa ipsius essentia* (*Propositio* XXXIV).

In the preceding Section *Remarks on the previous subject of consciousness: The relation between the spirit and mental functions in the West* we have already indicated that for Spinoza "Thinking is an attribute of God, or in other words God is a thinking thing": *Cogitatio attributum Dei est, sive Deus est res cogitans* (*Ethica, Pars Secunda, De natura et origine mentis, Propositio* I).

At the same time, Spinoza affirms that "extension is an attribute of God, or in other words God is an extended thing": *Extensio attributum Dei est, sive Deus est res extensa* (*Ethica, Pars Secunda, De natura et origine mentis, Propositio* II).

In the beginning of the *Appendix* which closes the first part of the *Ethica,* p. 77 of the quoted edition, Spinoza summarizes the explanation he gave in the previous pages and enumerates God's attributes:

> *His Dei naturam, ejusque proprietates explicui, ut, quòd necessariò existit; quòd sit unicus; quòd ex solâ suae naturae necessitate sit, & agat; quòd sit omnium rerum causa libera, et quomodò; quòd omnia in Deo sint, & ab ipso itá pendeant, ut sine ipso nec esse nec concipi possint; & denique quòd omnia á Deo fuerint praedeterminata, non quidem ex libertate voluntatis, sive absoluto beneplacito, sed ex absolutâ Dei naturâ, sive infinitâ potentiâ.*

"With what precedes I have explained God's nature and attributes, to wit: that He necessarily exists; that He is unique; that he exists and acts by the sole necessity of His nature; that He is the free cause of all things, and how [He is this]; that all things are in God and depends on Him, in such a way that without Him they cannot exist or be conceived; and finally that all things have been predetermined by God, not certainly according to the freedom of His will or to his absolute approval, but according to the absolute nature of God, i.e. His infinite power".[23]

III.14 The presence of the *Īśvara* in Indian culture. Religiosity and spirituality in the West

Brahman, which is mainly conceived of as a personal Supreme Principle, i.e. as an *Īśvara* (Lord, God), has always occupied an important position in Indian culture. Great thinkers such as Rāmānuja, Nimbārka, Vallabha, Madhva, etc. adopt the concrete-personal interpretation of the Upanishadic *Brahman*; Śaṅkara on his side adopts the abstract-impersonal interpretation but posits, besides the abstract-impersonal *Brahman*, an *Īśvara* who, although an illusory creation of the human mind, is treated as a real Supreme Being.

The *Īśvara* is at the center of a profound theistic religiosity and spirituality. He is the worthy object of cult and devotion; to His sacred person are dedicated a large emotive religious literature and splendid works of art; many philosophical systems have Him as the central all-supporting Principle, as the foundation of their theories; and an intense mystical life is centered around Him. Taking into account the powerful religious and spiritual importance given to the *Īśvara*, it is possible to say that India is "the land of spirituality" – this is the common opinion. Of course, we must not forget that, besides the systems which postulate the *Īśvara* as the

---

[23] Cf. E.E. Powell, *Spinozas Gottes Begrieff*, Yirmiyahu Yovel, *Spinoza and other Heretics*, and Michel Hulin, "Spinoza l'oriental?", in *Cahiers Spinoza* 4, Paris: Éditions Réplique, pp. 139-170, where are shown in a detailed way a series of interesting points of contact between Spinoza's and Indian doctrines, which could be added to those we have pointed out.

Supreme Principle, there have been several important philosophical systems in India which had nothing to do with an *Īśvara,* for instance Buddhism, Jainism, Mīmāṃsā, Sāṃkhya and the Materialists.

We think that, at least until the 16th century, Europe can also be rightly called "a land of spirituality and wisdom", to judge by the intensity of cult and devotion directed towards God, the magnificent literary and artistic works which He inspired and the important function which He has in the works of many Western philosophers, who also posited Him as the foundation of their theories.

The characteristic of being a "land of spirituality" was almost exclusively attributed to India; and European spirituality was not taken into account, and this was usually done with the purpose of denying the existence of rationalistic thought in India. It is another aspect of the myth with which we are dealing.

III.15 Other concepts of the "arche" (ἀρχή) in the *Upaniṣads* and in Greece

Brahman / Ātman represents the apex of the Upanishadic reflection in the search for that Principle which is the ultimate foundation, the first cause, the primordial origin and the definitive end of all that exists. However, before reaching this point, the *Upaniṣads* reveal that there were intents to bring various elements, generally of a material nature, to the level of that Principle.

For instance, if we limit ourselves to the oldest *Upaniṣads,* the *Bṛhadāraṇyaka-Upaniṣad* V, 5, 1, proclaims that

> *āpa evedam agra āsuḥ:*
>
> "in the beginning all this [= the world] was water",

and the *Chāndogya-Upaniṣad* VII, 10, 1, states that everything, including the earth, space, the sky, the mountains, Gods and men, animals and plants, all is solidified water:

āpa evemā mūrtā yeyaṃ pṛthivī yad antarikṣaṃ yad dyaur yat parvatā yad devamanuṣyā yat paśavaś ca vayāṃsi ca tṛṇavanaspatayaḥ śvāpadānyākīṭapataṅgapipīlikam āpa evemā mūrtāḥ.

The *Chāndogya-Upaniṣad* I, 9, 1, declares:

sarvāṇi ha vā imāni bhūtānyākāśād eva samutpadyanta ākāśaṃ pratyastaṃ yāntyākāśo hyevaibhyo jyāyān ākāśaḥ parāyaṇam.

"All beings comes forth from space (*ākāśa*) and in the space are dissolved. Space is older than they; space is the final goal".

The *Taittirīya-Upaniṣad* II, 7, 1 (*asad vā idam agra āsīt / tato vai sad ajāyata*) and the *Chāndogya-Upaniṣad* VI, 2, 1 (*asad evedam agra āsīd ekam evādvitīyam*) state the opinion that, in the beginning, all that "existed" was the inexistent non-being (*asat* in Sanskrit) and that the existent, being (*sat*), came forth from the inexistent.

It is necessary to mention one fact here which manifests the metaphysical trend in Indian thought: of the *arches* (principles) of which the Indian thinkers conceived, that of *Brahman / Ātman* was the one which acquired the greatest importance. This was an abstract metaphysical notion whose characteristics we have already indicated.

Several centuries after the *Upaniṣads*, many Greek thinkers were interested in determining the *arche* (ἀρχή) of all things, each offering different solutions. According to the testimonies gathered by H. Diels/W. Kranz in *Die Fragmente der Vorsokratiker*, let us give the examples that Thales thought that "water" was the universal *arche*, Anaximander thought it was the "unlimited" and "undefined" (*tò ápeiron*) and Anaximenes considered it to be the "air".[24]

III.16 Triadic conception in the *Upaniṣads*

In the *Upaniṣads*, we can find a series of texts which affirm that the world is a triad and that everything in it is in turn constituted by three elements or components. Examples of triads are:

---

[24] Cf. Eduard Zeller, *Die Philosophie der Griechen in ihrer geschichtlichen Entwicklung*, Vol. I.

Bṛhadāraṇyaka-Upaniṣad I, 6, 1, 3:
(1) *Trayaṃ vā idaṃ nāma rūpaṃ karma* ... (3) *tat etat trayaṃ sad ekam ayam ātmā, ātmo ekaḥ sann etat trayam.*
(1) "Verily this [= the empirical reality, the world, the Universe] is a triad: name, form, action ... (3) This, being a triad, is one, the *ātman* [spiritual principle, Supreme Principle, the Absolute]; the *ātman* being one is this triad".

Bṛhadāraṇyaka-Upaniṣad I, 5, 1-10:

(1) yat saptānnāni medhayā tapasājanayat pitā /... trīṇyātmane 'kuruta; (3) ... mano vācaṃ prāṇaṃ ...; (4) trayo lokā eta eva vāg evāyaṃ loko mano 'ntarikṣalokaḥ prāṇo 'sau lokaḥ; (5) trayo vedā eta eva vāg evargvedo mano yajurvedaḥ prāṇaḥ sāmavedaḥ; (6) devāḥ pitaro manuṣyā eta eva vāg eva devā manaḥ pitaraḥ prāṇo mānuṣyāḥ; (7) pitā mātā prājaita eva mana eva pitā vāṅ mātā prānah prajā; (8) vijñātaṃ vijijñāsyam avijñātam eta eva yat kiñ ca vijñātaṃ vācas tad rūpaṃ ...; (9) yat kiñ ca vijijñāsyaṃ manasas tad rūpaṃ ...; (10) yat kiñ cāvijñātaṃ prāṇasya tad rūpaṃ.

(1) "When the Father [Prajāpati God] produced by His wisdom and asceticism the seven kinds of food ... three He made for himself: ... (3) ... mind, speech, breath ... (4) These same are the three worlds: speech is this world [the earth], mind is the atmospheric world, breath is that world [the heaven]. (5) These same are the three Vedas: speech is the Ṛg Veda, mind is the Yajur Veda, breath is the Sāma Veda. (6) These same are the Gods, the Manes, the men: speech is the Gods, mind is the Manes, breath is the men. (7) These same are the father, the mother, the offspring: mind is the father, speech is the mother, breath is the offspring. (8) These same are what is known, what is to be known, what is unknown: what is known is the form of speech ... (9) What is to be known is the form of mind ... (10) What is unknown is the form of breath".

Chāndogya-Upaniṣad VI, 2, 3-4:

(3) *tad aikṣata bahu syāṃ prajāyeyeti tat tejo 'sṛjata / tat teja aikṣata bahu syāṃ prajāyeyeti tad apo 'sṛjata ...* (4) *tā āpa aikṣanta bahvyaḥ syāma prajāyemahīti tā annaṃ asṛjanta ...*

(3) "That [Being: the Primordial Principle] thought: 'Let me be many, let me procreate'. He emitted heat. That heat thought:

'Let me be many, let me procreate'. It emitted the waters. (4) Those waters thought: 'Let us be many, let us procreate'. They emitted food [= the earth according to Shaṅkara]".

Chāndogya-Upaniṣad VI, 4, 1-4:

(1) *yad agne rohitaṃ rūpaṃ tejasas tad rūpaṃ yac chuklaṃ tad apāṃ yat kṛṣṇaṃ tad annasya ... (2) yad ādityasya rohitaṃ rūpaṃ tejasas tad rūpaṃ yac chuklaṃ tad apāṃ yat kṛṣṇaṃ tad annasya ...* (3) *yac candramaso rohitaṃ rūpaṃ tejasas tad rūpaṃ yac chuklaṃ tad apāṃ yat kṛṣṇaṃ tad annasya ... (4) yad vidyuto rohitaṃ rūpaṃ tejasas tad rūpaṃ yac chuklaṃ tad apāṃ yat kṛṣṇaṃ tad annasya ...*
(1) "The red form of fire is the form of heat, the white that of waters, the dark that of food ... (2) The red form of the sun is the form of heat, the white is that of waters, the dark is that of food ... (3) The red form of the moon is the form of heat, the white is that of waters, the dark is that of food ... (4) The red form of the lightning is the form of heat, the white is that of waters, the dark is that of food".

Other examples of Upanishadic triads are to be found in *Bṛhadāraṇyaka-Upaniṣad* I, 2, 3 (*mṛtyu*, Death, presented as the Creator Principle, divides itself into three: fire, sun and wind); *Ibidem*

V, 2, 1 (the triple offspring of Prajāpati: Gods, men, Asuras);

Chāndogya-Upaniṣad II, 23, 1 (the three branches of religious life: 1. sacrifice, study, the giving of alms, 2. asceticism, 3. student's life in the house of the teacher); *Ibidem*

III, 16, 1-5 (three periods in man's life: those corresponding to the three libations of soma: that of the morning: the first 24 years of his life, that of the midday: the 44 following years, that of the night: the last 48 years of his life); *Ibidem*

VI, 3, 1 (the three possible origins of beings: to be born from an egg, from a living being, from a sprout); *Ibidem*

VI, 5, 1 (food when eaten, water when drunk, heat when absorbed, divide themselves in three inside the human body: respectively in faeces, flesh and mind; urine, blood and breath; bones, marrow, speech).

Although the *Upaniṣads* do not offer indications, which fix the nature of the relation among the elements constituting the triads they present, it is nevertheless possible to think that, in the same way as in the later Sāṃkhya system, the *Upaniṣads* also conceive of the triads as data of reality (*dravyasat*) and not as mental constructions (*prajñaptisat*).

In the *Ṛg Veda* and in the *Brāhmaṇas*, which are texts which precede the *Upaniṣads* chronologically, we can already find many examples of triadic groups.

The triadic concept of reality, which manifests itself in the Upanishadic texts quoted was to be developed a few centuries later by the Sāṃkhya philosophical system in its theory of the three *guṇas*, which are conceived of as the components of Matter. Matter, by virtue of its evolution, gives rise to the entire material and psychic empirical reality. The *guṇas* as constituents of Matter are present in everything and the diversity of beings and things depends on the diversity of the proportions in which they are mixed together in beings and things.

Evidently, for the Sāṃkhya system, the three elements (*guṇas*), which constitute Matter are linked amongst themselves by a necessary and essential relation; they can thus not be replaced by others. The triad for the Sāṃkhya is a datum of reality and not a creation of the mind, it is not a mental superimposition on three elements of reality chosen at random. The three *guṇas are* the essential nature of Matter.[25]

---

[25] Cf. the article "Numbers (Aryan)" by A.B. Keith, in *Encyclopaedia of Religion and Ethics*, Vol. 9, pp. 407-408, dedicated to India; A.B. Keith, *The Religion and Philosophy of the Veda and Upanishads, General Index, sub* "Numbers", "Three", "Five", "Seven", "Nine"; H. Oldenberg, *Vorwissenschaftliche Wissenschaft. Die Weltanschauung der Brāhmaṇa-Texte*, pp. 46-50. See also Isidorus Hispalensis (Isidore of Seville), *Liber numerorum, Le livre des nombres*, where numbers are conceived as "principles of the organization and explanation of the macrocosm and microcosm, as well as of the Bible and Christian revelation" (p. XVIII). In this treatise number six is considered as the first perfect number, because God created the world in six days. Let us remark that Isidore of Seville enjoyed the esteem of his contemporaries and greatly influenced Western Medieval culture.

In a general way, primitive or archaic people or people in the first stages of their cultural evolution considered that certain numbers were privileged, and they used some of them as criteria for grouping together things and elements of reality in wholes with an existence of their own.[26]

In culturally more advanced epochs, we can also find manifestations of this archaic tendency to give a special significance to a number and its use as a criterion of classification, either because this archaic belief in privileged numbers has been preserved or because it has spontaneously reappeared or been revived in imitation of the beliefs of past epochs or through the influence of a doctrine (mainly of a religious nature) which imposed itself. Probably this last reason has been the predominant factor in the case of the three authors we present as examples in what follows: Saint Augustine, Raimundus Lullus and Hegel.

III.17 Remarks on the previous subject: Triadic conception in Western thinkers

Many Greek and European thinkers developed the idea that the number three possesses a special hierarchical value, and consequently they utilized that number in their explanations and concepts of reality, thus giving rise to the constitution of triads. Among them are: the Pythagoreans, Plato and the ancient Academy, Plutarch, Middle Platonism, Neo-Platonism: Plotinus, Iamblichus and Proclus, St. Augustine, Roger Bacon, St. Thomas, Nicolaus of Cusa, Raimundus Lullus, Agrippa of Nettesheim, Giordano Bruno, Kant,

---

[26] On this matter see the quoted article "Numbers (Aryan)" by A.B. Keith, in *Encyclopaedia of Religion and Ethics* Vol. 9, pp. 408-413, dedicated to Iran, Greece, Rome and German and Slavic people; the article by William Cruickshank "Numbers (Semitic)", Vol. 9, pp. 413-417, in the mentioned *Encyclopedia*, dedicated to Semitic people; Eric Hornung, *Der Eine und die Vielen. Ägyptische Gottesvorstellungen*, Chapter VII, dedicated in a great part to the numerical-genealogical system of distribution of the Egyptian Gods; and the excellent monography of Henry Goudy, *Trichotomy in Roman Law*, where is found a series of remarks on the privileged numbers in general.

Hegel, Marx, Lenin, etc.[27]

Here we shall refer briefly only to Saint Augustine, Raimundus Lullus and Hegel.

1. In his important treatise *De Trinitate* Saint Augustine (354-430) intends to show that the Holy Trinity is reflected in the human mind, or in other terms that the human mind offers an image of it. He studies for this purpose a series of triads that exists in the human being, specifically in the psychic processes that take place in it. These triads are, according to him, a reflection, an image of the Trinity Father, Son and Saint Spirit, which form the true one and trine God according to whose image and resemblace man was

---

[27] Cf. the article by F.P. Hager and E. von Samsonow "Trias; Triaden", in *Historisches Wörterbuch der Philosophie*, Vol. 10, col. 1479-1483; and "Tres" by J. Ferrater Mora, Vol. IV, pp. 3579-3580; and Michel Piclin, *Les philosophies de la Triade ou l' histoire de la structure ternaire.*

It is interesting to point out, outside the limits of philosophy, the numerous studies done by George Dumézil (already mentioned in Chapter II of this book) on the tripartite ideology of the Indo-European societies, and the work *Trichotomy in Roman Law*, by Henry Goudy, who studies the triadic structures in Roman law. Lucien Gerschel in the book *Jupiter Mars Quirinus IV* by G. Dumézil, pp. 170-176, also deals with some cases of triadic structures in Roman law and in the Greek world relating them to Dumézil's theory of the three functions.

We give some examples of triadic legal structures in Roman law: Gaius, *Institutiones*: *Omne autem ius quo utimur uel ad personas pertinet uel ad res, uel ad actiones*, I, 8: "All the law we use has to do with persons or with things or with legal actions", *libertinorum tria sunt genera, nam aut cives romani aut latini aut dediticiorum numero sunt*, I, 12: "There are three classes of freedmen, since they are Roman citizens or Latin citizens or the individuals who have surrendered unconditionally to Rome", *Diuini iuris sunt ueluti res sacrae et religiose*, II, 3 ... *Sanctae quoque res, ueluti muri et portae, quodammodo diuini iuris sunt* II, 8: "Belong to divine law the sacred things [consecrated to the superior gods] and the religious ones [which have to do with dead persons]... and the saint things, as walls and doors [of the city] are equally in a certain way of divine law"; Ulpianus, in Iustinianus' *Digesta, Liber Primus* I, 1: *Publicum ius in sacris, in sacerdotibus, in magistratibus consistit. privatum ius tripertitum est: collectum etenim est ex naturalibus praeceptis aut gentium aut civilibus*: "The public law deals with sacred things, priests and magistrates. The private law is divided into three parts, since it derives from natural precepts, from [precepts] of human people or from civil [precepts]".

created. The Holy Trinity is one of the most difficult Christian dogmas that Saint Augustine carefully studies in his treatise.[28]

In Book XV of *De Trinitate* Saint Augustine gives a résumé of the subjects he deals with in each of the Books into which is divided his treatise. We transcribe some passages of this résumé that let know which was the aim Saint Augustine intended to carry out, and which was the directive idea of his speculation on the subject of the triadic structures. We quote by the edition of Johann Kreuzer, Darmstadt: Wissenschaftliche Buchgesellschaft, 2001, which limits itself to the texts of the Books of this treatise which specifically refer to the subject that interests us. The edition by Kreuzer we follow reproduces the text of the *Corpus Augustinianum Gissense*, whose editor is C. Mayer, Basel, 1996:

> p. 256 [3.5, 77] *in nono ad imaginem dei quod est homo secundum mentem peruenit disputatio, et in ea quaedam trinitas inuenitur, id est mens et notitia qua se nouit et amor quo se notitiamque suam diligit, et haec tria aequalia inter se et unius ostenduntur esse essentiae.*
>
> "In the ninth [Book] [our] research reaches that image of God, which is man according to mind, and in it a certain trinity is discovered, namely: the mind, and the knowledge by which it knows itself, and the love through which it loves itself and its knowledge, and these three [mind, knowledge, love] are shown to be equal among them and of the same essence".
>
> p. 258 [3.5, 81] *in decimo hoc idem diligentius subtiliusque tractatum est atque ad id perductum ut inueniretur in mente euidentior trinitas eius, in memoria scilicet et intelligentia et uoluntate.*
>
> "In the tenth [Book] this same [subject] is dealt with in a more careful and meticulous way and is developed in order that a more

[28] Cf. J. Brachtendorf, ed., *Gott und sein Bild. Augustins De Trinitate im Spiegel gegenwärtiger Vorschungen.* In this work many triadic structures are mentioned referred to by Saint Augustine in pp. 57-58, 74, 155, 162-163. Specially see the article by E. Booth, O.P., "Saint Thomas Aquinas's Critique of Saint Augustine's Conceptions of the Image of God in the Human Soul", pp. 219-239, and the text of Saint Thomas edited by the same Booth, in pp. 249-273.

evident trinity be discovered in the mind as belonging to it, consisting namely in memory, intelligence and will".

p. 258 [3.5, 91] *in undecimo ergo electus est sensus oculorum in quo id quod inuentum esset etiam in ceteris quattuor sensibus corporis et non dictum posset agnosci, atque ita exterioris hominis trinitas primo in his quae cernuntur extrinsecus, ex corpore scilicet quod uidetur et forma quae inde in acie cernentis imprimitur et utrumque copulantis intentione uoluntatis apparuit.*

"In the eleventh [Book], thus, the sense of the eye has been chosen in order that what has been discovered in relation to it - and had not been said before – could also be recognized in relation to the other four senses of the body, and in this way the trinity of the exterior man [i.e. man in his relation with the world] appeared in first place – [trinity consistent] in those things which are seen outside, namely the object which is perceived, the form which is impressed in the eye, and the attention of will which relates both".[29]

And in what follows the text of Saint Augustine adds another triadic structure related with the previous one:

p. 258 [3.5, 96] *sed haec tria non inter se aequalia nec unius esse substantiae claruerunt. deinde in ipso animo ab his quae extrinsecus sensa sunt uelut introducta inuenta est altera trinitas ubi apparerent eadem tria unius esse substantiae, imaginatio corporis quae in memoria est et inde informatio cum ad eam conuertitur acies cogitantis et utrumque coniungens intentio uoluntatis. sed ideo et ista trinitas ad exteriorem hominem reperta est pertinere quia de corporibus inlata est quae sentiuntur extrinsecus.*

"But it is evident that these three things [= body, form, attention of the will] are not equal among them nor of the same substance. Then, another trinity is discovered in the same soul as if introduced by those things which are externally perceived,

[29] In Buddhism it is also found that in order to explain the coming forth of sensory cognition the coming forth of the visual cognition is studied as an example (privileging vision as Saint Augustine also does), and then that study is applied to the other senses. Similarly on analyzing the coming forth of the visual cognition are pointed out the different factors that produce it: the eye, the form (the object), the light, the space, the attention, etc. See for instance *Śālistambasūtra*, in F. Tola and C. Dragonetti, *Cinco Sūtras del Mahāyāna*, p. 55, where the coming forth of the visual cognition is analyzed (= p. 15 of N. Aiyaswami Sastri edition).

> [trinity] where those three same things would appear as being of a same substance: the representation of the object which is in the memory, and the information from there [which is produced] when the insight of the thinking person is directed towards it, and the attention of the will which unites both. But for that reason it has been established that this trinity also belongs to the exterior man [i.e. man in his relation with the world], since it has been introduced by the objects which are externally perceived".

Finally, Saint Augustine concludes his synthesis with the résumé of Book XIV where he reiterates:

> p. 264 [3.5, 100, 112] *in cuarto decimo ... eo peruenit disputatio ut trinitas appareat in imagine dei quod est homo secundum mentem.*
>
> "In the fourteenth [Book] ... [our] research reaches [the conclusion] that trinity is manifested in that image of God, which is man according to mind".

It is interesting to point out other triadic structures indicated by Saint Augustine in the same treatise: p. 20 [*Liber* VIII, 5.8, 35] *aeternitas, aequalitas, unitas* ("eternity, equality, unity") as attributes of the Trinity; p. 44 [*Liber* VIII, 10.14, 3] *amans, quod amatur, amor* ("lover, what is loved, love"); p. 54 [Liber IX, 4.4, 3] *mens, amor, notitia eius* ("mind, love, its knowledge"); p. 80 [Liber IX, 12.18, 30] *mens* [*cognitor*], *cognitum, cognitio* ("mind [knower"], what is known, cognition"); p. 122 [*Liber* X, 11.18, 28] *memoria, intelligentia, uoluntas* ("memory, intelligence, will"); p. 130 [*Liber* XI, 2.2, 2] *res, uisio, animi intentio* ("thing, vision, attention of the mind [focussed in a thing]"); p. 140 [*Liber* XI, 2.5, 122] *species corporis quod uidetur, imago eius impressa sensui, uoluntas animi quae rei sensibili sensum admouet* ("the form of the object which is perceived, its representation impressed in the sense-organ, the will of the mind, which brings the sense-organ near to the sensible thing"); p. 142 [*Liber* XI, 2.6, 1] *memoria, interna uisio, uoluntas quae utrumque copulat* ("memory, internal vision, will which unites both"); p. 176 [*Liber* XI, 11.18, 26] *mensura, numerus, pondus* ("mesure, number, weight", criteria which guided God in his ordering of reality).

A last example, in which Saint Augustine directly relates the human triads with the divine Trinity, is found on p. 204:

> [*Liber* XIV, 8.11, 14] *mens meminit sui, intellegit se, diliget se. Hoc si cernimus, cernimus trinitatem, nondum quidem deum sed iam imaginem dei.*

> "Mind remembers itself, knows itself, loves itself. If we see that, we are seeing a trinity, not yet certainly God but already the image of God".

In Book XV of his *De Trinitate*, p. 344 [24.44, 53], Saint Augustine points out in which manner it is necessary to look for God through the knowledge of the Trinity's image, which is found in the human mind:

> *qui ergo uident suam mentem quomodo uideri potest et in ea trinitatem istam de qua multis modis ut potui disputaui nec tamen eam credunt uel intellegunt esse imaginem dei. speculum quidem uident sed usque adeo non uident per speculum qui est per speculum nunc uidendus ut nec ipsum speculum quod uident sciant esse speculum, id est imaginem. quod si scirent fortassis et eum cuius est hoc speculum per hoc quaerendum et per hoc utcumque interim uidendum esse sentirent fide non ficta corda mundante ut facie ad faciem possit uideri qui per speculum nunc uidetur.*

> "Therefore, those persons who see their mind as it can be seen and in it this Trinity, which I discussed in many ways as I could, and notwithstanding they do not believe nor understand that it [= the mind] is the image of God, certainly they see the mirror, but to such an extent they do not see by means of the mirror Him who must be seen by means of the mirror, that they do not know that the mirror itself, which they see, is a mirror, i.e. an image. If they knew, perhaps they would feel that He, of whom that mirror is, should be looked for by means of this [mirror] and by means of it in whatever manner in the meantime He should be seen, while a non feigned faith purifies the hearts in order that He who now is seen [only] by means of the mirror could be seen face to face".

In *De Trinitate* Saint Augustine makes some interesting philosophical analyses of the mental processes and of the functioning of consciousness with the religious aim to demonstrate that man, who according to Christianity has been created by God in His own image and resemblance, presents in the functioning of his mind triads, which are the reflection of the divine Trinity. Saint Augustine supplies thus the support for a better understanding of the nature of the incorporation of triads in the thought of many Western philosophers.

2. Raimundus Lullus, who was born in Mallorca in 1232 and died in 1316, expounds a completely Trinitarian concept of the world, endeavouring to discover in creation a reflex and an image of the Christian Trinity, giving universality to the triadic model, and finding triadic structures in all the aspects of reality.

Lullus establishes nine *praedicata absoluta* ("absolute predicates") or *principia transcendentia* ("transcendent principles") or most usually called by him in Catalan *dignitats* ("dignities"), which express the nature of God insofar as He can be known to man, and which are reflected in any aspect of creation, being the instruments of His creative activity: *Bonitas* ("Goodness"), *Magnitudo* ("Greatness"), *Aeternitas* ("Eternity"), *Potestas* ("Power"), *Sapientia* ("Wisdom"), *Voluntas* ("Will"), *Virtus* ("Virtue"), *Veritas* ("Truth"), *Gloria* ("Glory").

There is another set of principles, called *praedicata relata* ("predicates of relation"), which governs the relations between the *praedicata absoluta* and the universe. The *praedicata relata* are nine and are grouped also in three triads: *Differentia-Concordantia-Contrarietas* ("Difference-Concordance-Opposition"), *Principium-Medium-Finis* ("Beginning-Middle-End"), *Maioritas-Aequalitas-Minoritas* ("The fact of being greater-The fact of being equal-The fact of being smaller").[30]

Other examples of triads to be found in Raimundus Lullus are: the three forms of existence: *Deus-Creatura-Operatio* ("God-Creature-Act"); form, matter and the relation between both; the tridimensionality of bodies; the two premises and the conclusion as components of the

[30] Cf. R.D.F. Pring-Mill, "The Trinitarian World Picture of Ramon Lull", pp. 229-256.

syllogism;[31] the capacity or *agent* (Catalan), the object or *patient* ("passive element", in Catalan) and the action or *act* (Catalan) as components of all activity: *actionativum, actionabile, actionare* (p. 116 C2), *bonificativum, bonificabile, bonificare* (p. 58 C3, etc.), *calefactivum, calefactibile, calefacere* (p. 110 D3), *collocativum, collocabile, collocare* (p. 142 C2), *corruptivum, corruptibile, corrumpere* (p. 108 C4), *intellectivus, intelligibilis, intelligere* (p. 106 B, etc.), *naturativum, naturatibile, naturare* (p. 274 C2), *relativum, referibile, referre* (p. 108 C2), *situativum, situabile, situare* (p. 132 C2), *substantiativum, substantiabilis, substantiare* (p. 88 D2), etc.[32]

As in the case of the *Upaniṣads,* for Raimundus Lullus the triads were also real, since they reflect the Christian Trinity, they are not mere mental creations.

3. The triadic arrangements have special importance in Hegel. As M. Piclin, op. cit, p. 151, says:

> "It is with Hegel that the triadic structure comes to inhabit in all the moments of the philosophical research" and p. 155:
>
> "... the triplicity inspires the general lines [of the Hegelian philosophy]".

The importance of the triads in Hegel derives from his concept of dialectics as a method to conform the *concept,* which possesses an exceptional *status,* since it is the sole reality, the absolute *ens.* The conformation of the concept takes place by means of an evolutive process through the three moments of the thesis (affirmation), the antithesis (negation) and the synthesis (integration and overcoming); this evolutive process gives rise to ever more determinate concepts, endowed with greater content and more concrete, grouped in triads. The result of this process is thus the conformation of a succession of triads. In the treatises *Phänomenologie des Geistes, Wissenschaft der Logik* and

---

[31] Cf. Raimundus Lullus, *Die neue Logik. Logica Nova,* Charles Lohr ed., Vittorio Hösle and Walburga Büchel trans., pp. LI and LII of the Introduction by Vittorio Hösle.

[32] The pages refer to the quoted edition of Lullus' work.

Enzyklopädie der philosophischen Wissenschaften Hegel enumerates and studies a good number of concepts put together in triadic groups. As examples, let us now indicate a few of these concepts and the triads which they originate.

The *Phänomenologie des Geistes, Werke* 3, pp. 178-323, Suhrkamp edition, includes the following description of the evolutive process of the concept of *reason* (*Vernunft*):

A. Observational reason (*Beobachtende Vernunft*),
B. The realization of rational self-consciousness by itself (*Die Verwirklichung des vernünftigen Selbstbewusstseins durch sich selbst*),
C. The individuality, which for itself is real in itself and for itself (*Die Individualität, welche sich an und für sich reell ist*).

A. Observational reason is on its turn divided in:
a. Observation of nature. Observation of the organic (*Beobachtung der Natur. Beobachtung des Organischen*),
b. The observation of self-consciousness in its purity and in its relation to external reality; logical and psychological laws (*Die Beobachtung des Sebstbewusstseins in seiner Reinheit und in seiner Beziehung auf äusere Wirklichkeit; logische und psychologische Gesetze*),
c. Observation of the relation of self-consciousness to its immediate reality (*Beobachtung der Beziehung des Selbstbewusstseins auf seine unmittelbare Wirklichkeit*).
B. The realization of rational self-consciousness is on its turn divided in:
a. Pleasure and necessity (*Die Lust und die Notwendigkeit*),
b. The law of the heart and the madness of conceit (*Das Gesetz des Herzens und der Wahsinn des Eigendlnkels*),
c. Virtue and the way of the world (*Die Tugend und der Weltlauf*).
C. The individuality is on its turn divided in:
a. The animal spiritual kingdom and the deception or the thing itself (*Das geistige Tierreich und der Betrug oder die Sache selbst*),
b. Reason as giver of laws (*Die gesetzgebende Vernunft*),
c. Reason as tester of the laws (*Die gesetzprlfende Vernunft*).

In his *Wissenschaft der Logik* II, *Werke* 6, pp. 469-487, Suhrkamp edition, Hegel deals with The life (*Das Leben*) which gives rise to the following triad:

A. The living being (*Das lebendige Individuum*),
B. The process of life (*Der Lebensprozess*),
C. The gender (*Die Gattung*).

Finally, in the *Enzyklopädie der philosophischen Wissenschaften* II, *Werke* 9, pp. 41-108, Suhrkamp edition, Hegel deals with The mechanics (*Die Mechanik*) which gives rise to the following triad:

A. Space and time (*Raum und Zeit*),
B. Matter and movement. Finite mechanics (*Materie und Bewegung. Endliche Mechanik*),
C. Absolute mechanics (*Absolute Mechanik*).

A. Space and time is in turn divided into:
a. Space (*Der Raum*),
b. Time (*Die Zeit*),
c. Place and movement (*Der Ort und die Bewegung*).
B. Matter and movement is on its turn divided in:
  a. Inert matter (*Die träge Materie*),
  b. Impulse (*Der Stoss*),
  c. Fall (*Der Fall*).

Other examples of triads in Hegel are given by José Ferrater Mora (in his *Diccionario de Filosofia*, Vol. I, p. 870, *sub* "Dialéctica" after indicating that Hegel's Dialectics "operates through triads"), and are considered by him as "the principal ones":

"The Idea articulates itself in the triad are:
(1) *Being*, (2) *Essence* and, (3) *Concept*.
1. *Being*, in the triad: (A) Quality, (B) Quantity and, (C) Measure. (A) Quality, in (a) indeterminate Being, (b) determinate Being and (c) Being for itself. The indeterminate Being, in (α) pure Being, (β) Nothingness and (γ) Becoming. The determinate Being, in (x) This, (y) Other and (z) Change. Being for itself, in (f) One, (g)

Repulsion, and (h) Attraction [...]
2. The *Essence*, in (A) Reflection of itself, (B) Appearance and (C) Reality. The Reflection of itself, in (a) Appearance, (b) reflective Determinations and (c) Reason [...]
3. *Concept*, in (A) subjective Concept, (B) objective Concept and (C) Idea [...] and (C) Idea, in (a) Life, (b) Knowledge and (c) absolute Idea [...]".

Taking into account (a) Hegel's religious (Lutheran) education; (b) his religious faith, which is present in his works; (c) that all through his life he was interested in historical and doctrinaire questions related to religion; (d) the presence in his works of numerous expositions on religious subjects such as the Christian Trinity (as for instance in *Enzyklopädie der philosophischen Wissenschaften* III, *Werke* 10, pp. 372-378, §§ 564-571; in *Phänomenologie des Geistes, Werke* 3, pp. 495-574, where the final part (VII.) is dedicated to "Religion"; in *Texte zur philosophischen Propädeutik in Nürnberger Schriften, Werke* 4, sections 8 [*Religionslehre*] and 9 [*Religionslehre*], pp. 272-290; and also in the two volumes of his *Vorlesungen über die Philosophie der Religion*); (e) the importance which the subject of the Christian Trinity has in Hegel, to the extent that Ludger Oeing-Hanhoff (in his article "Hegels Trinitätslehre, zur Aufgabe ihrer Kritik und Rezeption" in *Theologie und Philosophie*, No. 52, 1977, pp. 378-407, following J. Moltmann "Gedanken zur 'trinitarischen Geschichte Gottes'" in *Evangelische Theologic*, No. 35, 1975, pp. 208-222), calls Hegel "the philosopher of Trinity" (*Philosoph der Trinität*) - taking into account the above facts, it could be thought that, not only the frequent triadic classifications of Kant and his notion of the concept but also (as in the case of Raĭmundus Lullus) the religious Christian dogma of the Trinity contributed to Hegel's triadic structures.

Let us indicate here that Vittorio Hösle, one of the editors of Raimundus Lullus' *Die neue Logik. Logica Nova*, says on p. 52: "In a certain sense it could be said that the Enzyklopädie of Hegel is until today the last intent for accomplishing

Lullus' goal".

III.18 Correspondences and identifications between the macrocosm and the microcosm. The unity of the world in the *Upaniṣads*

1. Besides the central concept of *Brahman / Ātman*, the *Upaniṣads* develop other doctrines. Of them, the doctrine, which deserves a special mention is that related to the correspondences and identifications. A frequent procedure of the *Upaniṣads* is to establish correspondences and identifications between component elements of the microcosm and component elements of the macrocosm or just between component elements of either of them.

A typical case of this archaic form of thinking is given in the *Bṛhadāraṇyaka-Upaniṣad* I, 1, which points out the correspondences between the horse which had to be sacrificed in the ritual called *Aśvamedha* (Horse Sacrifice) and the Dawn as well as diverse elements of nature. The text expresses that the head of the horse is the Dawn, its eye the sun, its breath the wind, its open mouth the *vaiśvānara* fire, its *ātman* (essence) the year, its back the sky, its belly the atmosphere and so on, in a very minute and comprehensive enumeration.

Other cases are offered by the same *Bṛhadāraṇyaka-Upaniṣad*:

II, 1, 2 (identification of *Brahman* with the being which is in the sun), 3 (with the being which is in the moon), 4 (with the being which is in the lightning), 5 (with the being which is in the space) and so on with different beings in the celebrated dialogue between the brahmin Gārgya and Ajātaśatru, king of Benares;

III, 1, 3 (identification of the voice with the *hotṛ* priest and fire), 4 (identification of the eye with the adhvaryu priest and the sun), 5 (identification of breath with the *udgātṛ* priest and the wind), 6 (identification of mind with the *brahman* priest and the moon) in a dialogue of ritualistic speculation between the greatest Upanishadic thinker *Yājñavalkya* and *Aśvala*, the priest in the service of Janaka, king of Videha;

III, 9, 6 (identification of the God Indra with thunder and of the God *Prajāpati* with the sacrifice) in a debate between the brahmin *Vidagdha Śākalya* and *Yājñavalkya*;

VI, 2, 9-13 (identification of the atmospheric world, clouds, this world, man and woman with fire: in each case it is indicated which element of the macrocosm or microcosm corresponds with fire-wood, smoke, flame, charcoal or sparks) in the teaching of the doctrine of the five fires imparted by king Pravāhaṇa Jaivali.[33]

The identification of *Brahman*, which can be considered as the Cosmic Soul, with *Ātman*, the individual soul, is the foremost example of these identifications.

The discovery of these identifications and correspondences is not a childish game; its aim is much more important and serious. The knowledge of these identifications and correspondences is a means to acquire material and spiritual benefits; it is an instrument of power and control. This fact can be clearly seen in *Chāndogya-Upaniṣad* II, sections 1-23, where the text indicates the benefits to be obtained through the knowledge of each of the identifications or correspondences which the text examines. The same thing happens with many other Upanishadic texts, which also contain a series of identifications and correspondences.

It is obvious that an important consequence of these identifications and correspondences is that a network of tight links, bonds and relations is established between the components of the macrocosm and the microcosm and between the components of each of the two taken separately.

The distant origin of these identifications and correspondences is the widespread magical idea that whoever dominates an entity and is able to control or affect

[33] Cf. for other examples *Chāndogya-Upaniṣad* II, sections 1-21; V, 4, 1; 5, 1; 6, 1; 7, 1; 8, 1; 12, 1; 13, 1; 14, 1; 15, 1; 16, 1; 17, 1; 18, 2.

it can also dominate, control or affect other entities similar to it, or which are related to it by any kind of relationship such as one of ownership. This idea is the essence of magic by similarity, analogy, sympathy or homeopathy.[34]

2. The idea that the world constitutes a unitary whole in which the parts are interlinked is implicit in the doctrine of *Brahman / Ātman* conceived of as a *Universal Soul* and also in the doctrine of the identifications and correspondences just referred to.

However, this idea is also explicitly expressed in the text of the *Bṛhadāraṇyaka-Upaniṣad* III, 7, which contains the famous dialogue between the two most important thinkers of the *Upaniṣads*: Uddālaka, son of Aruṇa and Yājñavalkya. Uddālaka asks Yājñavalkya whether he knows which "thread" (*sūtra*) keeps this world and the other world tied like a bundle (*sandṛbdha*) and which Internal Governor (*antaryāmin*) rules them all from inside. Yājñavalkya answers that he does know the "thread" and the Internal Governor.

We must make it clear here that the "thread" and the Internal Governor are one and the same entity: *Brahman / Ātman*. This identification not only becomes apparent from the exposition which Yājñavalkya is to make – it is also explicitly expressed in paragraph 1 of section III, 7, in which we are told that a *gandharva* (supernatural being) called Kabandha had on a previous occasion revealed the doctrine of the "thread" and of the Internal Governor to Uddālaka. Kabandha had said on that occasion that

> *yo vai tat kāpya sūtraṃ vidyāt taṃ cāntaryāmiṇam iti sa brahmavit sa lokavit sa devavit sa vedavit sa bhūtavit sa ātmavit sa sarvavid iti* [35]

---

[34] On this subject see H. Oldenberg, *Vorwissenschaftliche Wissenschaft, Die Weltanschauung der Brāhmaṇa-Texte*, pp. 110-123; H. Oldenberg, *Die Religion des Veda*, pp. 484-485 and 506-509; A.B. Keith, *The Religion and Philosophy of the Veda and Upanishads*, pp. 388-390; and Mario Bunge, *La Causalidad. El principio de la causalidad en la ciencia moderna*, pp. 316-320, and in page 60 a brief reference to the theory of the universal causal interconnection.

[35] See also *Bṛhadāraṇyaka-Upaniṣad* III, 7, 3-23, analyzed in the section *Brahman as Universal Spirit*.

"he who knows that 'thread' and the Internal Governor, knows *Brahman*, knows the worlds, knows the Gods, knows the *Veda*, knows the beings, knows the *Ātman*, knows all".

This is the old Upanishadic theory which states that knowledge of the *Supreme Principle* means the knowledge of all and the unification of all in *Brahman / Ātman.*

At the intimation of Uddālaka, Yājñavalkya answers:

vāyur vai Gautama tat sūtraṃ vāyunā vai Gautama sūtreṇāyaṃ ca lokaḥ paraś ca lokaḥ sarvāṇi ca bhūtāni sandṛbdhāni bhavanti ... (III, 7, 2).

"The Wind, O Gautama [another name of Uddālaka], is that thread, because by the Wind as a thread, O Gautama, this world and the other world and all beings are maintained tied as in a bundle [*sandṛbdha*]".

In this paragraph, the word *vāyu* meaning the 'wind' is used with the meaning of *prāṇa*, 'vital air or breath' in a cosmic sense, and as such it is a name for *Brahman / Ātman.*

In the *Bṛhadāraṇyaka-Upaniṣad* III, 6, 1, in the dialogue between Gārgī and Yājñavalkya referred to in the section entitled 'Brahman as a substance', it is taught that all the worlds which constitute the universe are all "interwoven" (*ota, prota*) and are all "interwoven" in *Brahman / Ātman.*

Several centuries later, Buddhism was to give expression to the idea of the unity of all reality in its concept of universal interdependence. This is nothing other than the corollary of the theory of strictest causality, which according to Buddhism governs the whole of empirical reality: everything without exception has a cause. It is well-known that causality is the central concept of Buddhism and was established as such by the Buddha himself, and this fundamental principle underlies the *nairātmya* Buddhist theory of the absolute negation of the existence of any substance, whether it be God or the soul.

III.19 Remarks on the previous subject: The correspondences and identifications between the macrocosm and the microcosm and the unity of the world in the West

A similar concept to the Indian one is also to be found in the West. According to Festugière, *La Révélation d'Hermès Trismégiste*, Vol. I, p. 90:

> "Since the Hellenistic epoch and until the Renaissance, this doctrine of the unity of the Cosmos and of the sympathy that binds all its members has had the value of a dogma".

See also note 1 on the same page. According to this archaic doctrine, all reality constitutes a fully organized whole in which the inferior components (animals, plants, stones etc.) are related or linked to the superior components (Gods, demons etc.). Also, thanks to this relation or link, the inferior components possess powers similar to those possessed by the superior ones, although to a more or less reduced degree depending on the distance, which separates them. Whatever affects one of these components also affects the others. And whoever controls one of them is able to control some of the others too.

We shall now quote a few texts in which these ideas are present.

1. In Volume II of *Stoicorum veterum fragmenta*, J. von Arnim ed., under numbers 473 lines 7-9, 475 line 15, 534 lines 32-33, 543 lines 17-19, 912 lines 7-8, 1013 lines 23-25, we can find testimonies which inform us that Chrysippus (282-209 B.C.) and his disciples, all of them adhering to Stoicism, thought that the cosmos was "one" and that "sympathy" reigned between its different parts:

473, Alexander of Aphrodisias, *De mixtione*, p. 216, 14, I. Bruns ed., expresses that, according to Chrysippus' opinion:

> ἡνῶσθαι μὲν ὑποτίθεται τὴν σύμπασαν οὐσίαν, πνεύματός τινος διὰ πάσης αὐτῆς διήκοντος, ὑφ' οὗ συνέχεταί τε καὶ συμμένει καὶ συμπαθής ἐστιν αὑτῷ τὸ πᾶν
>
> "all the substance is unified, for throughout it all is spread a

spirit (πνεῦμα), by which all is kept and held together, and the whole is sympathetic with itself";

475, Alexander of Aphrodisias, *De mixtione*, p. 226, 34, refers to the Stoic doctrine of the
ἡ τοῦ παντὸς ἕνωσις τε καὶ συμπάθεια πρὸς αὑτό
"unification of the all and the sympathy (of the all) with itself";
534, Cleomedes, *Circul. doctr.* I, Chapter I, p. 1, Bake ed., has a reference to a Stoic doctrine according to which
ἐκ τῆς συμπαθείας τῶν ἐν αὑτῷ μερῶν πρὸς ἄλληλα
"through the mutual sympathy of the parts that exist in it [= the all]";
it is proved that the world has a nature which pervades the whole of it;
543, Diogenes Laërtius, VII, 140, mentions the Stoic theory that the cosmos knows no empty space, that the whole cosmos is unified and that this fact is the cause of
τὴν τῶν οὐρανίων πρὸς τὰ ἐπίγεια σύμπνοιαν καὶ συντονίαν
"the consent and syntony of celestial things with earthly things";
912, [Plutarch], *De fato*, Chapter XI, p. 574 d, resuming Chrysippus' doctrine on Fate, also states that the cosmos itself is possessed of consent (σύμπνους) and of sympathy (συμπαθής) with itself;

1013, Sextus Empiricus, *Adversus mathematicos* IX, 78, in his exposition of the Stoic doctrines, informs us that, according to them,

> ἐπὶ δὲ τῶν ἡνωμένων συμπάθειά τίς ἐστιν, εἴ γε δακτύλου τεμνομένου τὸ ὅλον συνδιατίθεται σῶμα.
>
> "in the things that are unified there exists some sympathy, since, when a finger is cut, the entire body is affected at the same time".

2. Plotinus (204-270 A.D.) in the fourth treatise of the *Ennead* IV (Difficulties with regard to the soul) develops his concept of the world, using some ideas of the Stoic Posidonius as a source of inspiration and thus introduces in his concept the idea that the world is a unitary whole in which the parts influence each other.[36] Plotinus explained

[36] Cf. Beate Nasemann, *Theurgie und Philosophie in Jamblichs de Mysteriis,*

divination practices, astrological predictions, magic and in particular the success of magical prayers addressed to the Gods via the theory of cosmic "sympathy".

3. Iamblichus (died circa 330 A.D.) in his *De Mysteriis* also refers to the theme of cosmic "sympathy", thus adopting the basic ideas of Plotinus.[37]

4. Synesius of Cyrene (375-415 A.D.) adheres to the same doctrine in his treatise "On dreams" (Περὶ ἐνυπνίων), in *Synesii Cyrenensis, Opuscula,* p. 147, N. Terzaghi ed. Here Synesius declares:

> ἔδει γάρ, οἶμαι, τοῦ παντὸς τούτου συμπαθοῦς τε ὄντος καὶ σύμπνου τὰ μέλη προσήκειν ἀλλήλοις, ἅτε ἑνὸς ὅλου μέλη τυγχάνοντα ... καὶ σοφὸς ὁ εἰδὼς τὴν τῶν μερῶν τοῦ κόσμου συγγένειαν. ἕλκει γὰρ ἄλλο δι' ἄλλου, ἔχων ἐνέχυρα παρόντα τῶν πλεῖστον ἀπόντων, καὶ φωνὰς καὶ ὕλας καὶ σχήματα· ὥσπερ ἐν ἡμῖν σπλάγχνου παθόντος ἄλλο συμπέπονθε, καὶ τὸ τοῦ δακτύλου κακὸν εἰς τὸν βουβῶνα ἀπερείδεται, πολλῶν τῶν μεταξὺ μὴ παθόντων· ἑνὸς γὰρ ἦν ἄμφω ζῴου, καὶ ἔστιν αὐτοῖς τι μᾶλλον ἑτέρων πρὸς ἄλληλα. καὶ δὴ καὶ θεῷ τινι τῶν εἴσω τοῦ κόσμου λίθος ἐνθένδε καὶ βοτάνη προσήκει, οἷς ὁμοιοπαθῶν εἴκει τῇ φύσει καὶ γοητεύεται.

> "It was necessary, I think, that the members [= component parts] of this whole [= the Universe], which is affected by the same feelings and is animated by the same Spirit, be mutually linked, because they are the members of a unique whole [= the Universe] ... and is wise he who knows the relations of the parts of the cosmos among themselves, because he is able to attract one by means of the other, having words, matters and forms as a present guarantee of things which are far away. As in our case when an internal organ was affected other also was affected, and the pain of a finger is transferred to the virile gland, without the intermediate zones being affected, since both [= the finger and the virile gland] belong to a unique living being, and they have in common between them something that they do not have with others. Also a stone or a herb from here [= the earth] is linked with some God

pp. 106-107, and her erudite bibliographic references, and also É. Bréhier's *Notice* in his edition of the *Enneads* IV, 4, pp. 46-57.

[37] See Nasemann, Beate, *ibidem.*, pp. 105-121.

who is inside the Universe, and He, experiencing the same thing [as the stone or the herb], yields to nature, and is bewitched".

Synesius develops similar ideas in his treatise entitled *Egyptians or on the providence*, p. 128, in the same quoted edition of Opuscula by Terzaghi.

5. In Proposition 145 of his *The Elements of Theology*, Proclus (420-485 A.D.) expounds ideas similar to those of the quoted authors:

> κομίζηται γὰρ ἕκαστον ἀπὸ τῆς οἰκείας προσεχοῦς αἰτίας τὴν ἰδιότητα ... λέγω δὲ οἷον εἴ τις ἔστι θεότης καθαρτική, καὶ ἐν ψυχαῖς ἔστι κάθαρσις καὶ ἐν ζώοις καὶ ἐν φυτοῖς καὶ ἐν λίθοις.
>
> "Each thing receives from its own immediate cause [which gave origin to it] its peculiar way of being ... for instance if it is [the case of] a purifying deity, the purification [i.e. the purity and the purifying power] is also found in the souls, in the animals, in the plants, in the stones [which belong to the series of that deity]."

Let us now indicate with Dodds, the editor of Proclus' *The Elements*, in his commentary to Proposition 145, that one of the purposes of that proposition is to provide a philosophical basis for theurgist practices; that the virtues attributed to plants and stones, such as that of purification, are not of a medical nature, but are magical; that a single plant or stone can put us into contact with some form of divine activity; and that this doctrine has its origin in Iamblichus (cf. Iamblichus, *De mysteriis*, in Jamblique, *Les Mystères d'Égypte*, p. 233, lines 10 ff.), who took it from Egyptian magic. Lists of symbolic stones, plants, animals, etc. frequently appear in the magical papyri, and many of the names of these stones etc. are common to Proclus and the Egyptian texts.

Proclus uses the principle behind this proposition to explain the existence of oracles and of sacred places and to justify astral determinism.

Proclus ends Proposition 145 by affirming that: "All things are full of Gods": μεστὰ δὲ πάντα θεῶν. This is a maxim of Thales, which became a favourite with the Stoics. Its animistic inspiration is obvious. Nevertheless, E.R. Dodds, who is also the author of *The Greeks and the Irrational*, qualifies this maxim as venerable in his commentary without taking its irrational nature into account.

6. In the treatises on the Greek lapidaries, edited by R. Halleux and J. Schamp, *Les lapidaires grecs*, we can find references to the correspondences which exist between the stones and the signs of the Zodiac, for example between the stone keraunius and the sign Sagittarius, which corresponds to the planet Jupiter. The *lapides* (stones) are "healthy and powerful" (*sani et potentes*). They protect the persons who carry them and give them health and security. Their power increases if certain engravings, indicated in the text, are added to them.[38] And the authentic stones (*veras species*) - not the falsified ones are accompanied by extraordinary effects (*effectus miri*) when they have been duly consecrated (*rite sacre*), as teaches Marbodus (11th century A.D.) in his treatise *Liber lapidum*, verses 726-727.

7. Cornelius Agrippa (1485-1535) in his important treatise *De occulta philosophia*, already quoted, dedicates many pages to establishing the correspondences between each star and the corresponding sign of the zodiac, which are considered as divine beings, and all of the things of this world such as animals, plants, stones, metals, regions, places, colours, faces, gestures etc.

For example, he attributes Spain, Arabia Felix and other regions to Jupiter along with Sagittarius (p. 143, lines 25-26), whereas he attributes Britain, Gallia, Germania etc. to Mars along with Aries, (p. 143, lines 27-28); he derives hardness from Mars, life from the sun, grace and beauty from Venus (p. 143, lines 15-16); "the stinking, gloomy, underground, unlucky, and fatal places as the cemeteries, the funeral pyres, etc." correspond to Saturn; (p. 176, lines 6-8), "the workshops, the schools, the taverns, the markets

[38] See pp. 219-221 of the *Notice* and pp. 232-233 of the text of the Latin lapidary attributed to Damigeron-Evax, a Latin text created on the basis of ancient Greek treatises.

and similar places" correspond to Mercury (p. 176, lines 21-22); "the reddish, blazing, igneous, flaming, violate, purple, sanguine, and iron colours" are proper to Mars (p. 179, lines 27-29); "the golden, yellow, purple, and more brilliant colours" correspond to the Sun (p. 179, line 29-p. 180, line 1); "the sad and grieving gestures as those of weeping and those of knocking one's own head, and also the religious gestures, as genuflection with the eyes looking downwards as imploring, those of striking one's own chest, etc." correspond to Saturn (p. 185, lines 21-22); whereas "the cheerful and elegant faces, the honourable gestures, joining of hands as for applauding and praising, genuflection with the head raised as in a adoration mood" correspond to Jupiter (p. 185, line 29-p. 186, line 2).

8. It is interesting to indicate that several centuries after the quoted author we find in Leibniz (1646-1716) the assertion of the existence of a universal sympathy, which links all that exists in the universe. In support of this idea Leibniz quotes Hippocrates. In the compilation of Louis Couturat, *Gottfried Wilhelm Leibniz, Opuscules et fragments inédits*, pp. 14-15, is included the following text where Leibniz refers to the "sympathy" which links all the things among themselves and to the mutual influence that all exerts on all:

> *Et sciendum est per naturam rerum fieri, ut quemadmodum in corpore animalis Hippocrates ait, ita in toto universo sint σύμπνοια πάντα; et quidvis cuivis certa quadam ratione conspiret ... Hinc sequitur unumquodque corpusculum ab omnibus universi corporibus pati, et ab iis varie affici, ita ut omniscius in unaquaque particula universi cognoscat omnia quae in toto universi fiunt ...*
>
> "It is necessary to know that, owing to the nature of things, it happens that, in the same way as Hippocrates says [it happens] in the body of a living being, so in the whole universe all the things are animated by a common spirit, and whatever you will harmonizes with whatever you will by some definite motive ... Hence it follows that any corpuscle is influenced by all the bodies of the universe, and through them it is affected diversely, in such a way that an omniscient person could know in each particle of

the universe all the things that occur in the totality of the universe ..."

This idea of identifications and correspondences provided a philosophical basis for the magical practices, which employed different objects which are provided in this way, according to the traditional belief, with extraordinary powers for healing and other purposes.[39]

Here we have another example of the use of philosophical speculation for purposes, which are not theoretical but practical.

III.20 Conclusion

We can conclude this Chapter III with the following words taken from the lucid book by Paolo Rossi *La naissance de la science moderne en Europe*, pp. 41-42. They refer to 16th century Europe, but they can also be applied to India of the same epoch and of several centuries before:

> "The limits between the philosophy of nature and the mystic knowledge ... frequently presented themselves to the men of this epoch as very fragile and faint. The *nature*, as it is conceived of by magic culture, is not only a continuous and homogeneous matter filling the space; it is a Living-all that possesses a soul, a principle of internal and spontaneous activity ... Each object of this world is full of hidden sympathies which link them to the All. Matter is pervaded by the Divine ... Between the great world or macrocosm and the microcosm or the world in a small scale (and such is man) there exist correspondences point by point ... The magician is he who knows how to penetrate that infinitely complex reality, this system of correspondences and insertions which remit to the All, and in which the All is enclosed ... Vitalism and animism, organicism, anthropomorphism, such are the categories of the magic thought".

The *Upaniṣads*, which are dated at quite a few centuries B.C., constitute the magnificent entrance door to Indian

---

[39] Cf. José Ferrater Mora, *Diccionario de Filosofía*, Vol. III, article *Macrocosmo*, pp. 2239-2241; and *Historisches Wörterbuch der Philosophie*, Vol. 5, article "Makrokosmos-Mikrokosmos" by M. Gatzemeier, col. 640-642.

thought. They reveal the powerful metaphysical impulse, which was to characterize that thought in the centuries that followed. In the *Upaniṣads* we can find bold intuitions and often also the overcoming of archaic forms of thought, not by eliminating them but by transforming them into new forms more in accordance with a more sophisticated and demanding way of thinking. Both forms of thought were to find their counterparts in the Western thought of the same epoch and of several centuries to come.

Chapter IV
The *Sāṃkhya* system: A pinnacle of Indian Rationalism

IV.1 Introduction

The Sāṃkhya system has its origin a few centuries before the Christian era and manifests itself in the form of several schools. Of these, we shall now expound the doctrines of the classical Sāṃkhya school, which puts the intuitions and theoretical concepts of the Indian thinkers who lived several centuries B.C. into a definitive form.

One of the fundamental texts of this school are the *Sāṃkhya-kārikās* (Stanzas of the Sāṃkhya) attributed to Īśvarakriṣṇa and whose composition must be located in the 4th or 5th centuries A.D. The *Sāṃkhya-kārikās* were translated into Chinese by Paramārtha between 557 and 569 A.D. This work gave the classical Sāṃkhya its definitive form and exerted an enormous influence on Indian thought. Another fundamental text of the Sāṃkhya are the *Sāṃkhya-sūtras* (Aphorisms of the Sāṃkhya) attributed to Kapila, the sage, founder of the system according to the tradition, but they are in fact a late work composed several centuries after the beginning of the Christian era, perhaps in the 14th or 15th centuries.

There is a very valuable commentary on the *Sāṃkhya-kārikās* which is traditionally attributed to Gauḍapāda. Other commentaries of equal value are that by Vācaspati Miśra entitled *Tattvakaumudī* and the *Yuktidīpikā* by an anonymous author, both commentaries on the *Sāṃkhyakārikās*, and the *Vṛtti* of Aniruddha as well as the *Sāṃkhyapravacanabhāṣya* by Vijñānabhikṣu, both commentaries on the *Sāṃkhyasūtras*.[1]

We shall mainly expound the Sāṃkhya system on the basis of the *Sāṃkhya-kārikās* and of the commentary by Gauḍapāda. In some cases we shall also have recourse to the *Sāṃkhya-sūtras* and the other commentaries mentioned.

IV.2 Dualism

The Sāṃkhya is a dualist system in the sense in which this term is defined by Christian Wolff and other authors in the context of Western philosophy.

In *Psychologia rationalis methodo scientifica pertractata*, Jean École ed., p. 26, § 39, Christian Wolff says:

> Dualistae *sunt, qui & substantiarum materialium, & immaterialium existentiam admittunt, hoc est, & corporibus realem extra ideas animarum existentiam concedunt, et animarum immaterialitatem defendunt.*
>
> "*Dualists* are those who admit the existence of material and immaterial substances, i.e. they concede to the bodies a real existence outside the ideas of the souls, and they uphold the immateriality of the souls".

The term "dualism," according to Rudolf Eucken, *Geschichte der philosophischen Terminologie*, p. 195:

> *"... designated firstly (in Hyde, Bayle, Leibnitz) the religious doctrine that admitted both a good Cosmic Principle* (Weltwesen) *and a evil one, but, since Wolff* [whose definition we quote in the next paragraph], [it

[1] For a history and exposition of the system see G.J. Larson, *Classical Sāṃkhya*; Michel Hulin, *Sāṃkhya Literature*; R. Garbe, *Die Sāṃkhya-Philosophie*, Chapter II, of the First Part; E.H. Johnston, *Early Sāṃkhya*; and G.J. Larson and R.S. Bhattacharya, *Encyclopaedia of Indian Philosophies*, Vol. IV, *Sāṃkhya, A Dualist Tradition in Indian Philosophy.*

designates] *the philosophical theory according to which the spiritual* (Geistiges) *and the material* (Körperliches) *are substantially different".*

Let us add here that "the religious doctrine" to which Eucken refers is the Zoroastrian religion with its opposing principles Ormazd and Ahriman, that this definition can also be applied to Manichaeism and that Zoroastrism as well as Manichaeism attributed an absolute character to the two cosmic principles – Good and evil.

"In this strict philosophical sense, the term 'dualism' is opposed to monism."

In his fourth transcendental paralogism (*der vierte Paralogism der Idealität*), *Kritik der reinen Vernunft,* p. 483 Felix Meiner ed. (= A 367), and from a gnoseological point of view, Kant opposes dualism to idealism:

Also ist das Dasein aller Gegenstände äusserer Sinne zweifelhaft. Diese Ungewissheit nenne ich die Idealität äusserer Erscheinungen und die Lehre dieser Idealität heisst der Idealism, in Vergleichung mit welchem die Behauptung einer möglichen Gewissheit von Gegenständen äusserer Sinne, der Dualism gennent wird.

"Thus, the existence of all the objects of the external senses is doubtful. I call this uncertainty the Ideality of the external phenomena and the doctrine of this Ideality is called idealism, in confrontation to which the affirmation of a possible certainty regarding the objects of the external senses is called Dualism".

In p. 500 (A 389), Kant defines "a certain transcendental dualism" as follows:

... der jene äussere Erscheinungen nicht als Vorstellungen zum Subjekte zählt, sondern sie, so wie sinnliche Anschauung sie uns liefert, ausser uns als Objekte versetzt und sie von dem denkenden Subjekte gänzlich abtrennt.

"... which does not consider those external phenomena as [mere] representations in the subject, but, just as the sensible intuition provides them to us, places them outside ourselves as objects, and completely separates them from the thinking subject".

In p. 501 (A 391) Kant gives the definition of matter from the point of view of dualism, which completes the previous definition of dualism itself:

> ... *Materie, als solche, nicht Erscheinung, d. i. blosse Vorstellung des Gemüts, der ein unbekannter Gegenstand entspricht, sondern der Gegestand an sich selbst sei, so wie er ausser uns und unabhängig von aller Sinnlichkeit existiert.*
>
> "... matter as such is not phenomenon, i.e. a mere representation of the spirit to which corresponds an unknown object, but the object in itself just as it exists outside us independently from any sensibility".

Thus, in the philosophical sense in which Kant uses the term "dualism", "dualism" is opposed to "idealism" insofar as the latter negates the existence of an external object of knowledge, which is independent of the subject. This type of idealism has more relation in India with idealism as conceived of in the Buddhist context than with the idealism of Śaṅkara, which is closer to the transcendental idealism of Kant since it affirms the existence of "a thing in itself", *Brahman*, which is incorrectly known or not known at all but nevertheless exists.

Due to the extension of its meaning beyond the opposition between matter and spirit (Wolff) and between realism (independent existence of matter) and idealism (doubt concerning the independent existence of matter or even the negation of it) (Kant), in the history of Western philosophy the term "dualism" is applied to all confrontations between two entities, principles, tendencies or realities, each of which cannot be reduced to the other, such as for instance the opposition between the intelligible world (ideas) and that of the senses (empirical reality) in Plato, between good and evil in Manichaean and Gnostic speculation and between *res cogitans* and *res extensa* in Descartes etc.

The relationship between the two entities, which are opposed in dualism, can assume various forms, for example mere coexistence, open hostility or collaboration in order to accomplish certain creative processes. It must be taken into account that there is a tendency to give a greater qualitative evaluation to one of the two entities.

It can be said that, in the dualism of religious inspiration, there is a hostile relationship between both entities, and one of them is placed on a level superior to that of the other.

In Sāṃkhya, dualism implies a relationship between both entities–Matter and Spirit–which is characterized by mere juxtaposition and cooperation.[2]

IV.3 *Sāṃkhya* Dualism and Realism: Primordial Matter and Spirit

The Sāṃkhya system is dualist since it maintains the existence of two absolute principles, neither of which depends on the other, neither do both together depend on another principle different from them and above them: Primordial Matter (*Prakṛti*) and the Spirit (*Puruṣa*) (*Sāṃkhyakārikā* 3), neither of which can be reduced to the other and both of which are *real*.[3]

The Sāṃkhya system rejects idealism: *na vijñāna-mātram, bāhya-pratīteḥ:* "[the theory that] 'only-consciousness [exists]' is not [logical] because of the knowledge of external objects" (*Sāṃkhyasūtra* I, 42, R. Garbe ed.).

Sāṃkhya holds that even the texts of the *Śruti* (Revelation) and the *Smṛti* (Tradition), which are of an idealistic tendency, do not however negate empirical existence as such, but negate its existence in absolute terms only. *Bhāṣya* of Vijñānabhikṣu *ad* I, 43, p. 21, lines 5-7, R. Garbe ed. says :

---

[2] Cf. in *Encyclopaedia of Religion and Ethics*, Vol. 5, pp. 100-101, article "Dualism (Introductory)" by R. Eucken; J. Ferrater Mora, *Diccionario de Filosofía*, Vol. I, pp. 941-942, article "Dualismo"; *Historisches Wörterbuch der Philosophie*, Vol. 2, col. 297-299, article "Dualismus" by W. Nieke; and *Enzylopädie Philosophie und Wissenschaftstheorie*, Band 1, pp. 503-504, article "Dualismus" by K. Mainzer.

[3] On the terms *prakṛti* and *puruṣa* see Knut A. Jacobsen, *Prakṛti in Sāṃkhya-Yoga* the articles by K. Rüping, in *Historisches Wörterbuch der Philosophie*, Vol. 7, col. 1252-1253 and 1718-1719 respectively; R. Garbe, *Die Sāṃkhya-Philosophie, Dritter* and *Vierter Abschnitt*; and G.J. Larson, *Classical Sāṃkhya*, pp. 160-171. We shall refer later on to both Principles.

vijñāna-mātra-satyatā-pratipādaka-śruti-smṛtayas tu kūṭasthatva-rūpām pāramārthika-sattām eva bāhyānām pratiṣedhanti, na tu pariṇāmitva-rūpāṃ vyāvahārika-sattām api

Finally, the Sāṃkhya system emphatically denies the unreality of the world. *Sāṃkhya-sūtra* I, 79 says :

abādhāt aduṣṭa-kāraṇa-janyatvāc ca nā 'vastutvam.

"[The world is] not unreal, because there is no fact contradictory [to its existence] and also because it is not produced by faulty causes [as a defect of the sense-organs]".

Cf. *jagat-satyatvam, aduṣṭa-kāraṇa-janyatvād, bādhakā-'bhāvāt* (*Sāṃkhya-sūtra* VI, 52), which expresses the same idea.

IV.4 Remarks on the previous subject: Dualism outside India: Manichaeans, Paulicians, Bogomils, Priscillians and Cathars

The peculiar affirmation on the part of Sāṃkhya of the absolute character of the two opposing principles brings the Sāṃkhya system close to the type of dualism proper to Manichaeism and other religious/philosophical/theological movements such as the Cathars or Albigenses in the West.

The following remarks show the enormous diffusion of dualism on the religious level and also on the philosophical and theological levels, both in the East and in the West.

Manichaeism

1. For Manichaeism, two Principles exist: Spirit-Light-Good and Matter-Darkness-Evil, which are eternally and essentially opposed. Manichaeism was founded in Persia by Mani, Māni or Manes, a religious man who was born in Persia in 216 A.D. and died in 276/277. It is a syncretistic religion which combines elements taken from various religious traditions of the epoch such as elements from late Hellenism, especially Gnosticism, Judaism, Christianity, Zoroastrianism, Buddhism, etc. Manichaeism had an enormous importance and influence, spreading from Central Asia up to France and

Spain and penetrating into Syria, Armenia, Asia Minor, Palestine, Northern Arabia, Egypt, North Africa, the Balkans and Rome and generally into the regions occupied by the Byzantine empire. In the Byzantine world, it suffered persecution by the emperors Juṣtin (518-527 A.D.) and Justinian (527-565 A.D.) and disappeared from it almost completely. In Persia, which had been conquered by the Moslem Arabs, it also fell victim to harsh attacks and persecutions at the end of the 8th century.[4]

As a proof of the influence exercised by Manichaeism, let us indicate here that St. Augustine, born in Numidia in North Africa in 354 A.D., adhered to Manichaeism from 373, when he was 19 years old, to 382 A.D. In Books III-VI of his *Confessions*, he repeatedly refers to Manichaeans and the attraction that their doctrines exercised on him as well as to his gradual withdrawal from those doctrines and his conversion to Christianity. As he informs in *Liber Sextus* I, 1, when he was in Milan in 384 A.D., he could declare to his mother Monica that he was no longer a Manichaean (*non me quidem iam esse manichaeum*). After his conversion, St. Augustine wrote a good number of treatises against Manichaeism, which are included in Volumes XXX and XXXI of his *Complete Works* (Latin and Spanish translation) (*Obras Completas de San Agustín, Escritos antimaniqueos*, Biblioteca de Autores Cristianos).[5] Julian, the opponent of St.

[4] On Manichaeism in general, see in *Encyclopaedia of Religion and Ethics*, Vol. 8, pp. 394-402, the article "Manichaeism" by A.A. Bevan; in *Historisches Wörterbuch der Philosophie*, Vol. 5, col. 714-716, the article "Manichaïsmus" by S. Lorenz and W. Schröder; in J. Ferrater Mora, *Diccionario de Filosofía*, Vol. III, pp. 2269-2271, the article "Maniqueísmo"; M.D. Lambert, *Medieval Heresy*, pp. 3-36; Fernand Niel, *Albigeois et Cathares*, pp. 11-44; and *Mani et le Manichéisme* of several authors, in *Connaissance des Péres de l'Èglise* No. 83. On the history of Manichaeism in Mesopotamia and in the Roman Empire of Orient see Samuel N.C. Lieu, *Manichaeism in Mesopotamia & the Roman East.*

[5] Cf. Alberto Pincherle, *Sant'Agostino*, pp. 24-34; Pierre de Labriolle, *Histoire de la Littérature Latine Chrétienne*, pp. 530-532, 541-542.

Augustine, asserted that Saint Augustine's thought still showed remains of his original Manichaean position.[6]

2. Soon after the death of Mani, the founder of Manichaeism (end of 3rd century), his disciple Mar Amu created a Manichaean church in the city of Samarkand in the region of Sogdian, Central Asia, which became the center of proselytist activities. In the next centuries, these spread to the oasis of the Tarim basin and the cities of the present Kan-su in China and also to Mongolia and Tibet.[7]

In the 20th century, numerous texts of the Manichaean communities of Central Asia were found in the Turfan oasis and in the Tun-huang caves in Chinese Turkestan. They were written in Middle Persian, Parthian, Sogdian, Uighur and Chinese.[8]

3. Manichaeism was introduced into China in 694 A.D. It enjoyed the tolerance of the empress Wu tse-t'ien (reigned 684-704 A.D.) of the T'ang Dynasty (618-907 A.D.). Later on, however, in an imperial edict pronounced by the emperor Hiuan-tsong in 732 A.D., it was considered a "heretical doctrine" which falsely passed itself off as Buddhism in order to attract adherents, and because of this - as the edict affirmed - it should be strictly prohibited. But this did not happen, due to its being "the local religion of the Hu of the West [Iranian or Indo-European people] and others", which were part of the Chinese Empire, and "so long as they practice it personally, have not to be accused of any crime". Finally, the Manichaean religion, in conjunction with all of the other foreign religions, including Christianity,

[6] Cf. A. von Harnack, *Lehrbuch der Dogmengeschichte*, Vol. III, p. 185, and the "Introduction" of Pio de Luis in *Obras Completas de Sãn Agustín*, Vol. XXX, pp. 158-163.

[7] Cf. Hans Wilhem Haussig, *Die Geschichte Zentralasiens und der Seidenstrasse in Vorislamischer Zeit*, chapter entitled "Mani und die Mission seiner Jünger in Mittelasien und in China", p. 233 ff.

[8] Cf. Samuel N.C. Lieu, *Manichaeism in Central Asia and China*, pp. 1-75; Julien Ries, "Bouddhisme et Manichéisme. Les étapes d'une recherche", in *Indianisme et Bouddhisme. Mélanges offerts á Mgr Étienne Lamotte*, pp. 283-287; and Jens Wilkens, *Alttürkische Handschriften.* Teil 8. *Manichäisch-türkische Texte der Berliner Turfansammlung.*

was prohibited in the whole of China in 843 A.D. This decision was not of a religious nature, but instead had a more economic aim, since it allowed the Chinese state to seize all of the money accumulated in the temples by the foreign religious communities established in China at a time in which the principal problem of the Chinese state was the scarcity of the money circulating.[9]

As a curious manifestation of the presence of Manichaeism in China, the *Taishō* edition of the *Chinese Buddhist Canon* includes two Chinese texts discovered in Tun-huang by the *Mission Pelliot* [*Taishō* Vol. LIV, No. 2140: *Mo ni kiao hia pou tsan* (Stanzas in Praise of the Sect of the adherents to the Doctrine of Mani)] and by the *Mission Stein* [*Taishṣo* Vol. LIV, No. 2141: *Mo ṇi kouang fo kiao fa yi lio* (The Compendium of the Doctrines and the Rites of Mani, the Buddha of Light), translated into English by G. Haloun/ W.B. Henning, in *Asia Major* (N.S.) 3, 1953, pp. 184-212.[10]

4. According to the testimony of the trilingual inscription in Chinese, Uighur (Turkish) and Sogdian discovered in Qara Balgasun, Manichaeism became the official religion of the Turkish empire of the Uighurs in Mongolia in 762 A.D. The Uighurs, one of the peoples of Turkish origin established in Mongolia, had come to power in 744 A.D., replacing the Eastern Turks in the governing of Mongolia. They became the allies of the Chinese empire of the T'ang at a difficult moment for the Chinese government due to internal rebellions. They acquired considerable power

---

[9] Cf. Samuel N.C. Lieu, *Manichaeism in Central Asia and China*, pp. 126-131; Hans Wilhem Haussig, *Die Geschichte Zentralasiens und der Seidenstrasse in Vorislamischer Zeit*, p. 233; W. Eberhard, *Histoire de la Chine*, pp. 203-204; and R.A. Stein, "Une mention du Manichéisme dans le choix du Bouddhisme comme religion d'Ètat par le roi Tibetain Khri-sroṅ lde-bcan", in *Indianisme et Bouddhisme. Mélanges offerts á Mgr Étienne Lamotte*, p. 334.

[10] Cf. Samuel N.C. Lieu, *Manichaeism in Central Asia and China*, pp. 49-54; G. Uray, "Tibet's connections with Nestorianism and Manicheism in the 8th-10th centuries", in *Contributions on Tibetan Language, History and Culture*, Vol. I, pp. 411-412.

throughout the northern part of Central Asia. Thanks to their relationship with China, they made contact with Manichaeism, which, as we have already said, was proclaimed to be their state religion in 762 A.D. In 840 A.D., the capital of the Uighur empire was conquered by another Turkish people, the Kirghiz, thus putting an end to Uighur power, which had until then served as protection for the Manichaeans in China.[11]

5. Manichaeism also became known in Tibet. The *Tibetan Buddhist Canon*, Tanjur, Tōhoku 4352 and Peking 5839, includes a treatise under the name of: *Bkaḥ yaṅ-dag-paḥi tshad-ma-las mdo-btus-pa* (Brief Exposition of the Proofs of the Correct Word [= the Buddhist Doctrine]) (*Samyagvākpramāṇoddhṛtasūtra* in Sanskrit: attributed to the Tibetan king Khri-sroṅ lde-bcan (or bstan) of the 8th century, and whose aim was to base the decision for Buddhism as the state religion of Tibet on logical proofs (*pramāṇa* in Sanskrit / *tshad-ma* in Tibetan). This treatise includes a passage (p. 403, lines 5-6, *Sde dge* edition, Dharamsala, India) which contains a criticism of Mani (= *Mar ma ni* (or *ne)* in Tibetan = *Mo mo ni* in Chinese), the founder of Manichaeism, who is said to be "the great Persian liar" (*par sig gyon chen Mar ma ni*) who, "with the aim to create a single (doctrine) different to all the (other) doctrines, extracted (elements) from all the (other) doctrines and combining (them) deliberately in a different way gave rise, by means of the other doctrines, to a not-founded doctrinaire position (*siddhānta* in Sanskrit, *grub paḥi mthaḥ* in Tibetan)": ... *gtsug lag kun daṅ mi mthun pa gcig bya baḥi phyir gtsug lag kun nas draṅs te / byas pa lta bu ched du mi mthun par sbyar na / gtsug lag gźan gyis grub paḥi mthaḥ yod par gyur te / ma grub pa la sogs paḥo /*. According to the present text, it would seem that Manichaeism was

[11] Cf. René Grousset, *L'empire des steppes. Attila, Gengis-Khan, Tamerlan*, pp. 172-178; W. Eberhard, *Histoire de la Chine*, pp. 202-205; Hans Wilhem Haussig, *Die Geschichte Zentralasiens und der Seidenstrasse in Vorislamischer Zeit*, pp. 233-234; Annemarie von Gabain, *Einführung in die Zentralasienkunde*, pp. 49-50; G. Hambly (editor), *Historia Universal Siglo Ventiuno, Asia Central*, pp. 61-63.

rejected by the Tibetans because of its syncretistic character, to which we have already referred, and which could be considered as a stratagem for gaining Buddhist adepts. As a consequence of this, Manichaeism was accused of being a false and deceitful doctrine.[12]

Paulicians and Bogomils

6. Let us now move on to the West. In the Byzantine empire, after the disappearance of Manichaeism due to the persecution by Justin and Justinian mentioned above (6th century A.D.), there were manifestations of dualist beliefs in Christian communities such as those of the Byzantine Paulicians and the Bogomils.

The Byzantine Paulicians were the successors of the Armenian Paulicians, whose religious and political organizations were destroyed by the persecution carried out by the Christian Byzantine emperors (Theodora in 842-857 A.D., Basilius I, who destroyed Tephrikē, capital city of the Armenian Paulicians, in 871-872 A.D., John Tzimiskes in 970 A.D.). The Armenian Paulicians were deported to Bulgaria where they spawned the sect of the Bogomils or amalgamated with it.[13]

7. The Bogomils were another heretical Christian sect. It was created by a Bulgarian monk called Bogomil in the first half of the 10th century under the reign of Tsar Peter (927-969 A.D.). The doctrines of this sect contained elements taken from the sect of the Byzantine Paulicians established in Bulgaria.

---

[12] Cf. R.A. Stein, "Une mention du Manichéisme dans le choix du Bouddhisme comme religion d'État par le roi Tibetain Khri-sroṅ lde-bcan", pp. 333-335; G. Uray, "Tibet's connections with Nestorianism and Manicheism in the 8th-10th centuries", in *Contributions on Tibetan Language, History and Culture*, Vol. I, pp. 407-412; G. Tucci, *Minor Buddhist Texts*, Part II, pp. 122-125.

[13] Cf. the article "Paulicians" by C.A. Scott, in *Encyclopaedia of Religion and Ethics*, Vol. 9, pp. 695-698; M.D. Lambert, *Medieval Heresy*, pp. 10-12; and Raoul Vaneigem, *Les hérésies*, pp. 72-73. On the Paulicians in Spain see Marcelino Menéndez y Pelayo, *Historia de los heterodoxos españoles*, Alphabetical Index of subjects *sub* "Paulicianos" (Vol. III, pp. 152-154).

They advocated a special form of dualism according to which Satanael, the first son of God, stricken with pride, revolted against his father. He was expelled from Heaven, but as a son of God he retained the power to create, and this allowed him to create a second Heaven as his personal residence and then the visible, material world; the opposition between God and Satanael was thus established. Moreover, Cain, adulterous son of Satanael and Eve, represented the Evil Principle in mankind while Abel, son of Adam and Eve, represented the Good Principle.

In the 11th century, the sect spread across the Byzantine empire, including Constantinople. In 1119, in the time of the emperor Alexius and the Patriarch Nicholas, the Bogomils were persecuted. The monk Basil was burnt on a pyre and became the first Bogomil martyr, while other Bogomils were condemned to life-long imprisonment. In the Synods of 1140 and 1143, the doctrines of the Bogomils were condemned. In 1230, the Patriarch Germanos II referred to the intense activity of the sect. In Bulgaria, there were references to this sect even in the 17th century. Today some popular legends with vague dualistic elements are all that remains of this most powerful heretic sect of the Balkan region.[14]

Priscillianism

8. In Spain Manichaean doctrines were maintained among others by Priscillian and his followers. The bishop Priscillian, born in Merida, Lusitania, in the middle of 4th century A.D., was the founder of this Christian heretic sect influenced by the Manichaen and Gnostic ideas, and owing to these ideas he was finally put to the torture and, afterwards together with his followers Armenius, Felicissimus, the poet

---

[14] Cf. the article "Bogomils" by Fred. J. Powicke, in *Encyclopaedia of Religion and Ethics*, Vol. 2, pp. 784-785; M.D. Lambert, *Medieval Heresy*, pp. 12-23, and *The Cathars*, Chapter 2 (German translation *Geschichte der Katharer*, pp. 26-47); Dmitri Obolensky, *The Bogomils. A Study in Balkan Neo-Manichaeism*; Raoul Vaneigem, *Les hérésies*, pp. 73-74; and *Le livre secret des Cathares*.

Latronianus and Euchrocia, the widow of Delphidius, was condemned to be beheaved by resolution of the bishops summoned in a Synod at Bordeaux, who with that aim asked for the authorization of Emperor Maximus (reigned 383-388). Thus all of them became the first heretic martyrs sent to the scaffold by the Church. The condemnation of a bishop by other bishops caused indignant protests throughout the Christian world, as for instance those of Saint Ambrose and Saint Martin of Tours, who in an attitude of more Christian charity implored the Emperor to spare the life of Priscillian.[15]

Cathars (Albigenses, Bulgars and Patarenes)

9. Another dualistic sect of the West was that of the Cathars, also known as Albigenses, Bulgars and Patarenes etc. Their doctrines constituted the most powerful heresy within Christianity in Europe in the 13th century, but their existence can be traced back to the beginning of the 11th century. The Cathars spread especially in Italy and the South of France (Languedoc), and also in Germany and the Low Countries. They disappeared almost completely in the 14th century due to the violent and cruel persecutions they suffered. As Michel Roquebert, *Histoire des Cathares. Hérésie, Croisade, Inquisition du Xe au XIVe siécle*, p. 15, says:

> "*To write the history of the Cathars is more or less to write the history of their persecution. Very brief were the periods during which they could live their faith with all freedom*".

---

[15] On Priscillian see the articles by C.A. Scott "Priscillianism", in *Encyclopaedia of Religion and Ethics*, Vol. 10, pp. 336-338, and by A. Olivares Guillem, "Prisciliano entre la ortodoxia y la heterodoxia. Influencia del ambiente político y religioso en la evolución histórica del priscilianismo (ss. IV-VI d.C.)", in *'Ilu, Revista de ciencias de las religiones*, Madrid, 2002, Vol. 7, pp. 97-120; and the work of Marcelino Menéndez y Pelayo, *Historia de los heterodoxos españoles*, Tomo II, pp. 85-150, and the Appendices III-IX, pp. 409-556, which include texts by Priscillian or concerning Priscillianism. In pages 99-101 Marcelino Menéndez y Pelayo, with his habitual spirit of intolerance and fanaticism, ardently defends the execution of Priscillian and his companions and in a general way the punition of the heterodox even with the capital punishment.

Of the persecutions of the Cathars, the most important was the so-called "Albigensian Crusade" which took place between 1209 and 1229.[16]

The doctrines of the Paulician and Bogomil sects of the Byzantine empire influenced the doctrines of the Cathars through merchants, devout travellers and missionaries. Let us remark here that the bishop Nicetas, principal chief of the Paulicians of Constantinople, and to whom the title of *(Pope of the heretics)* "Papa haereticorum" was given, journeyed to the South of France and presided over a council of Catharian bishops at Saint-Felix de Caraman in 1167. Before returning to his country, Nicetas confirmed or designated several Cathar bishops.

The organization of the Cathars was very similar to that of the Church of Rome.

Of the Cathar doctrines, it is interesting to stress the dualist doctrine here, which was presented in two forms. It was either asserted, as the Bogomils did, that an evil angel, Satan, revolted against God and was the origin of Evil, or it was affirmed in a more radical form that there is an evil God. This evil God had his retinue of evil angels, was as eternal as the good God and possessed equal powers. He created the material world and the material bodies, and captured good angels and confined them in material bodies. It is possible to think that the second form of Cathar dualism contained remote influences from Manichaeism, which had "in fact" influenced all of the dualist doctrines of the Western world. The Cathars were dualist in the sense in which this word is used by Hyde, Bayle and Leibniz. The Cathars were often called Manichaeans because it was an established habit to apply this name to dualist sects in general. This is because Manichaeism was the best-known form of the dualist heresy,

---

[16] Cf. *Les Cathares. La croisade albigeoise* by different authors; the just quoted work of Roquebert, pp. 129-301; Georges Bordonove, *La tragédie Cathare*, Henri-Charles Lea, *Histoire del' Inquisition au Moyen Âge*, Tome I, pp. 133-191; and Jörg Oberste, *Der Kreuzzug" gegen die Albigenser.*

partly because of its link to St. Augustine, who was so venerated in the Christian world.

During the pontificates of Innocentius III (1198-1216), Honorius III (1216-1227), Gregorius IX (1227-1241) and Innocentius IV (1243-1254), the Church took drastic measures against the Cathars. The persecution of the Cathars also had a political aspect, since many of the feudal lords of the South of France protected or tolerated the Cathars, as was the case with Count Raymond VI of Toulouse. When Innocentius III ordered a crusade against the Cathars and those who protected or tolerated them, many of the feudal lords of Northern France joined it, eager to take possession of the lands and riches of the feudal lords of the South, whom they accused of being heretics.

The Cathars were the object of cruel persecutions. On March 16, 1244, in the morning, immediately after the surrender of the Monségur fortress, redoubt of the Cathars, about 220 Cathars dedicated to the religious life, were burnt in a unique huge pyre specially prepared for that aim. Those who had the strength to do it, climbed up to the pyre by themselves; those who were ill, wounded, crippled, and women were thrown as parcels by the soldiers into the flames (cf. G. Bordonove, *La tragédie Cathare*, p. 428).

The Albigenses, Cathars or Patarenes left "slight traces" in Spain, according to the opinion of Marcelino Menéndez y Pelayo, *Historia de los heterodoxos españoles*, Tomo III, p. 152, and lasted for a short time, p. 183. This was not an obstacle to their being persecuted with the same cruelty as in France. Menéndez y Pelayo, in the quoted work, p. 192, refers to the "zeal of San Fernando" for fighting "the great although transient ... danger" of the Albigenses in the region of León. Firstly he quotes Father Juan de Mariana, an author at the end of the 16th century and beginning of 17th century, and then he says:

> "[San Fernando] *was so enemy of the heretics (Mariana says), that not being satisfied with ordering his ministers to punish them, he himself, with his own hand, brought the firewood close to the condemned and set fire to*

them. In the law codes that this saint monarch gave to Cordoba, Seville and Carmona capital punishment and confiscation of their possessions were imposed on the heretics. In Castilla there was not Inquisition, and perhaps owing to this fact the punishments were harder. The Anales Toledanos refer that in 1233 San Fernando hanged many persons and cooked many others in big kettles".

- an image pathetically surrealist that of a "saint" cooking heretics.

The cruel persecutions which the Cathars had to suffer as well as the increasing activity of the Papal Inquisition (which in fact arose in the time of Gregorius IX) with its consequent capital condemnations involving being burnt at the stake gradually caused the Cathars to disperse and decrease in numbers. The result was that, during the 14th century, the Cathars disappeared almost completely from Western Europe. Remnants of the sect survived in Bosnia and in some valleys in the Pyrenees.[17]

The interest for Dualism introduced by Manichaeism and the other sects, derived from it or influenced by it, was always alive inasmuch as it constitutes an answer to the problem of evil in the world. For instance, Leibniz dedicates several pages of his *Théodicée* to it (II, §§ 135-139 and 144-145 = I, pp. 438-442 and 452-454, Insel Verlag ed.) and Pierre Bayle (1647-1706) gives detailed information on Manichaeism in his *Dictionnaire historique et critique* .

The adherents of the dualist Sāṃkhya.system in India had better luck than those who adhered to Dualism in Europe: they did not suffer any persecution whatsoever. In addition, their system of thought was considered as one of

[17] See in *Encyclopaedia of Religion and Ethics*, Vol. 1, pp. 277-287, the article "Albigenses" by J. Bass Mullinger; in *Historisches Wörterbuch der Philosophie*, Vol. 5, col. 714-716, the article "Manichaïsmus" by S. Lorenz and W. Schröder; M.D. Lambert, *Medieval Heresy*, pp. 108-164, and of this same author especially *The Cathars*; M. Roquebert, *Histoire des Cathares*; F. Niel, *Albigeois et Cathares*; *Les Cathares* of several authors; Jörg Oberste, *Der Kreuzzug" gegen die Albigenser* and Raoul Vaneigem, *Les hérésies*, pp. 82-85. On the Albigenses and Cathars in Spain see M. Menéndez y Pelayo, *Historia de los heterodoxos españoles*, Alphabetical Index of subjects *sub* "Albigenses" and "Cátaros".

the orthodox Hindu systems in the rich history of Indian philosophy, and even at present, as a philosophical system in itself and as the philosophical foundation of the Yoga system, it still maintains its validity.

IV.5 The Principle of *ex nihilo nihil*, the foundation of *Sāṃkhya* causality

Even in one of the oldest *Upaniṣads*, the *Chāndogya Upaniṣad* VI, 6.2.1 and 2, there is a reference to the theory that the existent (*sat*) was born from the inexistent (*asat*) (*asataḥ sad ajāyata iti*) in order to reject it: "How from the inexistent the existent could be born?": *katham asataḥ saj jāyeta*. The idea of the *Upaniṣad* is that, in the beginning, only Being (*sat*) existed, and everything else emerged from it. This is the orthodox position of the *Upaniṣads*.

Before the *Upaniṣads*, in the creation theories found in *Ṛg Veda,* we find the idea that this world came forth from something which existed previously. Creation is conceived of as a construction task similar to building a house. Consequently, the hymns refer to measurements (of space), to the materials used (wood), to columns (which support the sky and the earth), to doors (the East from which light comes forth) and to chains (to fix the earth) etc., as we have already said. At other times, the *Ṛg Veda* presents creation as an act of pro-creation on the part of the Sky (*Dyaus*) and the Earth (*Pṛthivī*), which were considered as the universal Father and Mother. In one instance, creation is described as a ritualistic act in which the world is created from the body of a gigantic primordial being (*puruṣa*). The famous Hymn of Creation (*Ṛg Veda* X, 129) affirms that creation originated from the One *(Eka)*.[18]

The Sāṃkhya system maintains the same Upanishadic position in regard to the relationship of cause and effect. Then *Sāṃkhyasūtras* I, 78 says :

nā 'vastuno vastu-siddhiḥ.

[18] See in *Chapter II* of this book the sections related to Creation and the text and translation of *Ṛg Veda* X, 129.

"An existing thing (*vastu*) does not come to being from a non-existing thing (*avastu*)".

Vijñānabhikṣu *ad locum* glosses:

avastuno 'bhāvān na vastu-siddhir bhāvo-'tpattiḥ.

"From a non-existing thing [i.e. from inexistence] it is not possible that something be, [i.e. it is not possible] the coming forth of existence".

The same Vijñānabhikṣu *ad* I, 113, adduces as the foundation of the *satkāryavāda* (Sāṃkhya theory of causality), the principle of *sad-asatoḥ sambandhā-'nupapatteḥ:* "impossibility of connection between the existent and the non-existent" and *ad* I, 63, in his reasoning to demonstrate the existence of *ahaṃkāra,* (ego-consciousness) (a notion which will be dealt with later in connection with the theory of evolution in the Sāṃkhya), he refers to the fact that *dravyasyāi 'va loke dravyo-'pādānatva-darśanāt:* "in the world it is seen that only a substance can be the material cause of a substance". Gauḍapāda commenting on *kārikā* 9 of the *Sāṃkhya-kārikās,* which enumerates the reasons supporting the theory of the *satkārya,* concludes (with reference from Anne-Marie Esnoul edition of the kārikās):

tasmāt sata utpattir nāsata iti.

"Consequently, from the inexistent the existent does not originate".

The Sāṃkhya position, based on the principle of *ex nihilo nihil,* constitutes the *pariṇāmavāda* or "theory of the transformation or evolution" (from the seed, the fruit): the cause is transformed into the effect and there is no creation of something new, there is no creation *ex nihilo.* The *pariṇāmavāda* is opposed by the *ārambhavāda* or "theory of the beginning", asserted by the Nyāya and Vaiśeṣika schools, according to which a series of component elements are joined together to give rise to something new (from the threads, the cloth): the effect is something essentially new and different from the cause, something new is created, but there is no creation *ex nihilo.*

IV.6 Remarks on the previous subject: The Principle of *ex nihilo nihil* in Greco-Roman Antiquity

This Sāṃkhya principle, *nāsataḥ sat* (from the inexistent no existent), corresponds to the *ex nihilo nihil* (from nothing, nothing) which found wide acceptance in Greco-Roman Antiquity.

In his *Metaphysica*, K, 6. 1062 b 24-26, Aristotle supplies the following information:

> τὸ γὰρ μηθὲν ἐκ μὴ ὄντος γίγνεσθαι πᾶν δ' ἐξ ὄντος, σχεδὸν ἁπάντων ἐστὶ κοινὸν δόγμα τῶν περὶ φύσεως.
>
> "That nothing comes forth from something inexistent and all from something existent, is a dogma common almost to all the Physicists".

This principle was maintained by thinkers such as Melissus of Samos (5th century B.C.) and Empedocles of Acragas (483-430 B.C.) in Greece as well as by Lucretius in Rome and was generally used to prove the eternity of the world.

1. A fragment from Melissus on the subject, preserved by Simplicius in his *Commentary of the Physics of Aristotle*, p. 162, 24 [30 B 1. Diels / Kranz], says:

> ἀεὶ ἦν ὅ τι ἦν καὶ ἀεὶ ἔσται. εἰ γὰρ ἐγένετο, ἀναγκαῖόν ἐστι πρὶν γενέσθαι εἶναι μηδέν· εἰ τοίνυν μηδὲν ἦν, οὐδαμὰ ἂν γένοιτο οὐδὲν ἐκ μηδενός·
>
> "Always existed what existed and always will exist, because if it had come to being, then it would be necessary that it were nothing before [its] coming to being; if it were nothing, then in no way something could have come to being from nothing".[19]

In the same commentary 103, 13, in which he gives a paraphrase of some fragments of Melissus, Simplicius says that Melissus maintained that "it is not possible that from the inexistent something comes to being": οὔτε ἐκ μὴ ὄντος οἷόν τε γενέσθαι τι [Diels / Kranz, p. 268, paraphrase 1].

[19] Cf. Aristotle, *De sophisticis elenchis*, p. 167 b 14-15.

The same opinion was attributed to Melissus in the treatise on Melissus, Xenophanes and Gorgias handed down under the name of Aristotle, *Aristotelis de Melisso, Xenophane, et Gorgia Disputationes*, p. 1, lines 1 and 2, and p. 12, lines 2 and 3, F. W. A. Mullach ed. [p. 259 lines 38 and 39 and p. 261, line 20, Diels/Kranz].

2. In two fragments [31 B 11. y 31 B 12. Diels/Kranz], Empedocles expresses his support for the same principle:

νήπιοι ...
οἳ δὴ γίγνεσθαι πάρος οὐκ ἐὸν ἐλπίζουσιν
"foolish ... [are those] who deem
that what does not exist before can come to being"

ἔκ τε γὰρ οὐδάμ' ἐόντος ἀμήχανόν ἐστι γενέσθαι
"from what does not exist at all
it is impossible that something comes to being"

3. The Epicureans also maintained this principle. In the letter of Epicurus to Herodotus, paragraph 38, it is affirmed:

οὐδὲν γίνεται ἐκ τοῦ μὴ ὄντος.
"Nothing comes to being from the inexistent".

4. Finally, in verses I, 146-214 of his poem *De rerum natura*, Lucretius adheres to this principle and gives reasons in its favor:

I, 150
nullam rem e nilo gigni divinitus umquam.

"no thing was ever divinely created from nothing".

I, 155-156
... nil posse creari
de nilo ...

"... nothing can be created from nothing ..."

I, 205
nil igitur fieri de nilo posse fatendumst
"it is necessary to admit
that nothing can be produced from nothing".

The reasons given by Lucretius in favor of this principle present remarkable similarities with those adduced by the

Sāṃkhya school in defense of its theory of causality, to which we shall refer in the next section.

For Lucretius, if this principle is not accepted, absurd consequences would be produced, such as:

a. Anything could be produced from anything:

I, 159-160
Nam si de nilo fierent, ex omnibu' rebus /
omne genus nasci posset, nil semine egeret
"For if things came forth from nothing,
from anything any species could be born,
nothing would be in need of a seed",

as for instance (I, 162) ... *volucres erumpere caelo* : "... that birds rush out from space", but experience reveals that this absurdity does not happen.

b. There would not be material causes proper to each species:

I, 167-173
... ubi non essent genitalia corpora cuique, /
qui posset mater rebus consistere certa?
"... where there would not be procreating elements
[specifically] for each species,
how things would have a certain mother?",

but experience also reveals (I, 169-170) that ... *seminibus ... certis quaeque creantur, / inde enascitur ... / materies ubi inest cuiusque et corpora prima*: "each thing is created from determinate seeds", and "[each thing] is born from there where are found its matter and its first elements".

c. There would be no determination of place and time for the coming forth of things, and on the contrary flowers, fruits, etc:

(I, 180)
... subito exorerentur /
incerto spatio atque alienis partibus anni

"... suddenly would emerge
in an uncertain place
and at inappropriate moments of the year",

and (I, 174-175) the flowering of the rose in spring, the maturing of the wheat in summer and the spreading of the vine in autumn would not be seen, neither (I, 186) would graduality exist in growth: ... *fierent iuvenes subito ex infantibu' parvis*: "... little children would become suddenly young men".

Lucretius, who has recourse to factual evidence in the same way as Sāṃkhya does, concludes that none of the above mentioned absurd consequences of the non-acceptance of the principle of *ex nihilo nihil* is given in reality: (I, 188) *Quorum nil fieri manifestum est*: "It is evident that none of the indicated things happens".

The arguments presented by Lucretius against the non-acceptance of the principle of *ex nihilo nihil* and the arguments adduced by the Sāṃkhya in order to found its own particular theory of causality (which is based on that principle) both aim to safeguard causality, which is considered as a datum of reality.

IV.7 *Sāṃkhya* theory of Causality, *satkāryavāda*: The effect is existent (before its manifestation)

The idea of *ex nihilo nihil*, "from nothing, nothing" or in Sanskrit *nāsataḥ sad ajāyata*, "from the inexistent the existent was not born" or *sata utpattir nāsata iti*, "the coming forth of the existent is not from the inexistent", is the basis on which the *satkāryavāda* is founded, "the doctrine (*vāda*) that the effect (*kārya*) exists really (*sat*) [before its manifestation]", i.e. the doctrine of causality in Sāṃkhya.

According to this theory, on the one hand the effect pre-exists in the cause in a potential condition, and the effect is only a manifestation of something which is already in the cause in some way; on the other hand, the effect is only a transformation, development or evolution (*pariṇāma*) of the cause; the effect is nothing other than the cause in a transformed, developed and evolved form. The cause thus has the capacity to transform itself into the effects. In other terms, the cause is potentially the effect, and it is also possible to say that the effect "is" already in the cause. There is identity between the cause and the effect. Before its manifestation, the effect exists in the form of the cause. The cause as well as the effect really exist: the effect is not something which passes from inexistence to existence. There is no creation of something new.[20] (See section *The principle of* ex nihilo nihil, *the foundation of Sāṃkhya causality.*) This Sāṃkhya theory of causality is opposed to the *asatkāryavāda*, which is, for example maintained by the Hindu orthodox Nyāya and Vaiśeṣika systems. According to the *asatkāryavāda*, the effect does not exist before its production but is a new creation.

IV.8 *Sāṃkhya* arguments in favour of *satkāryavāda*

The existence of the effect "before its manifestation" (*utpatte prāk*, according to the expression of Vijñānabhikṣu *ad Sāṃkhyakārikā* I, 118) is asserted in *Sāṃkhyakārikās* 9 using the following arguments, which are also expounded in *Sāṃkhyasūtras* I, 113-121:

1. *asadakaraṇāt*: an expression which can be understood as "due to the absence of action (*akaraṇa*) on the part of the inexistent (*asat*)" or as "due to the fact that there is no production (*akaraṇa*) of the inexistent (*asat*)". In the first translation, *asad°* in the compound is interpreted subjectively: the non-existent cannot be the *subject* of any activity, in this case that of coming forth or of being born; in the second translation, *asad°* is interpreted objectively: the non-existent cannot be the *object* of any activity; nobody can act or influence something which is inexistent. The commentary of Gauḍapāda makes this clear through an example: "In the same way as the arising of oil from the sand": *yathā sikatābhyas tailotpattiḥ* [= oil inexistent in the sand cannot arise from the sand or be produced from it], so

[20] Cf. S. Bhaduri, *Studies in Nyāya-Vaiśeṣika Metaphysics*, pp. 306-313; M.M. Gopinath Kaviraj, "The problem of causality – Sānkhya-Yoga view", pp. 114-136.

the effect [non-existing in the cause] cannot arise or be produced from the cause. To be able to arise from the cause the effect has to pre-exist in it. Cf. *Sāṃkhyasūtras* I, 114, *nāsatutpādo nṛśṛiṅgavat*: "It is not possible that the inexistent arise as [it is not possible that] a horn [arise] in a man".

2. *upādānagrahaṇāt*: "due to the fact of the resort to (*grahaṇa*) the material cause (*upādāna*) [which is proper of the effect]". To use the example of the commentator Gauḍapāda *ad kārikā* 9, if somebody wants to make curds, he gets milk but not water, because he knows by experience (*iha loke*: here in the world) that, if he performs certain actions, milk will transform into curds, that there will thus be a *pariṇāma* (transformation) of the milk into curds. The way in which a thing is transformed is determined; it is not arbitrary, and thus for every product there is a determination of the material cause (the matter with which something is made). The *sūtra* I, 115 of the *Sāṃkhyasūtras* says: *utpādānaniyamāt*, "because of the determination of the material cause".

3. *sarvasambhavābhāvāt*: "due to the fact that there is no production of anything [from anything]". Experience also shows that things are not produced arbitrarily in any way; as gold cannot, for example, be produced with earth, one cannot make a gold bracelet with a handful of earth. There is determinism with regard to the production of things; if there were none, anything could be produced from anything.

4. *śaktasya śakyakaraṇāt*: "due to the fact that the production of something capable of being made (*śakya*) [can only be accomplished] by the person or things capable (*śakta*) [of accomplishing them]". For example, a potter provided with all of the necessary elements of his craft (clay, water, wheel, rope, etc.) is able to transform a mass of clay into a pot of clay, which is something that can be made with clay. The same potter, although provided with the same elements of his craft, could not produce a clay pot with a mass of gold. It is necessary to conclude that this impossibility to produce a clay pot with something which is not clay is due to the fact

that the clay pot, the effect, is only the transformed clay (the material cause) and nothing else.

5. *kāraṇabhāvāt*: "due to the nature (*bhāva*) of the cause (*kāraṇa*) [being the same as that of the effect]". There is identity of nature of the cause and of the effect. From rice seeds, only rice is produced and nothing else. To explain this fact, it is necessary to suppose that the seed, the cause, is in a potential condition and that the rice is the effect which will come out of it.

The impossibility of the non-existent's functioning either as subject or object (1.), the determinism of the material cause (2.), the impossibility of a cause turning into whatever effect (3.), the incapability of the agent to transform determinate matter into something which does not participate in that matter (4.) as well as the identity of nature of cause and effect (5.) lead us to posit that the cause is in a potential way the effect, that the effect is in the cause, and that the cause can therefore transform itself or be transformed into that effect only.

It is necessary to bear in mind that, in order for an effect to be produced from a determinate material cause, the presence of other accessory causes is also necessary. Gauḍapāda *ad kārikā* 9 mentions several accessory causes, which intervene in the production of the clay pot, which is accomplished by the potter as the efficient cause and the clay as the material cause.

With regard to the apparently astonishing identity of the cause and the effect, let us point out here that the transformation of the cause into the effect is not an act taking place at a certain fixed time but a gradual process which can have many stages of evolution, in each of which the cause goes on adopting new forms which gradually set it apart from its initial form and bring it nearer to the final form which it will have as an effect. Each of these new forms maintains a relation of similarity which includes less and less of the form of the cause from which it proceeds and more and more of the form of the effect towards which it is making its way. As a result of this, when the effect appears, it no longer reveals any relation of similarity with the remote cause which produced it. An example of this kind of gradual and invisible transformation is offered by the evolution of Matter, which passes from its *avyakta* (non-manifested) state to its *vyakta* (manifested) state. Cf. the Section Sāṃkhya *Theory of Evolution* in this Chapter.

The Sāṃkhya affirms that, in spite of the external dissimilarity between the effect and the cause, the effect is identical to the cause because the effect is nothing other than the cause which has undergone a process of transformation: the cause and the effect possess identity of nature.

For the contrary thesis of the *asatkāryavāda*, maintained, as we have said, by other Indian philosophical schools, the external dissimilarity supports the assertion that, when the cause gives rise to the effect, something new is created.

IV.9 Remarks on the previous subject: Identity of cause and effect in Hegel, Proclus, St. Thomas and Leibniz

The idea that the effect is identical to the cause was also maintained in the West.

1. Hegel in his *Wissenschaft der Logik*, first part, second book, third section, third chapter B. *Das Kausalitätsverhältnis* (The relation of causality), refers in detail to the theory of the identity of the cause and the effect. Hegel bases this thesis on a series of reflections on the substance and on cause and effect and the relation which links them. Here we give the translation of some texts by Hegel which present points of contact with the Sāṃkhya theory of causality and can help us to understand and assess it. We quote Hegel from the Suhrkamp edition: Volume 6 of *G.W.F. Hegel Werke.*

> *Die Ursache ist das* Ursprüngliche *gegen die Wirkung* (p. 223).
>
> "The cause is the *original* with regard to the effect".
>
> *die Ursache ist in der Wirkung als ganze Substanz manifestiert* (p. 223).

"... the cause manifests itself as complete substance in the effect... "

Die Substanz hat daher erst als Ursache Wirklichkeit. *Aber diese Wirklichkeit ... ist die* Wirkung; *die Substanz hat daher die Wirklichkeit, die sie als Ursache hat,* nur in ihrer Wirkung. – *Dies ist die* Notwendigkeit, *welche die Ursache ist* (p. 224).

"Therefore the substance has *effective existence* firstly as cause. But this effective existence ... is the *effect;* thus the substance, *only in its effect,* has the effective existence that it possesses as cause.–This is the *necessity,* which the cause is".

...die Ursache ist daher erst in ihrer Wirkung das wahrhaft Wirkliche und mit sich Identische (p. 224) .

"... therefore the cause is, firstly in its effect, the truly effectively existing and the identical to itself".

Die Wirkung ist daher notwendig, *weil sie eben Manifestation der Ursache oder diese Notwendigkeit ist, welche die Ursache ist* (p. 224).

"The effect is therefore *necessary,* because it is just manifestation of the cause or that necessity, which is the cause".

Die Wirkung enthält daher überhaupt nichts, was nicht die Ursache enthält. Umgekehrt enthält die Ursache nichts, was nicht in ihrer Wirkung ist. *Die Ursache ist nur Ursache, insofern sie eine Wirkung hervorbringt; und die* Ursache ist nichts als diese Bestimmung, eine Wirkung zu haben, und die Wirkung nichts als dies, eine Ursache zu haben. *In der Ursache als solcher selbst liegt ihre Wirkung und in der Wirkung die Ursache.*

"The effect does not contain therefore anything that the cause does not contain. On its turn, *the cause does not contain anything, which is not in its effect.* The cause is only cause in so much as it produces an effect and *the cause is nothing else than this determination of having an effect and the effect is nothing else than this: to have a cause.* In the cause as such is found its effect and in the effect the cause".

In dieser Identität der Ursache und Wirkung ... (p. 225).

"In this identity of cause and effect ... ".

Die Identität *der Ursache in ihrer Wirkung mit sich ist das Aufheben ihrer Macht und Negativität, daher die gegen die Formunterschiede gleichgültige Einheit, der* Inhalt.

"The *identity* of the cause to itself in its effect is the suppression of its power and negativity, and consequently the indifferent unity with regard to the difference of form, the *contents*".

Durch diese Identität des Inhalts *ist diese Kausalität ein* analytischer *Satz. Es ist* dieselbe Sache, *welche sich das eine Mal als Ursache, das andere Mal als Wirkung darstellt, dort als eigentümliches Bestehen, hier als Gesetztsein oder Bestimmung an einem Anderen. ... es wird nur ein und derselbe Inhalt wiederholt; man hat in der Ursache nichts anderes als in der Wirkung* (p. 226).

"Through this *identity of the contents* is this causality an *analytical* proposition. It is the *same thing* which presents itself sometime as cause, at other time as effect, there as specific existing, here as being established or determination on something other. ... one and the same contents is repeated; one has in the cause nothing else than in the effect".

... *denn die Wirkung ist nichts weiter als die Manifestation der Ursache* (p. 228).

"...since the effect is nothing more than the manifestation of the cause".

2. Even before Hegel Proclus in his *Elements of Theology*, Proposition 35 E.R. Dodds edition, had expressed an idea similar to that of Hegel and of the *Sāṃkhya* concerning the identity of cause and effect:

Πᾶν τὸ αἰτιατὸν καὶ μένει ἐν τῇ αὐτοῦ αἰτίᾳ καὶ πρόεισιν ἀπ' αὐτῆς καὶ ἐπιστρέφει πρὸς αὐτήν.

"Each effect remains in its cause, comes from it and returns to it".

In this Proposition Proclus refers to

"the three moments of the Neoplatonic world-process, immanence in the cause, procession from the cause, and reversion to the cause - or identity, difference and the overcoming of difference by identity. This triad is one of the governing principles of Pr.'s [= Proclus'] *dialectics ...* ".

as Dodds, the editor of the treatise, p. 220, note to the Proposition 35, says.

3. St. Thomas in *Summa Theologiae* I, 2, 19, 5, also expresses a similar idea in his demonstration that God's will is the cause of things:

Respondeo ... Tertio, ex habitudine effectuum ad causam. Secundum hoc enim effectus procedunt a causa agente, secundum quod praeexistunt in ea: quia omne agens agit sibi simile. Praeexistunt autem effectus in causa secundum modum causae. Unde, cum esse divinum sit ipsum eius intelligere, praeexistunt in eo effectus eius secundum modum intelligibilem. Unde et per modum intelligibilem procedunt ab eo.

"Thirdly, on account of the relation between the effects and the cause. According to this [relation], the effects indeed proceed from an efficient cause, according to what they preexist in it [in the cause]: because any agent [= efficient cause] gives rise to something similar to itself. Moreover, effects preexist in their cause according to the mode [of being] of the cause. Whence, since to be [a] divine [being] is just His being possessed of intelligence, His effects preexist in Him [= the divine being] according to His intelligible mode [of being]. Whence, they [= the effects] proceed from Him in an intelligible mode."

4. Finally, G.W. Leibniz in his *Catena mirabilium demonstrationum de summa rerum*, in *Philosophische Schriften* I, p. 6, Insel Verlag edition, expressed an idea similar to that of the Sāṃkhya, St. Thomas, Proclus and Hegel with regard to the identity of cause and effect:

Effectus integer aequipollet causae plenae, *quia aequatio quaedam debet esse inter causam et effectum, transiens ex uno in aliud.*

"*The whole effect is equivalent to the complete cause,* since a certain equality has to exist between the cause and the effect, passing from one to the other".[21]

IV.10 Names for Primordial Matter

Primordial Matter is given several names in the Sāṃkhya system:

Prakṛti: literally "producer element", generally translated as "Matter", but whose original meaning must always be taken into account (*kārikās* 3, 8, 22, 42, 45, etc.),

Mūlaprakṛti: 'Original Matter' (*kārikā* 3),

[21] Cf. Mario Bunge, *La Causalidad. El principio de causalidad en la ciencia moderna*, pp. 290-311.

Pradhāna: "the first", 'the principal', 'the primordial', which is the name reserved for the non-manifested *Prakṛti* (*avyakta*) (in the commentary of Gauḍapāda to the *kārikā* 3 and in *kārikās* 11, 21, 37, 57, 68).

IV.11 Attributes of Primordial Matter

The *Prakṛti* has two states or forms of being (*kārikā* 10): *vyakta*, "manifested", i.e. in its process of evolution, and *avyakta*, "non-manifested", i.e. before the beginning of the process of evolution, to which we shall refer afterwards.

When the *Prakṛti* is *vyakta* (*kārikā* 10) it is "caused (*hetumat*), non-eternal (*anitya*), non-pervading (*avyāpi*), active (*sakriya*), manyfold (*aneka*), founded (on another) (*āśrita*), liable to dissolution (*liṅga*) [according to Gauḍapāda's interpretation: *layayuktam*], with parts (*sāvayava*), depending on another (*paratantra*)".

When the *Prakṛti* is *avyakta*, it has attributes opposed to the previous ones (*viparīta*, *kārikā* 10).

According to the commentary of Gauḍapāda to the *kārikā* 10, the *Prakṛti* as *avyakta*

— has no cause, because there is nothing beyond it (or previous to it) (*na hi pradhānāt paraṃ kiñcid asti*);
— is eternal (*nitya*) because it is not produced and because it is not produced as the elements are (*nityam avyaktam anutpadyamāna-tvāt / na hi bhūtānīva kutaścid utpadyata iti*);
— is all-pervading (*vyāpin*) because (before presenting itself in its *vyakta* state there is no individualization or division and consequently) Matter is all of it in everything (*vyāpi pradhānaṃ sarvagatatvāt*);
— is inactive (*akriya*) due to the simple fact that all of it is in everything (*sarvagatatvād eva*) (which means that discontinuity, which is necessary for any activity, did not exist);
— is one (*eka*) in the sense that it is the only cause (*pradhānam ekaṃ kāraṇaṃ*) of empirical reality (= of the three worlds, *trayāṇāṃ lokānām*);

— is not founded on another (*anāśrita*) because it is not effect (*akāryatvāt*) and because there is nothing beyond the *Prakṛti* (= *Pradhāna*) of which it could be an effect (*na hi pradhānād asti kiñcit paraṃ yasya pradhānāṃ kāryaṃ syāt*) (cf. *Bṛhadāraṇyaka-Upaniṣad* III. 6, where it is affirmed that the Absolute (*Brahman*) is not woven onto anything since there is nothing beyond It);

— is non-liable to dissolution (*aliṅga*) because it is eternal (*nityatvāt*), in contrast to the products which arise from one another in the course of the process of evolution and which are dissolved (*pralīyate*) in one another (*parasparaṃ*) in the process of evolution while Matter is not liable to reabsorption or dissolution in anything else (*aliṅga*);

— is without parts (*niravayava*) because the *Prakṛti* (= *Pradhāna*) includes no object of the senses: sound, touch, taste, form/colour, smell (*śabda-sparśa-rasa-rūpa-gandha*);

— is dependent on itself (*svatantra*), is its own master (*prabhavatyātmanaḥ*) and depends on its own laws.[22]

Moreover, *Prakṛti* is *avikṛti* (*kārikā* 3), which Gauḍapāda's commentary *ad locum* explains as follows: *anyasmān notpadyate tena prakṛtiḥ kasyacid vikāro na bhavati*: "It does not arise from another, consequently it is not a transformation (*vikāra*) of anything": and the *Prakṛti saukṣmyāt tadanupalabdhir nābhāvāt*; "is imperceptible due to its subtlety and not to its inexistence.; and *kāryatas tadupalabdhiḥ* "it is perceptible from its effects" (*kārikā* 8 a-b). It is understood that these three characteristics (not caused, imperceptible, subtle) refer to the *Prakṛti* in its non-manifested (*avyakta*) state or mode of being.

The *Prakṛti* in its manifested (*vyakta*) mode of being and the *Prakṛti* in its non-manifested (*avyakta* = *Pradhāna*) mode

---

[22] Cf. Knut A. Jacobsen, *Prakṛti in Sāṃkhya-Yoga*, pp. 172-192, for the names, epithets and attributes of the Primordial Matter in the Proto-Sāṃkhya and, pp. 227-236, in Classical Sāṃkhya.

of being have common characteristics (*kārikā* 11 and its commentary):

— both are composed of the three *guṇas* (*sattva*, *rajas* and *tamas*);

— are non-differentiated (*avivekin*) in the sense that they are not different from the *guṇas* that constitute them: *na viveko 'syāstīti / idaṃ vyaktam ime guṇā iti na vivekaṃ kartuṃ yāti ... ye guṇās tad vyaktaṃ yad vyaktaṃ te ca guṇā iti* [commentary of *vyakta*]; *pradhānam api guṇair na bhidyate / anye guṇā anyat pradhānam evaṃ vivektuṃ na yāti* [commentary of *avyakta*];

— are an object (*viṣaya*) in the sense that they are experienceable (*bhojya*), i.e. that they can become an object of experience by the Spirit (*Puruṣa*);

— are general (*sāmānya*) in the sense that they are common to all (*sādhāraṇa*), i.e. they constitute the elements of which all is made;

— are non-conscious (*acetana*) since they do not experience sensations of any kind, whether agreeable or disagreeable, etc.;

— both have the attribute of productivity (*prasavadharmin*) in the sense that they give rise to everything and everything arises from them.

It is interesting to point out the fact that the attributes of matter in Sāṃkhya do not present anthropomorphic, theomorphic, deifying or animist elements. They are attributes which do not go beyond the material or physical realm. This fact is a manifestation of the rationalistic and atheistic tendency of the Sāṃkhya system, which also shows an obvious overcoming of myth.

Moreover, according to the Sāṃkhya system, Matter (*Prakṛti*) unconsciously fulfils a "generous", beneficial and positive function since it carries out a determinate finality fixed by its own rules with relation to the Spirit (*Puruṣa*) which, after Matter has accomplished its task and ceases in its activity, attains Liberation (*Sāṃkhyakārikās* 56, 60 and 68). Cf. *Sāṃkhyasūtra* III, 58. Of course, this function is fulfilled by Matter in an unconscious, spontaneous way, since the lack of consciousness is one of its main characteristics. It is interesting to remark that in the Buddhist *Śālistambasūtra* the unconscious character of the evolutive process in nature is frequently pointed out. Cf. pp. 4-7, 8-9, 15, of N. Aiyaswami Sastri edition, Adyar, Madras: The Theosophical Society, 1950.

IV.12 Remarks on the previous subject: The notion of matter in the West

The notion of Matter in Western philosophy has had a long history rich in very diverse concepts. It is interesting here to point out some of the ideas proper to four of these concepts, which allow us to value the richness and originality of the Sāṃkhya notion of Matter. In addition, when this Sāṃkhya notion is placed among its peers in that context, its special theses cease to surprise us and are perceived as another effort of the human mind, as valid as any other, to represent and explain reality - an effort in which reasoning and fancy often run together.

The Pre-Socratics in Greece tried to find the element or entity from which all originates or of which all is made, i.e. that which corresponds to what the Sāṃkhya thinkers called *Prakṛti.* We shall designate this primordial entity, the origin of all and the constitutive element of all, with the words ὕλή (hylē) and ἀρχή (arché). We shall briefly refer to the doctrines of some pre-Socratics related to ὕλη /ἀρχή, using for that purpose H. Diels/W. Kranz, *Die Fragmente der Vorsokratiker,* to which the square brackets refer.

According to Galenus, *Corpus Medicorum Graecorum* V, 9, 1, 17, 16 [30 A 6], it was only after Melissus of Samos (*floruit* 444-441 B.C.) that the word ὕλη was used to designate the common "substance (οὐσία), which underlies the four elements, unborn and indestructible". It is generally thought that Anaximander, disciple of and successor to Thales, was the first to use the word ἀρχή to designate the original substance of all, according to testimonies by Simplicius, *Commentary to the Physics of Aristotle,* p. 24, 13 [12 A 9.] and

Hippolytus, *Refutatio omnium haeresium* I, 6, 1 [12 A 11.]. These two words were employed by the Greek writers, such as for instance Aristotle, who expounded the doctrines of the pre-Socratics with regard to that primordial entity which was considered by the pre-Socratics to be the constitutive element of all or the origin of all, each of them attributing certain determinate characteristics to it which were not always the same.

1. Thales of Miletus (6th century B.C.) thought that water is the ὕλη /ἀρχή of everything. Aristotle, *Metaphysics*, A 3. 983 b 6, [11 A 12.] informs us:

> τῶν δὴ πρώτον φιλοσοφησάντων οἱ πλεῖστοι τὰς ἐν ὕλης εἴδει μόνας ᾠιήθησαν ἀρχὰς εἶναι πάντων· ἐξ οὗ γὰρ ἔστιν ἅπαντα τὰ ὄντα καὶ ἐξ οὗ γίγνεται πρώτου καὶ εἰς ὃ φθείρεται τελευταῖον, τῆς μὲν οὐσίας ὑπομενούσης τοῖς δὲ πάθεσι μεταβαλλούσης, τοῦτο στοιχεῖον καὶ ταύτην ἀρχήν φασιν εἶναι τῶν ὄντων, καὶ διὰ τοῦτο οὔτε γίγνεσθαι οὐδὲν οἴονται οὔτ' ἀπόλλυσθαι, ὡς τῆς τοιαύτης φύσεως ἀεὶ σωιζομένης ... (17) δεῖ γὰρ εἶναί τινα φύσιν ἢ μίαν ἢ πλείους μιᾶς, ἐξ ὧν γίγνεται τἆλλα σωιζομένης ἐκείνης. τὸ μέντοι πλῆθος καὶ τὸ εἶδος τῆς τοιαύτης ἀρχῆς οὐ τὸ αὐτὸ πάντες λέγουσιν, ἀλλὰ Θαλῆς μὲν ὁ τῆς τοιαύτης ἀρχηγὸς φιλοσοφίας ὕδωρ εἶναί φησιν.
>
> "Most of the first philosophers thought that principles in the form of matter were the only principles (ἀρχή) of all things. That of which all is constituted, from which, as [its] first [origin], all arises, and into which, as [its] ultimate [destiny], all is dissolved, the substance persisting although changed in its qualities, this they say is the original element (στοιχεῖον) and the original principle (ἀρχή) of existing things; and for this reason they think that nothing comes to be or passes away, since such a nature (φύσις) always persists ... for there must be some nature either one or more than one from which the other things come into being while it is preserved. As to the number and form of such original principle they do not say all of them the same thing: Thales, the founder of this sort of philosophy, says that it is water".[23]

---

[23] Cf. Simplicius, *Commentary to the Physics of Aristotle*, p. 23, 21 [11 A 13.]; Plutarch, *De Iside et Osiride*, 34 [11 A 11.]; Cicero, *De deorum natura* I, 10, 25 (*Thales ... aquam dixit esse initium rerum*); Diogenes Laertius, *Lives of Philosophers* I, 27 [11 A 1.]; and the fragment of Thales probably apocryphal quoted by

In relation to the idea mentioned by Aristotle that the substance persists although changed in its qualities (πάθος in the original = *quod quis patitur*), let us now quote a text from the *Mahābhāṣya* of Patañjali, the great Indian grammarian *approximately* 150 B.C., commentary to I, 1, Kielhorn edition, p. 6, lines 11-12 and 17-18, which says, referring to the substance and the forms it adopts:

dravyaṃ ... nityam ākṛtir anityā ... ākṛtir anyā cānyā ca bhavati, dravyaṃ punas tad eva / ākṛtyupamardena dravyam evāvaśiṣyate.

"The substance [as for instance earth] is permanent, the form [it adopts: clod, pots, pitchers etc.] is impermanent... the form undergoes successive changes; the substance however remains the same. On the destruction of the form the substance alone remains".

Besides the theory that water is the ὕλη /ἀρχή of all, it is interesting to point out that, according to the testimonies which we shall discuss, Thales claimed that all is animated and that all is full of gods.

Aristotle, *De anima*, A 5, p. 411 a 7 [11 A 22.]:
καὶ ἐν τῷ ὅλῳ δέ τινες αὐτὴν /τὴν ψυχήν/ μεμεῖχθαί φασιν, ὅθεν ἴσως καὶ Θαλῆς ᾠήθη πάντα πλήρη θεῶν εἶναι.
"Some say that it [the soul] is intermingled in the universe, for which reason Thales also thought that all things are full of gods".

Aristotle, *De anima*, A 2, p. 405 a 19 [11 A 22.]:
Ἔοικε δὲ καὶ Θαλῆς ἐξ ὧν ἀπομνημονεύουσι κινητικόν τι τὴν ψυχὴν ὑπολαβεῖν, εἴπερ τὸν λίθον ἔφη ψυχὴν ἔχειν ὅτι τὸν σίδηρον κινεῖ.
"It seems that also Thales, according to what is remembered, considered that the soul is something possessed of movement, since he says that the magnetic stone has a soul because it causes the steel to move".

And Diogenes Laertius, *Lives of Philosophers* I, 27 [11 A 1.] affirms that Thales said:

Galenus in his *Commentary on the Treatise of Hypocrates on the humours* I, 1 ed. C.G. Kühn [11 B 3.].

τὸν κόσμον ἔμψυχον καὶ δαιμόνων πλήρη.
"The cosmos is animated and full of daimons".

Diogenes Laertius, in § 24 *ibidem*, also adduces the example of the magnetic stone as used by Thales to prove the existence of a soul in everything.

It is evident that these two last theses of Thales, which present "animated" matter, reveal an animist attitude which does not appear at all in the Sāṃkhya concept of matter.[24]

2. Now we shall pass on to dealing with the original substance according to Anaximander (6th century B.C.).

Simplicius, *Commentary of the Physics of Aristotle*, p. 24, 13 [12 A 9.; cf. 12 B 1.] has conserved a fragment of Anaximander [in italics in our following translation of the Greek quotation] included in his commentary [also in italics in our translation] which reads:

> 'Αναξίμανδρος ... ἀρχήν τε καὶ στοιχεῖον εἴρηκε τῶν ὄντων τὸ ἄπειρον, πρῶτος τοῦτο τοὔνομα κομίσας τῆς ἀρχῆς. λέγει δᾶ αὐτὴν μήτε ὕδωρ μήτε ἄλλο τι τῶν καλουμένων εἶναι στοιχείων, ἀλλᾶ ἑτέραν τινὰ φύσιν ἄπειρον, ἐξ ἧς ἅπαντας γίνεσθαι τοὺς οὐρανοὺς καὶ τοὺς ἐν αὐτοῖς κόσμους· ἐξ ὧν δὲ ἡ γένεσίς ἐστι τοῖς οὖσι, καὶ τὴν φθορὰν εἰς ταῦτα γίνεσθαι κατὰ τὸ χρεών· διδόναι γὰρ αὐτὰ δίκην καὶ τίσιν ἀλλήλοις τῆς ἀδικίας κατὰ τὴν τοῦ χρόνου τάξιν ποιητικωτέροις οὕτως ὀνόμασιν αὐτὰ λέγων.
>
> "Anaximander says that *the original principle* (ἀρχή) and the original element (στοιχεῖον) *of the existing things* is *the ápeiron* (τὸ ἄπειρον), being the first to introduce this name for the ἀρχή. He said that it is neither water nor anyone of the other so-called original elements (στοιχεῖον), but some other indefinite (ἄπειρον) nature (φύσις), from which arise all the heavens and the universes in them, *from which there is the production of the existing things and in*

[24] Cf. E. Zeller, *Die Philosophie der Griechen in ihrer geschichtlichen Entwicklung*, Vol. I, 1, pp. 264-266; and on Animism in general see in *Historisches Wörterbuch der Philosophie*, the article "Animismus" by Klaus E. Müller, Band 1, col. 315-319; in *Enzyklopädie Philosophie und Wissenschaftstheorie*, the article "Animismus" by Jürgen Mittelstrass, Vol. 1, p. 117; in José Ferrater Mora, the article "Animismo", Tomo I, pp. 176-177.

which takes place their destruction according to necessity, because they pay penalty and retribution to each other for the injustice [they have committed] *according to the order of time,* expressing these things with more poetical words [than usual]".[25]

Let us now add two more testimonies in which *tó ápeiron* is identified with ὕλη· Aëtius, *De placitis philosophorum* I, 3, 3, in H. Diels, *Doxographi Graeci,* fragment 277 [12 A 14.]: τὸ γὰρ ἄπειρον οὐδὲν ἄλλο ἢ ὕλη ἐστιν· "The *ápeiron* is nothing else than ὕλη"; and Aristotle, *Physics* III, 7, p. 207 b 35, [12 A 14.]: φαίνονται δὲ καὶ οἱ ἄλλοι πάντες ὡς ὕλῃ χρώμενοι τῷ ἀπείρῳ· "Also all the others [philosophers] seem to use the *ápeiron* as ὕλη."

It is difficult to determine what Anaximander understood by "the ápeiron" (ἄπειρον). τὸ ἄπειρον was probably conceived of as a substance which is spatially infinite and indefinite in nature and form and may be like something intermediate among the four known elements: water, fire, earth and air or a mixture of them.[26]

Whatever the meaning attributed to that term, it is important for us here to emphasize the characteristics which, according to some testimonies, Anaximander attributed to τὸ ἄπειρον.

Aristotle refers to them in *Physics* III, 4, p. 203 b 6, [12 A 15.]:

ἅπαντα γὰρ ἢ ἀρχὴ ἢ ἐξ ἀρχῆς, τοῦ δὲ ἀπείρου οὐκ ἔστιν ἀρχή· εἴη γὰρ ἂν αὐτοῦ πέρας· ἔτι δὲ καὶ ἀγένητον καὶ ἄφθαρτον

---

[25] Other testimonies on *tò ápeiron* being the ἀρχή are offered by Simplicius, *Commentary to the Physics of Aristotle,* p. 154, 14 [12 A 9 a.]; Plutarch, *Stromata* 2 [12 A 10.]; Hippolytus, *Refutatio omnium haeresium* I, 6, 1-2 [12 A 11.]; Cicero, *Academica priora* II, 37, 118 [12 A 13.]: *is enim* [Anaximander] *infinitatem naturae dixit esse, e qua omnia gignerentur.* "for he [= Anaximander] said that the infinity of nature is that from which all things would have been born"; Aëtius, *De placitis philosophorum* I, 3, 3, [12 A 14.]; Aristotle, *Physics* III, 4, 203 b 6 [12 A 15.]; Alexander of Aphrodisias, *Commentary to the Metaphysics of Aristotle,* 60, 8, [12 A 16.]; Simplicius, *Commentary to De Caelo of Aristotle* 615, 13, [12 A 17.].

[26] See G.S. Kirk & J.E. Raven, *The Presocratic Philosophers,* pp. 104-114; E. Zeller, *Die Philosophie der Griechen,* Vol. I, 1, pp. 275-291.

ὡς ἀρχή τις οὖσα· τό τε γὰρ γενόμενον ἀνάγκη τέλος λαβεῖν, καὶ τελευτὴ πάσης ἐστὶ φθορᾶς. διὸ καθάπερ λέγομεν, οὐ ταύτης ἀρχή, ἀλλὰ αὕτη τῶν ἄλλων εἶναι δοκεῖ καὶ περιέχειν ἅπαντα καὶ πάντα κυβερνᾶν, ὥς φασιν ὅσοι μὴ ποιοῦσι παρὰ τὸ ἄπειρον ἄλλας αἰτίας οἷον νοῦν ἢ φιλίαν. καὶ τοῦτ᾽ εἶναι τὸ θεῖον· ἀθάνατον γὰρ καὶ ἀνώλεθρον, ὥς φησιν ὁ Ἀναξίμανδρος καὶ οἱ πλεῖστοι τῶν φυσιολόγων.

"All things either are *arché* or come out from an *arché*, the *ápeiron* has no *arché*, since [if it had one] it would have a limit. Moreover it is unborn (ἀγένητον) and imperishable (ἄφθαρτον), as it is an *arché*, for it is necessary that what comes to be has an end, and all destruction implies an end.[27] For this reason, as we say, of this [*arché* = the *ápeiron*] there is no *arché*, but it seems that it is [an *arché*] of all the other things, and that it contains all things, and that it governs all things, as it is said by all those who do not put besides the *ápeiron* other causes as mind [Anaxagoras] or love [Empedocles]. And [they say that] it [= the *ápeiron*] is the divine (θεῖον), since it is *immortal* (ἀθάνατον) and *indestructible* (ἀνώλεθρον), as Anaximander and the most part of the physiologists [or philosophers of nature] say".

It is considered that the Greek words ἀθάνατον and ἀνώλεθρον, "immortal" and "indestructible", which are employed by Aristotle in this passage, derived from terms employed by Anaximander himself. Thus Hippolytus, *Refutatio omnium haeresium* I, 6, 1 [12 A 11.], calls the nature of the *ápeiron* "eternal" (ἀΐδιον) and "beyond old age"

[27] The idea expressed by Aristotle that all that comes to be or is produced (γενόμενον) has an end, or is not eternal, constitutes a principle of Indian Philosophy. This principle is expressed in the commentary by Gauḍapāda to the *Sāṃkhyakārikās* 10, in which he affirms that non-manifested Matter is not eternal (*anitya*) just because it does come from or is produced from another (*yasmād anyasmād utpadyate*). It is a principle repeatedly expressed in the Buddhist texts since most ancient times in the well-known formula: *yaṃ kiñci samudayadhammaṃ, sabban taṃ nirodhadhamman ti*: "all that comes forth [from a multiplicity of causes according to Buddhism], is subject to destruction". This formula appears in the following texts, for instance: *Udāna* V, 3, p. 49, lines 15-16, *Mahāvagga*, p. 11 *in fine*, *Dīgha Nikāya* I (*Ambaṭṭhasutta*), p. 110, lines 12-13, *Saṃyutta Nikāya* IV (*Paṭhamagilānasutta*), p. 47, 107, *Majjhima Nikāya* III (*Cuḷarahulovādasutta*), p. 280, lines 10-11.

(ἀγήρω), and says that "it contains all the universes" (πάντας περιέχειν τούς κόσμους). The words ἀίδιον and ἀγήρω could also come from Anaximander himself, and both constitute Homeric epithets of the Gods. Cf. *Odyssey* V, 218.

The original substance thus has the following characteristics in Anaximander: it is ἀρχὴ and ὕλη of all, all arises from it, all returns to it, all is constituted by it; it is unlimited and indefinite in nature and form; it has no cause; it is unborn and imperishable; it contains in itself all the things and controls or governs all the things; it is of divine nature; it is immortal and indestructible or eternal and beyond old age.

Many of these characteristics are the same as those of the *Prakṛti* in the Sāṃkhya system, but not so others, since some of them ("unborn", "controls all", "of divine nature", "beyond old age') reveal the archaic theomorphic and even anthropomorphic concept of the primordial matter so frequent in the pre-Socratics, as remarked by G.S. Kirk J. & E. Raven, *The Presocratic Philosophers,* p. 115. This archaic concept is absent from the Sāṃkhya system, which liberated Matter from all divine or human subjectivity and did not attribute to Matter any degree of consciousness, keeping it on the level of purely material objects.

3. The notion of "matter" in Plato is integrated into his concept of reality considered in its absolute totality. This concept opposes *the intelligible world of the Ideas* (a fantastic world) and *the sensible world of empirical beings and things.* It is, as we have already said, a dualistic concept.

The Ideas or Forms are the truly and really existent. Plato in *Timaeus* 51 b-c, himself asks the rhetorical question as to whether the Idea of fire and the Ideas of all things in general are existent in themselves and by themselves (ἄρα ἔστιν τι πῦρ αὐτὸ ἐφ' ἑαυτοῦ καὶ πάντα περὶ ὧν ἀεὶ λέγομεν οὕτως αὐτὰ καθ' αὑτὰ ὄντα ἕκαστα). In the next passage (up to 52 a), he answers this question in the affirmative: they are indeed existent in themselves, and they are also all that is intelligible. Εἰ μὲν νοῦς καὶ δόξα ἀληθής ἐστον δύο γένη, παντάπασιν εἶναι καθ' αὑτὰ ταῦτα, ἀναίσθητα ὑφ' ἡμῶν εἴδη, νοούμενα μόνον· (*ibidem* 51 d): "If intellection and true opinion are two [different] genres [of knowledge], they [the Ideas of fire and of the other things] must anyhow exist in themselves and by themselves, [as] Ideas imperceptible to us and solely intelligible [i.e. objects only of intellection]." Cf. *Phaedo* 100 b, where there is a reference to the Ideas of the beautiful, the good and the great as being existent in themselves (ὑποθέμενος εἶναί τι καλὸν αὐτὸ καθ' αὑτὸ καὶ ἀγαθὸν καὶ μέγα καὶ τἆλλα πάντα). Of the two forms of cognition indicated, intellection (νοῦς) has a supreme quality which allows us to reach truth; and only the Gods and a small group of selected men partake of it. It is the νοῦς which reveals to us the specific mentioned quality of the Ideas: *to exist in themselves and by themselves.*

In the same text (52 a), Plato indicates other characteristics of the Ideas which it is convenient to mention here because they implicitly determine the characteristics which matter does not possess, and which we shall point out later on: the Idea is "one" (ἓν); "unborn" (ἀγέννητον); "indestructible" (ἀνώλεθρον); "it does not admit in itself something different coming from elsewhere" (οὔτε εἰς ἑαυτὸ εἰσδεχόμενον ἄλλο ἄλλοθεν) "it does not transform itself into another thing"; (οὔτε αὐτὸ εἰς ἄλλο ποι ἰόν) "not visible and not perceptible in another [sensory] way" (ἀόρατον δὲ καὶ ἄλλως ἀναίσθητον); "to perceive the Idea fell to the intellection's lot" (τοῦτο ὃ δὴ νόησις εἴληχεν ἐπισκοπεῖν). The Ideas, *Timaeus* 48 e - 49 a, are the paradigm (παράδειγμα) according to which all empirical things are made with the quality of imitation (μίμημα), and "possessed of birth and being perceptible" (γένεσιν ἔχον καὶ ὁρατόν). Cf. *Parmenides* 132 d, and *Phaedo* 100 d-e.

In the same passage of *Timaeus* 49 a, Plato says that he must refer to a third element, which is nothing other than matter (ὕλη) given the name of "place" (χώρα) (cf. Aristotle, *Physics* IV 2, 209 b, 10-12), the principal capacity of which is that it is a receptacle (ὑποδοχή) of the whole creation.

In several passages of *Timaeus,* Plato enumerates characteristics of matter. Thus, in 50 b-c:

— it never loses its capacity (ἐκ γὰρ τῆς ἑαυτῆς τὸ παράπαν οὐκ ἐξίσταται δυνάμεως);
— it always receives all the things (δέχεταί τε γὰρ ἀεὶ τὰ πάντα);
— it has never in any way adopted a form similar to anything which enters into it (μορφὴν οὐδεμίαν ποτέ οὐδενὶ τῶν εἰσιόντων ὁμοίαν εἴληφεν οὐδαμῇ οὐδαμῶς);
— it is like wax on which anything can be imprinted (ἐκμαγεῖον γὰρ φύσει παντὶ κεῖται);
— it is set in motion and is formally shaped by whatever penetrates into it (κινούμενόν τε καὶ διασχηματιζόμενον ὑπὸ τῶν εἰσιόντων);
— due to what penetrates into it, it manifests itself in a different way every moment (φαίνεται δὲ δι' ἐκεῖνα ἄλλοτε ἀλλοῖον). In 51 a:
— it is the mother and the receptacle of everything that is born, it is visible and is an object of sensation (τὴν τοῦ γεγονότος ὁρατοῦ καὶ πάντως αἰσθητοῦ μητέρα καὶ ὑποδοχὴν);
— it is none of the four elements earth, air, fire or water, nor is it whatever is born from them, nor that from which they emerged (μήτε γῆν μήτε ἀέρα μήτε πῦρ μήτε ὕδωρ λέγωμεν, μήτε ὅσα ἐκ τούτων μήτε ἐξ ὧν ταῦτα γέγονεν);
— it is an invisible element–without form and all-receiving (ἀνόρατον εἶδός τι καὶ ἄμορφον πανδεχές).

In Plato, Matter has a hierarchy, which is highly inferior to that of the Ideas which, we could say, are given from a rationalistic and intellectual perspective: Matter is invisible and amorphous and is the object of cognition on an inferior level (δόξα) qualified as "spurious (or bastard) reasoning" (λογισμῷ τινι νόθῳ) (52 b). Also, Matter is dependent on Ideas in order to be able to abandon its invisible and amorphous condition and acquire an identity which renders it visible and endows it with a form, however precarious; at the same time, this form makes it cease to be itself - although only transitorily.

4. In Plotinus, who developed Platonic tendencies and emphasized them, the status of Matter worsens. Its inferiority subsists from a rationalistic and intellectual perspective, but an ontic, moral and religious inferiority is added to it in an explicit and insistent manner. Plotinus collects the negative and pejorative characteristics of matter. Let us concisely point out some of these characteristics here, which gave rise to a notion of matter which was not to lose its preeminence in any remarkable way in the course of the 16th century, when what we can call the "modern notion" of matter slowly began to appear.

For Plotinus, Matter is the first evil (I, 8, 3; I, 8, 8), the cause of evil (I, 8, 4; I, 8, 8), it ruins the work of reason (II, 3, 16), it is the sinister depth of being (II, 4, 5), it is deprivation (II, 4, 13), it is evil and poverty (II, 4, 16), it is not being (II, 5, 4 and 5), a ghost (II, 5, 5), a real lie (*ibidem*), the cause of inferiority of beings (III, 2, 15), not-being, ghost, lie (III, 6, 7), shadow (III, 6, 18), it is symbolized by indigence (III, 5, 9), symbolized by the eunuchs who follow the Mother (III, 6, 19), it renders being corruptible (III, 9, 8), it is compared to darkness (IV, 3, 9 and 10), it is the cause of ugliness (IV, 4, 38) and it has an obscure being deprived of reason (VI, 3, 7).[28]

The negative evaluation of matter as presented in Plato and especially in Plotinus is opposed to the evaluation of matter in the Sāṃkhya system, for which Matter is located on the same level as the Spirit. Matter's attributes lack negative nuances and Matter carries out a beneficial and positive function.

---

[28] Cf. R. Arnou, *Le désir de Dieu dans la philosophie de Plotin*, pp. 64-66, 71 note 1, 89-90, 117.

5. The "modern notion" of matter manifests several tendencies pointed out by W. Breidert, in section III of the article "Materie", in *Historisches Wörterbuch der Philosophie,* Vol. 5, col. 905-912:

> "*a) the 'realization'* (Realisierung): *the matter* (Stoff) *related to the Form* (Form) *and as such non-independent becomes a universal, independent substance, producer of movements and forms* (Bewegungen und Gestalten), *which constitutes the whole reality* (Materialismus). *b) Structuration* (Strukturierung): *the matter devoid of form is endowed with general attributes that cannot be separated from it, as for instance extension, inertia, weight and/or atomic structure. c) Dynamization* (Dynamisierung): *the passive matter is provided with activity, force, own movement and the capacity to produce effects. d) Phenomenalization* (Phänomenalisierung): *matter is not conceived as a substance but as a phenomenon. e) Dissolution* (Dissolution): *matter loses all the attributes and limits itself to be the incognoscible bearer of attributes, and finally is considered as superfluous or dissolved in a nothingness*".

In a sense, the Sāṃkhya concept is close to the modern concept of matter. See the previous Section *Attributes of Primordial Matter.*

We shall now refer to two authors which can be located to a certain degree in this new concept of matter: Giordano Bruno and Paul Henri d'Holbach.

6. This modern concept of matter is present in the appraisals which Giordano Bruno makes with regard to David of Dinant (*floruit* 1200) and to the Spanish philosopher of Jewish lineage Ibn Gabirol (Avicebron) (*circa* 1020-1059) whom Bruno calls "*il moro*" (= the moor) in spite of his origins.

In the *Proemiale Epistola* (*Argomento del Terzo Dialogo*) of his treatise *De la causa, principio et uno,* p. 17, Giordano Bruno indicates:

> *prima si mostra che non fu pazzo nel suo grado David de Dinanto in prendere la materia come cosa eccellentissima e divina:*
>
> "firstly it is shown that David of Dinant was not senseless when he conceived matter as a most excellent and divine thing".

On p. 191 of the same treatise (*Dialogo Terzo),* Bruno refers to Avicebron with praise, including him among those philosophers who, after a thorough study of the subject, came to the conclusion that Matter is *un principio necessario eterno e divino* : "a necessary, eternal and divine principle", adding that Avicebron calls it *'Dio che é in tutte le cose'*: "God who is in all the things"; further down on the same page, Bruno affirms that, for Avicebron, matter is *stabile, eterna, progenitrice, madre*: "stable, eternal, progenitrix, mother".[29]

The *Dialogo Quarto* begins on p. 219 with an exposition of the Platonic and Aristotelic theory of matter carried out by Polihimnio, the pedantic personage of the *Dialogo*, who is presented in a ridiculous way. The epithets which Polihimnio attributes to matter in accordance with Greek thinkers include the following:

> *chaos, privationi admixtum, peccati causa, ad maleficium ordinata, per se non ens, tabula rasa, prope nihil, necque quid, necque quale, necque quantum:*
>
> "chaos, mixed with deprivation, cause of sin, determined for evil doing, not being in itself, *tabula rasa*, almost nothing, neither something, nor such, nor so much".

Polihimnio, in order to sum up all of the words in one, ends his exposition expressing that "(matter) is called woman": *faemina dicitur.*

The same Polihimnio adds on p. 223 of the *Dialogo* that it is at the end of the first book of his *Physics* that Aristotle compares primary matter with the feminine sex; and that gives Polihimnio occasion to enumerate a long series of pejorative epithets of the *sesso feminile* with which Aristotle, according to Polihimnio, compares matter and which do not deserve to be translated:

> ... *ritroso, fragile, inconstante, molle, pusillo, infame, ignobile, vile, abietto, negletto, indegno, reprobo, sinistro, vituperoso, frigido, deforme, vacuo, vano, indiscreto, insano, perfido, neghittoso, putido, sozzo, ingrato, trunco,*

---

[29] On David of Dinant and Avicebron, see J. Ferrater Mora, *Diccionario de Filosofía* I, p. 779, and I, pp. 282-284; the article "Ibn Gabirol, Salomon" by Ariane Azouvi, in *Dictionnaire des Philosophes*, Vol. I, pp. 1439-1443; and P. Duhem, *Le système du monde*, Tome V, pp. 3-37.

> *mutilo, imperfetto, incoato, insufficiente, preciso, amputato, attenuato, rugine, eruca, zizania, peste, morbo, morte...*

We shall now point out a few passages of the same work of Giordano Bruno *De la causa, principio et uno,* in which he manifests his own concept of matter.

In the *Proemiale Epistola* (*Argomento del Quarto Dialogo*), p. 23:

> *ogni numero, diversità, ordine, bellezza et ornamento è circa la materia:*
>
> "any number, diversity, order, beauty and ornament are in relation to matter".

On the same page, he expresses that matter does not receive its forms from outside but that matter itself, emitting them as from its own bosom, causes them to arise from its interior, whereby matter

> *non è un* prope nihil, *un quasi nulla, una potenza nuda e pura, se tutte le forme son come contenute da quella, e dalla medesima ... prodotte e parturite ...*
>
> "is not a *prope nihil,* an almost nothing, a nude and pure potency, if all the forms are as contained in it, and by it...are produced and begotten..."

Cf. p. 251, where he adds that matter is not *senza virtù e perfezzione*: "without virtue and perfection".

On page 251, speaking through Theophilo's mouth, Giordano Bruno affirms the following with reference to matter:

> *la dico privata de le forme e senza quelle, non come il ghiaccio è senza calore, il profonde è privato di luce: ma come la pregnante è senza la sua prole, la quale la manda e la riscuote da se.*
>
> "I say that it [matter] is deprived of the forms and it is without them, not as ice is without heat or as the abyss is deprived of light: but as a pregnant woman is without her offspring, that it produces and causes to arise from her".

On page 259, through the mouth of his disciple Alexander Dicson, Bruno maintains:

> *... deve essere chiamata cosa divina, et ottima parente, genetrice e madre di cose naturali: anzi la natura tutta in sustanza.*
>
> "... [matter] must be called a divine thing and best relative, genetrix and mother of natural things: even the whole nature in substance".

On page 267 of the same dialogue, Bruno says the following through Theophilo:

> *... se ben si contempla* [matter] *è uno esser divino nelle cose, come forse volea dire David de Dinanto:*
>
> "if it is well examined, [matter] is a divine being in things, as perhaps David of Dinant wanted to say".

In his treatise *De l'infinito universo et Mondi*, p. 43, Giordano Bruno asserts that *dall' infinito sempre nova copia di materia sottonasce*: "from the infinite always, once and again, is born a new mass of matter".

Although the concept of matter in Giordano Bruno has the absence of negative elements in common with that of the Sāṃkhya, it differs from this in that he endows matter with exalting attributes of a deifying, animistic, anthropomorphic, feminine nature, almost transforming it into a living creative feminine principle with a slight aureole of mysticism - attributes and tendencies absolutely absent from the concept of matter given in Sāṃkhya. In this regard, please see the words and expressions used by Giordano Bruno in his treatise *De la causa, principio et uno*, p. 17: *cosa eccellentissima e divina*; p. 23: *bellezza et ornamento, seno, parturite*; p. 191: *principio necessario eterno e divino, Dio che è in tutte le cose, progenitrice, madre*; p. 249: *seno;* p. 251: matter is compared to the *pregnante*; p. 259: *cosa divina, ottima parente, genetrice e madre*; p. 267: *esser divino* (divine being).

7. Paul Henri d'Holbach (1723-1789) was a German aristocrat who had lived in France since his childhood, a "patron of philosophers", a friend of the Encyclopedists, author of more than 400 articles on subjects of natural sciences for the *Encyclopédie* edited by Diderot and d'Alembert and of a good number of translations of scientific

works from German into French.[30] He adopted a materialist and atheistic philosophy. In his opinion, Matter is the only reality, and on it he constructs his explanation of all. His principal work is *Système de la Nature, ou Des loix du Monde Physique et du Monde Moral*, published for the first time under the pseudonym of "Jean Baptiste Mirabaud" in 1770. This book is considered as "the masterpiece of French materialism" (article by Charles B. Upton on "Atheism and anti-theistic theories", in *Encyclopaedia of Religion and Ethics*, Vol. 2, p. 177 b), as "the Bible of materialism" *(biblia materialismi)* by F. Klimke in his *Institutiones Historiae Philosophiae*, Vol. I, p. 352, and as a "true ideological bomb", according to the expression of Josiane Boulad-Ayoub, who took care of the edition of his *Système de la Nature* (Paris: Fayard, 1990) utilized by us. Together with other works by the same author, this work was condemned to be burnt by a decree of the Parliament of Paris of 18 August 1770 for the "crime of *laesa-majestate* human and divine".

In his *Système de la nature, Seconde Partie, Chapitre 4*, pp. 134-135, in a résumé of his ideas on matter expressed in the responses that had been given to the English theologian Clarcke,[31] d'Holbach says:

> *Ainsi pour résumer les réponses qui ont été faites à M. Clarcke l'on dira 1°. que l'on peut concevoir que la matière a existé de toute éternité, vu qu'on ne conçoit pas qu'elle ait pu commencer. 2°. Que la matière est indépendante, vu qu'il n'y a rien hors d'elle: qu'elle est immuable, vu qu'elle ne peut*

[30] On d'Holbach, see the article by Ferrater Mora, in his *Diccionario de Filosofía*, Vol. II, pp. 1676-1678; the article "Holbach" by Kuno Lorenz, in *Enzyklopädie Philosophie und Wissenschafts-Theorie*, Vol. 2, pp. 120-121; Jean Lefranc, "Holbach Paul Henri Thiry, baron d', 1723-1789", en *Dictionnaire des Philosophes*, Vol. I, pp. 1379-1381; Fritz Mauthner, *Der Atheismus und seine Geschichte im Abendlande*, Vol. III, pp. 132-159; and the *Préface* (*Redécouvrir d'Holbach*) de Jean Claude Bourdin en P.-H.Th. d'Holbach, *Oeuvres Philosophiques*, Tome I.

[31] On Samuel Clarcke (1675-1729), cf. José Ferrater Mora, *Diccionario de Filosofía*, Vol. I *sub* "Clarke, Samuel"; note 27 of page 103, Vol. II of the *Systéme* by d'Holbach; and the article by Jean-Marc Lachaud, "Clarke, Samuel, 1675-1729", in *Dictionnaire des Philosophes*, Vol. I, pp. 600-601.

changer de nature quoiqu'elle change sans cesse de forme ou de combinaisons. 3°. Que la matière existe par elle-même, puisque, ne pouvant pas concevoir que'elle puisse s'anéantir, nous ne pouvons pas concevoir qu'elle ait pu commencer d'exister. 4°. Que nous ne connoissons point l'essence ni la vraie nature de la matière, quoique nous soyons á portée de connoître quelques-unes de ses propriétés et qualités d'aprés la façon dont elle agit sur nous, ce que nous ne pouvons point dire de Dieu. 5°. Que la matière étant sans commencement, n'aura jamais de fin, quoique ses combinations et ses formes commencent et finissent. 6°. Que si tout ce qui existe, ou tout ce que notre esprit peut concevoir est matière, cette matière est infinie, c'est-á-dire ne peut être bornée par rien: qu'elle est présente par-tout, s'il n'y a point de lieu hors d'elle; s'il y avoit en effet un lieu hors d'elle, ce seroit le vuide et alors Dieu seroit le vuide. 7°. Que la nature est unique, quoique ses éléments et ses parties soient infiniment variées et douées de propriétés très différentes. 8°. Que la matière modifiée, arrangée, combinée d'une certaine façon produit dans quelques êtres ce que nous appellons l' intelligence; c'est une des ses façons d'être, mais ce n'est pas une de ses propriétés essentielles. 9°. Que la matière n'est point un agent libre, puisqu'elle ne peut agir autrement qu'elle ne fait en vertu des loix de sa nature ou de son existence; et qu'ainsi les corps graves doivent nécessairement tomber, les corps légers doivent s'élever, le feu doit brûler, l'homme doit sentir le bien et le mal, suivant la nature des êtres dont it éprouve l'action. 10°. Que la puissance ou l'énergie de la matière n'a d'autres bornes que celles que leur prescrit sa nature même. 11°. Que la sagesse, la justice, la bonté, etc. sont des qualités propres ā la matière combinée et modifiée comme elle se trouve dans quelques êtres de la nature humaine, et que l'idée de la perfection est une idée abstraite, négative, métaphysique, ou une manière de considérer les objets qui ne suppose rien de réel hors de nous. Enfin 12°. que la matière est le principe du mouvement, qu'elle le renferme en elle-même, puisqu'il n'y a qu'elle qui soit capable de le donner et de le recevoir, ce que l'on ne peut pas concevoir d'un être immatériel, simple, dépourvu de parties, qui privé d'étandue, de masse, de pesanteur, ne pourroit ni se mouvoir lui-même ni mouvoir d'autres corps, et encore moins les créer, les produire, les conserver.

"Thus in order to summarize the answers that have been given to Mr. Clarcke, it will be said 1°. That it can be conceived that matter has existed for all the eternity, since it is not conceived that it could have begun. 2°. That matter is independent, since nothing exists outside of it: that it is immutable, since it cannot change its nature although it incessantly changes its form or combinations. 3°. That matter exists by itself, since, not being possible to conceive that it can be annihilated, we cannot conceive that it might have begun to exist. 4°. That we do not know at all the essence or the true nature of matter, although we are able to know some of its properties and qualities according to the form in which it acts on us, what we cannot say about God. 5°. That being matter without a beginning, it will never have an end, although its combinations and its forms begin and end. 6°. That if all that exists, or all that our mind can conceive is matter, this matter is infinite, i.e. it cannot be limited by anything: that it is present everywhere, if there is in no way a place out of it; if there were a place out of it, it would be the void and then God would be the void. 7°. That nature is one, although its elements and its parts are infinitely varied and possessed of very different properties. 8°. That matter, on being modified, disposed, combined in a certain way produces in some beings what we call intelligence; this is one of its forms of being, but it is not one of its essential properties. 9°. That matter is not at all a free agent, since it cannot act in a way different from the way it acts according to the laws of its nature or of its existence; and that thus heavy bodies must necessarily fall, light bodies must go up, fire must burn, man must experience good and evil according to the nature of the beings whose action he suffers. 10°. That power or energy of matter has not other limits than those which are prescribed by its own nature. 11°. That wisdom, justice, goodness, etc. are qualities proper of matter combined and modified according to how it is found in some beings of human nature, and that the idea of perfection is an abstract, negative, metaphysical idea, or a form to consider the objects which does not imply the existence of anything real out of us. Finally, 12°. that matter is the principle of movement, which it includes in itself, since there exist only it [matter] being able to give and to receive it [movement], what is not possible to think in relation to an immaterial, simple being, deprived of parts, which being without extension, mass, weight, could not move itself or move other bodies, and much less create, produce, conserve them".[32]

[32] On the concept of matter in the West, see the articles "Materia", in José Ferrater Mora, *Diccionario de Filosofía,* Vol. III, pp. 2315-2323; "Materie" by diverse authors, in *Historisches Wörterbuch der Philosophie,* Vol. 5, col. 870-924; and "Materie" by Klaus Mainzer, in *Enzyklopädie Philosophie und Wissenschaftstheorie,* Vol. 2, pp. 296-299. On the history of materialism in the West see F.A. Lange, *Geschichte des Materialismus.*

Abraham Gaultier can be considered as an interesting predecessor of d'Holbach. His work *Reponse en forme de dissertation à un théologien sur les sentiments des sceptiques,* published in 1714 and reprinted by Olivier Bloch in 2004, contains a series of theses of materialistic inspiration, which were later developed by French materialists as La Mettrie, Helvetius, Diderot, and d'Holbach himself.

IV.13 Constitutive elements (*guṇa*) of Matter

Matter, whether manifested or non-manifested, has three constitutive elements called *guṇas,* which make up its essence. In *sūtra* VI, 39 of the *Sāṃkhyasūtras,* it is said that the *guṇas* are not attributes of the *Prakṛti* because they are its essence (*sattvādīnām ataddharmatvaṃ tadrūpatvāt*). Literally, *guṇa* means: "thread", "filament", which implies the image of the weft of a cloth, and which by extension has been translated in the context of the Sāṃkhya system, not very correctly, as "quality", "attribute", "property". The *guṇas* are the *Prakṛti*: as cloth is nothing other than the weft of the threads which constitute it, in the same way Matter (*Prakṛti*) is nothing other than its essential constitutive elements (*guṇa*). The best way to translate the term *guṇa* in the context of the Sāṃkhya system is therefore "essential constitutive element".[33]

The word *guṇa* is mentioned in *kārikās* 11, 12, 14, 16, 20, 27, 36, 46. *Kārikā* 11 presents as the first attribute of Matter that of *triguṇa*: "constituted by the three *guṇas*", and the commentary explains that these three *guṇas* are *sattva, rajas* and *tamas,* to whose meanings we shall refer afterwards. The three *guṇas* are also expressly mentioned in *kārikās* 13 and 54, and *tamas* alone in *kārikā* 48. In Gauḍapāda's commentary, they are referred to in several places.

---

[33] Cf. what has been previously expressed in relation to the attribute of Matter *avivekin,* "not-differentiated", *kārikā* 11; the *sūtra* VI, 39 of the *Sāṃkhyasūtras* where it is said that the *guṇas* are not attributes of the *Prakṛti* because they are its essence (*sattvādīnām ataddharmatvaṃ tadrūpatvāt*); and R. Garbe, *Die Sāṃkhya-Philosophie,* pp. 209-212.

Kārikās 12 and 13 and their commentaries indicate the characteristics of each of the three *guṇas*:

According to *kārikā* 12 the *guṇa sattva* has as its essence *prīti* (pleasure), glossed by *sukha* (happiness). *Prīti* is a term of great semantic extension here; it comprises all of the manifestations of psychological life that can be termed "positive", like *prasāda*, (calm), *lāghava* (lightness), *abhiṣvaṅga*, (affection), *prīti*, (joy), *titikṣā*, (patience), *sāntoṣa* (contentment), etc.[34] The *guṇa sattva* is moreover *prakāśa-artha*, "which has as its aim light, manifestation", glossed by *prakāśa-samārtha*, "to which belongs light, manifestation". According to *kārikā* 13 the *guṇa sattva* is "light" (*laghu*) and "manifesting" (*prakāśaka*).

According to *kārikā* 12, the *guṇa rajas* has as its essence *aprīti* (displeasure), glossed by *duḥkha* (pain). Here, too, *aprīti* as well as *prīti* is a term of great semantic extension, which includes all of the manifestations of the psychological life, which can be termed "negative", like *śoka* (sorrow), etc.[35] The *guṇa rajas* is also *pravṛtti-artha*, "which has as its aim activity", "to which belongs activity". According to *kārikā* 13, the *guṇa rajas* is "activating" (*upaṣṭambhaka*) and "mobile" (*cala*).

According to *kārikā* 12 the *guṇa tamas* has as its essence *viṣāda*, (depression), glossed by *moha*: (confusion). *Viṣāda* is also a collective term of great semantic extension which comprises all of the manifestations of psychological life which partake of dejection, despondency and insensibility, like *nidrā* (deep sleep).[36] The *guṇa tamas* is moreover *niyama-artha*, "which has as its aim stopping", "to which belongs stopping". According to *kārikā* 13, the *guṇa tamas* is "heavy" (*guru*) and "hiding", "covering, hindering" (*varaṇaka*).

---

[34] See afterwards the references to *Sāṃkhyasūtra* I, 127, to the opinion of Pañcaśikha (quoted by Vijñānabhikṣu *ad* I, 127), and to Vijñānabhikṣu himself *ad* I, 127, who adopts the interpretation of Pañcaśikha.

[35] Cf. the previous note 34.

[36] Cf. the previous note 34.

Of the attributes assigned in *kārikās* 12 and 13 to each of the three *guṇas,* the first (*kārikā* 12 a) has to do with psychology, the others (*kārikās* 12 b and 13) referring to the physical reality, and it must be taken into account that, for the Sāṃkhya, the psychological as well as the physical reality are products of the evolution of Matter, as we shall see later.

Also, according to the well-known Sāṃkhya theory of causality (*Satkāryavāda*), already explained, all which is in the effect, i.e. in the manifested Matter (empirical reality) already has to exist in the cause, i.e. in the non-manifested Matter and *vice versa.* It is understood that the three *guṇas,* which are the essence of Matter and that which constitutes Matter, have to contain in themselves all that Matter produces in its manifestation and evolution. Consequently, the characteristics assigned to the *guṇas* in *kārikās* 12 and 13 (which in a sense express what they contain) are not at all exhaustive, being more like examples, and they do not comprehend the whole reality of the *guṇas*: they are that and much more besides.

The reasons for this interpretation are as follows:

1. *Sāṃkhyasūtra* I, 127, which adds to the words indicating the essence of each *guṇa,* i.e. to *prīti,* (pleasure), *aprīti* (displeasure) and *viṣāda,* (depression), the word *ādi* with the meaning of "et cetera";

2. the opinion of Pañcaśikha (quoted by Vijñānabhikṣu *ad* I, 127), who expresses that, from a psychological point of view, each *guṇa* comprises an "infinite diversity" (°*anantabheda*) and enumerates some of them in each case (*prasāda,* (calm), *lāghava* (lightness), *abhiṣvaṅga,* (affection), *prīti,* (joy), *titikṣā,* (patience), *sāntoṣa* (contentment), etc.); and

3. Vijñānabhikṣu *ad* I, 127, who adopted Pañcaśikha's interpretation. The extensive interpretation of the attributes of psychological order indicated in *kārikās* 12 and 13 is also valid for those attributes of physical nature.

Literally, the word *sattva,* related to the root *AS-,* "to be", "to exist", can mean: the fact of being, being, existence, true essence, life, etc.;

the word *rajas* usually means: passion, impurity and is related to the root *RAÑJ-,* "to be affected" or "to be moved" or "to be excited";

the word *tamas* usually means: obscurity, ignorance, error and is related to the root *TAM-,* "to become motionless", "to become immobile", "to get stiff".

In relation to the *guṇas* in the Sāṃkhya system, it is not possible to restrict or limit oneself to taking only one of those literal values for these words. The meaning of the three names of the *guṇas* is in fact symbolic; they designate realities of great complexity, a complexity, which cannot be expressed by one word only.

If we wanted to indicate with a sole notion the essential nature of each of the three *guṇas* in agreement with the Sāṃkhya tradition, with the usual meanings applied to the words (*sattva*: existence, "it reveals"; *rajas*: passion, "it incites"; *tamas*: darkness, "it immobilizes") and, finally, with the relating of the three names of the *guṇas* to their respective roots, it could be said that *sattva* refers to "existence", which implies manifestation, *rajas* refers to "impulse", which sets in motion, and *tamas* refers to "inertia", which stops.

The *guṇas* are not isolated, but are related amongst themselves in various ways: they dominate one another (*anyo'nyābhibhava*), (Gauḍapāda's *Bhāṣya ad kārikā* 12 c-d), one of them acquiring predominance over the others; they support one another (*anyo'nyāśraya*) (*ibidem*); they produce one another (*anyo'nyajanana*) (*ibidem*); they unite one with the other (*anyo'nyamithuna*) (*ibidem*); they incite one another to action (*anyo'nyavṛtti*), (*ibidem*).

Due to this complex relation among the *guṇas*, and especially to the predominance of one of them over the other as well as to the various proportions in which each of them is found in the beings and things which constitute our empirical reality, diversity and multiplicity take place in it.[37]

As we have said, the *guṇas* are the essence of Matter, whether manifested (*vyakta*) or non-manifested (*avyakta*), but there is a difference: *Prakṛti* proper, i.e. non-manifested Matter, is the total equilibrium of the *guṇas*, their absolute harmony (*sāmyāvasthā*, "state of balance", *guṇasāmānya*, "equality of the guṇas", *akāryāvasthā*, "state in which the condition of non-effect is given") (Gauḍapāda's *Bhāṣya ad Sāṃkhyakārikās* 23: *iyaṃ prakṛtiḥ sattvarajastamasāṃ sāmyāvasthā* and *Sāṃkhyasūtras* I, 61). This equilibrium excludes all differentiation, all multiplicity and all diversity. When this equilibrium is broken, the evolution of Matter begins.

IV.14 Remarks on the previous subject: The Homoeomeries of Anaxagoras. The two forces of Schelling

1. The Sāṃkhya theory of the *guṇas* brings a few theses of the pre-Socratic Anaxagoras (5th century B.C.) to mind. Anaxagoras asserted that there is not as ἀρχή (original substance from which all comes forth and of which all is made) a unique substance, such as for instance water according to Thales, but that an infinite number of *archés* exist. Simplicius in his *Commentary to the Physics of Aristotle* 27, 2 beginning [59 A 41. Diels / Kranz]: τὰς μὲν σωματικὰς [ἀρχὰς] ἀπείρους ποιήσας: "... as [Anaxagoras] considered the material [literally: corporeal] [*archés*] to be infinite"; Hippolitus, *Refutatio omnium haeresium* I, 8, 1 [59 A 42.]; Aristotle, *Metaphysics* A 3. 984 a 11 [59 A 43.]: ἀπείρους εἶναί φησι τὰς ἀρχάς: "[Anaxagoras] says that the *archés* are infinite".

These original substances are constituted by infinite, extremely small, totally invisible and absolutely diverse particles of all things which exist in our reality. Cf. the

[37] Cf. *Sāṃkhyakārikās* 23 and 25, Gauḍapāda's *Bhāṣya ad locum*, and *Bhagavad-Gītā*, Chapters XIV and XVII.

fragment of Anaxagoras quoted by Simplicius, in his *Commentary to the Physics of Aristotle* 155, 23 [59 B 1. and 4.], a text which refers to the condition of the original substance before its diversification into individual beings and things:

> ὁμοῦ πάντα χρήματα ἦν, ἄπειρα καὶ πλῆθος καὶ σμικρότητα ... πάντων ὁμοῦ ἐόντων οὐδὲν ἔνδηλον ἦν ὑπὸ σμικρότητος·
> "all things were together, infinite in quantity and smallness ... as all things were together nothing was visible due to their smallness" [59 B 1.];

and

> πρὶν δὲ ἀποκριθῆναι ταῦτα πάντων ὁμοῦ ἐόντων οὐδὲ χροιὴ ἔνδηλος ἦν οὐδεμία· ἀπεκώλυε γὰρ ἡ σύμμιξις πάντων χρημάτων ... καὶ γῆς πολλῆς ἐνεούσης καὶ σπέρματων ἀπείρων πλῆθος οὐδὲν ἐοικότων ἀλλήλοις·
> "before being separated, as all things were together, no color was visible, since the mixture of all things hindered it ... as there were much earth and seeds infinite in quantity, and in nothing similar one to the other" [59 B 4.].

As all was in this state of lack of differentiation, νοῦς or mind came in order to accomplish the distribution and arrangement of things, according to the information given by Hippolitus, *Refutatio omnium haeresium* I, 8, 1 [59A 42.], νοῦς ἐπελθὼν διεκόσμησεν.

Other texts (quoted by Anaxagoras and testimonies of other authors to follow) refer to the situation of the original substance *after* differentiation, expressing that *there are seeds (i.e. particles) of everything in everything* and that *things are characterized as what they are, in their diversity, due to the predominance of one or the other kind of particles.*

The fragment of Anaxagoras quoted by Simplicius in his *Commentary to the Physics of Aristotle* 155, 23 [59 B 4.]: χρὴ δοκεῖν ἐνεῖναι πολλά τε καὶ παντοῖα ἐν πᾶσι τοῖς συγκρινομένοις καὶ σπέρματα πάντων χημάτων καὶ ἰδέας παντοίας ἔχοντα καὶ χροιὰς καὶ ἡδονάς: "It is to be considered that in all the things brought into combination there are many and varied components and seeds of all the things, which have diverse forms, colors and tastes".

Another fragment of Anaxagoras, also quoted by Simplicius, in ibidem 164, 22 [59 B 11.]: ἐν παντὶ παντὸς μοῖρα ἔνεστι: "In all there is a part of all"; and 164, 24 [59 B 12.] where the same idea is repeated with the same words; in this same fragment it is said moreover that "all the other things [with the exception of the *nous*] have a part of all": τὰ μὲν ἄλλα παντὸς μοῖραν μετέχει.

The scholium of Gregory of Nazianzus (*circa* 329-389/90 A.D.) *ad* XXXVI, 911, Migne edition [59 B 10.], reproduces a fragment which contains an argument of Anaxagoras in favor of his theory: πῶς γὰρ ἂν ...ἐκ μὴ τριχὸς γένοιτο θρὶξ καὶ σὰρξ ἐκ μὴ σαρκός: "How from what is not a hair a hair could come out, and flesh from what is not flesh?"

In [Plutarch], *Opinions des philosophes*, in *Plutarque, Oeuvres morales, Tome XII, 2e partie*, Belles Lettres edition, p. 73 [876 A] we find a reference to an interesting argument in favor of Anaxagoras' theory: the food that man consumes must contain imperceptible particles of sinews, bones, blood, etc., since these components of the human body develop and grow thanks to ingestion of food.

Simplicius, in his *Commentary to the Physics of Aristotle* 27, 2 [59 A 41.]: ... πάντων μὲν ἐν πᾶσιν ἐνόντων, ἑκάστου δὲ κατὰ τὸ ἐπικρατοῦν ἐν αὐτῷ χαρακτηριζομένου: "... being all things in all, and being each one of them characterized according to what predominates in it".

Lucretius, *De rerum natura* I, 830-844 begins his exposition of Anaxagoras' theory with the following verses:

Nunc et Anaxagorae scrutemur homoeomerian
quam Grai memorant, nec nostra dicere lingua
concedit nobis patrii sermonis egestas...

"And now let us investigate
what the Greeks call homoeomeries of Anaxagoras:
the poverty of our native language
does not grant us to express [that notion] in our speech".

and in I, 876-879 he expressly says:

...omnibus omnis
res putet immixtas rebus latitare, sed illud
apparere unum cuius sint plurima mixta
et magis in promptu primaque in fronte locata.

"... [Anaxagoras] thinks that all the things, mixed,
are hidden in all the things,
but only appears that of which there exists,
in the mixture,
more quantity, more at hand,
and placed in the first line".

2. It is surprising and therefore interesting to indicate that the German philosopher F.W.J. Schelling (1775-1854) begins his important treatise *Von der Weltseele* ["On the soul of the world"] (third edition of 1809) by pointing out the existence of two forces in nature: an impelling force which would correspond to the *guṇa rajas* and a stopping force which would correspond to the *guṇa tamas*:

> *Jede in sich selbst zurückkehrende Bewegung setzt, als Bedingung ihrer Möglichkeit, voraus eine positive Kraft, die (als* Impuls*) die Bewegung anfaht, ... und eine negative, die (als* Anziehung*) die Bewegung* in sich selbst zurücklenkt, *(oder sie verhindert in eine gerade Linie auszuschlagen).*
>
> *In der Natur strebt alles continuirlich* vorwärts; *dass diess so ist, davon müssen wir den Grund in einem Princip suchen, das, eine unerschüpfliche Quelle* positiver *Kraft, die* Bewegung *in der Welt immer von neuem anfaht und ununterbrochen unterhält. Dieses* positive *Princip ist die* erste Kraft der Natur.
>
> *Aber eine unsichbare Gewalt führt alle Erscheinungen in der Welt in dem ewigen Kreislauf zurück. Dass diess so ist, davon müssen wir den letzten Grund in einer* negativen *Kraft suchen, die, indem sie die Wirkungen des positiven Princips continuirlich beschränkt, die allgemeine Bewegung in ihre Quelle zurückleitet. Dieses* negative *Princip ist die* zweyte *Kraft der Natur.*

"All movement that returns on itself presupposes as a condition of its possibility a *positive* force that (as *impulse*), *incites* motion ...

and a *negative* one that (as *attraction*), *causes* motion *to retrace its steps* (or it prevents it to continue in a straight line).

In the Nature all continuously tends *forward*; we must look for the reason of this in a principle that, as an inexhaustible source of *positive* force, always renewedly incites motion in the world, and uninterruptedly maintains it. This *positive* principle is the *first force of Nature.*

But an invisible force leads backwards all manifestations in the world in an eternal circular movement; we must look for the ultimate reason of this in a *negative* force that, while it continuously limits the effects of the positive principle, leads the universal movement back to its sources. This *negative* principle is the *second* force of Nature".

IV.15 *Sāṃkhya* Theory of Evolution

From Matter, *Prakṛti*, not only the material things of our world arise, but also the material components (body, sensory organs) and the psychic components (mind, senses, ego-consciousness) of man.

The Sāṃkhya describes in detail the process of evolution whereby the arising of the whole empirical reality out of Matter, i.e. the transformation of Matter into reality, is accomplished. During this process of evolution, Matter passes from a form of imperceptible subtlety into forms which become gradually coarser. Each of the new forms assumed by Matter during its evolution acquires new attributes which are added to the attributes already possessed by Matter in its previous form, as Vijñāṇabhikṣu interprets it in his commentary of the *Sāṃkhyasūtras ad* I, 99, p. 48, lines 27-28, Garbe ed. (*sāmānya-guṇā-'tirikta-dharmo-'tpattāv eva pariṇāma-vyavahārād iti*: "because it is spoken of evolution only when [new] properties are produced besides the general qualities"). Also, the process of evolution is governed by the principle of continuity, as is clear from the description of that process in the *Sāṃkhyasūtras* I, 61- I, 65 and I, 71 - I, 73.

The *Sāṃkhyakārikās* 22-38 describe this process of evolution of Matter.

At the very beginning, *Mahat* "arises" from the Primordial Matter, which is non-manifested and devoid of qualifications, i.e. the Primordial Matter manifests itself in an extremely subtle form which constitutes the *Mahat*, the Great (Principle). This term is glossed by Gauḍapāda with the words *buddhi*, meaning intellect or intelligence; *mati*, meaning thought; *khyāti*, meaning discursive knowledge and *jñāna*, *prajñā*, meaning knowledge; which the commentator presents as synonyms of *Mahat*. Of these words, the one used most frequently to designate *Mahat* is *buddhi*, which fundamentally includes the capacity, aptitude or power to know the object of the cognitive act as what it is: "this is a pot", "this is a cloth", i.e. the power to determine the being of things, to "assert" something, to make an affirmation (*Sāṃkhyakārikās* 23; *Sāṃkhyasūtras* I, 71, and Vijñānabhikṣu *ad locum*, and II, 13).

From *Mahat* "arises" *Ahaṃkāra*, the ego, the principle of subjectivity, the principle of individuation, glossed by Gauḍapāda with the word *abhimāna*, meaning egotism or ego-consciousness. We must understand the act of "arising" as a process by virtue of which Matter, which at the very beginning manifested itself in the form of *Mahat/buddhi*, continues its evolution or transformation and immediately manifests itself in a less subtle form than that of *Mahat*, i.e. in the form of *Ahaṃkāra*.

From that *Ahaṃkāra* "arises" the group of sixteen, which is constituted by the five "subtle elements" or *Tanmātras* and by the eleven organs of sense or *Indriyas*.

The five *Tanmātras* are: the subtle element of sound (*śabda*), the subtle element of touch (*sparśa*), the subtle element of form/color (*rūpa*), the subtle element of taste (*rasa*) and the subtle element of smell (*gandha*). The *Tanmātras* are the objects of each one of the sensory organs.

The eleven *Indriyas* are the five organs of knowledge (*buddhīndriya*) which are: ear (*śrotra*), skin (*tvac-*, as the organ of touch), the two eyes (*cakṣus*), tongue (*jihvā*), nose (*ghrāṇa*, as the organ of smell); and the five organs of action (*karmendriya*) which are: voice/tongue (*vac*), hands (*pāṇi*), feet (*pāda*), the anus (*pāyu*) and the generative organs (*upasthā*); and as the eleventh the mind (*manas*), which partakes of both the sensory organs and the organs of action.

Manas is the mind in its capacity to build up concepts, create images and organize ideas, which it grasps in the same way as each of the five sensory organs grasps its own object.

The products of the evolution of Matter mentioned until now are considered as *subtle* in opposition to the *coarse* elements, which are mentioned immediately afterwards.

Finally, from each one of the five *Tanmātras* (sound, etc.) "arise" the five *Mahābhūtas* (*Sāṃkhykārikās* 22) or *sthūla-bhūtas* ("coarse elements") (*Sāṃkhyasūtras* I, 61): from the subtle element of sound arises "space" (*ākaśa*), from the subtle element of touch arises "wind" (*vāyu*), from the subtle element of form/color arises "fire" (*tejas*), from the subtle element of taste arises "water" (*ap*) and from the subtle element of smell arises "earth" (*pṛthivī*). With these five coarse elements, the five great elements, the *coarse* material empirical reality is constructed.

IV.16 The *antaḥkaraṇa* or internal organ

The *buddhi*, the *ahaṃkāra*, and the *manas* or mind, all products of the evolution of Matter (*Prakṛti*), build up the *antaḥkaraṇa* or internal organ (*kārikā* 33), which in Western terms is equivalent to the "psychic" aspect of the individual in contrast to the physical aspect formed by the ten first *indriyas.* It is necessary to bear in mind at all times that, for Sāṃkhya, the psychic component of the individual is a product of the evolution of Matter and is therefore, like it, deprived of consciousness. However, as we shall see later on, the Spirit (*Puruṣa*) is reflected in the *antaḥkaraṇa,* and thanks to this reflection the *antaḥkaraṇa* acquires an appearance of consciousness which allows it to act as a real conscious being. The reflection of the Spirit takes place as soon as Matter manifests itself in the form of each and every one of the components of the *antaḥkaraṇa.*

The function of the *antaḥkaraṇa* as a whole is essentially to transform into knowledge, i.e. into contents of consciousness, the data provided by the sensory organs of knowledge when these are in contact with the *Tanmātras* (sound, etc.) and are affected by them.

IV.17 The *sui generis* Materialism of *Sāṃkhya*. Radical Materialism in India

It could be said that Sāṃkhya in a sense adheres to the doctrine of "materialism", since all that constitutes the empirical reality has its origin in *Matter* and is nothing other than *Matter* in any of its stages of evolution. However, it is not materialism in absolute terms, since Sāṃkhya equally admits the existence of the Spirit, which is apart from Matter and is opposed to it. For Sāṃkhya, all that is empirically existent thus possesses a fundamental and absolute homogeneity, and from this point of view it is possible to speak, as proper to the Sāṃkhya system, of a "materialist monism" on the empirical level, which does not exclude the "Matter/Spirit dualism" on the level of the whole of reality.

However, in India there was also a "radical materialism" which manifested itself as early as the 6th and 5th centuries B.C. and which acquired its systematically settled form in the first centuries A.D. Indian materialism was given several names: *Bārhaspatya, Nāstikamata, Cārvākadarśana, Lokāyata.* The materialists are known to us thanks to references to them and quotations from their texts by other authors. Their principal doctrines are as follows: 1. matter, constituted by the four elements earth, water, fire and air and its products, are all that exists, and there is no entity of a spiritual nature; 2. consciousness, intelligence, arises from these four elements in a process similar to that of fermentation; 3. negation of the existence of God: the only "God" that exists is the king, i.e. the state; 4. negation of a *post mortem* life: all ends with death; 5. the only valid means of knowledge is perception; 6. negation of *Śruti*, Revelation, of religious life in any of its forms, of religious prescriptions, of ritual traditions, of the castes and the hierarchical superiority of brahmins, the so-called priests who dealt with rites; 7. amoralism: they do not accept any moral order in the world; from the moral point of view, all was indifferent for them; 8. they favored the most unbridled hedonism: the aim of life was to enjoy sensual pleasures, the *carpe diem.*[38]

The notion of materialist as conceived of in the West and in general terms could be related not to the *sui generis* materialism of the Sāṃkhya system but to the last philosophical current of Indian "radical materialism" referred to.

Chr. Wolff, *Psychologia rationalis,* pp. 24 and 25, §§ 33 and 34, defines materialist philosophers in the following terms:

> (§ 33) Materialistae *dicuntur philosophi, qui tantummodo entia materialia, sive corpora existere affirmant.* (§ 34) Materialistae *nonnisi corporum existentiam admittunt, immo nonnisi eadem possibilia esse contendunt; nonnisi unum substantiarum genus existere affirmant, adeoque* Monistae *sunt.*
>
> (§ 33) "Are called *Materialists* the philosophers who affirm that only the material entia or bodies exist". (§ 34) "The *Materialists* only admit the existence of bodies, even uphold that only they are able to exist; even they assert that there exists only one kind of substances, and therefore they are called *Monists*".

IV.18 Remarks on the previous subject: The notion of evolution in the West

The notion of evolution, which implies the transformation of one thing into another, was also maintained in the West. There were hints of a theory of evolution in some presocratic thinkers. For example, according to the information of

[38] On Indian Materialism see G. Tucci, "Linee di una storia del Materialismo indiano", in *Opera Minora,* Vol. I, pp. 49-155; F. Tola, "Tres concepciones del hombre", in *Pensamiento,* Vol. 42, 1986, pp. 29-46; F Tola and C. Dragonetti, *Filosofia de la India,* pp. 573-581; K.K. Mittal, *Materialism in Indian Thought;* S. Pāthak, *Cārvāka Darśana ki Śāstrīya Samīkṣā;* and Ramkrishna

[Plutarch], *Stromata* 3 D 579 [13 A 6.], Anaximenes (6th century B.C.) asserted that all things are produced by condensation and rarefaction of the air (γεννᾶσθαί τε πάντα κατά τινα πύκνωσιν τούτου καὶ πάλιν ἀραίωσιν). According to Galenus, *De elementis secundum Hippocratem* I, 4 [22 A 5.] Heraclitus also taught that a similar process of condensation had taken place with regard to fire in the genesis of the universe. However, this theory did not develop further, and it was rather the static concept of the world upheld by Plato and Aristotle which predominated. It was not until the 18th century that the theory of evolution became influential in the West in various scientific disciplines such as cosmogony, chemistry, biology, and in its most unique form in the latter: "pre-formation".

The concept of "pre-formation" arose in the field of biology (embryology) to explain how the evolution of an organism takes place. According to this notion of "pre-formation", the components of organism in the last state of its evolution (i.e. in its definitive form) pre-exist and are in some way "preformed" in the egg or sperm; and in the development of embryo and all phases of its further development, the only thing that takes place is its "unfolding" or "unwrapping" in a gradual, ordained and fixed process. It is in a sense the process explained by the *satkāryavāda* of the Sāṃkhya: the effect pre-exists in the cause in a subtle or invisible form. Cf. the previous section *The Homoeomeries of Anaxagoras.*

1. Leibniz, "Essai de Théodicée sur la bonté de Dieu, la liberté de l'homme et l'origine du mal, Préface", in *Philosophische Schriften* Band II. 1, Insel Verlag edition, p. 44, refers to the concept of "preformation" in these terms:

Bhattacharya "Cārvāka Fragments: a new collection", in *Journal of Indian Philosophy*, Vol. 30, No. 6, December 2002 (2003), pp. 597-640. On the notion of "Materialism" in Philosophy see Mario Bunge, *Chasing Reality: Strife over Realism*, pp. 26-27.

... préformation *déjá tout organique dans les semences des corps qui naissent, contenues dans celles des corps dont ils sont nés, jusqu'au semences premières; ce qui ne pouvait venir, que de l'auteur des choses, infiniment puissant et infiniment sage, lequel faisant tout d'abord avec ordre, y avait préétabli tout ordre, et tout artifice futur* ...

"... *pre-formation* already completely organic in the seeds of the bodies which are born, contained in the seeds of the bodies from which they have been born, up to the first seeds; this could only come from the author of things, infinitely powerful and infinitely wise, who doing all from the beginning according to order, had established there all future order and device".

and on p. 46 of the same book, he adds:

... *il faut juger que Dieu a* préformé *les choses, en sorte que les organisations nouvelles ne soient qu'une suite mécanique d'une constitution organique précédente; comme lorsque les papillons viennent des vers à soie, oú M. Swammerdam a montré qu'il n'y a que du développement.*

"... it is necessary to think that God has *preformed* things in such a way that the new organizations are nothing else than a mechanic continuity of a preceding organic constitution; as for instance when butterflies originate from the silk worm, in relation to which fact mister Swammerdam has demonstrated that there is only development".

In "Principes de la nature et de la grace, fondés en raison," included in his *Philosophische Schriften*, Band I, Insel Verlag edition, which is one of his last works, Leibniz says, § 6, pp. 422 and 424 (= Band VI, p. 601, C.I. Gerhardt ed.):

Les recherches des Modernes nous ont appris, et la raison l'approuve, que les vivans dont les organes nous sont connus, c'est à dire, les plantes et les Animaux, ne viennent point d'une putrefaction ou d'un Chaos, comme les anciens ont crû, mais de semences préformées, *et par consequent de la* Transformation *des vivans préexistans. Il y a des petits animaux dans les semences des grands, qui par le moyen de la conception prennent un revestement nouveau, qu'ils approprient, et qui leur donne moyen de se nourrir et de s'aggrandir, [ils ne passent point dans la mort, mais il quittent] pour passer sur un plus grand theatre, et faire la propagation du grand animal.*

"The investigations of the Moderns have taught us, and reason approves it, that living beings whose organs are known to us, i.e.

plants and Animals, do not come in any way from a putrefaction or a Chaos, as the Ancients have believed, but from *preformed* seeds, and therefore from the *Transformation* of the pre-existing living beings. There are small animals in the seeds of the big ones, which through the conception assume a new covering that they appropriate, and that gives them a means to feed and to grow, [they do not pass into death, but they leave] in order to pass to a bigger theatre, and to do the propagation of the big animal".

And in the same paragraph, p. 424 (= Band VI, p. 601, C. I. Gerhardt ed.), he affirms:

> *Ainsi non seulement les Ames, mais encore les animaux sont ingenerables et imperissables: ils ne sont que developpés, enveloppés, revêtus, depouillés, transformés ...*
>
> "Thus not only the Souls, but also the animals are unable to be generated or to perish: they are only developed, wrapped, covered, stripped, transformed..."

Leibniz in his treatise *Causa Dei*, § 81, which is a methodic résumé written in Latin of his *Theodicée*, in *Philosophische Schriften*, Band II, Insel Verlag edition, pp. 350-352, also refers to the theory of the *Preformatio* in order to explain the transmission of the original sin of Adam and Eve to their descendants:

> *Sequitur* Propagatio Contagii *a lapsu Protoplastorum orti perveniens in animas posterorum. Ea non videtur commodius explicari posse quam statuendo animas posterorum in Adamo jam fuisse infectas. Quod ut intelligatur rectius, sciendum est ex recentiorum observatis rationibusque apparere, animalium et plantarum formationem non prodire ex massa quadam confusa, sed ex corpore jam nonnihil praeformato in semine latente et dudum animato. Unde consequens est, vi benedictionis divinae primaevae, omnium viventium rudimenta quaedam organica (et pro animalibus quidem, animalium licet imperfectorum forma) animasque quodammodo ipsas dudum in Protoplasto cujusque generis extitisse; quae sub tempore omnia evolverentur. Sed animas animantiaque seminum humanis corporibus destinatorum, cum caeteris animalculis seminalibus talem destinationem non habentibus, intra gradum naturae sensitivae substitisse dicendum est, donec per ultimam conceptionem a caeteris discernerentur, simulque corpus organicum ad figuram humanam*

disponeretur, et anima ejus ad gradum rationalitatis (ordinaria an extraordinaria Dei operatione non definio) eveheretur.

"[Now] it is the turn [in our explanations to speak] of the *Propagation* [= transmission] of *Contagion* originated by the fall of the firstly created [human beings, Adam and Eve], which reaches the souls of their later [descendants]. It does not seem that that [Propagation, transmission] could be explained more easily than accepting that the souls of the later [descendants] were already infected in Adam. In order to understand better this fact it is necessary to know from the observations and the reasonings of the more recent [scientific researchers] that the formation of animals and plants does not come from some confuse mass, but from a somewhat already preformed body, latent in the seed and animated long since. Whence it follows that, by the force of the primordial divine blessing, some organic rudiments of all living beings (and even in the case of animals, although the form of the animals is imperfect), and in some way the souls themselves long since existed in the first created [living being] of each species; [rudiments] that in the course of time had all of them evolved. But it is to be said that the souls and the principles of life of the seeds destined to human bodies - together with the other seminal small animals which do not have such a destination - maintain themselves within the limits of the sensitive nature, until by means of their last conception they differentiate from the other [beings], and at the same time [their] organic body is arranged in a human form, and its soul [= the soul of the body with human form] is brought to the level of rationality (I do not decide whether by an ordinary or by an extraordinary act of God)".

The philosopher Leibniz thus utilizes an erroneous scientific theory of his epoch in order to demonstrate the validity of a religious tradition which is many centuries old and is accepted as a dogma by Christianity.

2. In his work *Considérations sur les corps organisés,* edited for the first time in Paris in 1762 and censored and prohibited in France by Abbot Lignac, Charles Bonnet (1720-1793), an author of Swiss origin relying on observations concerning animals, expresses similar ideas to those of Leibniz concerning

a theory of evolution, but does not use his theory to support a religious dogma.[39] On p.14, Fayard ed., 1985, he says:

J'avois admis l'évolution, comme le principe le plus conforme aux faits et à la saine Philosophie. Je supposois que tout Corps organisé préexistoit à la fécondation, et que celle-ci ne faisoit que procurer le développment du Tout organique dessiné auparavant en miniature dans la grain ou dans l'oeuf.

"I had admitted the *evolution* as the principle the most in accordance with facts and sound Philosophy. I supposed that all organized Body preexisted the fertilization, and that this did nothing else than provide the development of the organic All, previously sketched in miniature in the grain or in the egg".

Je ne cessois pas un instant de penser qu'il n'y avoit point de génération proprement dite, et que tout se réduisoit à un simple développment.

"I did not cease even for an instance to think that there was not at all generation properly said, and that all was reduced to a simple development".

Cependant il restoit toujours à démontrer que le Germe appartenoit à la femelle, qu'il préexistoit ainsi à la fécondation, et que l'évolution étoit la loi universelle des Êtres organisés.[40]

"Nevertheless, there always remained to demonstrate that the Germ belonged to the female, that it preexisted thus the fertilization, and that evolution was the universal law of all organized beings".

On page 21 he says:

... la raison envisage avec plaisir la graine d'une plante ou l'oeuf d'un animal, comme un petit monde peuplé d'une multitude d'Etres organisés, appellés à se succéder dans toute la durée des siecles.

"... reason observes with pleasure the seed of a plant or the egg of an animal, as a small world inhabited by a multitude of organized beings, summoned to succeed each other during all the centuries".

[39] On Bonnet see J. Ferrater Mora, *Diccionario de Filosofía*, Vol. I, p. 407; and *Dictionnaire des philosophes*, article by François Azouvi, "Bonnet Charles 1720-1793", Vol. I, pp. 389-391.

[40] According to Bonnet this discovery was announced to him by Baron of Haller in 1757.

On page 23:

L'état actuel d'un Corps, est la suite ou le produit de son état antécédent; ou pour parler plus juste, l'état actuel d'un Corps est déterminé par son état antécédent.

"The present state of a Body is the continuation or the product of its preceding state; or to speak with more accuracy, the present state of a Body is determined by its preceding state".

On page 24:

Si nous observons au microscope, la graine d'une plante ou l'oeuf d'un animal, nous nous convaincrons que le Corps organisé qui en doit naître, y existe déja en petit avec toutes ses parties essentielles.

"If we observe through a microscope the seed of a plant or the egg of an animal, we will be fully convinced that the organized Body, which has to be born out of it, already exists in it in a small scale with all its essential parts".

On page 33:

On dit que le germe est une ébauche ou une esquisse du Corps organisé.

"It is said that the germ is a sketch or an outline of an organized Body".

Let us finish these quotations from Bonnet with a text from page 88 in which he has recourse to poetical devices in order to enhance his thesis:

Pour moi j'aime à reculer le plus qu'il m'est possible, le borne de la création. Je me plais à considérer cette magnifique suite d' Êtres organisés, renfermés comme autant de petits mondes, les uns dans les autres. Je les vois s'éloigner de moi par degrés; diminuer suivant certaines proportions, et se perdre enfin dans une nuit impénétrable. Je goûte une secrette satisfaction à contempler dans un gland *le germe d'où naîtra, dans quelques siecles, le* Chêne *majestueux, à l'ombre duquel les Oiseaux de l'air et les bêtes des champs iront se réjouir. J'ai encore plus de plaisir á découvrir dans le sein d'Émilie le germe du Héros qui fondera dans quelques miliers d'années un gran empire, ou plutôt celui d'un Philosophe qui découvrira alors au monde la cause de la* Pesanteur, *le mystère de la génération, la méchanique de notre Être.*

"As for myself, I like to cause the limit of creation to go back as much as possible. I find pleasure in considering this magnificent succession of organized Beings, enclosed as so many small worlds one in the other. I see them moving gradually away from me; decreasing according to certain proportions, and finally disappearing in a impenetrable night. I enjoy a secret satisfaction contemplating in an *acorn* the germ from which will be born after some centuries the majestic *Oak*, under whose shadow the Birds of the air and the animals of the fields will go to enjoy. I find even more pleasure discovering in the womb of Emily the germ of the Heroe that will found after several thousands of years a great empire, or better that of a Philosopher who will discover then to the world the cause of *Gravitation*, the mistery of generation and the mechanic of our Being".[41]

For similar ideas, see of the same author *La palingénésie philosophique*, published in 1783, reedited in Paris: A. Fayard, 2002, pp. 130-131, 156, 200-204, 207-211, 260-273, 298-303.

IV.19 Appraisal of the *Sāṃkhya* Theory of Evolution

In Chapter II we referred to the myths of creation in the Vedic tradition. In all of them, creation is conceived of as a task carried out by a divinity of some description.

In same Chapter II we also indicated that one exception is the *Hymn* X 129 of the *Ṛg Veda*, which postulates the One as the origin of all in a way which, already in the *Vedas*, constitutes an overcoming of myth.

The One is a pre-figuration of the notion of the Absolute or *Brahman* which in the Upaniṣads and the Vedānta schools occupies an important position, is conceived of as the Spiritual Principle, origin, support and end of all, and is the central notion of a huge metaphysical construction.

The Sāṃkhya theory of creation considered as the product of the evolution of Primordial Matter (*Prakṛti*) is

[41] On the general principles of the theory of evolution in the West, see the articles "Evolución, Evolucionismo", by J. Ferrater Mora, in *Diccionario de Filosofía*, Vol. II, pp. 1158-1164; "Entwicklung" by several authors, and "Evolutionstheorie" by B. Rensch, in *Historisches Wörterbuch der Philosophie*, Vol. II, col. 550-560, and col. 836-838 respectively; "Evolution" and "Evolutionstheorie" by G. Wolters, in *Enzyklopädie Philosophie und Wissenschaftstheorie* I, pp. 610-614; and "Evolution (biogical)" by R.C. Punnette, in *Encyclopaedia of Religion and Ethics*, Vol. V, pp. 615-623.

opposed to the mythical (*Vedas*) and spiritualist (*Upaniṣads* and *Vedānta*) traditions.

No-one can avoid recognizing the originality inherent in the fact that, in the 4th century A.D., the Saṃkhya system gave a bold materialistic and evolutionist explanation of creation which went far beyond mythical thinking and did not have recourse to a Spiritual Principle or Divine Being. This is one of the most important aspects of Sāṃkhya rationalism.

IV.20 The alternation of creations and disappearances of the world

According to the Sāṃkhya system, the genesis of empirical reality from Matter or, in other terms, the transformation of Matter into that empirical reality through the process of evolution, is not a fact which took place once only.

In the commentary of Vijñānabhikṣu *ad sūtra* II, 2, the following is said:

> *nāi'kadā sṛṣṭer mokṣaḥ, kiṃ tu bahuśo janma-maraṇa-vyādhy-ādi-vividha-duḥkhena bhṛśaṃ taptasya.*
>
> "Liberation is not [produced] through a sole creation, but [it takes place] only for him who has repeatedly been excessively tormented by the varied suffering of birth, death, illness, etc".

The same Vijñānabhikṣu in his commentary *ad sūtra* II, 4, speaks of "the current or series of creations": *sṛṣṭi-pravāha.*

In an eternal alternation, creations (*sṛṣṭi*) and disappearances (*pralaya*) of the world follow one another. When the stage of existence of the world which emerged via a process of evolution ends, the world disappears by a process of in-volutions which are the opposite of e-volution. Involution follows the same stages as evolution in the opposite direction.

The commentary of Gauḍapāda to *kārikā* 15 (at the end) of the *Sāṃkhyakārikās* explains involution in the following way:

pṛthivy āpas tejo vāyur ākāśam ity etāni pañca mahābhūtāni pralayakāle sṛṣṭikrameṇaivāvibhāgaṃ yānti tanmātreṣu pariṇāmiṣu tanmātrāṇy ekādaśendriyāṇi cāhaṃkāre 'haṃkāro buddhau buddhiḥ pradhāne/ evaṃ trayo lokāḥ pralayakāle prakṛtāvavibhāgaṃ gacchanti.

"These five Great material Elements: earth, water, fire, air, and space, at the time of universal dissolution in the same order as that of creation return to [the state of] in-differentiation [or undivision or unification] into the [five] *Tanmātras* [or subtle Elements or objects proper of each one of the sense-organs] [which are still in their] evolute [form]; the *Tanmātras* and the eleven *Indriyas* [the five organs of knowledge, the five organs of action and the mind, *manas*] into the *Ahaṃkāra* [the ego, the principle of subjectivity, the principle of individuation]; the *Ahaṃkāra* into the *Buddhi* [= *Mahat* or Great (Principle), the intellect]; and the *Buddhi* into the *Pradhāna* [or the Primordial non-manifested Matter]. Thus the three worlds [all the empirical reality] at the time of universal dissolution return to [the state of] indifferentiation into Matter, *Prakṛti*".

In the stage of disappearance, the three *guṇas* enter into a state of equilibrium in which no single one of them prevails over the other two, and Matter remains in a state of indifferentiation and rest. It is said that Matter is *avyakta* (non-manifested) as long as the period of its inexistence in the form of the world and the beings lasts; and that it is *vyakta* (manifested) when it reappears in the form of the world and the beings and the equilibrium of the *guṇas* comes to an end.[42]

According to R. Garbe, *Die Sāṃkhya Philosophie*, pp. 220-222, the doctrine of the alternation of creations and disappearances of the world could be a doctrine which originated in the Sāṃkhya system, and from there it passed on to the other orthodox systems as well as to Buddhism and Jainism. The process according to which the alternation takes place is the same in all of the systems indicated.

---

[42] See the *Appendix* II in R. Garbe's edition of the *Sāṃkhyasūtras*, under the Sanskrit terms *sṛṣṭi* and *pralaya*; and of the same author *Die Sāṃkhya Philosophie*, pp. 220-228; and on the Indian theory of the periods of the cyclic time see Luis González Reimann, *Tiempo cíclico y eras del mundo en la India.*

In the *Sāṃkhyakārikās* and the *Sāṃkhyasūtras*, there is no complete and systematic description of the alternative process which governs the world, but in both we can find numerous references to the creation and disappearance of the world, and to the condition which in both cases corresponds to the *antaḥkaraṇa* (internal organ) or to its components.

IV.21 Remarks on the previous subject: The Doctrine of Eternal Return in the West. Ἀποκατάστασις πάντων· "Universal Restoration". Evolution. Involution. Salvific ἀποκατάστασις

In the West, there was also the concept of successive and alternating creations and dissolutions of the universe, which is usually called the "Doctrine of Eternal Return". The doctrine of eternal return was already maintained by Greek thinkers like Heraclitus, the Stoics and others.

We shall refer to the concept of "eternal return" in Heraclitus and in the Stoics, to Aristotle's idea of a universe endowed with cyclical eternal movement, to the doctrine of ἀποκατάστασις as described by Leibniz and sustained by J. W. Petersen, and to the way Proclus conceives evolution and involution, similar to that of the Sāṃkhya.

1. The fragment of Heraclitus preserved by Clemens of Alexandria, *Stromata* V, 105 [22 B 30.] says:

> κόσμον τόνδε, τὸν αὐτὸν ἁπάντων οὔτε τις θεῶν οὔτε ἀνθρώπων ἐποίησεν, ἀλλ' ἦν ἀεὶ καὶ ἔστιν καὶ ἔσται πῦρ ἀείζωον ἁπτόμενον μέτρα καὶ ἀποσβεννύμενον μέτρα.
>
> "This universe, the same for all, did none of Gods or men make, but it always was and is and shall be an everliving fire, kindling according to measures and going out according to measures".

Diogenes Laertius IX, 8 [22 A 1.] glosses this fragment of Heraclitus in the following way:

γεννᾶσθαί τε αὐτὸν ἐκ πυρὸς καὶ πάλιν ἐκπυροῦσθαι κατά τινας περιόδους ἐναλλὰξ τὸν σύμπαντα αἰῶνα· τοῦτο δὲ γίνεσθαι καθ' εἱμαρμένην.

"[Heraclitus said that] it [= the cosmos] had arisen from fire and [after existing as such] again it catches fire [becoming again fire] according to a certain periodicity, alternately, for all the eternity, and that this takes place according to destiny".[43]

2. The Stoics asserted a doctrine of eternal return which was similar to that of Heraclitus but was more sophisticated and enriched with new and extremely fanciful aspects, according to which there is an alternation of destruction by fire (ἐκπύρωσις) and re-creation (παλιγγενεσία).

J. von Arnim, in his *Stoicorum Veterum Fragmenta*, Volume II, pp. 183-191 (*Conflagrationis et restaurationis mundi aeternae vices*), has gathered a great number of testimonies by different authors regarding the Stoic teaching of the doctrine of eternal return. We shall quote some of them here, indicating the number of the fragments in J. von Arnim's edition in square brackets.

Eusebius, *Praeparatio Evangelica* XV, 18, 1-3 [596], expresses:

'Αρέσκει γὰρ τοῖς Στωϊκοῖς φιλοσόφοις τὴν ὅλην οὐσίαν εἰς πῦρ μεταβάλλειν οἷον εἰς σπέρμα, καὶ πάλιν ἐκ τούτου αὐτὴν ἀποτελεῖσθαι τὴν διακόσμησιν, ὅια τὸ πρότερον ἦν.

"The Stoic philosophers accepted the idea that all the reality transforms itself into fire, as if in its original element, and again from it the orderly arrangement of the universe is accomplished as it was before".

Simplicius, commentary to the *Physics* of Aristotle, p. 480, line 27, H. Diels ed. [603], says:

ἔλεγε γὰρ 'Ηράκλειτος ἐκ πυρὸς πεπερασμένου πάντα εἶναι καὶ εἰς τοῦτο πάντα ἀναλύεσθαι. εἶεν δ' ἂν καὶ οἱ Στωϊκοὶ ταύτης τῆς δόξης.

---

[43] Aëtius I, 3, 11 [22 A 5.]; Aristotle, *De caelo* I, 10, p. 279 b line 12, [22 A 10.]; and Simplicius, commentary to *De caelo* of Aristotle, p. 94 line 4, Heiberg ed. [22 A 10.], contain a similar information on this doctrine of Heraclitus.

"Since Heraclitus said that all the universe comes out from the limited fire and all is dissolved in it. The Stoics also would be of the same opinion".

A very peculiar feature of eternal return as it was conceived of by the Stoics is that, in each new re-creation of the universe, all reality recurs in exactly the same way as previously: individuals and things are reproduced in the same number and form and with the same qualities.[44]

For instance, Nemesius, *De natura hominis*, Chapter XXXVIII, p. 277, Ch. F. Matthae ed. [625], after explaining the process of eternal return, adds:

οἱ δὲ Στωϊκοί φασιν ... ἔσεσθαι γὰρ πάλιν Σωκράτη καὶ Πλάτωνα καὶ ἕκαστον τῶν ἀνθρώπων σύν τοῖς αὐτοῖς καὶ φίλοις καὶ πολίταις· καὶ τὰ αὐτὰ πείσεσθαι καὶ τὰ αὐτὰ μεταχειριεῖσθαι, καὶ πᾶσαν πόλιν καὶ κώμην καὶ ἀγρὸν ὁμοίως ἀποκαθίστασθαι· γίνεσθαι δὲ τὴν ἀποκατάστασιν τοῦ παντὸς οὐχ ἅπαξ, ἀλλὰ πολλάκις· μᾶλλον δὲ εἰς ἄπειρον καὶ ἀτελεύτητον τὰ αὐτὰ ἀποκαθίστασθαι ... οὐδὲν γὰρ ξένον ἔσεσθαι παρὰ τὰ γενόμενα πρότερον, ἀλλὰ πάντα ὡσαύτως ἀπαραλλάκτως ἄχρι καὶ τῶν ἐλαχίστων.

"The Stoics say thus that Socrates and Plato and each man together with the same friends and fellow citizens will exist again; that they will experience the same and they will deal with the same; and that all the cities, villages and countries in the same way [as before] will be re-established; and that the re-establishment of all will take place not only once but many times; and that, moreover, the same things will be re-established *ad infinitum* and forever ... and that there will be nothing different from what has happened before, but all in the same way will be the same up to the slightest".

---

[44] Testimony on this Stoic doctrine is given by the following authors: Lactantius, *Divinae institutiones* VII, 23 [623]; Alexander of Aphrodisias, *Commentary to the First Analytics* of Aristotle, p. 180, line 31, p. 182, line 25, M. Wallis ed. [624]; Nemesius, *De natura hominis*, Chapter XXXVIII, p. 277, Ch. F. Matthae ed. [625]; Origen, *Contra Celsum* IV, 68, Vol. I, p. 338, 3 y IV, 12, Vol. I, p. 282, 9, P. Koetschau ed. [626 y 628]; Simplicius, *Commentary to the Physics* of Aristotle, p. 886, 11, H. Diels ed. [627]; Plutarch, *De defectu oraculorum*, Chapter XXIX [632]; etc.

According to the text of Origen, *Contra Celsum* [626], mentioned in note 44 above, the Stoics say that individuals will not be born again, but that individuals similar to them will be produced: an individual similar to Socrates will be born, and he will marry a woman similar to Xanthippe and will be accused by two persons similar to Anytus and Melytus; and according to the mentioned text by Plutarch [632], for the Stoics there will be infinite Zeuses, Suns, Moons, Apollos, Artemises and Poseidons in the infinite periods of the universes.[45]

3. Aristotle accepts the theory of eternal return in the past and in the future, for the incorruptible and eternal superior world (heavens and planets) (ἄνω καὶ μέχρι σελήνης) as well as for the sub-lunar world (κάτω σελήνης) as a consequence of the eternal circular movement of the superior world. That movement of the superior world governs the movement and the tasks of the inferior sub-lunar world. Also, thanks to this circular movement of the superior world, the position of those heavens and planets above and the position of the sub-lunar world below also periodically return to the same position that they had before the beginning of the concluding cycle. In opposition to the idea of Heraclitus and that of the Stoics, the eternal return of Aristotle does not involve alternative creations and destructions.

These ideas are expressed in the texts of Aristotle which we shall now present.

In *Physics* VIII, p. 267 b, lines 8-9, he refers to "the movement of the whole": ἡ τοῦ ὅλου κίνησις, and in *De Caelo* II, 4, p. 287 a, lines 11 and 12, he affirms that that movement is circular:

ἔτι δὲ ἐπεὶ φαίνεται καὶ ὑπόκειται κύκλῳ περι φέρεσθαι τὸ πᾶν ...

"Since it is evident and it is established that the whole turns in circle ..."

---

[45] Cf. E. Zeller, *Die Philosophie der Griechen*, Vol. III, 1, pp. 154-159; and Carlos Lévy, *Les Philosophies hellénistiques*, p. 151.

The movement of the whole, of the universe, is eternal (*Physics* VIII, p. 251 b, line 13, and 252 a, lines 3-4: δῆλον ὡς ἔστιν ἀΐδιος κίνησις· "It is evident that the movement is eternal", cf. *ibidem*, p. 259 b, line 25);

indestructible (*ibidem*, p. 251 b, lines 28-29: ... ἄφθαρτον εἶναι τήν κίνησιν: "...that the movement is indestructible");

even (*ibidem*, p. 267 b, line 4: ὁμαλὴς αὕτη: "it is even");

continuous (*ibidem*, p. 259 a, line 16: ἀνάγκη καὶ συνεχῆ εἶναι· "it is necessary that it be continuous", cf. *ibidem*, p. 258, line 10);

everlasting and immortal (*ibidem*, p. 259 b, line 25: ἄπαυστός τις καὶ ἀθάνατος κίνησις: "an everlasting and immortal movement").

The circular or cyclic movement is incessant: *Metaphysics* XI, p. 1072 a, lines 21 and 22:

> καὶ ἔστι τι ἀεὶ κινούμενον κίνησιν ἄπαυστον, αὕτη δ' ἡ κύκλῳ. "And there is something that always moves with an incessant movement, and this is the cyclic [movement]".

In *De generatione et corruptione* II, 11, p. 338 a, line 10-b, line 4, besides affirming that the movement of the whole is circular, Aristotle expresses that this movement is eternal and constant and that it "returns" [to its point of origin of course]:

> διὸ ἀνάγκη κύκλῳ εἶναι. ἀντιστρέφειν ἄρα ἀνάγκη ἔσται, οἷον εἰ τοδὶ ἐξ ἀνάγκης, καὶ τὸ πρότερον ἄρα· ἀλλὰ μὴν εἰ τοῦτο, καὶ τὸ ὕστερον ἀνάγκη γενέσθαι. καὶ τοῦτο ἀεὶ δὴ συνεχῶς· ... ἐν τῇ κύκλῳ ἄρα κινήσει καὶ γενέσει ἐστὶ τὸ ἐξ ἀνάγκης ἁπλῶς· καὶ εἴτε κύκλῳ, ἀνάγκη ἕκαστον γίνεσθαι καὶ γεγονέναι, καὶ εἰ ἀνάγκη, ἡ τούτων γένεσις κύκλῳ. ταῦτα μὲν δὴ εὐλόγως, ἐπεὶ ἀΐδιος καὶ ἄλλως ἐφάνη ἡ κύκλῳ κίνησις καὶ ἡ τοῦ οὐρανοῦ, ὅτι ταῦτα ἐξ ἀνάγκης γίνεται καὶ ἔσται, ὅσαι ταύτης κινήσεις καὶ ὅσαι διὰ ταύτην· εἰ γὰρ τὸ κύκλῳ κινούμενον ἀεί τι κινεῖ, ἀνάγκη καὶ τούτων κύκλῳ εἶναι τὴν κίνησιν, οἷον τῆς ἄνω φορᾶς οὔσης ὁ ἥλιος κύκλῳ ὡδί, ἐπεὶ δ' οὕτως, αἱ ὦραι διὰ τοῦτο κύκλῳ γίνονται καὶ ἀνακάμπτουσιν, τούτων δ' οὕτω γινομένων πάλιν τὰ ὑπὸ τούτων.

"Consequently [= because of the reasons already expounded] it is necessary that [the movement] be cyclic, and then it will be necessary that it return [to its starting point]. If this [happens] by necessity [at present], then also [it necessarily had to happen] before; moreover if this is [so], it is necessary that it happen in the future, and this unceasingly for ever ... For, as regards the cyclic movement and creation, to happen by necessity is an absolute fact. And then, if [the movement and the creation are] cyclic, it is necessary that everything come into being and have come into being, and, if [this is] necessary, [also] that their creation be cyclic. And [all] this is according to reason, that - since the cyclic movement and that of heaven besides [being necessary] have been shown [in *Physics* VIII, 7-9] to be eternal - these things happen at present and should happen in the future by necessity, [i.e.] all the movements of this [creation] and all the [movements] that take place because of it [= creation]. For if what moves in circle always moves other things, it is necessary that the movement of these [other] things be [also] circular. For instance, if the above movement exists, [then] the sun [moves] here in circle; and being so, seasons for this reason are produced and return in cycles. And if [upper] things happen in this way [i.e. move in circle], at their turn things that are below them [also move in circle]".

Of the attributes of the circular movement, the one that interests us is that of the "return". The text of *De generatione et corruptione* II, 11, p. 338 a, line 10-b, line 4 (already quoted) refers several times to the "return" of the movement. In *Physics* VIII, p. 264 b, lines 27-28, it is said that the circular movement is the only perfect one, because it returns to its starting point, and this is what allows it to be continuous:

ἡ δὲ τοῦ κύκλου συνάπτει, καὶ ἔστι μόνη τέλειος.
"The circular [movement] unites [the end with the beginning], and is the only perfect".

In *Physics* VIII, p. 264 b, lines 10-11, Aristotle asserts:
ἡ δᾶ ἐπὶ τῆς περιφεροῦς ἔσται μία καὶ συνεχής ... τὸ γὰρ ἐκ τοῦ Α κινούμενον ἅμα κινήσεται εἰς τὸ Α κατὰ τὴν αὐτὴν πρόθεσιν.
"The circular [movement] will be one and continuous ... since what moves from [the point] A equally will move towards [the point] A according to the same purpose".

Cf. *ibidem*, p. 262 a, lines 16-17.

The movements of the superior world influence and govern the sub-lunar world: *Meteorologica* I, 2, p. 339 a, lines 21-24:

> ἔστι δ' ἐξ ἀνάγκης συνεχής πως οὗτος ταῖς ἄνω φοραῖς, ὥστε πᾶσαν αὐτοῦ τὴν δύναμιν κυβερνᾶσθαι ἐκεῖθεν.
>
> "This [world] is in some way necessarily connected with the movements [that take place in the world] above, in such a way that all its power is governed therefrom".

The sub-lunar world then imitates the cyclic movement of the world which is above and beyond the moon. This text and the theory it expresses will be the origin and the foundation of the astrological beliefs that so much importance would have in the Western world, in Greece and in Europe. Cf. Pierre Duhem, *Le Système du Monde*, Tome I, p. 164.[46]

4. Many centuries after the Stoics, in a few texts edited by Michel Fichant in his book *Gottfried Wilhelm LEIBNIZ, De l'horizon de la doctrine humaine (1693)* 'Αποκατάστασις πάντων *(La Restitution Universelle) (1715)*, Leibniz refers to the "restitution" or "restoration" of all things in a way very similar to the peculiar Stoic doctrine of eternal return as exposed by Nemesius, Origen and other authors.

In two paragraphs of a text written by Leibniz, text VI of Fichant (Leibniz' Briefwechsel in Hannover Library 705, folio 72 recto), we find an evident acceptance by Leibniz of the 'Αποκατάστασις πάντων in its extreme form. But these two paragraphs of the text, are absent from the new version given by Leibniz himself in text VII of Fichant (Leibniz' Briefwechsel in Hannover Library 705, folio 73 recto). This makes it difficult to decide whether Leibniz adhered to that doctrine or not, abandoned it after having adhered to it at first, merely considered it an interesting

[46] On the theories of time in the Greek philosophy after Aristotle see the quoted work by Pierre Duhem, Tome I, Chapter V, sections I-VII, pp. 242-297. Cf. Luis González Reimann, also already quoted, for interesting approximations between Greek and Indian theories on the "Great Year".

hypothesis or even adhered to it but for some reason preferred not to express it.

After a few numerical reflections, Leibniz writes on page 62 (text VI of Fichant):

> *Itaque si genus humanum in statu qualis nunc est per annos plus quam N duret, necesse est redire priores annales Historias. Q. E. D. Itaque Leopoldum et Ludovicum, et Guilielmum et Georgium nostrum cum suis gestis intra hoc temporis spatium redire necesse est.*

> "Thus if mankind lasts in the state in which it is now more than N years [= an infinite number of years], it is necessary that the previous yearly Histories return. Thus it is necessary that Leopold [I, Emperor of Germany, died in 1705] and Louis [XIV, King of France, died in 1715], William [III, King of England, died in 1702] and Georges [Louis of Hannover, who would become King of England, died in 1727] return with their actions in this space of time".

On page 64 (of the same text VI of Fichant) he adds:

> *Hinc jam sequitur: si genus humanum satis diu duret in eo qui nunc est statu, affore tempus quo singulorum etiam vita minutatim per easdem circumstantias redeat. Ego ipse verbi gratia sedens in urbe Hanovera dicta, ad Leinam fluvium sita, occupatus in Brunsvicensi Historia, scribens literas ad amicos eosdem, sensibus iisdem.*

> "Hence follows: if mankind lasts enough time in the state in which it is now, a time will come when the life of the individuals will return passing exactly by the same circumstances - for instance, myself sitting in the town called Hannover, located by the river Leine, dedicated to the History of Brunswick, writing letters to the same friends, with the same meaning".

It is certain that Leibniz did not adhere to the doctrine of 'Αποκατάστασις in its religious salvific form as developed by Johann Wilhem Petersen his contemporary, to whom we shall refer afterwards. Leibniz expresses himself in a very favourable way about Petersen and had correspondence with him. Cf. the quoted work of Fichant, pp. 22-24.[47]

---

[47] On the apocatastasis doctrine, besides the edition of M. Fichant (especially the bibliographical note 13 and pages 17-18 of the Introduction,

We thus have four models of the doctrine of eternal return: evolution and involution of Primordial Matter (Sāṃkhya), conflagrations and re-creations (Heraclitus), periodical conflagrations and re-creations of the same universe with the same or similar individuals, things, events, and behaviors (Stoics, Leibniz [?]) and the circular movement of the cosmic sphere *ad aeternitatem* (Aristotle) – four efforts of human imagination and reason with which to describe the reality in which we live in such a way as to give a satisfactory answer to the human anxiety to find solutions to the questions it poses.

Let us add here two ideas related to the "eternal return": one has to do with the Sāṃkhya theory (referred to in the previous section) that the *involution* takes place following in an inverted direction the same stages of the *evolution,* theory which also appears in Proclus; the other idea could be called "the unavoidable return to the beginning", and appears very early in the context of Christian thought: the doctrine of religious or salvific 'Αποκατάστασις.

Evolution. Involution

5. In Proclus the process of evolution and involution that partakes of all the same stages in the direct and in the inverted order, is connected in some way with the theory of the "eternal return", as it is a process of returning to a starting point. In his Treatise *Elements of Theology,* Proposition 38, Proclus affirms:

---

and the notes and the "Postface", pp. 125-210) see the articles "Apocatastase" by Jean-Yves Lacoste, in *Dictionnaire critique de théologie,* Paris: Quadrige / PUF, 1998, pp. 70-72; "Apokatastasis" by G. Bien / H. Schwabl, in *Historisches Wörterbuch,* Vol. I, col. 440-441, and "Eterno retorno" and "Universalismo", in J. Ferrater Mora, *Diccionario de Filosofia,* Vol. II, pp. 1140-1141, and Vol. IV, pp. 3608-3609, respectively; and "Universalism" by James Edwin Odgers, in *Encyclopaedia of Religion and Ethics,* Vol. 12, pp. 529-535, especially pp. 530-535, in which there is a reference to the third meaning of the term "universalism": "*the final Salvation of all mankind*", and on J.W. Petersen, *ibidem,* p. 531.

Πᾶν τὸ προϊὸν ἀπό τινων πλειόνων αἰτίων, δι' ὅσων πρόεισι, διὰ τοσούτων καὶ ἐπιστρέφεται· καὶ πᾶσα ἐπιστροφὴ διὰ τῶν αὐτῶν, δι' ὧν καὶ ἡ πρόοδος.

"All that comes forth from a plurality of causes, through as many [causes] as it came forth, through so many does it return. And all return is through the same [causes or stages] through which was the coming forth".

Dodds, Proclus' editor, comments this Proposition in the following terms:

"The stages of the return repeat those of the procession, but in the reverse order: thus, e.g. body proceeds from the One through Intelligence and Soul, and reverts to it through Soul and Intelligence: cf. Propos. 128, 129".

Salvific 'Αποκατάστασις

6. We shall refer now to the doctrine of the 'Αποκατάστασις in the religious, salvific meaning, as conceived by Johann Wilhem Petersen (1649-1727), a prominent dignitary of the Lutheran Church in Germany, who between 1701 and 1710 compiled in a book in three volumes, entitled Μυστήριον ἀποκαταστάσεως πάντων *oder das Geheimniss der Wiederbringung aller Dinge*, a series of works on the subject of "the restauration of all things", among other controversial subjects of his epoch.

This doctrine of Petersen is inserted in the current of Christian thought called "Universalism". According to this doctrine, the whole of mankind would be reintegrated into the moral and spiritual perfection which it possessed before Adam's fall, what implied the final Salvation for everybody. In the opinion of some members of this current of thought Salvation would extend even to the demons.

In a general way Universalism and with it the doctrine of the religious Αποκατάστασις had an extensive diffusion in Protestant countries as Germany and in the Anglo-Saxon world: England, Scotland and North America (United States and Canada).

This doctrine of Petersen was condemned by the German Church in 1692 and he was removed from his office in the same year.

7. Eleven centuries before, Pope Virgilius (537/540-555) has condemned a similar thesis by Origen, which was probably the source of that of Petersen.

The doctrine of Origen receives the name of *Restitutio* in the Latin translation by Rufinus of Origen's treatise *De Principiis*, preserved in its integrity only in that Latin translation and, in a fragmentary form, in Greek. This doctrine is mentioned in several passages of the Treatise, especially in Chapter 6 of Book I, pp. 214-230, H. Görgemanns and H. Karpp ed. (= pp. 78-85 Koetschau ed.).

The condemnation of Origen's thesis said:

> Εἴ τις λέγει ἢ ἔχει, πρόσκαιρον εἶναι, τὴν τῶν δαιμόνων καὶ ἀσεβῶν ἀνθρώπων κόλασιν, καὶ τέλος κατά τινα χρόνον αὐτὴν ἕξειν, ἤγουν ἀποκατάστασιν γενέσθαι δαιμόνων, ἢ ἀσεβῶν ἀνθρώπων, ἀνάθεμα ἔστω.
>
> "If somebody says or believes that the chastisement of demons and impious men is temporary, and that it will have an end after some time, that is to say that there will be an apocatastasis [= doctrine of the final restoration of all sinful beings to God and to the state of blessedness] of demons and impious men, *anathema sit* [let him be cursed]".[48]

The apocatastasis imagined by Petersen is similar to the inclusivist and compassionate Buddhist Mahāyānist thesis that at the end of time all living beings without exception, even the most perverse and depraved ones (*icchāntikas*), will be saved, acquire Supreme Enlightenment and become *Buddhas.*[49]

---

[48] Cf. Henricus Denzinger, *Enchiridion Symbolorum*, p. 97, § 211 can. 9.

[49] Cf. Ming-Wood, Liu, "The Doctrine of the Buddha-Nature in the Mahāyāna *Mahāparinirvāṇasūtra*", in *The Journal of the International Association of Buddhist Studies*, Vol. V, No. 2, 1982, pp. 63-94 (Spanish version in *Revista de Estudios Budistas*, No. 6, Octubre 1993-Marzo 1994, pp. 9-46), and "The Problem of the *icchantikas* in the Mahāyāna *Mahāparinirvāṇasūtra", ibidem*, Vol. VII, No. 1, 1984, pp. 57-82; and F. Tola and C. Dragonetti, "Aportes desde la Filosofía de la India: Multilateralidad, Perspectivismo, Tolerancia, Inclusivismo, rechazo de todo Etnocentrismo", in *América*, Vol. IX, Córdoba, Argentina: Editorial Alejandro Korn, 2003 (Proceedings of the International Congress of Philosophy, held at Cordoba, November 2003.

IV.22 Proofs of the existence of non-manifested Matter (*pradhāna*)

In the treatises of the Sāṃkhya system, we can generally find a great preoccupation with "proof", i.e. to demonstrate through rational arguments the existence of diverse entities which are postulated in the course of the exposition of the ideas and which are not evident by themselves. This is how it, for example, happens in the case of the existence of the *Puruṣa*, the non-manifested *Prakṛti*, the *Ahaṃkāra*, the *Tanmātras* and the *Antaḥkaraṇa*.

As an example of this exposition, we have selected the case of proof of the existence of Primordial Matter. In *kārikā* 15 of the *Sāṃkhyakārikās*, we can find five arguments which are very synthetically expressed and aim at demonstrating the existence of Primordial Matter (*pradhāna*) in its non-manifested aspect (*avyakta*) because Matter in its manifested (*vyakta*) aspect does not need a demonstration since its existence is evident by itself through the perception of the components which constitute empirical reality. We shall now give the development of these five arguments:

1. *bhedānāṃ parimāṇāt*: "*by reason of the measure proper to the particular objects* (non-manifested Primordial Matter exists as a cause although it is not perceived)".

According to the commentary of Gauḍapāda, experience (*loke*, "in the world") reveals that, wherever there is a creating or producing agent (*kartṛ*), this agent is seen to have recourse to measure (*parimāṇa*) in the sense that, to accomplish his work, he uses portions of prime matter endowed with measure, delimited, finite, or to which he imposes a measure. For instance, the potter makes jars possessing a certain measure, using lumps of clay which also possess measure, or on which he imposes a measure, and which are "extracted" from a prime matter (clay), which lacks measure. Without that clay, he would not be able to carry out his task. Similarly, the intellect, the individuation principle, the five subtle elements, the eleven sensory organs and the five great elements (which constitute the totality of empirical reality) must be produced by *delimitation* from something, a Primordial Matter, which is thus its prime matter and its material cause. This argument is founded in the idea, confirmed by the experience of the senses, that every thing (effect) implies the existence of a material cause of which it is made through a process of "partition" or "delimitation".

2. *samanvayāt*: "*by reason of the essential connexion* (or correlation or coherence or consistence) (between the effect and its cause) (non-manifested Primordial Matter exists a as cause although it is not perceived)".

In order to explain this argument, the commentary of Gauḍapāda has recourse to the following example, which is also based on the observation of the senses (*iha loke prasiddhir dṛṣṭā* : "in this world the demonstration is evident"): one sees a boy engaged in a rite which exclusively corresponds to brahmins, and one infers that his parents, who gave birth to him, are brahmins. In order to understand the example, it is necessary to take into account that, according to the Hindu concept of the castes, a *brahmin* son can only be born from *brahmin* parents. If there is an effect with determinate characteristics, there must be a cause of that effect which is essentially coherent with it: this is a consequence of the Sāṃkhya theory of causality which postulates that the effect is in the cause and that both are essentially identical. Therefore, according to common experience exemplified by the brahmin boy and his parents, and by applying the theory of causality mentioned above, the material cause of the intellect and the other products, which are possessed of unique characteristics, has to be a cause possessing the same characteristics as these products.

3. *śaktitaḥ pravṛtteś ca*: "*by reason of the activity depending upon the efficiency or capacity* (non-manifested Primordial Matter exists as a cause although it is not perceived)".

The present argument is also based on everyday experience (*iha*, "here, in the world"): any creating or producing agent can create or produce *only* that for which it is qualified. Thus, the potter, who uses clay (the material cause of the jar) as prime matter, is able to make a jar but he is not able to produce a cloth or a chariot. His productive capacity is conditioned by the capacity (*śakti*) of the matter he uses. Through reasoning similar to that used in the previous arguments, one has to infer that the material cause of the intellect etc., admitted by the reasoning of the first argument and provided - according to the second argument - of the same characteristics as their effects, must be possessed of the capacity or efficiency consisting in the fact that the intellect etc. can be produced from it.

4. *kāraṇakāryavibhāgāt*: "*by reason of the difference between cause and effect* (non-manifested Primordial Matter exists as a cause although it is not perceived)".

Cause and effect are different in the sense that both have specific functions which belong exclusively to each of them: "it makes, so it is cause" (*karotīti kāraṇam*), "it is made, so it is effect" (*kriyata iti kāryam*); a jar, the effect of the potter's activity applied to the prime matter of clay, can serve as a recipient, but not so the clay; also, clay can produce a jar, but a jar cannot produce clay.

The difference consisting in the diversity of the functions does not affect the essential identity of the cause and the effect affirmed by the theory of causality, *satkāryavāda*, to which Sāṃkhya adheres: the effect can exist in the cause and therefore be identical with it, but both are different inasmuch as the function of the cause is *to produce* and that of the effect is *to be produced*, and inasmuch as the effect (a plant) is able to do things that the cause (seed) cannot, and *vice versa*.

To return to the initial explanation, we must apply the remarks concerning the jar as an effect and the clay as a cause for empirical reality. Empirical reality cannot be the material cause itself; it has to have a material cause different from it (*asti vibhaktaṃ tat kāraṇaṃ yasya vibhāga idaṃ vyaktam iti*: "There exists as something different that cause of which this manifested [reality] is the separate and different [product]"), also provided with a specific capacity.

5. *avibhāgād vaiśvarūpyasya*: "*by reason of the indifferentiation which belongs to multiplicity* (non-manifested Primordial Matter exists as a cause although it is not perceived)".

All of the things that constitute the multiple and diverse empirical reality possess common qualities as indicated under Section *Attributes of Primordial Matter* as proper to the *Prakṛti* in its *vyakta* (manifested) form, like "caused", "impermanent", etc. In this sense it can be said that there is no difference between things in the multiple and diverse empirical reality. Consequently, a common material cause has to be admitted for that multiplicity, and this common material cause produces the identity of the qualities.

The material cause whose existence must be accepted by the force of the five arguments presented is given the name of *Pradhāna* or *Prakṛti avyakta.* Its attributes are those indicated in relation to the arguments: coherence with its effect (empirical reality), the capacity to originate that effect, the possessing of functions different from those of the effect and also the attributes enumerated as belonging to the *Prakṛti avyakta* the Section *Attributes of Primordial Matter*, where their basis is also pointed out.

It is convenient here to apply the commentary of Aniruddha on *sūtra* I, 137 of the *Sāṃkhyasūtras* to the present case of demonstration of existence of Matter as a cause. The commentary asks whether that cause, Matter, *Pradhāna,* is an effect of another cause or not, and answers that it is not, because if it were an effect, the same question would have to be asked in relation to it, and so on *ad infinitum,* and we would have the logical defect of the *anavasthā* or *regressus ad infinitum.* For this reason, concludes Aniruddha, the *Pradhāna* cannot be the effect of anything else, and not being an effect of anything else, it is the first or original cause (*mūlakāraṇa*).

Let us add that, as the Sāṃkhya does not admit the existence of a God or creative principle and the arising of empirical reality is due to the evolution of Primordial Matter itself, which acts according to its own laws, Primordial Matter is not only the material cause of its products (intellect, etc.) but can also be considered as its efficient cause. In the analogy developed in Gauḍapāda's commentary, the Primordial Matter corresponds both to the clay and to the potter.

IV.23 Remarks on the previous subject: Proofs of the existence of God in the West

In the Sāṃkhya demonstration of the existence of Primordial Matter, we can find a few elements which also appear in Aristotle's Theory of Causality and in St. Thomas' Proofs of the Existence of God.

That the Sāṃkhya system presents for demonstrating the existence of Primordial Matter proofs, which possess remarkable similarities with the proofs utilized by Saint Thomas for demonstrating the existence of God may seem to be a paradoxical and amazing fact. Nevertheless, let us point out that in the *Opus postumum* of Kant is found a similar case, to which refers Vittorio Mathieu of the Universitā di Torino, in his article "L'argomento ontologico per dimostrare l'esitenza dell'etere nell' "Opus postumum" di Kant", in *L' argomento ontologico*, p. 271 in the following way:

> *"In his projected work on the passage from the metaphysics of nature to physics, whose fragments are known under the name of Opus postumum, Kant does not return except in a cursory way to the ontological argument, whose refutation takes for granted. The importance of the Opus is rather in the paradox of using an argument that, by its form, is exactly <ontological> (even if Kant does not call it explicitly with that name) in order to demonstrate* a priori *the existence, not of God, but of the <caloric>, or <ether>, <or as one wishes to call it>".*

The same Mathieu comments on pp. 272-273:

> *"That it is an <ontological> argument is confirmed by the assertion that <here, but only in this case, it is licit to say* a posse ad esse valet consequentia> *(XXI, 592, 12, 10: Spring 1799), i.e. the consequence, invalid in the case of God, is valid in the case of the ether, or caloric ... It is sufficient* to think *the concept of ether in order to know that it necessarily exists".*

From the oddity of this situation - according to Mathieu, p. 273 - did not escape Kant himself (XXI, 538, 3 y XXII, 615, 9, etc.).

Coming back to our subject, let us indicate some ideas common to Sāṃkhya (in relation to the existence of Primordial Matter), to Aristotle (in relation to his theory of causality), and to Saint Thomas (in relation to the proofs of the existence of God):

1. The need for an efficient cause (in the West) and a material cause (in the Sāṃkhya).

Aristotle, *Metaphysica* VIII, section 8, p. 1049 b, lines 28-29, asserts the general principle:

> ἅπαν τὸ γιγνόμενον γίγνεται ἔκ τινός τι καὶ ὑπό τινος.
>
> "All that comes into being comes to be something out of something [*material cause*] and by means of something [*efficient cause*]".

In the second proof of the existence of God offered by St. Thomas in *Summa Theologiae* I, 2, 3, we can find the idea that every effect requires a cause to produce it, i.e. an efficient cause (agent) without any reference to the material cause:

> *Respondeo ... Secunda via est ex ratione causae efficientis. Invenimus enim in istis sensibilibus esse ordinem causarum efficientium.*
>
> "The second method [of the demonstration of the existence of God] is by reason of the efficient cause, since we find that in sensible things there exists an order of efficient causes".

The Sāṃkhya postulates the necessary existence of a material cause for the production of anything, which in the case of the Primordial Matter is also the efficient cause.

2. The impossibility of the *regressus ad infinitum* (in both the West and the Sāṃkhya).

Aristotle in *Metaphysica* I, ʼΕΛΑΤΤΟΝ, section 2, p. 994 a, line 1-b, line 31, maintains another important general principle: the impossibility of a *regressus ad infinitum* for any kind of cause, including material, efficient, final and formal causes. In this text, Aristotle does not relate this principle to the notion of an efficient cause in order to demonstrate the existence of God, although he utilizes this principle in his expositions on movement which conclude the necessary existence of a first motor (for instance in *Physics* VII, p. 242 a, lines 15-20; p. 242 b, lines 32-34) which, in Book XI, Chapter 7 of *Metaphysica*, p. 1072 a, line 19; p. 1073 a, line 13, is identified with God and exalted as such.

St. Thomas, *Summa Theologiae* I, 2, 3, *Respondeo ... Secunda via est ...*, in his second proof of the existence of God, starts from the Aristotelic principle, which he enunciates thus:

> *Non autem est possibile quod in causis efficientibus procedatur in infinitum.*
>
> "Now, it is not possible to proceed *ad infinitum* in the efficient causes",

in order to reach the conclusion that there must be a *prima causa efficiens*: "first efficient cause", "that all call God": *quam omnes Deum nominant.*

This principle which, in Sanskrit, is given the name of *anavasthā*, is employed by Aniruddha in his commentary (previously quoted) on the *Sāṃkhyasūtras* I, 137 in relation to argument number one of the five arguments offered by *kārikā* 15 of the *Sāṃkhyakārikās* in order to demonstrate the existence of Primordial Matter.

3. It is impossible for the effect to be the cause of itself (in the West and in the Sāṃkhya), and this demands the existence of a cause different from the effect..

Aristotle in *Magna Moralia* II, 8, p. 1207 b, lines 7-8, expresses this idea:

> ἡ γὰρ αἰτία καὶ οὗ ἐστὶν αἰτία ἄλλο ἐστί.
>
> "Because the cause and that of which it is the cause are different things".

This idea is adopted by St. Thomas in his second proof of the existence of God:

> *nec est possibile, quod aliquid sit causa efficiens sui ipsius.*
>
> "It is not possible that something be the efficient cause of itself".

In the Sāṃkhya system, this idea appears in the fourth argument of *kārikā* 15 of the *Sāṃkhyakārikās*.

4. The empirical ascertainment of a fact as the basis of the argumentation (in the West and in the Sāṃkhya).

It is interesting to remark that, in the arguments of the Sāṃkhya used to demonstrate the existence of Primordial Matter as well as in the proof of the existence of God in St. Thomas, the argumentation starts from the observation of the common sensible things, i.e. from factual evidence.

In his commentary, Gauḍapāda uses (in the first argument) the words *loke*, "in the world", *dṛṣṭam*, "it is seen", "it is evident", and the example of the *kulāla*, "the potter"; (in the second argument) *iha loke*, "in this world", *dṛṣṭā*, "it is seen", "it is evident", *dṛṣṭvā*, "seeing", and he resorts to the example of the boy performing a rite; (in the third argument) *iha*, "here", and he resorts also to the example of the *kulāla*; (in the fourth argument) he uses the example of the jar and the term *dṛṣṭvā*, "seeing"; (in the fifth argument) there is a reference to the five material great elements (*mahābhūta*) (*pṛthivī*, "the earth", etc.) and the example of the milk and the curds.

Similarly, St. Thomas uses the following expressions: in the first proof (I, 2, 3, *Respondeo...*) *certum est enim, et sensu constat*: "It is true, and is ascertained by the senses"; in the second proof (*ibidem*) *invenimus enim in istis sensibilibus*: "since we find in this sensible things..."; in the third proof (*ibidem*) *invenimus enim in rebus*: "since we find in the things..."; in the fourth proof (*ibidem*) *quarta via sumitur ex gradibus qui in rebus inveniuntur*: "the fourth method is taken from the positions that are found in things..."; and in the fifth proof (*ibidem*) *videmus enim*: "since we see..."

5. Recourse to the principle of causality (in the West and in the Sāṃkhya).

A characteristic feature of the Sāṃkhya proofs for demonstrating the existence of Primordial Matter as well as of the argumentation of St. Thomas for demonstrating the existence of God is the use of notions and principles, which are related to causality. All of the argumentation of the Sāṃkhya and that of St. Thomas have to do with the theory of causality.[50]

IV.24 An interesting marginal note: The "Ontological Proof" in the West and the Distinction *in intellectu / in re* in Bhartṛhari

The "ontological proof" in the West

In the West there existed another proof of the existence of God, already mentioned before, which has no correspondence at all in Indian philosophy that developed diverse proofs of the existence of the *Īśvara* (God). On the proofs of the existence of God in Nyāya and Vaiśeṣika systems of Indian philosophy, see C. Bulcke, *The Theism in Nyaya-Vaisesika,* Chapter VI.

We refer to the so-called "ontological proof" or "proof of Saint Anselm" or "cartesian proof", which had numerous defenders among outstanding philosophers that admit it although some of them with variants and diverse grounds: Alexander of Hales (1185-1245), Bonaventura (1221-1274), William of de Auxerre (died in 1231), Duns Scotus (1266-1308), Descartes (1596-1650), Leibniz (1646-1716), Malebranche (1638-1715), Hegel (1770-1831); and also opposers, who reject it as Gaunilo (a monk in an Abbey near Tours, who died in 1083), Saint Thomas Aquinas (1225-1274), Gassendi (1592-1655), Locke (1632-1704), Hume (1711-1776), and Kant (1724-1804) for instance. A. Sertillanges (1863-1948), one of the most active and influential modern neo-Thomist philosophers according to Ferrater Mora, in his book *Les grandes thèses de la philosophie thomiste,* p. 55, points out that the evidence of God has been looked for by Saint Anselm "more philosophically" but "a

---

[50] Cf. É. Gilson, *Le Thomisme, Introduction au système de Saint Thomas d'Aquin,* p. 91.

little sophistically" with the inclusion of the existence in the notion of God itself.

We bring up here the "ontological proof", because it gives us the opportunity to indicate an interesting point of coincidence between the argument of rejection of this proof utilized in the West by the philosophers that were opposed to it, and a principle of Indian thought expounded by Bhartṛhari, the great Indian philosopher of language; and also because it gives a good idea of the nature of the *cultural dogmas* or *principia prima*, which in general are at the basis of philosophical thinking. Let us say that the bold type in all the texts and translations that we quote in what follows is ours.

The ontological proof was expounded by Saint Anselm (1035-1109) in his Treatise *Proslogion*, Chapter II, Les Éditions du Cerf ed., 1986, pp. 244-246:

> *Et quidem credimus te esse aliquid quo nihil maius cogitare possit. An ergo non est aliqua talis natura, quia <dixit insipiens in corde suo: non est Deus>? Sed certe ipse idem insipiens, cum audit hoc ipsum quod dico: 'aliquid quo maius nihil cogitari potest', intelligit quod audit; et quod intelligit* ***in intellectu*** *eius est, etiam si non intelligat illud esse. Aliud enim est rem esse* ***in intellectu****, aliud intelligere rem esse. Nam cum pictor praecogitat quae facturus est, habet quidem* ***in intellectu****, sed nondum intelligit esse quod nondum fecit. Cum vero iam pinxit, et habet in intellectu et intelligit esse quod iam fecit. Convincitur ergo etiam insipiens esse vel* ***in intellectu*** *aliquid quo nihil maius cogitari potest, quia hoc cum audit intelligit, et quidquid intelligitur* ***in intellectu*** *est. Et certe id quo maius cogitari nequit, non potest esse* ***in solo intellectu****. Si enim vel* ***in solo intellectu*** *est, potest cogitari esse et* ***in re****, quod maius est. Si ergo id quo maius cogitari non potest, est* ***in solo intellectu****: id ipsum quo maius cogitari non potest est quo maius cogitari potest. Sed certe hoc esse non potest. Existit ergo procul dubio aliquid quo maius cogitari non valet,* ***et in intellectu et in re****.*

"And indeed we believe that You are something greater than which nothing can be thought. Or such a nature does not exist, because <the fool said in his heart: God does not exist>? [Psalm 14, 1; 53, 1]. But certainly when this same fool hears what I say: 'Something greater than which nothing can be thought', he understands what he hears; and what he understands exists **in** his **intellect**, even if he does not know that that exists. For one thing is that the object exists **in intellect**, and quite another to know that that object exists [**in reality**]. When a painter for example thinks in advance what he is going to do, he certainly has **in** his **intellect** what he has not yet done, but he knows that [that] does not yet exist [**in reality**]. But once he has painted it, he has **in** his **intellect** what he already did, and knows that it exists [**in reality**]. So even the fool is convinced that something greater than which nothing can be thought actually exists **in** his **intellect**, because he understands this when he hears [it], and whatever is understood exists **in** the **intellect**. And certainly that something greater than which nothing can be thought cannot exist only **in intellect**. For if it actually exists only **in intellect**, it can be thought that [that] exists also **in reality** - what would be greater than [that which exists only **in intellect**]. Consequently, if that greater than which nothing can be thought exists only **in intellect**, [then] that greater than which nothing can be thought is [at the same time] something greater than which something can be thought. But that is clearly impossible [since it is contradictory]. Therefore, there is no doubt that something greater than which nothing can be thought exists **in intellect as well as in reality**".

1. The monk Gaunilo, in his small Treatise *Quid ad haec respondeat quidam pro insipiente*, included on pp. 288-297 of First Volume of the quoted edition of the works of Saint Anselm, refutes the arguments of Saint Anselm. Gaunilo begins synthesizing Saint Anselm's reasoning for demonstrating the existence of God:

> *Dubitanti utrum sit vel neganti quod sit aliqua talis natura, qua nihil maius cogitari possit, cum esse illam hinc dicitur primo probari, quod ipse negans vel ambigens de illa iam habeat eam* ***in intellectu****, cum audiens illam dici id quod dicitur intelligit; deinde quia quod intelligit, necesse est ut non* ***in*** *solo* ***intellectu*** *sed etiam* ***in re*** *sit, et hoc ita probatur quia maius est esse et* ***in re*** *quam* ***in*** *solo* ***intellectu****, et si illud* ***in*** *solo est* ***intellectu****, maius illo erit quidquid etiam* ***in re*** *fuerit, ac sic maius omnibus minus erit aliquo et non erit maius omnibus, quod utique repugnat; et ideo necesse est ut maius omnibus, quod esse iam probatum est* ***in intellectu****, non* ***in*** *solo* ***intellectu*** *sed et* ***in re*** *sit, quoniam aliter maius omnibus esse non poterit ...* (p. 288).

"Someone who either doubts or denies that there is any such a nature greater than which nothing can be thought is told that it is proved that it exists, first because he himself, on denying or doubting about it [= that nature], has already it **in intellect**, since on hearing it spoken of he understands what is said; further, because what he understands must exist not only **in intellect**, but also **in reality**. And this is proved thus: since to exist [**in intellect** and] also **in reality** is greater than [to exist] only **in intellect**, and if that [= the mentioned nature] exists only **in intellect**, [then] greater than that will be whatever also would exist **in reality**. And thus the greater than anything else will be less than something else and will not be greater than everything else [as it has been claimed], which is of course a contradiction. And so what is greater than everything else, which has already been proved to exist **in intellect**, must exist not only **in intellect** but also **in reality**, since otherwise it could not be greater than everything else".

Gaunilo makes then the following remark:

Nonne et quaecumque falsa ac nullo prorsus modo in seipsis existentia in intellectu habere similiter dici possem, cum ea dicente aliquo, quaecumque ille diceret, ego intelligerem? (p. 288).

"And, could I not also be said to have similarly **in** my **intellect** [ideas corresponding] to things that are false and not existing at all in themselves, since when someone speaks of them, I would understand whatever he could say?"

The fact of being understood and therefore to exist in the intellect (*in intellectu*) of somebody does not guarantee the real (*in re*) existence of those ideas, i.e. in the intellect can exist ideas that have false correlates or no correlates at all in reality, and that are fully understood.

But the central nucleus of Gaunilo's refutation of Anselm's demonstration of the existence of God is found in sections 5 and 6 of his Treatise, pp. 292-294. Gaunilo's reasoning is as follows:

... ad hoc respondeo: Si esse dicendum est ***in intellectu****, quod secundum veritatem cuiusquam rei nequit saltem cogitari: et hoc in meo sic esse non denego. Sed quia, per hoc, esse quoque* ***in re*** *non potest ullatenus obtinere: illud ei esse adhuc penitus non concedo, quousque mihi argumento probetur indubio. Quod qui esse dicit hoc quod maius omnibus aliter non erit omnibus*

maius: non satis attendit cui loquatur. Ego enim nondum dico, immo etiam nego vel dubito ulla re vera esse maius illud, nec aliud ei esse concedo quam illud, si dicendum est "esse", cum secundum vocem tantum auditam rem prorsus ignotam sibi conatur animus effingere. Quomodo igitur inde mihi probatur maius illud rei veritate subsistere, quia constet illud maius omnibus esse, cum id ego eo usque negem adhuc dubitemve constare, ut ne ***in intellectu*** *quidem vel cogitatione mea eo saltem modo maius ipsum esse dicam, quo dubia etiam multa sunt et incerta? Prius enim certum mihi necesse est fiat re vera esse alicubi maius ipsum, et tum demum ex eo quod maius est omnibus, in seipso quoque subsistere non erit ambiguum.* (5)
"... to that [argument] I reply: If it must be said that something exists **in intellect** that cannot be thought according to the truth [= true nature] of anything whatever, then I do not deny that this thing exists also **in** my [**intellect**]. But since from this [affirmation of the sole existence **in intellect**] it is not at all possible to infer the existence also **in reality**, [then] I do not concede at all to him [= the opponent] that this thing [that exists only **in intellect**] exists [also **in reality**] until [such a thing] is proved to me by a not doubtful argument. For he who says: 'That [greater than which nothing can be thought] exists [not only **in intellect** but also **in reality**] since otherwise that which is greater than everything else will not be greater than everything else – he does not fully realize whom he is speaking with. For I do not say – even more, I even deny or doubt – that this [greater than everything else] is greater than any real thing, nor do I concede to it an existence (if it is possible to speak of 'existence') different from that [existence one has in mind] when the soul tries to imagine from a word that has been only heard a thing completely unknown to it. How, then, is it proved to me that this greater [than everything else] really exists simply because that is greater than everything else, when until this moment I am denying or doubting that this [= the fact of being greater than everything else] has been established, so that I do not [even] say that this greater than everything else exists **in** my **intellect** or **in** my **thought** at least in the way that many doubtful and uncertain things exist [**in** my **intellect**]? For it is necessary that first I become certain that that greater [than everything] exists somewhere **in** true **reality**, and only then, due to the fact that it is greater than everything else, it will not be doubtful that it also exists in itself".

Next Gaunilo gives his well-known example of the Lost Island in order to make clear his thought:

> *Aiunt quidam alicubi oceani esse insulam, quam ex difficultate vel potius impossibilitate inveniendi quod non est, cognominant aliqui 'perditam', quamque fabulantur multo amplius quam de fortunatis insulis fertur, divitiarum deliciarumque omnium inaestimabili ubertate pollere, nulloque possessore aut habitatore universis aliis quas incolunt homines terris possidendorum redundantia usquequaque praestare. Hoc ita esse dicat mihi quispiam, et ego facile dictum in quo nihil est difficultatis intelligam. At si tunc velut consequenter adiungat ac dicat: non potes ultra dubitare insulam illam terris omnibus praestantiorem vere esse alicubi in re, quam et in intellectu tuo non ambigis esse; et quia praestantius est, non in intellectu solo sed etiam esse in re; ideo sic eam necesse est esse, quia nisi fuerit, quaecumque alia in re est terra, praestantior illa erit, ac sic ipsa iam a te praestantior intellecta praestantior non erit; - si inquam per haec ille mihi velit astruere de insula illa quod vere sit ambigendum ultra non esse: aut iocari illum credam, aut nescio quem stultiorem debeam reputare, utrum me si ei concedam, an illum si se putet aliqua certitudine insulae illius essentiam astruxisse, nisi prius ipsam praestantiam eius solummodo sicut rem vere atque indubie existentem nec ullatenus sicut falsum aut incertum aliquid in intellectu meo esse docuerit.* (6)

"Some say that somewhere in the ocean exists an island, which, because of the difficulty or rather impossibility to find what does not exist, some call '[The] Lost [Island]'. And they narrate that this island thrives much more than what it is said of the Blessed Islands with an inestimable abundance of riches and delights, and that, not having possessor or inhabitant, it is superior to all the other lands that human beings inhabit, because of the redundancy of all things worthy to be possessed. If somebody tells me that it is so, I will easily understand what he says - in this there is no difficulty. But if then, as it were a logical consequence, he would add and say: 'You cannot any longer doubt that this island, more pre-eminent than all other lands, and which you do not doubt to exist **in** your **intellect**, truly exists somewhere **in reality**. And, since to exist not only **in intellect** but also **in reality** is more pre-eminent [than to exist only **in intellect**], therefore, this island must exist so [= also **in reality**], because if it did not exist [also **in reality**], any other land which exists also **in reality** will be more pre-eminent than it; and thus this same [island], which has been recognized by you to be the most pre-eminent, will not be the most pre-eminent.' If - I say - by these [arguments] he would try to demonstrate to me that, in regard to this island, it is not possible to doubt anymore that it truly exists: either I would think he is joking or I do not know whom I ought to think more foolish, myself if I accept [his proof], or him, if he thinks that he has demonstrated with any certainty the existence of that island, without having instructed me before that the pre-eminence of that [island] exists **in** my **intellect** as a real and undoubtedly existing thing only, and not at all as something false and uncertain".

2. As it is said by Battista Mondin of the Pontificia Università Urbaniana, in his article "L'argomento <ontologico> nella metafisica dell'essere di San Tommaso d'Aquino", included in the already quoted book *L'argomento ontologico,* pp. 161-171:

> *"It is something universally admitted that Saint Thomas is resolutely against the ontological argument of the Anselmian type, argument that intends to prove the existence of God starting from the definition of His essence* (id cuius maius cogitari nequit). *According to Saint Thomas this way of proceeding is incorrect, because it is founded on the false assumption that human reason has a pure (and not simply nominal) concept of the divine essence even before it has known His existence".*

Saint Thomas, in *Summa Theologiae, Prima Pars, Qu.* 2, A, I (*Resp. ad secundum*), expresses his idea on the ontological argument limiting his criticism to two aspects of that argument, which he clearly distinguishes: 1. "that not everybody does understand that the word *God* means *that greater than which nothing can be thought*", and 2. "the logical argument that from thinking something it does not follow its existence in reality, but only its existence in the mind" (Herwy Rikhof, of the University of Nijmegen, "Aquinas and the "ratio Anselmi". A theological analysis of Aquinas' criticism", in the already quoted work *L'argomento ontologico,* p. 137). Saint Thomas declares thus:

> *... dicendum quod forte ille qui audit hoc nomen* Deus, *non intelligit significari aliquid quo maius cogitari non possit, cum quidam crediderint Deum esse corpus. Dato etiam quod quilibet intelligat hoc nomine Deus*

> *significari hoc quod dicitur, scilicet illud quo maius cogitari non potest; non tamen propter hoc sequitur quod intelligat id quod significatur per nomen, esse* ***in rerum natura****; sed* ***in apprehensione intellectus*** *tantum. Nec potest argui quod sit* ***in re****, nisi daretur quod sit* ***in re*** *aliquid quo maius cogitari non potest: quod non est datum a ponentibus Deum non esse.*
>
> "... it must be said that perhaps he who hears this word *God*, does not understand that it means something greater than which nothing can be thought, since some have believed that God is a body. Even if it is conceded that anybody understands that by this word *God* is meant what is expressed, i.e. that greater than which nothing can be thought, nevertheless from this fact does not follow that anybody understands [Battista Mondin, *op. cit.* p.161, translates: *non segue ... la persuasione*: 'does not follow ... the conviction'] that what is signified by the word exists **in the nature of things** – but only **in the intellect's comprehension**. It is not possible to argue that it exists **in reality**, unless it is [previously] proved that something greater than which nothing can be thought exists **in reality**, what is not accepted by those who affirm that God does not exist".

3. Immanuel Kant (1724-1804) all along his work was interested in the problem of the ontological proof of the existence of God and dedicated to it many pages of his books, always adopting in relation to it a rejecting attitude, in which is prevalent, as in Gaunilo and Saint Thomas, the contraposition of the existence *in intellectu* and *in re*. We transcribe and translate some passages of Kant concerning this subject, taken from his treatises *Kritik der reinen Vernunft* and *Der einzig mögliche Beweisgrund zu einer Demonstration des Daseins Gottes*:

> *Kritik der reinen Vernunft*, p. 662 Meiner ed. = A 583-584: *Ungeachtet dieser dringenden Bedürfnis der Vernunft, etwas vorauszusetzen, was dem Verstande zu der durchgängigen Bestimmung seiner Begriffe vollständig zum Grunde liegen könne, so bemerkt sie doch das Idealische und bloss Gedichtete einer solchen Voraussetzung viel zu leicht, als dass sie dadurch allein überredet werden sollte, ein blosses Selbstgeschöpf ihres Denkes sofort für ein wirkliches Wesen anzunehmen...*

"Notwithstanding this urgent necessity of reason of presupposing something [i.e. an Absolute Being, God] that could fully serve the understanding as ground for the complete determination of its concepts [in order not to incur in a *regressus ad infinitum*], however reason notices **the idealistic** and **merely ficticious** [nature, i.e. existing only ***in intellectu***] of such a presupposition too easily to be persuaded by that alone to assume as **an actual being** [existing ***in re***] a **mere creation of his own thinking** [existing only ***in intellectu***]..."

Kritik der reinen Vernunft, p. 668 Meiner ed. = A 592: *Mann siehet aus dem bisherigen leicht: dass der Begriff eines absolut notwendigen Wesens* ***ein reiner Vernunftbegriff****, d. i.* ***eine blosse Idee*** *sei, deren* ***objective Realität*** *dadurch, dass die Vernunft ihrer bedarf, noch lange nicht Bewiesen ist ...*

"From what precedes it is easily seen that the concept of an absolutely necessary being [= God] [that reason needs, looks for and constructs] is **a pure concept of reason**, i.e. **a mere idea** [existing ***in intellectu***], whose **objective reality** [= existence ***in re***] is not at all proved by the fact that reason needs it"...

Kritik der reinen Vernunft, p. 675 Meiner ed. = A 601: *Unser* ***Begriff*** *von einem Gegestände mag also enthalten, was und wie viel er wolle, so müssen wir doch aus ihm heraugehen, um diesem die* ***Existenz*** *zu erteilen.*

"Our **concept** of an object may thus contain whatever and however much it wants, nevertheless we must go out of it in order to provide it with **existence**".

Kritik der reinen Vernunft, p. 676 Meiner ed. = A 602: *Es ist also an dem so berühmten ontologischen (cartesianischen) Beweise, vom Dasein eines höchten Wesens, aus* ***Begriffen****, alle Mühe und Arbeit verloren, und ein Mensch möchte wohl eben so wenig aus* ***blossen Ideen*** *an Einsichten reicher werden, als ein Kaufmann an Vermögen, wenn er um seinem Zustand zu verbessern, seinem Kassenbestande einige Nullen anhängen wollte.*

"Thus, all effort and labour given to this famous ontological (Cartesian) proof of the existence of a Supreme Being from **concepts** is lost, and a man could from **mere ideas** become richer in insight, not much more than a merchant in money, if he, in order to improve his economic situation, would add a few zeros to his cash balance".

Der einzig mögliche Beweisgrund zu einer Demonstration des Daseins Gottes, p. 730 Suhrkamp ed. = A 191-192: *Indessen haben wir einen berühmten*

Beweis, der auf diesen Grund erbauet ist, nämlich den so gennanten Kartesianischen. Man erdenket sich zuvörderst einen ***Begriff*** *von einem möglichen* ***Dinge****, in welchem man alle wahre Vollkommenheit sich vereinbart vorstellt. Nun nimmt man an, das* ***Dasein*** *sei auch eine Vollkommenheit der Dinge; also schliesst man aus der Möglichkeit eines vollkommensten Wesens auf seine* ***Existenz****. Eben so könnte man aus dem* ***Begriffe*** *einer jeden Sache, welche auch nur als die vollkommenste ihrer Art vorgestellt wird, z. E. daraus allein schon dass eine vollkommenste Welt zu gedenken ist, auf ihr* ***Dasein*** *schliessen.*

"However we have a famous proof, which is based on that principle [= from the **concept** of something possible its **existence** is deduced], i.e. the so-called Cartesian [proof or argument]. One conceives firstly the **concept** of a possible **thing** in which one imagines that all true perfection is reunited. Now one assumes that **existence** is also a perfection of things, so from the possibility of a most perfect being one deduces its **existence**. Equally from the **concept** of anything, which is also imagined as the most perfect of its kind - as for instance, only from the fact that a most perfect world is thought – one could deduce its **existence**".

Kant in *Kritik der reinen Vernunft*, p. 699 Meiner ed. = A 630, after referring, in pages 668 to 699 Meiner ed. = A 592-630, to the impossibility of the ontological, cosmological and physico-theological proofs of the existence of God, concludes affirming that the ontological proof is the basis of the other two and that besides these three proofs there is not another proof for the speculative reason:

So liegt demnach dem physikotheologischen Beweise der kosmologische, diesem aber der ontologische Beweis, vom ***Dasein*** *eines einigen Urwesens als höchsten Wesens, zum Grunde, und da ausser diesen dreien Wegen keiner mehr der spekulativen Vernunft offen ist, so ist der ontologische Beweis, aus lauter* ***reinen Vernunftbegriffen****, der einzig mögliche, wenn überall nur ein Beweis von einem so weit über allen empirischen Verstandesgebrauch erhabenen Satze möglich ist.*

"Thus, the cosmological [proof] underlies the physico-theological proof, and the ontological proof of the **existence** of a unique original Being as the Supreme Being [underlies] this [last] one [= the cosmological one]; and since besides these three paths no more are open to the speculative reason, so the ontological proof, from **pure concepts of reason**, is the only possible one - if even a proof of a proposition so extraordinarily above any empirical use of the understanding is possible at all".

Cf. *Kritik der reinen Vernunft*, p. 667 Meiner ed. = A 590-591, where Kant affirms that:

> ... *mehr gibt es ihrer nicht, und mehr kann es auch nicht geben.*
>
> "more than these three [proofs] there are no more, and also there cannot be more".

It is obvious that, being the ontological proof the basis of the other proofs mentioned by Kant that are adduced for demonstrating the existence of God, all these proofs are deprived of any value, when the ontological proof, which is their foundation and reason, is descarded. In a similar way É. Gilson, in his commented edition of Descartes' *Discours de la Méthode*, p. 349, expresses:

> *"If it is wanted to prevent Descartes to deduce from an idea* [the existence of] *a* [really existing] *nature to force him to deduce from an idea only an idea,* [then] *it is not only the second proof* [of the existence of God = the ontological one in the case of Descartes] *but all the Cartesian philosophy that is called in question".*

Given the impossibility of demonstrating the existence of God, one understands Kant's conclusion in his treatise *Der einzig mögliche Beweisgrund zu einer Demonstration des Daseins Gottes*, p. 738 Suhrkamp ed. = A 205:

> *Es ist durchaus nötig, dass man sich vom Dasein Gottes überzeuge; es ist aber nicht eben so nötig, dass man es demonstriere.*
>
> "It is absolutely necessary to be convinced of the existence of God; but it is not equally necessary to demonstrate it".

The previous remarks show the great presence that the controversial "ontological proof" had in Western thought in theologians as well as in philosophers.

4. The "ontological proof" carries us back to India. For the Hinduists Śiva for some, Viṣṇu for others, is the Supreme Being, endowed with the most excellent qualities, perfect, infinite, omnipotent, etc. See C. Bulcke S.J., *The Theism of Nyaya-Vaisesika, Its Origin and Early Development*, and Chapters

V, VI and VII in our book, *Filosofia de la India* (2010), where we have dealt with the conception of God (*Īśvara*) in three Vedānta systems.

Applying the reasoning of the ontological proof, utilized in the West for demonstrating the existence of God, to the Supreme Being as conceived in Indian philosophy - either under the name of Śiva or under the name of Viṣṇu, and adding an example more to those imagined by Gaunilo (*The Lost Island*), and by Kant (*eine vollkommenste Welt,* and the "*caloric*" or "*ether*"), previously referred to, one could affirm that Śiva and/or Viṣṇu conceived as Beings endowed with all the perfections, must possess, among these, that of real existence. This conclusion cannot be but disturbing for any monotheist religion, which pretends that its God exists and is unique.

5. We think that it could be thought that the "ontological proof" as all the proofs adduced to give a rational basis to the cultural dogmas or *principia prima* (as the soul, God, the first principle, reincarnations, beginninglessness, the absolute value of the Scriptures: Bible or Veda), in the West as well as in India, lack any proving value, or at least are of a very precarious or not at all indisputable value, which does not justify the profound adhesion they enjoy. In the last analysis the true foundation of the *cultural dogmas* or *principia prima* in each culture is faith. And, although faith is worthy of all respect out of consideration for those who possess it, anyhow it does not belong to the field of rational processes, which is claimed to be that of philosophy. The book of J.P. Revel of the *Académie Française,* entitled *Descartes inutile et incertain,* clearly shows the nature of "cultural dogma" of the dogma of the existence of God in Western philosophy. Revel presents in it a masterly criticism of the proofs of the existence of God developed by Descartes. Let us remember that the title of Revel's work is the *Pensée* number 78 of the Article II in the book *Pensées* of Blas Pascal.

The distinction "in intellectu" *and* "in re" *in Bhartṛhari*

Concerning the central point of the problem of the "ontological proof ", which lies in the admission of two types of existence, one *in intellectu* and the other *in re,* and in the impossibility to pass from the first to the second, it is interesting to remind here what expresses Bhartṛhari, the Indian philosopher who in the 5th century A. D. dealt with the subjects which constitute the so-called Philosophy of Language and to whom we shall dedicate a special work in the future.

According to Bhartṛhari, in his *Vākyapadīya, Sambandha-samuddeśa* 39-51, there are two types of existence (*sattā*), one the "principal" (*mukhya*), "direct" (*saṃprati*), "external" (*bāhya*) existence, which corresponds to the things of the external world, and the other, the "secondary" or "metaphorical" (*aupacāriki, upacāra°*) existence of all what is expressed by the words. The commentator Helārāja *ad Sambandha-samuddeśa* 48, III, 1, p. 158, line 10, K.A. Subramania Iyer ed., gives to this second type of existence the epithet of *bauddha,* "mental". The Bhartṛhari's "principal existence" is the "existence *in re*" of Western authors, the "metaphorical existence" is the "existence *in intellectu*".

We give the text and the translation of the *kārikās* III, 3 (*Sambandha-samuddeśa*), 39 and 51, of the Bhartṛhari's *Vākyapadīya,* which have to do with this subject:

vyapadeśe padārthānām anyā sattaupacārikī/
sarvāvasthāsu sarveṣām ātmarūpasya darśikā//39//

"When something is named,
there is another existence, the metaphorical one,
which is proper of things designated by words;
it shows the form of all things in all situations"//39//

Bhartṛhari in *Sambandha-samuddeśa, kārikās* 49, 50 and 51 refers to the metaphorical existence (*aupacārikī*) pointing out in *kārikās* 49 and 50 some of its characteristics. But the *kārikās* 50 d and 51 are those which directly have to do with the subject of the distinction between *in intellectu* and *in re*:

...aupacārikīm//50//

etāṃ sattāṃ padārtho hi na kaścid ativartate/
*sā ca sampratisattāyāḥ pṛtag bhāṣye nidarśitā//*51//

"Nothing expressed by a word
can go beyond this metaphorical [or mental] existence.[a]
And in the *Bhāṣya* it has been thaught
that it is different from the principal existence".//50 d-51//[b]

[a] The existence to which this stanza refers (*etaṃ sattām*) is, as we said, the *aupacārikī* or "metaphorical" existence that Bhartṛhari characterizes in *kārikās* 49 and 50 attributing to it several epithets. The notion or idea that a word expresses can never pretend to have an existence other than the metaphorical one, i.e. *in intellectu*; it is obliged to remain within the limits of mere "metaphorical", "secondary" or "mental" existence, which by essence corresponds to it. Obviously, the "principal" or "external" *in re* existence can be attributed to the object, which is expressed by the notion or idea the w ord refers to, if and only if those who affirm that existence adduce solid arguments with that purpose - as the commentator Helārāja expresses in his introductory remarks to *kārikās* 40 and 41. The existence of something (for instance: God) *in intellectu* does not guarantee by itself alone its existence *in re*. The existence of God or any other existence supposed to be *in re* would have to be demonstrated by other means of proof, and not only by the fact that the corresponding notion or idea exists *in intellectu*.

[b] Bhartṛhari in *kārikā* 51 c-d and Helārāja in the beginning of his commentary *ad locum* indicate that the foundation of the theory of the two types of existence is found in the *Mahābhāṣya* or "Great Commentary" (as the *kārikā* says: "*in the Bhāṣya*"), written by Patañjali around 150 B.C. The *Mahābhāṣya* is a commentary of the *Aṣṭādhyāyī* or "The Eight Chapters", the masterly analysis of the Sanskrit language done by Pāṇini in the 5th or perhaps 6th century B.C., as well as of Kātyāyana's *Vārttikas* (between 250 B.C. and Patañjali's date). The *Vārttikas* are technical remarks on the Aphorisms (*Sūtras*) of Pāṇini. The three mentioned authors are eminent representatives of the great linguistic Indian

tradition, which has had no comparison in Western antiquity.[51]

Let us add, as another, more ancient, antecedent in India of the distinction between the existence *in intellectu* and the existence *in re*, the distinction between an existence *dravyataḥ* (as a real entity), and an existence *prajñaptitaḥ* (as a mere concept, i.e. without objective reality) that correspond, the first, to the principal, external, *in re* existence, the second, to the secondary, metaphorical, mental, *in intellectu* existence, and that appear in the oldest Buddhist texts.[52]

IV.25 The Spirit, *Puruṣa*: names, plurality and attributes

Now we return to the Indian philosophical Sāṃkhya system, whose exposition was interrupted by the marginal note on the "ontological proof" in the West and the distinction *in intellectu* and *in re* in Bhartṛhari.

Opposed to Matter are the Spirits, which are designated with the Sanskrit terms *puruṣa, puṃs, ātman,* but it is usual to unify all of the Spirits under the collective name of "Spirit", *Puruṣa,* and thus to speak of the opposition between *Primordial Matter* and the *Spirit* in Sāṃkhya.

The plurality of the *Puruṣas* or Spirits (*puruṣabahutva*) is affirmed in several texts: *kārikā* 18 of the *Sāṃkhyakārikās* with the commentaries of Gauḍapāda and of Vācaspati Miśra (*Tattvakaumudī*), Srinivasa Ayya Srinivasan (ed.)'; and *sūtras* I, 149-154 and VI, 45 of the *Sāṃkhyasūtras* with the commentaries of Vijñānabhikṣu and Aniruddha. The acceptance of a multiplicity of *Puruṣas* by the Sāṃkhya opposes this system to the non-dualist Vedānta system of

---

[51] Ver Hartmut Scharfe, *Grammatical Literature*; F. Tola and C. Dragonetti, "Los estudios lingüísticos en la India Antigua I", in *Argos* 25 (2001), pp. 127-150, and "Los estudios lingüísticos en la India Antigua II" (Pāṇini), in *Argos* 26 (2002), pp. 159-185.

[52] Cf. pp. XXXII-XXXIV of the Introduction of our book *Being as consciousness.*

Śaṅkara, which only accepts the existence of one sole Spirit, *Brahman/Ātman*.

The Spirit has the following attributes:

- it is neither a producing element (*prakṛti*, cf. the section *Names for Primordial Matter*),
- nor a transformation of something else (*vikṛti*, cf. the section *Attributes of Primordial Matter*) (*kārikā* 3 d);
- it has characteristics which are contrary (*viparīta*) to those pointed out for Primordial Matter (*pradhāna*) as affirmed in *kārikā* 11 and its commentary by Gauḍapāda:
- it is devoid of constitutive elements (*aguṇa*);
- it is differentiated (*vivekī*) in the sense that it has nothing to do with the *guṇas* while Matter is the *guṇas*;
- it is not an object (*aviṣaya*) in the sense that it is not an object of experience;
- it is not general and not common (*asāmānya*), in the sense that it does not partake of anything, material or spiritual;
- it is a conscient being (*cetana*) since its essence is pure knowledge, pure consciousness;
- it does not carry out any productive function and is therefore not productive (*aprasavadharmin*), "since nothing originates from the *Puruṣa*": *na hi puruṣāt kiṃcit prasūyate.*

The *Puruṣa* also has some of the characteristics of the non-manifested Primordial Matter (*pradhāna*) referred to by the expression *tathā ca* of *kārikā* 11 and glossed by Gauḍapāda in his commentary *ad kārikā* 11 (cf. kārikā 10):

– it is not caused (*ahetumant*),
– eternal (*nitya*),
– all-pervading (*vyāpin*),
– without activity (*akriya*),
– one (*eka*),
– not founded (on another) (*anāśrita*),
– not liable to dissolution (*aliṅga*),
– without parts (*niravayava*),
– dependent on itself (*svatantra*).

Moreover the *Puruṣa,* in the same way as the non-manifested Primordial Matter, is subtle (*sūkṣma*) and therefore imperceptible, and its existence can only be inferred (*anumitāstitva*) (commentary of Gauḍapāda to *kārikā* 17).

Kārikā 19 mentions a few important characteristics of the *Puruṣa*:

– to be the witness (*sākṣitva*),
– isolation (*kaivalya*),
– indifference (*mādhyasthya*),
- to be the seer (*draṣṭṛtva*), and
- to be a non-agent (*akartṛbhāva*).

All of these attributes of the *Puruṣa* express that it is the unalterable witness and seer of everything that occurs, submerged in absolute isolation and in absolute indifference and completely beyond action.

The *Sāṃkhyasūtras* add other attributes of the *Puruṣa* such as:

– *asaṅga,* "devoid of connection, association or attachment" (*sūtra* I, 15),
– *nityaśuddha,* "eternally pure",
– *nityabuddha,* "eternally in possession of knowledge",
– *nityamukta,* "eternally liberated" (*sūtra* I, 19),

upon which Vijñānabhikṣu *ad locum* comments in the following terms:

> *... nitya-śuddhatvaṃ sadā-pāpa-puṇya-śūnyatvaṃ nitya-buddhatvam alupta-cid-rūpatvaṃ nitya-muktatvaṃ sadā-pāramārthika-duḥkhā-'yuktatvam ...*
>
> "... The fact of being eternally pure means the fact of being always devoid of evil and good; the fact of being eternally in possession of knowledge means the fact of possessing a nature of indestructible consciousness; and the fact of being eternally liberated means the fact of never being connected with true suffering ...",

and Vijñānabhikṣu adds a text of the *Śruti* that says:

> *ayam ātmā san-mātro nityaḥ śuddho buddhaḥ satyo mukto nirañjano vibhur iti ...*

"This *Ātman* [= *Puruṣa*] is only being, eternal, pure, in possession of knowledge, true, free, stainless, omnipresent.... "[53]

IV.26 The relation between Matter and Spirit and its effects

Matter (*Prakṛti*) and Spirit (*Puruṣa*), two principles endowed with such opposing attributes, are since beginningless (*anādi*) eternity interconnected through a peculiar relation which some texts consider as mere *proximity* (*saṃnidhāna, sannidhi, sānnidhya*) and other texts as *connection* (*saṃyoga*).[54]

Let us now see the important consequences which derive from this relation between the *Puruṣa* and the *Prakṛti*.

In the first place, "through this contact (between both) the creation is accomplished" (*tatkṛtaḥ* [= *tena saṃyogena kṛtaḥ*] *sargaḥ*: *kārikā* 21 and commentary of Gauḍapāda *ad locum*). Creation, as we have already explained, is the evolution of Matter into its material components (the five material great elements *(mahābhūta)* of which the cosmos and the "coarse body" *(sthūlaśarīra)*, of the diverse beings are made) as well as its "psychic" components (the *buddhi*, intellect, intelligence, the *ahaṃkāra*, ego, and the *manas*, mind, which constitute the so-called *antaḥkaraṇa*, i.e. the "internal organ", which together with the five *Tanmātras* and the remaining ten *Indriyas* build up the "subtle body" *(sūkṣmaśarīra, liṅga)*, of the various beings (cf. *kārikā* 40 with the commentary of Gauḍapāda and *sūtra* III, 9 of the *Sāṃkhyasūtras* and its commentaries). These psychic components arise at different stages in the evolution of the

---

[53] Cf. R. Garbe, *Die Sāṃkhya Philosophie*, pp. 296-302.

[54] For the notion of "proximity", see Vācaspati Miśra, *Tattvakaumudī ad kārikā* 37; Māṭhara, *Vṛtti, ad kārikā* 2, p. 18; Vijñānabhikṣu, *Sāṃkhyapravacanabhāṣya ad* I, 99; Vindhyavāsin, an ancient master of the Sāṃkhya tradition, quoted by Malliṣeṇa, *Syādvādamañjarī*, p. 97; Vyomaśiva, *Vyomavatī*, p. 521; and Haribhadrasūri, *Yogabindu*, Lalbhai Dalpatbhai Series stanza 449). For the notion of connection, see *Sāṃkhyakārikās* 20 and 21, and commentary of Gauḍapāda *ad kārikā* 21; Vijñānabhikṣu, *Sāṃkhyapravacanabhāṣya ad* I, 99; and *Yuktidīpika ad kārikā* 20, p. 87, line 18.

Prakṛti. It is appropriate to call to mind here that the evolution of *Prakṛti* is a mechanical act without the intervention of consciousness or the will. Cf. *kārikā* 57 and commentary of Gauḍapāda on *kārikās* 56-57.

Then, thanks to this "proximity" or "connection", the *Puruṣa* reflects itself in the *Prakṛti*, and the *Prakṛti* is in turn reflected in the *Puruṣa*. Cf. Vijñānabhikṣu, *Sāṃkhyapravacanabhāṣya ad* I, 99, p. 48, lines 31-32:

> *ayam eva ca saṃyoga-viśeṣo buddhy-ātmanor anyo-'nya-pratibimbane hetuḥ.*
>
> "This particular connection between the buddhi and the Ātman (= Puruṣa) is the cause of the reflection of one in the other".

Vijñānabhikṣu himself, p. 49, lines 5-6, *ibidem*, expresses that "this mutual reflection has been logically demonstrated by the divine Vyāsa in his *Bhāṣya* [Commentary] *on Yoga* [*ad* IV, 22]": *sa cā'yam anyo-'nya-pratibimbo Yoga-bhāṣye Vyāsa-devāiḥ siddhāntitaḥ*; and adds that he [= Vijñānabhikṣu] has dealt with this subject in his *Yogavārttika* [*ad* IV, 22, *Yogavārttika of Vijñānabhikṣu*, Volume IV, pp. 93-98].[55]

The theory of mutual reflection (*parasparapratibimba*) is expounded in the context of the Yoga system by Vyāsa, Vācaspati Miśra, Śaṅkara, Bhoja, Vijñānabhikṣu.[56]

The *Puruṣa* is reflected (cf. *pratibimba, chāyā*, "reflected image" in the *Prakṛti* in its entirity, but it is specifically to the *antaḥkaraṇa*, i.e. to the *buddhi*, etc. (internal organ), that it transmits an appearance of consciousness, as is explained in the following texts.

Gauḍapāda, commenting on *kārikā* 20, says:

---

[55] On the mutual relation between *Puruṣa* and *Prakṛti* in the Sāṃkhya system, cf. Shinkan Murakami, "What is *caintanya*?...", in *Asiatische Studien* LIII. 3. 1999, pp. 645-665, specially points 3. and 4.

[56] Cf. *Yogavārttika of Vijñānabhikṣu, Appendix* 9, pp. 195-202, where the editress deals with the "double reflection" in the philosophical Yoga system (this Appendix was published as an article in *Journal of Indian Philosophy*, 1988, No. 4, pp. 367-376).

... puruṣaś cetanāvān / tena cetanāvabhāsasaṃyuktaṃ mahadādiliṅgaṃ cetanāvad iva bhavati / yathā loke ghaṭaḥ śītasaṃyuktaḥ śīta uṣṇasaṃyukta uṣṇaḥ / evaṃ mahadādiliṅgaṃ tasya saṃyogāt puruṣasaṃyogāc cetanāvad iva bhavati.

"...The *Puruṣa* is endowed with consciousness. The subtle body constituted by the *buddhi,* etc., in contact with the light of consciousness, appears as provided with consciousness; in the same way as experience shows that a jar in contact with something cold becomes cold, in contact with something hot becomes hot, so the subtle body, constituted by the *buddhi,* etc., due to its contact with this, i.e. due to its contact with the *Puruṣa,* appears as provided with consciousness".

Vijñānabhikṣu, *Sāṃkhyapravacanabhāṣya ad* I, 99, p. 48, lines 34-36, affirms:

... buddhāu cāitanya-pratibimbaś cāitanya-darśanā-'rthaṃ kalpyate, darpaṇe mukha-pratibimbavat.

"...The reflection of consciousness [= *Puruṣa*] in the *buddhi* [= *Prakṛti*] is assumed for the vision of consciousness, as [it happens with] the reflection of the face in a mirror".

Vācaspati Miśra in his *Tattvakaumudī ad* I, 37:

buddhir hi puruṣasaṃnidhānāt tacchāyā'pattyā tadrūpe'va.

"Since the *buddhi,* thanks to the reflection [in it] of the *Puruṣa* due to the proximity of this one, appears as provided with its [= of the *Puruṣa*] nature".

Cf. *ibidem ad kārikā* 5, the last sentence.

Yuktidīpikā, commenting on *kārikā* 20, p. 87, line 18, *evaṃ puruṣasaṃyogāviśeṣe buddhighaṭayoḥ...buddhir eva cetanārūpāpannevopalabhyate, na ghaṭaḥ.*

"Thus being the same the union of the *Puruṣa* with the *buddhi* and with the jar [or any other material product]... only the *buddhi* is perceived as provided with a conscious nature, but not so the jar [or the other material products]".

Māṭhara, *Vṛtti ad kārikā* 2, p. 18:

saḥ puruṣaḥ / sannidhisattāmātreṇa cumbaka iva lohasya pravṛttihetur ayam asti ...

"The *Puruṣa,* due only to its proximity, is the cause of the movement [= activity, evolution, functioning] [of the *Prakṛti*], as the magnet [is the cause of the movement] of the steel".

Vindhyavāsin quoted by Malliṣeṇa in his *Syādvādamañjarī*, p. 97, has the following stanza:

puruṣo 'vikṛtātmaiva svanirbhāsam acetanam /
manaḥ karoti sāṃnidhyād upādhiḥ sphaṭikaṃ yathā // 449

"The *Puruṣa* whose essence is unalterable
makes the non-conscious mind similar to itself
[i.e. as possessed of consciousness]
due to its proximity,
as the accessory
[= any colored thing that is attached to a crystal]
[makes] the crystal [as possessed of a color that is not its]".

Vyomaśiva, quotes this verse by Vindhyavāsin in his *Vyomavatī*, pp. 521-522, and comments upon it. We reproduce now a part of his commentary:

...evam ayaṃ puruṣo 'vikṛtasvarūpo 'cetanaṃ manaḥ svanirbhāsaṃ cetanam iva karoti sānnidhyān na punar vastutas tasya caitanyaṃ vikāritvāt.

"... in the same way this *Puruṣa*, whose nature is unalterable, makes the non-conscious mind as possessed of an appearance that is its own [= that of the *Puruṣa*, i.e.], as endowed with consciousness due to its proximity, but the consciousness of it [= of the mind] does not really exist because it is subject to change".

There is also, as we have said, a reflection of the *Prakṛti* - or rather of the *buddhi*, which is a stage in the evolution of the *Prakṛti* - in the *Puruṣa*, to which the texts quoted in the following refer.

Vijñānabhikṣu, *Sāṃkhyapravacanabhāṣya ad* I, 99, p. 48, lines 38-49, line 5:

yaś ca caitanye buddheḥ pratibimbaḥ, sa cā'rūḍha-viṣayaiḥ saha buddher bhānā-'rtham iṣyate; arthā-'kāratayāi 'vā'rtha-grahaṇasya buddheḥ sthale dṛṣṭatvena [,] *tāṃ vinā saṃyoga-viśeṣa-mātreṇā'rtha-bhānasya puruṣe 'py anāucityāt; ... sa cā'rthā-'kāraḥ puruṣe pariṇāmo na sambhavatī'ty arthāt pratibimba-rūpa eva paryavasyati ... /*

"The reflection of the *buddhi* in consciousness [= *Puruṣa*] is postulated for the manifestation of the *buddhi* together with the objects that have come [within the range of its knowledge], because of the logical impossibilty of the manifestation of the object in the *Puruṣa* by means of the sole peculiar connection without it [= the *buddhi*], for it is seen [= known] that, in the case of the *buddhi*, the apprehension of the object [takes place] only when it [= the *buddhi*] assumes the form of the object ... and since such a transformation in the form of the object is not possible in the case of the *Puruṣa*, it is concluded that [the form of the object in the *Puruṣa*] is only something which has the nature of a reflection ..."

Vācaspati Miśra, in his *Tattvakaumudī ad kārikā* 5, comments:

puruṣas tu sukhādyananuṣaṅgī cetanaḥ. so 'yam [,] *buddhitattva-vartinā jñānasukhādinā tatpratibimbitas* [,] *tacchāyāpattyā jñānasukhādimān iva bhavatīti tenānugṛhyate.*

"And the *Puruṣa* is indifferent to pleasure, etc., conscious. Therefore it [= the *Puruṣa*] - in which it [= the *buddhi*] is reflected under the form of knowledge and pleasure, etc. which exist [only] in it [= the *buddhi*] - due to the arising of this reflection [in it], is conceived of as endowed with knowledge, pleasure, etc".

Āsuri, an ancient master of the Sāṃkhya, quoted by Vyomaśiva, in his *Vyomavatī*, p. 521, (cf. Malliṣeṇa, *Syādvādamañjarī*, p. 97) says:

viviktadṛkpariṇatau buddhau bhogo 'sya kathyate/
pratibimbodayaḥ svacche yathā candramaso 'mbhasi.

"When the *buddhi* is transformed
being the seer [= *Puruṣa*] apart [from that process],
[nevertheless] the experience
is considered to be his [= of the *Puruṣa*],
as in the case of the arising
of the reflected image of the moon in crystalline water
[when it is thought that it is the moon that is in the water]."

The Spirit is in fact not associated with anything, it is eternal, pure, free, inactive, devoid of qualities and unalterable, it is not enchained by reincarnations and is eternally liberated from them. Cf. *kārikā* 62 a-b:

...na badhyate nāpi mucyate nāpi saṃsarati kaścit.

"no *[Puruṣa]* is enchained or is liberated or transmigrates".

Nevertheless, these qualities which isolate the Spirit do not hinder that what the living individual (*jīva*) experiences be reflected in the Spirit and be attributed to it. It is a mere reflection, and it can only metaphorically be said that the experiences of the living individual take place in the Spirit and belong to it. In actual fact, though, this reflection has no effect on the Spirit: it does not alter it at all and does not trouble it at all, just as the image of an object reflected in a mirror does not alter the mirror, and just as a red flower under a crystal does not affect the crystal, although the reflection of the color of the flower gives the crystal the appearance of being red in color.

IV.27 Remarks on the previous subject: The problem of the union of the soul and the body in the West

The "union" of the soul and the body, which the Sāṃkhya explains as a "mutual reflection" was a much-discussed question in the West, and many extremely fanciful (even extravagant) solutions were imagined in order to determine the nature and form of that "union".

1. Descartes starts from the idea, expressed in *Passions de l'ame* (in *Oeuvres des Descartes,* Charles Adam & Paul Tannery ed., Vol. XI, p. 351, lines 6-8), *Première Partie,* Article XXX, that:

> *... l'ame est veritablement jointe à tout le corps, & qu'on ne peut pas proprement dire qu'elle soit en quelcune de ses parties, à l'exclusion des autres*
>
> "...the soul is really united to the whole body, and it cannot be properly said that it is in some of its parts to the exclusion of others".

In Article XXXI, (p. 351, line 27 - p. 352, line 2) after reiterating the previous idea, he affirms:

> *... il y a neantmoins en luy quelque partie, en laquelle elle exerce ses fonctions plus particulierement qu'en toutes les autres.*

"... there is notwithstanding in it [= the body] a part in which it [= the soul] carries out its functions more particularly than in all the others".

Descartes on p. 352, Lines 10-20 of Article XXXI says that this part of the body

> ... *n'est nullement le coeur; ny aussi tout le cerveau, mais seulement la plus interieure de ses parties, qui est une certaine glande fort petite, située dans le milieu de sa substance, & tellement suspenduë au dessus du conduit par lequel les esprits de ses cavitez anterieures ont communication avec ceux de la posterieure, que les moindres mouvemens qui sont en elle, peuvent beaucoup pour changer le cours de ces esprits; & reciproquement, que le moindres changemens qui arrivent au cours des esprits, peuvent beaucoup pour changer les mouvemens de cette glande.*
>
> "... is not at all the heart or all the brain but only the most interior of its parts, which is a certain very small gland, located in the middle of its substance, and suspended in such a way above the channel, through which the spirits from their front cavities have communication with those [spirits] of the rear [cavity], that the slightest movements which take place in it [= the gland] have great capacity to change the course of these spirits; and reciprocally, that the slightest changes which take place in the course of the spirits have great capacity to change the movements of that gland".

The small "gland" to which Descartes refers in this text is the *pineal gland* and the "spirits" are the *animal spirits* imagined by him.

In Article X, p. 334, Line 27-p. 335, Line 9, in the same part of the treatise, which has the title "Comment les esprits animaux sont produits dans le cerveau" (How the animal spirits are produced in the brain) Descartes explains what the animal spirits are:

> ...*ces parties du sang tres-subtiles composent les esprits animaux ... ne sont que des corps, & ils n'ont point d'autre proprieté, sinon que ce sont des corps tres-petits, & qui se meuvent tres viste, ... En sorte qu'ils ne s'arestent en aucun lieu.*
>
> "... these very subtle parts of the blood compose the animal spirits ... [they] are nothing but bodies and have no other property that being very small bodies that move very rapidly ... in such a way that they do not stop anywhere".

In Article XXXIV, p. 354, Descartes points out that these spirits, carried by the blood, also circulate through the whole body via the arteries, which transport them to the various nerves and muscles.

The unique function (*fonction*) of the soul (Article XVII, p. 342) is to think and thus give rise to thoughts (*pensées*), which are of two kinds, namely: "the actions of the soul" (*les actions de l'ame*), which are all our wills or acts of will (*toutes nos volontés*), and "the passions of the soul" (*les passions de l'ame*), which are all kinds of perceptions or cognitions which are to be found in us (*toutes les sortes de perceptions ou connoissances qui se trouvent en nous*).

In Article XLI, p. 360, lines 2-6 Descartes says that when an "action of the soul" takes place, i.e. when thc soul wants something,

> *par cela seul qu'elle veut quelque chose, elle fait que la petite glande, a qui elle est estroitement jointe, se meut en la façon qui est requise pour produire l'effect qui se raporte á cette volonté.*
>
> "by the very fact that it wants something, it causes that the small gland, to which it is tightly united, moves in the required way to produce the effect related to that will".

Article XLIII, p. 361, lines 12-15, exemplifies what goes before:

> *Ainsi enfin, quand on veut marcher, ou mouvoir son corps en quelque autre façon, cette volonté fait que la glande pousse les esprits vers les muscles qui servent à cet effect.*
>
> "Thus, finally, when one wants to walk, or to move his body in some other way, this will [which starts "from the soul"] makes the gland push the spirits towards the muscles which serve for this purpose".

The mechanism involved in this process is that whereby the soul moves the pineal gland to which it is united, and this in turn propels the animal spirits towards that part of the body concerned with this action of the soul in order to produce the desired movement in that part of the body.

Something similar happens with the "passions of the soul", but in an inverse direction, i.e. "towards the soul": when an external stimulus makes an impact on one of the senses, such as, for instance, the vision of a terrifying image, a movement of the spirits is produced, and some of these spirits excite a particular movement in the pineal gland, which originates a certain reaction in the soul, for instance, a "passion of fear" (Article XXXVI, Part I, p. 357, line 5). As Article LI (first Article, Part II), p. 371, lines 9-12, says:

> *...la derniere & plus prochaine cause des passions de l'ame n'est autre que l'agitation, dont les esprits meuvent la petite glande qui est au milieu du cerveau.*
>
> "... the last and nearest cause of the passions of the soul is not other than the agitation with which the spirits move the small gland, which is in the middle of the brain".

– this being a movement which affects the soul.

As Descartes himself says on pages 351 and 360 above quoted, all of the previous explanations imply a *close union* of the soul with the body.

In other passages of his work, Descartes refers to the relation of the soul with the body and claims in a general way that *between the soul and the body there is a relation of extremely tight union.* We quote some of these passages.

In Volume III of his works, p. 424, lines 19-29, in *Responsio ad Hyperaspistem* of August 1641, Descartes says that mind is different from the body but is nevertheless united to it (*coniuncta*) and that it can be affected by the body and can also affect it (*afficere*).

In Volume III, p. 493, lines 4-17, in a letter from Descartes to Regius (January 1642), he expresses that the soul is really and substantially (*realiter et substantialiter*) united (*vnita*) to the body through a true mode of union (*per verum modum vnionis*).

In Volume III, p. 665, lines 15-24, there is a reference to the union, to the force that the soul has to move the body, and that the body has to act on the soul, causing feelings and passions in it.

In Volume III, p. 694, lines 15-21, in a letter to Elisabeth dated June 28, 1643, Descartes accepts the proposition of Elisabeth to attribute matter and extension to the soul:

> *car cela n'est autre chose que la conceuoir vnie au corps*;
>
> "because that is nothing else than to conceive it united to the body".

In Volume IV, p. 166, lines 11-20, in a letter to Father Mesland of February 9, 1645 (?), Descartes expresses that it is the body itself which remains "substantially joined and united" (*ioint & vny*) to the soul itself.

In Volume V, pp. 221, line 30-222, line 3, Descartes points out that the way in which the soul sends the animal spirits to the diverse parts of the body depends on the union of the soul with the body.

In Volume VII, p. 81, lines 1-5, Meditation VI, he says:

> *Docet etiam natura, per istos sensus doloris, famis, sitis &c., me non tantùm adesse meo corpori ut nauta adest navigio, sed illi arctissime esse conjunctum et quasi permixtum, adeo ut unum quid cum illo componant.*

In its French version, Volume IX, quoted edition of Descartes, p. 64:

> *La nature m'enseigne aussi par ces sentimens de douleur, de faim, de soif, &c., que ie ne suis pas seulement logé dans mon corps ainsi qu'vn pilote en son nauire, mais, outre cela, que ie luy suis conioint tres-étroittement & tellement confondu & meslé, que ie compose comme vn seul tout auec luy.*
>
> "Nature teaches me also through these feelings of pain, hunger, thirst, etc., that I do not only dwell in my body as a pilot in his vessel, but that besides that I am very tightly united to it, and to such an extent confounded and mixed that I compose with it - as it were - a sole whole".

In the text just quoted, we must understand the word *ie* = *I* as referring to the "soul", as is evident from a conversation between Descartes and Burman dated April 16, 1648, registered in Vol. V, pp. 144-179. In this conversation Burman, commenting on the Latin expression *arctissime esse conjunctum et quasi permixtum*, asks (p. 163) how the "soul" can be affected by the body and *vice versa*, both being of a completely different nature; and Descartes answers:

> *hoc explicatu difficillimum; sed sufficit hîc experientia, quae hîc adeo clara est, ut negari nullo modo posit.*
>
> "This is very difficult to explain, but the experience in this case is sufficient, experience which is so clear that in no way it can be negated".

This is also confirmed by the comparison of the "pilot" and the "vessel" utilized by Descartes and which could have its origin in Aristotle, *De anima*, p. 413 a.

The idea of a *"close union"* and even of "confusion" and "mixture" of the soul and the body is in obvious opposition to the idea that the soul and the body are essentially different and of a very contrary nature: the nature of the soul is thought, whereas the nature of the body is extension. The distinction of soul and body, with the dualism that it implies, constitutes a fundamental element of the Cartesian system. Descartes for example affirms it in *Discours de la Méthode, Quatriesme Partie,* Volume VI, p. 33, lines 7-9, and in *Principes* I, § 8, Volume IX, p. 28.[57]

2. The union of the soul with the body as explained by Descartes was the object of much criticism. In Chapter XVII of Hamelin's quoted book, several thinkers who criticized Descartes' thesis are mentioned. Let us add to them Leibniz who, in his article "Système nouveau de la nature et de la communication des substances, aussi bien que de l'union qu'il y a entre l'ame et le corps", p. 216, Insel Verlag edition, in *Philosophische Schriften* Band I, expresses:

> *Car je ne trouvois aucun moyen d'expliquer comment le corps fait passer quelque chose dans l'ame, ou* vice versa *ny comment une substance peut communiquer avec une autre substance creée.*
>
> "Since I did not find any way to explain how the body transmits something to the soul or *vice versa,* nor how a substance can communicate with another created substance".

---

[57] Cf. O. Hamelin, *Le systême de Descartes,* Chapter XVII, where are exposed in detail the proofs that Descartes gives in order to establish this distinction.

Also, in *Essais de Théodicée sur la bonté de Dieu, la liberté de l'homme et l'origine du mal, Première Partie*, p. 294 (59), Insel Verlag edition, in *Philosophische Schriften*, Band II, 1, Leibniz affirms:

> *Les philosophes de l'école croyaient qu'il y avait une influence physique rèciproque entre le corps et l'âme; mais depuis qu'on a bien considéré que la pensée et la masse étendue n'ont aucune liaison ensemble, et que ce sont des créatures qui différent* toto genere, *plusieurs modernes ont reconnu qu'il n'y a aucune* communication physique *entre l'âme et le corps, quoique la* communication métaphysique *subsiste toujours, qui fait que l'âme et le corps composent un même* suppôt, *ou ce qu'on appelle une* personne.[58]
>
> "The philosophers of the School [= the Scholastics] thought that there was a physical mutual influence between the body and the soul; but since it has been considered that thought and the extended mass have not any union between them, and that they are creatures which differ *toto genere*, many modern have come to know that there is no *physical communication* at all between the soul and the body, although the *metaphysical communication* always subsists, and this makes that the soul and the body compose a same *basis*, or what is called a *person*".

3. Then, in his quoted article "Système nouveau", p. 216, § 12 (Band I, Insel Verlag edition) Leibniz states that the disciples of Descartes, seeing that the opinion of their master in relation to the union of the soul and the body was inconceivable (*inconcevable*), adopted another explanation concerning that union, which Leibniz expounds in the following terms:

> ... *Ses disciples ... jugèrent que nous sentons les qualitès des corps, parceque Dieu fait naistre des pensées dans l'ame à l'occasion des mouvemens de la matiere; et lorsque nostre ame veut remuer le corps à son tour, il jugérent que c'est Dieu qui le remue pour elle. Et comme la communication des mouvements leur paroissoit encor inconcevable, ils ont crû que Dieu donne du mouvement à un corps à l'occasion du mouvement d'un autre corps. C'est ce qu'ils*

[58] Cf. the following passages in which Leibniz reiterates his opinion that the soul cannot influence the body making it act in a determinate form, nor the body provoke the soul to determinate reactions: *Essais de Théodicée*, Band II, 1, *Préface*, pp. 54-55; *ibidem*, Band II, 1, *Première Partie*, p. 296 (61); "Système nouveau", in *Philosophische Schriften*, Band I, p. 216 (13); *Monadologie*, *ibidem*, § 51.

> *appellent* le Systeme des Causes occasionelles, *qui a esté fort mis en vogue par les belles reflexions de l'Auteur de* La Recherche de la Verité.[59]
>
> "... His disciples ... came to the conclusion that we feel the qualities of the body, because God produces thoughts in the soul on the occasion of the movements of matter; and when our soul wishes to move the body at its turn, they adopted the view that it is God who moves it on the soul's behalf. And as the communication of the movements seemed to them still inconceivable they believed that God gives movement to a body on the occasion of the movement of another body. It is what they call *the System of the occasional Causes*, which has become popular thanks to the beautiful reflections of the Author of *La Recherche de la Verité* [Malebrache]".

According to this *system of occasional causes*, any connection between the soul and the body, in fact any communication between them, is interrupted: if the soul wants to produce something (a movement) in its body, God performs it, and if the body has an experience of any kind (contact with something disagreeable or frightful), God provokes in the soul the corresponding reaction (displeasure or fear). All possibilities for one to affect the other then disappear. God's intervention is permanent: on every *occasion* He is always the direct *cause* owing to which the body behaves in a way which corresponds exactly to what is happening in the soul and *vice versa.*[60]

According to Leibniz ("Eclaircissement des difficultés", in *Philosophische Schriften*, Band I, p. 262, an article which contains the criticisms presented by Bayle to his system), if the theory of *occasional causes* were accepted, it would be necessary to also accept that God would be accomplishing miracles all the time or that He would be able to count on the assistance of angels expressly charged with that task.

---

[59] Cf. Leibniz, *Essais de Théodicée, Première Partie*, in *Philosophische Schriften* Band II, 1, pp. 296-297 (61), Insel Verlag edition.

[60] Cf. J. Ferrater Mora, *Diccionario de Filosofia, sub* "Ocasionalismo", Vol. III, pp. 2612-2615; *Historisches Wörterbuch der Philosophie, sub* "Occasionalismus" by E. Braun, Band 6, col. 1090-1091; and the article "Okkasionalismus" by Jürgen Mittelstrass, in *Enzyklopädie Philosophie und Wissenschaftstheorie*, Vol. 2, pp. 1067-1068.

From a theological point of view, the intervention of angels would not constitute a difficulty, since the driving force for the performance of movements requiring much more effort, such as the movements of the stars, was attributed to them.[61]

4. Leibniz replaces the *system of occasional causes* of the disciples of Descartes by his own system, the famous *system of pre-established harmony*.

The basic idea of this system is that the soul and the body, although constituting a single person, are like two robots, each of which has been programmed down to the smallest detail by God at the moment at which He created them, in such a way that there is an absolute correspondence between what happens in one and what happens in the other. If, for instance, the soul wishes to move an arm at a certain moment due to how it has been programmed, at that same moment the movement corresponding to that desire in the soul is produced in the body, also due to its programming.

In the system of *occasional causes* of the disciples of Descartes, God is constantly intervening at every moment in order to put into effect the correspondence between what happens in the soul and what has to happen in the body, and *vice versa*, while in Leibniz's system of *pre-established harmony*, God intervenes once and for all to establish the programming of the soul and the body in an absolute correspondence.

Leibniz's concept of *pre-established harmony* is especially developed 1. in the article "Système nouveau de la nature et de la communication des substances, aussi bien que de l'union qu'il y a entre l'ame et le corps", published in Paris in 1695 in the *Journal des Scavans* (= Insel Verlag edition *Philosophische Schriften* Band I, pp. 191-226) and 2. in a series of "explanations" (*Eclaircissement du nouveau systeme de la communication des substances, pour servir de reponse à ce qui en est*

[61] Cf. Tiziana Suarez-Nani, *Les anges et la philosophie.*

dit dans le journal du 12 septembre 1695) which appeared in the year 1696 as answers to criticism of his system of *pre-established harmony* (*ibidem*, pp. 226-319).[62]

We shall now present a few passages taken from texts by Leibniz which refer to two aspects of the doctrine of *pre-established harmony*, the advance "programming" of the soul and the body and the "coordination" of both.

In *Discours de métaphysique*, § 13, in *Philosophische Schriften*, Band I, p. 84 he writes:

> *Nous avons dit que la notion d'une substance individuelle enferme une fois pour toutes tout ce qui luy peut jamais arriver.*
>
> "We have said that the notion of an individual substance encloses, once and for all, anything that can happen to it at any time".

In the same paragraph 13 of the *Discours de métaphysique*, pp. 86-88, Leibniz gives an example:

> ... *puisque Jules Cesar deviendra Dictateur perpetuel et maistre de la Republique, et renversera la liberté des Romains, cette action est comprise dans sa notion ... et puisque Dieu luy a imposé ce personnage, il luy est desormais necessaire d'y satisfaire.*
>
> "... since Julius Caesar will become perpetual Dictator and master of the Republic, and will destroy the freedom of Romans, this action is included in his notion ... and, since God has imposed on him this role, it is for him necessary from that moment to comply with that imposition".

In paragraph 16 of the same treatise, p. 102, Leibniz expresses:

---

[62] Leibniz conception of the *pre-established harmony* is also found in isolated passages of his essay written in Latin in 1694, entitled *De primae philosophiae emendatione et de notione substantiae* (= P. Schrecker ed. and trans., in *Leibniz. Opuscules philosophiques choisis*, pp. 160-167); of another of his essays entitled *Discours de métaphysique* of 1686 (= Insel Verlag ed. *Philosophische Schriften* Band I, p. 51-172); and also of his treatise *Essais de Théodicée*, published in 1710 (= Insel Verlag ed. *Philosophische Schriften* Band II, 1, *Préface*, pp. 44, 48, *Première Partie*, p. 298, Band II, 2, *Troisième Partie*, pp. 238, 244; in the *Monadologie* of 1714 (= Insel Verlag ed. *Philosophische Schriften* Band I, pp. 438-483: *Articles* 7, 51, 61, 64, etc.); and in the short treatise *De ipsa natura* of 1698 (in *Leibniz. Opuscules philosophiques choisis*, pp. 192-237, especially pp. 212-213).

... rien ne leur peut arriver d'extraordinaire ny de surnaturel, veu que tous leur evenemens ne sont que des suites de leur nature.

"... nothing extraordinary or supernatural can happen to them [men and other substances], because all the events are nothing else than a sequence of their nature".

In *Discours de metaphysique,* paragraph 33, p. 150, Leibniz affirms:

... tout ce qui arrive à l'ame et á chaque substance, est une suite de sa notion, donc l'idée même ou essence de l'ame porte que toutes ses apparences ou perceptions luy doivent naistre (sponte) *de sa propre nature, et justement en sorte qu'elles répondent d'elles mêmes à ce qui arrive, dans tout l'univers, mais plus particulierement et plus parfaitement à ce qui arrive dans le corps qui luy est afectée.*

"... whatever happens to the soul and to each substance, is an effect of their notion; consequently, the idea itself or the essence of the soul implies that all his appearances or perceptions must be born (*sponte*) [spontaneously] from its own nature, and just in such a way that they respond by themselves to what occurs, in all the universe, but more particularly and more perfectly to what occurs in the body which is assigned to it".

In the "Système nouveau", in *Philosophische Schriften,* Band I, p. 218, paragraph 14, he says:

C'est qu'il faut donc dire que Dieu a creé d'abord l'ame ou toute autre unité reelle de telle sorte, que tout luy doit naistre de son propre fonds, par une parfaite spontaneité *à l'égard d'elle-même, et pourtant avec une parfaite* conformité *aux choses de dehors ... les perceptions ou expressions des choses externes arrivant à l'ame á point nommé, en vertu de ses propres loix, comme dans un monde à part, et comme s'il n'existoit rien que Dieu et elle (pour me servir de la maniere de parler d'une certaine personne d'une grande elevation d'esprit, dont la sainteté est celebrée) il y aura un parfait accord entre toutes ces substances, qui fait le même effect qu'on remarqueroit si elles communiquoient ensemble par une transmission des especes, ou des qualités que le vulgaire des Philosophes s'imagine. De plus, la masse organisée, ... estant exprimée plus prochainement par elle, et se trouvant reciproquement preste à agir d'elle-même, suivant les loix de la machine corporelle, dans le moment que l'ame le veut, sans que l'un trouble les loix de l'autre, les esprits et le sang ayant justement alors les mouvemens qu'il leur faut pour repondre aux passions et aux perceptions de l'ame, c'est ce rapport mutuel reglé par avance dans chaque substance de l'univers, qui produit ce que nous appellons leur* communication, *et qui fait uniquement* l'union de l'ame et du corps.

"Then it is necessary to say that God has firstly created the soul and any other real unity in such a way that all must arise from its own ground, through a perfect *spontaneity* in relation to itself, and, notwithstanding, with a perfect *conformity* with things outside ... since the perceptions or expressions of the external things reach the soul in the precise moment, by virtue of its own laws, as in a world apart and as if only God and it existed (to use the way of speaking of a certain person of a great loftiness of spirit and whose saintliness is praised), there will be a perfect accord among all these substances, which produces the same effects that would be perceived if they communicate among themselves through a transmission of species or qualities, as the majority of the Philosophers imagine. Moreover, being the organized mass [= the body] ... expressed more directly by it [= the soul] and being, in its turn, ready to act by itself, following the laws of the corporeal machine, [just] in the moment in which the soul wants it, without the one troubling the laws of the other, having the spirits and the blood just in that moment the movements that are necessary for them to respond to the passions and perceptions of the soul - it is this mutual relation regulated in advance in each substance of the universe which produces what we call their *communication*, and that constitutes merely the *union of the soul and the body*".

In *Ibidem*, p. 220, paragraph 15, Leibniz asks:

Car pourquoy Dieu ne pourroit il pas donner d'abord à la substance une nature ou force interne qui luy puisse produire par ordre (comme dans un Automate spirituel ou formel, mais libre *en celle qui a la raison en partage) tout ce qui luy arrivera, c'est à dire, toutes les apparences ou expressions qu'elle aura, et cela sans le secours d'aucune creature? ... Et cette nature de l'ame estant representative de l'univers d'une maniere tres exacte (quoyque plus ou moins distincte), la suite des representations que l'ame se produit, répondra naturellement à la suite des changemens de l'univers même: comme en échange le corps a aussi esté accommodé à l'ame, pour les rencontres où elle est conçue comme agissante au dehors.*

"Why God could not give first to the substance a nature or an internal force which could be able to produce in it [= the substance], according to order (as in a *spiritual or formal Robot, but free* in that [part of it] which partakes of reason) all that will happen to it, i.e. all the manifestations or expressions which it will have, and this without the help of any creature? ... And being this nature of the soul representative of the universe in a very exact way (although more or less different), the succession of the representations that the soul produces in itself will naturally agree with the sequence of changes of the universe itself: in the same way as in its turn the body has also been adapted to the soul, for the instances where it is conceived of as acting outward".

In the second "explanation" (*Second Eclaircissement*), in *Philosophische Schriften,* Band I, p. 240 Leibniz says:

Ainsi il ne reste que mon hypothese, c'est á dire que la voye de l'harmonie pré-établie *par un artifice divin prevenant, lequel a formé dés le commencement chacune des ces substances, qu'en ne suivant que ses propres loix qu'elles a receues avec son estre, elle s'accorde pourtant avec l'autre, tout comme s'il y avoit une influence mutuelle, ou comme si Dieu y mettoit tousjours la main, au delà de son concours general.*

"Thus it remains only my hypothesis, i.e. *the way of the pre-established harmony* through a previous divine artifice, which has formed from the beginning each one of these substances [the soul and the body], in such a way that, although [each one] follows only its own laws which it has received with its [own] being, notwithstanding [each one] agrees with the other, as if there were a mutual influence [according to the traditional idea], or as if God always would put in His hand [as in the system of the occasional causes] besides His general participation".[63]

In the second "explanation" (*Second Eclaircissement*), p. 238, and in the letter from Leibniz on the difficulties presented by Bayle, pp. 242-244, Leibniz, to illustrate his theory of *pre-established harmony,* resorts to the image of two perfectly synchronized clocks. Today we could also add the image of two robots [*Automate*!] programmed in their

---

[63] Cf. Third "explanation" (*Eclaircissement*), extracted from a letter of Leibniz, in *Philosophische Schriften,* Band I, pp. 244-246; "explanation" of the difficulties presented by Bayle, *ibidem,* pp. 254, 256, 260, 262, etc.; *Essais de Théodicée,* in *Philosophische Schriften,* Band II, 1, *Préface,* pp. 44, 48, *Première Partie,* p. 298; Band II, 2, *Troisième Partie,* pp. 238, 244; *Monadologie* 7, 51, 61, 64, etc.

smallest details in such a way that, when a certain movement is produced in one, another movement occurs in the other, which exactly corresponds with the previous one. In the case of the two robots and in that of the two clocks, there are physical movements only; in the case of the soul and the body, there is a psychic "movement" in the soul and a physical "movement" in the body.

It is remarkable that the notion of God should play such an important role in the amazing philosophical explanations of the union of the soul and the body offered by the disciples of Descartes and by Leibniz. It is a case of the intervention of a *cultural dogma* concealed by philosophers under the name of the "philosophical use of God". See in the next section some remarks on the notion of *cultural dogma* in relation to transmigration, and also in the *Final Remarks* of this book, Section *The methodological coincidence. The "cultural dogmas"*.

IV.28 The *jīva*, "living individual", and the subtle body. Transmigration. Liberation

1. With the creation of the coarse body and the subtle body (see Section *The relation between Matter and Spirit and its effects)* and the reflection of the Spirit in Matter (*buddhi*, etc.), which as it were imparts a consciousness to it, a *jīva*, which we shall call a "living individual", is constituted. Thus the *jīva*'s existence and functioning is due partly to its material element (physical and psychic) and partly to the influence, which the proximity of the Spirit exerts on Matter in the form of reflection. Thanks to this reflection, the *jīva* is endowed with life, and consequently, it thinks, feels, desires, acts etc. The *jīvas* are the beings which our experience of empirical reality reveals to us. All of the processes indicated are given in the complex of physical components and psychical components, i.e. in the realm of Matter. They are alien to the Spirit, whose connection with or proximity to Matter is nevertheless the cause of the constitution of the living being.

2. In addition, one of the *jīva*'s components, the subtle body, whose composition we have already indicated (see previous Section *The relation between Matter and Spirit and its effects*), transmigrates, passing from one existence to the other, incarnating in different coarse bodies at each new birth, bringing with it the subliminal impressions which the experiences of the living individual left in him, in the subconscious level of his mind, and assuming the good or evil destiny which corresponds to him according to his *karman* (merits and demerits accumulated in his previous reincarnations). Cf. Gauḍapāda's Commentary *ad Sāṃkhya-kārikā* 39:

> *tair ārabdhaṃ śarīraṃ karmavaśāt paśumṛgapakṣisarīsṛp asthāvarajātiṣu saṃsarati dharmavaśād indrādilokeṣu / evam etan niyataṃ sūkṣmaśarīraṃ saṃsarati ...*
>
> "The body constituted by them [= the subtle elements] by the force of *karman* reincarnates in the species of cattle, savage beasts, birds, reptiles, plants, [and] by the force of the good [that man has performed] [he is reborn] in the worlds of Indra, etc.; thus this subtle body inevitably transmigrates ..."

And the *kārikā* 40 and the commentary of Gauḍapāda describe how the subtle body transmigrates.

Transmigration is, as it is well-known, a *cultural dogma* of Indian thought, i.e. a fundamental principle, a presupposition, a premise, a postulate which is taken into account by the majority of the Indian philosophical systems when they construct their theories. Transmigration (*saṃsāra*), beginninglessness (*anāditva*) of all that exists, and subliminal impressions (*vāsanā*) accumulated in the subconscious part of mind are the three most important Indian cultural dogmas, as we have already said. These cultural dogmas seem to possess an autonomous existence, are admitted even by persons who do not adhere to the official religious tradition and *a priori* do not need for their acceptance a rational foundation.[64]

[64] On transmigration in India, see the articles "Saṃsāra" by Lambert Schmithausen, in *Historisches Wörterbuch*, Vol. 8, col. 1163-1167, and the

Western Philosophy also had its own cultural dogmas, as the existence of God and the existence of the soul, and many Western philosophers constructed their systems giving an indisputable validity to them.

Although to a much lesser degree than in India, transmigration also attracted the interest, or obtained the acceptance, of many philosophers and thinkers in Greece and the West.[65]

3. Now, when the different living individuals (which constitute the same series of reincarnations and can as such be considered as one single individual) have accumulated abundant merits, thanks to their moral conduct, then, through study, rational reflection and direct intuition, one of those individuals (the one who will be the last in that series of reincarnations) acquires the *knowledge* that the Spirit and the living individual are totally different and that Matter has nothing to do with the Spirit. With that living individual (the complex formed by the coarse body and the subtle

---

bibliography in it; and F. Tola and C. Dragonetti, "Saṃsāra y Nirvāṇa", in *Filosofīa y Literatura de la India,* pp. 13-31; and on Indian philosophical principles, see F. Tola, "Fundamental Principles of Indian Philosophy", in *Proceedings of the Fifth World Sanskrit Conference,* New Delhi: Rashtriya Sanskrit Sansthan, 1985, pp. 680-688.

[65] On the belief in transmigration in the West, see: the articles "Transmigration" by different authors in *Encyclopaedia of Religion and Ethics,* Vol. XII, pp. 425-440; "Seelenwanderung" by W. Burkert and L. Sturlese, in *Historische Wörterbuch der Philosophie,* Band 9, col. 117-121; and "Seelenwanderung" by Jürgen Mittelstrass, Band 3, pp. 747-748; Manfred Krüger, *Ichgeburt;* and Helmut Zander, *Geschichte der Seelenwanderung in Europa. Alternative religiöse Traditionen von der Antique bis Heute;* and Michel Hulin, "Die Seelenwanderung: Indo-griechischer Mythos oder Herausforderung an das zeitgenössische Denken?", in Fritz Graf-Erik Hornung-Hrsg., *Wanderungen,* Wilhelm Fink Verlag. Among the philosophers and thinkers who accepted transmigration, mentioned by these authors, are found: the Orphics, Pythagoras, Empedocles, Plato, Herodotus, Plutarch, Albinos, Plotinus, Porphyry, Iamblichus; Basileides, Origen, Proclus; Marsilius Ficino, Giordano Bruno; Lessing, Bonnet, etc. It is interesting to point out that even at the end of the 20th century the Catholic Church felt the necessity to reject the belief in "transmigration of souls" or "reincarnation". Cf. M. Krüger, *Ichgeburt,* p. 319.

body), thanks to the knowledge mentioned, the series of reincarnations to which it belonged together with the other living individuals who also formed part of it and were his predecessors comes to an end. The subtle body of that living individual no longer transmigrates, and as existence is nothing other than transmigration, the existence of that living individual finishes. The *jīva*, the living individual, liberated from reincarnations, ceases to exist, the subtle body and the coarse body again become absorbed in Matter, and Matter "leaves the scene", disappearing for the Spirit which was connected to that liberated *jīva*.

When the relation of proximity, which united the Spirit with Matter is broken, the isolation (*kaivalya*) of the Spirit is re-established, remaining alone without anyone else and with nothing opposed to it. This is the transcendent condition of the Spirit.

On the preceding subjects, see the following texts: *Kārikā* 44 c-d:

jñānena cāpavargo viparyayād iṣyate bandhaḥ //

"It is postulated that through knowledge
liberation is obtained;
through the contrary [namely, through ignorance],
enchainment [to the reincarnations cycle]".

Kārikā 2 d and the commentary of Gauḍapāda say what kind of knowledge this is: the discriminative knowledge of what the manifested Matter, the non-manifested Matter and the knower [= the *Puruṣa*] really are (*vyāktāvyāktajñavijñānāt*).

Kārikā 59 compares Matter in the moment of Liberation with a dancer who "leaves the scene" at the end of her dance; after having presented herself, she ceases to perform.

Finally, *kārikā* 68 describes Liberation in the following terms:

prāpte śarīrabhede caritārthatvāt pradhānavinivṛttau /

aikāntikam ātyantikam ubhayaṃ kaivalyam āpnoti //

"Once the separation of the body is attained,
having Matter ceased in its functioning

because of having obtained its goal,
[the Spirit] reaches Isolation,
which is both absolute and definitive".

If, in the case of Śaṅkara's system, the soul was submitted to error since a beginningless eternity, the error which prevented it from seeing itself as it really is, as *Brahman*, the Absolute; for Sāṃkhya, also since a beginningless eternity, the Spirit has been in a state of connection with or proximity to a part of Matter and shaped as the living individuals integrated into an identical series of reincarnations - a connection or proximity which was maintained in the course of those reincarnations. The connection with or proximity to Matter was the destiny of penury, which fell to the Spirit's lot; for the Spirit, to finish with that connection or proximity and to isolate itself in itself is Liberation, its salvation.

In the case of Sāṃkhya, as well as in the case of Śaṅkara, it is not possible to ask when, how and why the Spirit "came into contact with" or "approximated to" Matter, since that connection or proximity always existed since a beginningless eternity, which has no origin.

If, for Śaṅkara, the aim of existence is to overcome error by knowledge, for the Sāṃkhya system the aim is for the Spirit to remain far away from Matter, thanks to the knowledge which arose in the material complex.

IV.29 Remarks on the previous subject: The "subtle body" in Leibniz

The Sāṃkhya notion of "subtle body" brings to mind the notion of *"corps subtil"* to which Leibniz refers in his treatise of 1702, *Considérations sur la doctrine d'un Esprit Universel Unique*, p. 533:

> *Car pourquoy l'ame ne pourroit elle pas tousjours garder un corps subtile, organisé à sa manière, qui pourra même reprendre un jour ce qu'il faut de son corps visible dans la resurrection, puisqu'on accorde aux bien-heureux un corps glorieux, et puisque les anciens peres ont accordé un corps subtile aux anges.*

"Why the soul could not conserve ever a subtle body, organized in its own manner, [in such a way] that it [the soul] could even take again some day in the resurrection what is necessary [for it = the soul] of its visible body, since it is granted to the blessed ones a glorious body and the ancient Fathers [of the Church] have conceded a subtle body to the angels"?

The patriarchs expressed various different opinions in relation to the body of the angels. According to René Roques in his Introduction to *Denis l' Aréopagite, La Hiérarchie Céleste,* p. LXXI (who follows Petau, *De Angelis,* in J.B. Thomas, *Opus de theologicis dogmatibus*), numerous patriarchs and great men have affirmed that the angels have a body (Justin, Clemens of Alexandria, Origen, Theognostes, Hilarius, Ambrosius, St. Augustine, etc.) (Petau, pp. 5-12). Basilius speaks of an intelligible creation for the angels (νοητὴν κτίσιν), but he also sometimes seems to attribute material bodies to them, although these are very subtle (*très subtils*) (Petau, p. 6). Gregory Thaumaturgus, Titus the Hunchbacked, Gregory of Nyssa, Eusebius, Epiphanius, Theodoret and Chrysostom etc. affirm the pure spirituality of the angels (Petau, pp. 12-14).

In his article "Systeme nouveau de la nature", in *Philosophische Schriften,* Band I, pp. 208-210 (§ 7), Insel Verlag, Leibniz expresses his adhesion to the idea of the conservation

non seulement de l'ame, mais encor de l'animal même et de sa machine organique, quoyque la destruction des parties grossieres l'ait reduit à une petitesse qui n'echappe pas moins à nos sens que celle où il estoit avant que de naistre.

"not only of the soul, but also of the animal itself and of its organic machine, although the destruction of the coarse parts had reduced it to such a smallness that it does not escape our senses less than that it had before being born".

Cf. *Opuscules et fragments inédits...,* edited by L. Couturat, p. 16 § 13:

... *ideo etiam corpus ejus [*animae*] ad magnam quidem subtilitatem redigi, penitus autem destrui non potest.*

... therefore its [= of the soul] body can be reduced indeed to a great subtlety".

IV.30. The Atheism of the *Sāṃkhya*

One of the characteristic features of the Sāṃkhya philosophical system, which opposes it to a large portion of the orthodox systems in India while connecting it to a long tradition of atheism, equally powerful in India, is its negation of the existence of the *Īśvara* (Lord, God), who is mainly characterized by two attributes, that of the creator and that of the governor of the universe.

Of the Indian philosophical systems with atheistic tendencies, Sāṃkhya and Mīmāṃsā are considered orthodox systems, Jainism and Buddhism are considered heterodox while accepting the existence of a moral order, and the materialists deny the existence of any moral order. See Section *The* sui generis *materialism* of *Sāṃkhya.*

In numerous passages of the *Sāṃkhyakārikās* and of the *Sāṃkhyasūtras* and in their respective commentaries, this atheistic position of Sāṃkhya is expressed emphatically.

In his commentary on the *sūtra* V, 46 Vijñānabhikṣu refers to the rejection or negation of the *Īśvara* on the part of Sāṃkhya (*īśvarapratiṣedha*); in his commentary on the *sūtra* V, 126 he openly expresses that the aim of this *sūtra* is to establish the inexistence of the *Īśvara* (*īśvarābhāva*); in the commentary on the *sūtra* V, 127, he holds that the thesis of the existence of the *Īśvara* has not been proved (*īśvarasya asiddher*, cf. *sūtras* I, 92: *īśvarāsiddheḥ*; I, 93: *neśvarasiddhir*, V, 2: *īśvarāsiddher*; and in the commentary of the same Vijñānabhikṣu *ad sūtra* V, 5 *in fine*, we can find a reference to the impossibility of an eternal "Lordship": *nityaiśvaryānupapater*).

Many other passages of the Sāṃkhya texts also develop arguments on which to base the thesis of the inexistence of God.

1. One of the central ideas of these arguments is that *there are no proofs which have demonstrated the existence of God*, or in terms proper to Indian philosophical language, that there is no means of valid knowledge (*pramāṇa*) [perception (*pratyakṣa*), inference (*anumāṇa*) and verbal testimony (= the Revelation or tradition) (*śabda*)] which supports the existence of God.

In *Sāṃkhyasūtras* V, 10, the inexistence of a *pramāṇa* (perception, inference or verbal testimony) which proves His existence (*pramāṇābhāvān na tadsiddhiḥ*) is asserted in a general way in relation to the *Īśvara*.

Sāṃkhyasūtras I, 89 gives a definition of perception (*pratyakṣa*), which requires contact between the sensory organ and the object. In the introduction of thc *sūtra* I, 92, a theistic opponent adduces that this definition is invalid because it is incomplete and cannot be applied to the "perception of the Lord or God" (*Īśvara*), an "object" with which there is no possibility of contact. The *sūtra* I, 92 rejects this objection, affirming that there is no room for this logical defect (*doṣa*) intended to invalidate the mentioned definition of perception, "because there is no proof of the existence of God": *Īśvarāsiddeḥ*, and, consequently, the objection is based on something which has not been proved, God or the *Īśvara*.

Sāṃkhyasūtra V, 11 denies the existence of the inference (*anumāṇa*) as a valid means of knowledge of the existence of God, since, even accepting that this world is an effect and consequently requires the existence of a cause for its creation, it is not possible to construct an inference which leads to the conclusion that the *Īśvara* is unavoidably that cause.

In addition, the *sūtra* V, 12 adds that Revelation (*śruti*) itself affirms that the creation is a product or effect of (the evolution of) the non-manifested Primordial Matter (*pradhāna*); and consequently, for the Sāṃkhya system, God is not necessarily the unavoidable cause of this effect, which is creation. The commentary by Vijñānabhikṣu *ad locum* quotes a text from the *Śvetāśvatara-Upaniṣad* IV, 5, and another from the *Bṛhadāraṇyaka-Upaniṣad* I, 4, 7, which both belong to the Revelation, in support of the assertion of the *sūtra*. Also, *sūtra* I, 95 maintains the thesis that, when Revelation speaks of a God *(Īśvara)*, it is only with the aim of extolling the Spirits (*Puruṣas*) which have achieved Liberation (the term *Īśvara* being used as a merely praiseful epithet in this case) or with the aim of inciting to the veneration of the traditional Gods, who are not eternal, are submitted to reincarnations and have nothing to do with the creation and government of the world. Finally, *Sāṃkhyasūtra* VI, 64 and commentary of Vijñānabhikṣu *ad locum*, affirm that it cannot be said that the effect (= creation) depends on God since there is no proof of His existence: *kāryasiddhir ne 'śvarādhīnā pramāṇā 'bhāvāt.*

The interpretation which Sāṃkhya gives of the Revelation (*Śruti*) in the *sūtras* I, 95 and V, 12 is an example of how thinkers in India dealt with traditional texts, adapting them to the new ideas they maintained.

It can be affirmed that, for the Sāṃkhya, which holds the theory of the evolution of Matter, the notion of God has become unnecessary.

2. Another central idea of these arguments against the existence of God is that *the very notion of God as creator and governor of the world implies* a contradictio in adiecto.

For Sāṃkhya, beings can be either enchained (*baddha*) or liberated (*mukta*).

If they are *enchained* (*baddha*), they belong to the field of Matter and of empirical reality, i.e. to the cycle of reincarnations and to impermanence, they are submitted to impurities and have limited knowledge and power.

If they are *liberated (mukta)*, they are absolutely transcendent: they belong to the range of the Spirit, they are totally beyond all that belongs to the empirical reality and are isolated and apart from all.

In the *Sāṃkhyasūtras* I, 93-94 and their commentary of Vijñānabhikṣu *ad locum*, it is expressed that, if God existed,

He would have to belong to one of these two conditions indicated for beings. If He belonged to the first one (enchained), He would not have the capacity of performing creation or governing it; if He belonged to the second one (liberated), He would have neither will or desire, nor would He possess either purpose or finality in order to create and govern.

The commentary of Vijñānabhikṣu *ad Sāṃkhyasūtra* V, 5 explains that, in the first case (enchained), God's incapability to create and govern would be due to His limitations, since there is a contradiction (*virodha*) between *being submitted to reincarnations* (*saṃsāritva*) [i.e. belonging to empirical reality and being enchained] and *the fact of not finding limits to His desires* (*apratihatecchatva*) [i.e. the fact of having the unlimited power necessary to carry out creation]. In the second case (liberated), His incapability to create and govern would be due to His absolute heterogeneity and transcendence.

Also, as follows from the *sūtras* V, 3-7 and their commentaries, if we attribute to God the function of governing or creating, this would imply that He had a will to perform, an impelling wish and a determined aim, and this means that, in the same way as a monarch of the world, He would have deficiencies, defects and unsatisfied desires, and this would produce the absurd consequence (*prasaṅga*) that He would, like men, be subjected to displeasure and to suffering.

The conclusion is that the existence of a God as creator and governor of the universe is a logical impossibility since none of the two conditions mentioned can include a being who could perform the actions of creation and government of the world.

Moreover, for Sāṃkhya, as we have already said, creation is the evolution of Matter, and the government of the universe falls to karmic causality by means of which any action is followed by a determined effect or result adequate to it. Cf. the *sūtra* V, 2 and the commentary of Vijñānabhikṣu.

The *contradictio in adiecto* to which we have referred consists in the fact that, for building a notion of a Creator and Governor God, it is necessary to assign to Him attributes which are contradictory among themselves and impede the realization of the functions which it is supposed that he must perform.

3. Another argument for the negation of the existence of a Creator and Governor God in Sāṃkhya is developed by Vācaspati Miśra in his commentary *ad Sāṃkhyakārikā* 57.

If there were a God who had the function of Creator, *He would have to perform creation either in pursuit of an aim of his own* (svārtha) *or inspired by a desire to benefit someone else*, by good wishes towards others, i.e. by a feeling of compassion (*kāruṇya*). However, both alternatives are excluded.

In fact, a Supreme Being, all of whose desires have been realized by Him, has no reason, motive or *finality* of personal character for creating.

With regard to compassion, it is necessary to bear in mind that, before creation, there were no beings to whom that feeling of compassion could be directed and for whose benefit He could perform His creation.

And if, in spite of the absurdity of a compassion without beings which can be its object, it is said that God creates the world by compassion and then, on seeing the beings plunged into sorrow after creation, He feels compassion for them, we would have the logical defect of the "vicious circle" (*itaretarāśrayatva*): creation is due to compassion and compassion is due to creation.

Also, it would be easier (*sukaratva*) for a God who feels compassion to create all living beings to be happy and not to be submitted to different destinies, some of them full of suffering and others full of happiness.

4. If a Lord or a God is postulated as the creator and governor of all, *the presence of evil, suffering, injustice and the inexplicable differences in the personal destinies of beings in the world would force to "accuse Him" of "cruelty"* (nairghṛṇya) *and "partiality"* (vaiṣamya), as Vijñānabhikṣu affirms in his commentary *ad Sāṃkhyasūtras* VI, 65.

By attributing the creation and government of the world to Matter and to *karman* only, which Sāṃkhya does, God, the *Īśvara* (in case His existence is accepted) would be "released" from that accusation. However, in this case, an *Īśvara* deprived of the functions of creator and governor and beyond purposes and emotions is nothing but another Spirit like the others.

Matter and *karman* act in a mechanical and unconscious way and thus do not give way to egotistical purposes or to any feelings of compassion which would impel them to action. Unconscious Matter and *karman* act in the manner of the laws of nature or as *kārikā* 57 says:

> *vatsavivṛddhinimittaṃ kṣīrasya yathā pravṛttir ajñasya.*
>
> "As the milk arises spontaneously from the cow for feeding the calf."

And unconscious Matter and *karman* cannot be "accused" of "cruelty" or "partiality".[66]

This last argument (4.) implies the awareness, which Sāṃkhya had, of the problem of existence of evil in the world when the existence of a personal God, creator and governor of the universe possessing the most sublime qualities as omnipotence, infinite goodness and supreme justice is postulated.

The atheistic Sāṃkhya confronted by the reality of evil and the problem of the existence of an *Īśvara*, God, utilizes this unquestioned existence of evil as another proof of His inexistence.

In turn the Hindu theistic philosophical systems put God beyond evil, thus safeguarding His exalted attributes, also assigning the responsibility of evil to *karman*, as Sāṃkhya does. The theistic systems put great emphasis on the concept of

---

[66] On the atheism of the Sāṃkhya system, see Jadunath Sinha, *A History of Indian Philosophy*, Vol. II, pp. 88-92; Richard Garbe, *Die Sāṃkhya-Philosophie*, pp. 191-195; Dale Riepe, *The Naturalistic Tradition in Indian Thought*, pp. 210-211; K.K. Mittal, *Materialism in Indian Thought*, Chapter VII; and Debiprasad Chattopadhyaya, *Indian Atheism. A Marxist Analysis.*

anāditva, "beginninglessness" (or eternity *a parte ante*) of the *karman*, for liberating God or the Lord, whose existence they accept, from any guilt concerning the existence of evil in the world: God has nothing to do with the evil of the world; the evil is merely an effect of the actions of men in the course of their existences *from an eternity without a beginning in time.*[67]

IV.31 Remarks on the previous subject: Atheism in the West

Atheism also had its history in the West, where it adopted multiple forms. The term "atheism" can designate the negation of the existence and/or divinity of the traditional gods of the state, the refusal to worship them assuming a more elevated concept of divinity - a thing which happened in Greece and Rome before the advent of Christianity; or, after the advent of Christianity, the negation of the existence of a Supreme Being, God, Creator and Governor of the universe. This negation could or could not be accompanied by elevation to the rank of an explanatory and founding principle of reality of another principle with a nature totally different to that of God.[68]

From very early in the history of human thought proofs for establishing the existence of God were devised. This fact was generally inspired by the desire to give a rational foundation to an established belief. These proofs were utilized against those who negated the existence of that Supreme Being.

We shall limit ourselves here to pointing out two elements related to the atheism proper to Sāṃkhya thought which are also found in the thought of d'Holbach, an author to whom we have already referred to before and a prominent representative of an absolute atheism.

---

[67] On the importance of the notion of *anāditva*, beginninglessness, see our article "Anāditva or beginninglessness in Indian Philosophy", in *Annals of the Bhandarkar Oriental Research Institute*, pp. 1-20.

[68] Cf. Fritz Mauthner, *Der Atheismus und seine Geschichte im Abendlande.*

D'Holbach as well as Sāṃkhya denies the possibility of demonstrating the existence of God.[69] D'Holbach initiates Chapter V of the second part of his *Système de la Nature,* emphatically affirming:

> *On nous parle sans cesse de Dieu, et jamais personne n'est parvenu jusqu'ici à démontrer son existence.*
>
> "People speak to us incessantly about God, and never anybody has been able up to now to demonstrate his existence" (p. 137).

And next he moves on to deal with the proofs for the existence of God given by Descartes, Malebranche, Newton, etc.:

> *afin de nous convaincre du peu de solidité que les grands personnages ont sçu donner aux preuves qu'ils ont successivement imaginées pour établir l'existence d'un Dieu* (p. 137).
>
> "with the aim of convincing us of the scarce solidity that the great personages have been able to give to the proofs that they have successively imagined for establishing the existence of God".

In various passages of his work, d'Holbach expresses similar ideas:

In I, p. 19, he indicates the impossibility of knowing God, and as a consequence the impossibility of deriving moral norms from Him:

> *Ne va point faire descendre d'un Dieu, que tu ne connaîtra jamais, ... les règles de tes devoirs ...*
>
> "Do not make descend from a God, that you will never know, ...the rules of your duties ...[70]"

In p. 21, d'Holbach refers to God as an

> *... pouvoir inconnu que l'ignorance a créé, et que l'enthousiasme a revêtu de mille qualités incompatibles.*

---

[69] See in the previous Section *The Atheism of the* Sāṃkhya the first argument adduced by the Sāṃkhya system in order to found the inexistence of God.

[70] For Sāṃkhya, also morality does not derive from a God that does not exist, and it is the *karman* to which corresponds the function of moral retribution of actions.

"...unknown power that ignorance has created, and that the enthusiasm has covered with thousands of incompatible qualities".

And in II, p. 103, he says:

> ... *dans le Dieu du Dr. Clarcke ainsi que dans celui des plus grands Thélogiens, on ne verra qu'une chimère établie sur des suppositions gratuites, et formée par l'assamblage confus de qualités disparates, qui rendent son existence totalement imposible* ...[71]

"... in the God of Dr. Clarcke as in that of the greatest theologians only will be seen a chimera established upon unfounded suppositions and formed by a confuse assemblage of contradictory qualities that makes his existence totally impossible ..."

Like the Sāṃkhya system, d'Holbach also adhered to a theoretical materialism which extolled Matter, assigning to it extreme attributes which have their counterparts in Sāṃkhya, and made it the ultimate reason of all.

In the Section *Remarks on the previous subject: The notion of matter in the West* we have given a large extract from d'Holbach in which he expresses his concept of matter. Let us now emphasize the following attributes of matter in that text:

1. eternal,
2. independent,
3. beginningless,
4. its qualities and properties can be known by inference,
5. endless, although its products begin and end,
6. it is all that exists and it is infinite,
7. it is unique, although its component parts are infinitely varied,
8. it produces intelligence,
9. it acts according to the laws of its nature and existence,
10. its power is limited only by its own nature,

---

[71] See the arguments 2. and 3. of section *The Atheism of the* Sāṃkhya where it is expressed that to the *Īśvara*, Lord, God, if it existed, qualities contradictory among themselves would have to be attributed.

11. the moral and spiritual virtues are qualities proper of the evolved Matter.

See the Section *Attributes of Primordial Matter* which are also in this chapter of the book.[72]

In the West, also, the indisputable existence of evil in the world on one hand and a belief in the existence of an almighty and compassionate God on the other caused a serious problem, which theologians and philosophers tried to solve by looking for a device to harmonize both existences with the aim of liberating God from all accusations of wickedness, injustice, powerlessness or even ignorance.

The most important and celebrated declaration of intent in this respect is constituted by the treatise of Leibniz entitled *Essais de Théodicée sur la bonté de Dieu, la libertè de l'homme et l'origine du mal*, published in Amsterdam in 1710.[73]

In the same year Leibniz also published a methodical abridgement of his *Théodicée*, written in Latin and intended especially for theologians and philosophers, entitled *Causa Dei asserta per justitiam ejus, cum caeteris ejus perfectionibus, cunctisque actionibus conciliatam* ("The Cause of God defended by means of his justice, harmonized with his other perfections, and with all his actions").

We shall give the text and the translation of the paragraphs 60-65 of this treatise in which Leibniz refers to the problem of evil and to the diverse positions adopted in relation to it in his own epoch.[74] We follow the text of the Insel Verlag edition, Band II, second half.

---

[72] Cf. Fritz Mauthner, *Der Atheismus und seine Geschichte im Abendlande*, already quoted, Vol. III, pp. 132-157.

[73] On this work, see the articles "Teodicea", in J. Ferrater Mora, *Diccionario de Filosofía*, Vol. IV, pp. 3468-3469; "Theodicy" by William Fulton, in *Encyclopaedia of Religion and Ethics*, Vol. 12, pp. 289-291; "Theodizee" by S. Lorenz, in *Historisches Wörterbuch der Philosophie*, Vol. 10, col. 1066-1074; and "Theodizee" by Jürgen Mittelstrass, in *Enzyklopädie Philosophie und Wissenschaftstheorie*, Band 4, pp. 247-249.

[74] On the problem of the existence of evil in the world and its relation with the lofty qualities attributed to God, in the context of the conflict between faith and reason in the 18th century in the West, see the article "Bayle et les

60. Gravissimae tandem sunt difficultates circa Sanctitatem Dei, *seu circa perfectionem ad bona malaque moralia aliorum relatam, quae eum amare virtutem, odisse vitium etiam in aliis facit, et ab omni peccati labe atque contagio quam maxime removet; et tamen passim scelera regnant in medio potentissimi Dei imperio. ...*

61. Objicitur *nempe Deum nimis concurrere ad peccatum, hominem non satis.* Deum autem nimis concurrere ad malum morale *physice et moraliter, voluntate et productiva et permissiva peccati.*

62. Concursum moralem locum habiturum observant, etsi Deus nihil conferret agendo ad peccatum, saltem dum permitteret seu non impediret cum posset.

63. Sed revera Deum concurrere ajunt moraliter et physice simul, quia non tantum non impedit peccantes, sed etiam quodammodo adjuvat vires ipsis occasionesque praestando ...

64. Hinc quidam inferre audent Deum vel utroque vel certe alterutro modo, peccati complicem, imo autorem esse atque adeo divinam sanctitatem, justitiam, bonitatem evertunt.

65. Alii malunt Divinam omniscientiam et omnipotentiam, verbo magnitudinem labefactare, tanquam aut nesciret minimeve curaret mala, aut malorum torrenti obsistere non posset.

"60. Finally, there exist very serious difficulties concerning *the Sanctity of God*, or concerning [His] perfection in relation to the moral good or evil of the other [beings], [perfection] which makes Him love virtue and hate vice also in others, and which moves Him away as much as possible from the impurity and the contagion of sin; and nevertheless crimes reign everywhere in the center of the empire of the most powerful God ...

61. *It is objected* that God collaborates too much in [the performance of] sin, man not sufficiently. [It is said] that *God collaborates too much in moral wickedness* physically and morally, with a productive and permissive will of sin.

62. They remark that moral collaboration [of God in sin] will take place, even if God does not contribute anything to sin with His own action, but allows it, or does not hinder it having the power to do that.

---

apories de la raison humaine" by Jean-Luc Solère, section *VI. De la cruauté de Dieu*, in *La raison corrosive. Études sur la pensée critique de Pierre Bayle. Réunies par Isabelle Delpla et Philippe de Robert*, Paris: Honoré Champion, 2003.

63. But in fact they say that God collaborates [in sin] at the same time morally and physically, since not only He does not hinder sinners [to act], but even in some way helps them, giving them forces and occasions...

64. Hence some dare to infer that God either in both ways [morally and physically] or at least in one way or the other, is accomplice of the sin, or even more its author; and in this way they destroy the divine sanctity, justice and goodness.

65. Others prefer to cause the Divine omniscience and omnipotence, in a word the greatness [of God], to totter, as if He were ignorant of evils or worried very little about them, or were unable to oppose the torrent of evils".

IV.32 Conclusion

We think that the information given in this Chapter dedicated to the exposition of the principal aspects of the Indian philosophical system Sāṃkhya and of the coincidences between notions, ideas, principles, conceptions and theories of this system and of the Western philosophical thought constitute another solid foundation in favor of the theses presented in the introduction of this book.

We think also that this brief exposition of the Sāṃkhya system exemplifies the philosophical interest which this system presents by itself because of the richness of its theories, such as, for instance, its concept of Matter, its notion of evolution, its theory of causality and its atheism, and also because of its rationalistic tendency, which is revealed in arguments such as those used to prove the existence of non-manifested Matter and in its reasoning in support of the inexistence of an *Īśvara* (God) - a richness whose value increases if we take into account how early it appeared.

Thus Sāṃkhya can rightly be considered as a pinnacle of Indian rationalism, which so often has been denied by the West.

Final Remarks

V.1 Thematic coincidences

We think that the information given on the previous pages, which is dedicated to the exposition of a few aspects of Indian philosophical thought as expressed in the *Vedas*, the *Upaniṣads* and the *Sāṃkhya* system while pointing out coincidences between notions, ideas, principles, concepts and theories originating in Indian as well as Western thought (traditionally considered as *philosophy*), represents a solid argument in favour of the **first thesis** expounded in the *Introduction*, i.e. that, *up to the 17th century at least, in India on the one hand and in Greece and Europe on the other, there was frequent reflection on the same philosophical subjects, and it was carried out in the same way.*

We are also doing research on other systems of Indian thought such as Yoga, Nyāya, Vaiśeṣika, Vedānta (Gauḍapāda, Śaṅkara, Rāmānuja, Madhva) and Mīmāṃsā following the same method used in this book in relation to the *Vedas*, the *Upaniṣads* and the *Sāṃkhya* system. Remarkable points of contact between Indian and Western thought are to be found everywhere. When published, the results of this research will corroborate the arguments developed in this book.

In his *Prolegomena*, p. 113, in *Werke* V, Suhrkamp ed. (= A 3, 4) Kant refers to some scholars (*Es gibt Gelehrte...*) "who think that nothing can be said, which has not been said before" (*...kann nichts gesagt werden, was ihrer Meinung nach nicht schon sonst gesagt worden ist*), and immediately afterwards he expresses the idea (which appears in the epigraph heading the *Introduction* to this book) that, as human understanding has reflected on innumerable themes in many different ways for many centuries now, it is difficult not to find new ideas to which some old and similar idea does not correspond.

In his treatise *Über eine Entdeckung nach der alle neue Critik der reinen Vernunft durch eine ältere entbehrlich gemacht werden soll*, Vol. V, p. 364, Suhrkamp edition (= BA 110, 111), Kant refers to the same subject, stating that "it is the usual destiny of any new scientific idea, when nothing can be opposed to it, that it be considered at least that that idea had already been known since long time before" (... *es ist auch schon das gewöhnliche Schicksal alles Neuen in Wissenschaften, wenn man ihm nichts entgegensetzen kann, dass man es doch wenigstens als längst bekannt bei Älteren antreffe*).

Kant rightly opposes the idea that nothing new can be said: it is possible for new ideas to arise which do not have as predecessors similar ideas. This is the condition *sine qua non* for the advancement of thought.

We would like to add to Kant's opinion that, just as it is not difficult to find new ideas to which some older, similar idea *does not* correspond, it is also not difficult to find many ideas which are supposed to be new but to which older, similar ideas *do* correspond – especially if we broaden the geographical and chronological field of investigation. This is the assumption that makes our research on the parallelisms between Indian and Western thought possible and that seems to us to give a much wider range to Indian and

European thought: they cease to be "Oriental" or "Western" thought and instead become "universal" thought.

V.2 The methodological coincidence: The "cultural dogmas"

The examples given in Chapters II, III and IV of this book refer to similarities related to *themes* or *contents* of the philosophical reflection. Now wc shall point out a most important similarity in relation to the *method* or *way of acting* frequently adopted by Indian and Western thinkers, which strongly reduces in both cases the credibility of their conclusions, since they cannot be considered as authentic products of rationality.

In the Brahmanical or Hinduist tradition of India, for instance, there are *beliefs*, which come from the *Past* – it would be better to say: which are imposed by the *Past*, such as the beliefs in reincarnation, in the existence of an *Īśvara* (Lord, God), and in the infallibility of the *Śruti* (Revelation). We call these beliefs *cultural dogmas* (similar to other dogmas, which are found in other Indian traditions). These beliefs are unconsciously taken for granted or assumed by a great number of thinkers, they are for them unavoidable assumptions that do not require to be demonstrated. These beliefs are based on *faith* rather than on observation and verification of facts or on valid rational arguments. The force that these beliefs possess is incomparably greater than the force of the arguments that sometimes are adduced in support of them by some thinkers and refuted by others, not being unanimity in relation to their validity.[1] It could be said that the fact of being based on faith gives to these beliefs a force that they would not have if they were only based in logical reasoning. We do not discuss or question here the

---

[1] For instance Buddhists do not accept the existence of God or of a soul, which constitute cultural dogmas of the Hindu tradition of India, and the Indian materialists deny furthermore reincarnation, which is a cultural dogma accepted by Buddhists and Hindus, utilizing all of them in order to found their positions *rational proofs* developed in their philosophical treatises.

value of faith as a ground for a belief, but we think that it cannot be asserted that *an act of faith is a rational mental process.* Many Hindu thinkers have had recourse to these cultural dogmas as starting points, bases, or postulates to construct upon them their doctrinaire systems.

It is necessary to remark here that, even if Indian thinkers used some of their cultural dogmas, to which authority is attributed *a priori* (a procedure which could be considered as an example of non-rational behaviour), as a starting point, basis or postulate to construct their doctrinaire (philosophical) systems, nevertheless these same thinkers in their argumentations subject themselves to the strictest requirements of reason and logic. We can question the validity of their *cultural dogmas* but we cannot find logical defects in what they construct on the basis of these dogmas.[2] They are real granite and steal constructions upon clay foundations.

We must acknowledge the fact that the previous remarks concerning the Brahmanic or Hindu thinkers apply equally and in their integrity to Western thinkers (we could even say they apply also to thinkers belonging to any culture): although following the most rational and logical requirements in their reasonings, they construct their theories on frail bases or postulates, which are nothing other than their own *cultural dogmas.* Among these Western *cultural dogmas* are the belief in the existence of God, the belief in the immortality of the soul, the authority of the Christian tenets, the infallibility of the Bible, etc. There is neither in the West unanimity in regard to the validity of the proofs adduced in favor of the Western *cultural dogmas.*[3]

---

[2] F. Tola, "Fundamental Principles of Indian Philosophy", in *Proceedings of the Fifth World Sanskrit Conference*, pp. 680-688.

[3] In *Chapter IV* of this book, in Section *Remarks on the previous subject: Proofs of the existence of God in the West,* we have referred to the proofs of the existence of God in the West as an example of proofs adduced in order to validate a Western *cultural dogma,* the existence of God, accepted by many Western thinkers.

Descartes, referring to himself in the preface to his *Discours de la méthode*, in *Oeuvres de Descartes*, Vol. VI, p. 1, clearly says:

> *l' existence de Dieu & de l'ame humaine, ...sont les fondaments de sa Métaphysique*
>
> "the existence of God and of the human soul are ...the foundations of his Metaphysics".

Also, in the *Sexta Responsio* to the objections made against his *Meditationes de prima philosophia*, in *Oeuvres de Descartes*, Vol. VII, pp. 429-430, he affirms:

> *...nempe incipiendum est a Dei cognitione ac deinde aliarum omnium rerum cognitiones huic uni sunt subordinandae.*
>
> "... certainly it is necessary to begin with the knowledge of God and thereafter the knowledges of all the other things have to be subordinated to that sole [knowledge]".

And in his *Epistola*, Vol. VII, p. 1, which precedes his *Meditationes De Prima Philosophia, in quibus Dei existentia, & animae humanae a corpore distinctio*, in a more forceful way, he says:

> *.. nam quamvis nobis fidelibus animam humanam cum corpore non interire, Deumque existere, fide credere sufficiat ... Et quamvis omnino verum sit, Dei existentiam credendam esse, quoniam in sacris scripturis docetur, & vice versa credendas sacras scripturas, quoniam habentur a Deo.*

In his French version, Vol. IX, *Oeuvres*, p. 4:

> *... Car bien qu'il nous suffise à nous autres qui sommes fideles, de croire par la Foy qu'il y a vn Dieu, & que l'ame humaine ne meurt point auec le corps, ... Et quoy qu'il soit absolument vray, qu'il faut croire qu'il y a vn Dieu, parce qu'il est ainsi enseigné dans les Saintes Escritures, & d'autre part qu'il faut croire les Saintes Escritures, parce qu'elles viennent de Dieu ...*
>
> "... Since, although for us who are believers (*fideles*), it is enough to believe by Faith that the human soul does not perish with the body and that God exists ... And although it is absolutely true that it is necessary to believe in the existence of God, because thus it is taught in the Sacred Scriptures, and *vice versa* it is necessary to believe in the Sacred Scriptures, because they come from God ..."

Geneviève Rodis-Lewis in her article on Descartes, in Ueberweg, *Grundriss der Geschichte der Philosophie. Die Philosophie des 17. Jahrhunderts*, p. 325, referring to the religiousness of Descartes, concludes with words which center on a Western cultural dogma, God, as ground of the philosophical reflection:

> *"In a general way it has been positively answered the question on the religious sincerity of Descartes (thus already in [*Gaston*] Milhaud 1921 [*Descartes savant*]). This fact in no way weakens the effort [*of Descartes*] for the knowledge and possession of the world, for which the philosopher needed that absolute ground in God that granted him his independence ... That necessity of a support to reach philosophy (which encompassed the science of nature in its entireness) and at the same time wisdom manifested itself already when Descartes explained his dreams of the year 1619. Anyhow it would be mistaken to speak here of a 'mystic crisis' (Milhaud 1921 [op. cit.] Chapter 2) or of a 'night of ecstasy or of inexplicable halucinations' ([P.] Janet 1868* ['Descartes, son caractère et son génie', in *Revue des deux Mondes* 38/73, Paris, 1868, pp. 345-369]) *or of the appearance of the 'genius malignus' ([*J.*] Maritain 1932 [*Le songe de Descartes, Paris, 1932*]) ".*

Nicolaus of Cusa (1401-1464) in his *De docta ignorantia* III, Chapter XI (*Mysteria fidei*), had exalted the value of faith in the revealed truths of Christianity as a starting point and fundament of knowledge and reason.

In what follows we give the text and translation of the passage of the mentioned work *De docta ignorantia* of Nicolaus of Cusa, where he exposes his idea of the value of faith, Wissenschaftliche Buchgesellschaft edition, Band 1, p. 74:

> *Mayores nostri omnes concordanter asserunt fidem initium esse intellectus. In omni enim facultate quaedam praesupponuntur ut principia prima, quae sola fide apprehenduntur, ex quibus intelligentia tractandorum elicitur. Omnem enim ascendere volentem ad doctrinam credere necesse est his, sine quibus ascendere nequit. Ait enim Ysaias: "nisi credideritis, non intelligetis." Fides igitur est in se complicans omne intelligibile. Intellectus autem est fidei explicatio. Dirigitur igitur intellectus per fidem, et fides per intellectum extenditur. Ubi igitur non est sana fides, nullus est verus intellectus. Error principiorum et fundamenti debilitas qualem conclusionem subinferant, manifestum est. Nulla autem perfectior fides quam ipsamet veritas, quae Iesus est.*

> "All our elders in agreement affirm that faith is the beginning of the [activity of] reason, since in every discipline certain things are presupposed as first principles, which are apprehended by the sole faith, starting from which is obtained the understanding of the themes to be dealt with. It is necessary that anyone who wants to reach [the truth of] a doctrine believe in these [principles], without which one cannot reach [that truth], since Isaiah has said: 'If you do not believe, you will not understand.' Faith then encompasses in itself all the intelligible. On its turn reason is the revelation of [the truth of] faith. Then reason is directed by faith, and faith is increased by reason. Then where there is not a correct faith [i.e. the Christian one, later the author will say: *Christi sanissima fides*: 'the most correct faith in Christ'], there does not exist any reason which leads to truth. It is obvious which kind of conclusion is provided by error in the principles [from which one starts] and weakness in the fundaments. There is no more perfect faith than the truth itself that is Jesus".

The "*cultural dogmas*", to which we refer correspond to the "*principia prima*" mentioned by Nicolaus of Cusa, but with the difference that for us the "cultural dogmas" are relative to each culture and for Nicolaus of Cusa, the "first principles" are the Christian truths to which he attributes an absolute value and which for us are simple *dogmas* proper to the Western Christian culture.

É. Gilson, in his work *L'Esprit de la Philosophie Médiévale*, points out that the Christian Philosophy – whose height period is Medieval Philosophy – is naturally subordinated to that criterion of truth which is the Revelation, object of faith, and he says:

> "*The errors of Plato and Aristotle are just those of pure reason; any philosophy which pretends to be self-sufficient will fall again in the same errors, or in others worst; so that from that moment* [i.e. from the very moment in which Christian religion appeared] *the only sure method for us lies in taking Revelation as a guide in order to reach some insight of its contents; and this insight of Revelation is philosophy itself*" (p. 4).

> "*For Neo-scholasticism faith subsists, and any disagreement between faith and philosophy is a sure sign of philosophical error*" (p. 6).

"*The contents of Christian Philosophy is, thus, the body of rational truths which have been discovered, deepened, or simply saveguarded thanks to the help that Revelation has lent to reason*" (p. 30).

"*I call, thus, Christian Philosophy* all philosophy that considers Christian Revelation as an indispensable aid of reason, although it makes a formal distinction between the two orders [that of faith and that of reason]" (p.32).

"*The weakness of human understanding in its present condition is such that, without faith, what to some would seem evidently demonstrated would be considered as doubtful to the others ... Thus in order to remedy that debilitas rationis man needs a divine help; and it is faith which offers it to him*" (p. 36).

From the quoted texts of Descartes, Nicolaus of Cusa and Gilson becomes clear the important function as *fundaments* of philosophical thought, which corresponds to the "*cultural dogmas*" or first principles – contained in the Holy Scriptures and objects of Christian faith – in Western philosophy.

V.3 Indemonstrability of the *principia prima* or "cultural dogmas"

The first principles or "cultural dogmas", starting from which are constructed the philosophical systems cannot be – according to many Indian and Western philosophers – an object of logical demonstration, faith is thus their unique ground.

V.3.1 Indian Philosophy

Brahman, privileged object of the Hindu metaphysical adhesion, *principium primum* of the major part of the Hindu philosophical systems, its pre-eminent "*cultural dogma*", is beyond senses (*atīndriya*) and thought (*acintya*). It is the *atīndriya* or suprasensuous *par excellence.* The knowledge of its existence, nature and attributes cannot be reached by senses and reasoning (*tarka*), it must be founded only in *Śabda,* the Word, the Sacred Text, the Scriptures, the Revelation, which is the whole of those formulations in which confidence and faith are deposited.

This idea is clearly expressed in Śaṅkara's commentary *ad* II, 1, 27, lines 19-20:

śabdamūlaṃ ca brahma śabdapramāṇakaṃ nendriyādipramāṇakaṃ tad yathāśabdam abhyupagantavyam

"*Brahman* has *Śabda* as its basis; *Śabda* [alone] is its means of correct knowledge, the sense-organs and the other means of correct knowledge are not its means of correct knowldge; It must be known according to *Śabda*".

And in the same passage, line 25, Śaṅkara quotes a text from a *Purāṇa*, which says:

acintyāḥ khalu ye bhāvā na tāṃs tarkeṇa yogayet.

"To things that are unthinkable one must not apply reasoning".

And Śaṅkara concludes, line 26:

tasmāc śabdamūla evātīndriyārthayāthātmyādhigamaḥ.

"Therefore the cognition of the real nature of a supersensuous object has *Śabda* as its source".

To these quotations can be added the emphatic assertion that Śaṅkara does in his commentary to *Vedāntasūtra ad* II, 1, 1, p. 434, line 16:

na cātīndriyān arthāñ śrutim antareṇa kaścid upalabhata iti śākyaṃ saṃbhāvayitum.

"It is not possible to think that without the *Śruti* somebody grasps a supersensuous object".

Being *demonstration* an activity of reason, a corolary resulting from these ideas is that *Brahman* is *rationally indemostrable.*

V.3.2 Western Philosophy

The idea that the *principia prima* are indemonstrable had also free course in Western Philosophy.

1. Aristotle already deals with the indemonstrability of the premises or principles, starting from which is constructed the *demonstration* that leads to scientific knowledge, especially in his *Analytica Posteriora.*

In *Topica* I, 4, p. 100a, lines 27-29, Aristotle defining the demonstration (ἀπόδειξις), expresses that a *demonstration* takes place when the conclusion of the syllogism that constitutes it is produced from true and first premises, or from premises that originated in other true and first premises:

> Ἀπόδειξις μὲν οὖν ἐστίν, ὅταν ἐξ ἀληθῶν καὶ πρότων ὁ συλλογισμὸς ᾖ, ἢ ἐκ τοιούτων ἃ διά τινων πρότων καὶ ἀληθῶν τῆς περὶ αὐτὰ γνώσεως τὴν ἀρχὴν εἴληφεν·

For Aristotle, *Analytica Posteriora* I, 2, p. 71b, lines 17-22, (scientific) knowledge (ἐπιστήμη) is the product of a demonstration (ἀπόδειξις) that must start from premises endowed with some characteristics, which he enumerates:

> ... φαμὲν δὲ καὶ δι' ἀποδείξεως εἰδέναι. ἀπόδειξιν δὲ λέγω συλλογισμὸν ἐπιστημονικόν. ἐπιστημονικόν δὲ λέγω καθ' ὃν τῷ ἔχειν αὐτὸν ἐπιστάμεθα. εἰ τοίνυν ἐστὶ τὸ ἐπίστασθαι οἷον ἔθεμεν, ἀνάγκη καὶ τὴν ἀποδεικτικὴν ἐπιστήμην ἐξ ἀληθῶν τ' εἶναι καὶ πρώτων καὶ ἀμέσων καὶ γνωριμοτέρων καὶ προτέρων καὶ αἰτίων τοῦ συμπεράσματος·
>
> "... We say that it is through a demonstration that knowledge is reached. I call demonstration a syllogism which produces knowledge. I call [syllogism] which produces knowledge that, by means of which, because of the mere fact of possessing it, we know. Now if to know is as we have established, it is necessary that the knowledge produced by a demonstration [= apodictic] be from true and first and immediate things [= premises], and more known than and prior to [the conclusion], and causes of the conclusion".

Another most important characteristic of the premises (πρόστασις), which serve as fundament to a demonstration is that they are indemonstrable (ἀναπόδεικτος). In *Analytica Posteriora* I, 2, p. 71b, lines 26-27, Aristotle asserts:

> ... ἐκ πρώτων δ' ἀναποδείκτων ...
>
> "... [demonstration is] from first, indemonstrable [premises] ..."

This affirmation is repeated by Aristotle, for instance in *Analytica Posteriora* I, 9, p. 76a, lines 16-17; II, 3, p. 90b, lines 24-27.

The characteristic of "immediate" (ἄμεσος) proper of the premises of the demonstration, mentioned already in *Analytica Posteriora* I, 2, p. 71b, lines 17-22, text quoted *supra*, corroborates the inexistence of demonstration of such premises or first principles. Aristotle explains in I, 2, p. 72a, lines 7-8, what he understands by the words "immediate principle", ἀρχή ἄμεσος:

> ἄμεσος δὲ ἧς μή ἐστιν ἄλλη προτέρα.
> "Immediate [Principle] is that for which does not exist another one before".

And further on, I, 2, lines 14-15, he specifies that:

> ἀμέσου δ' ἀρχῆς συλλογιστικῆς θέσιν μὲν λέγω ἣν μὴ ἔστι δεῖξαι,
> "I call affirmation of an immediate principle which is a part of a demonstrative syllogism that which is not possible to demonstrate".

According to the quoted texts it is seen that for Aristotle demonstration is grounded in indemonstrable universal principles, which are originated in a cognitive process of inductive nature – from sensation to reason – through an act of intuition. Cf. *Analytica Posteriora* II, Chapter XIX. And it is more necessary to deposit faith (πιστεύειν) in these principles so established than in the conclusions which are deduced from them by syllogistic reasoning, and which constitute the contents of scientific knowledge as it was generally conceived at least up to the end of 17th century in Europe.

It can be considered that in a great extent Western philosophical thought follows the lines of the Aristotelian thinking in relation to the first principles.

2. Saint Thomas' testimony. The *primum principium* or *cultural dogma par excelence* of European thought is *God*. Cf. the textes of Descartes and Nicolaus of Cusa quoted in the previous section, and Saint Thomas, *Summa contra gentiles* I, Chapter 10, Volume 1, p. 30, in which he expresses that without the existence of God, "any reflection concerning divine things is necessarily eliminated" (*omnis consideratio de rebus divinis necessario tollitur*) – let us add: as would be also

eliminated any doctrine which in some way has its ground in God, that of Descartes for instance.

It is true that the endeavours to demonstrate the existence of God have been frequent in the history of Western Philosophy: Saint Anselm, Saint Thomas, Descartes, elaborated proofs with that aim. See in *Chapter IV* of this book the sections *An interesting marginal remark: The ontological proof in the West* and *Remarks on the previous subject: Proofs of the existence of God in the West.*

But the same Saint Thomas admits that among Christians there are thinkers (whom he does not mention by name with the exception of John Damascenus), who are against the demonstrability of that *primum principium*, which is God.[4]

Thus in *Summa contra gentiles, Liber Primus,* Chapter X, entitled *De opinione dicentium quod Deum esse demonstrari non potest cum sit per se notum,* pp. 30-34, Saint Thomas mentions those who consider that God, because of being known by himself, cannot be demonstrated and presents the arguments adduced in favor of this thesis, which he refutes in Chapter XI.

Similarly in *Summa contra gentiles, Liber Primus,* Chapter XII, entitled *De opinione dicentium quod Deum esse demonstrari non potest sed sola fide tenetur,* pp. 38-40, he refers to those who consider that God cannot be demonstrated and is known by the sole faith.

And in *Summa Theologiae, Prima Pars, Qu. 2, A. 2, Utrum Deum esse sit demonstrabile,* he deals also with the question of the indemonstrability of God. Saint Thomas exposes here in paragraphs 1, 2 and 3 of this article the fundaments which are adduced by those who asserted this thesis:

[4] Among the "doctors" referred to by Saint Thomas, who maintained the indemonstrability of God see É. Gilson, *Le Thomisme,* Chapter III, where he mentions among Saint Thomas' predecessors John Damascenus (675-749) and Jean de la Rochelle (*circa* 1200-1245), and among his contemporaries Saint Bonaventura (1221-1274), "according to whom all the other proofs [apart from the innate knowledge that one has of God] have only the value of dialectic exercises".

1. Deum enim esse est articulus fidei. Sed ea quae sunt fidei, non sunt demonstrabilia: quia demonstratio facit scire, fides autem de non apparentibus est, ut patet per Apostolum ad Heb. *II. Ergo Deum esse non est demonstrabile.*

2. *Praeterea, medium demonstrationis est* quod quid est. *Sed de Deo non possumus scire* quid est, *sed solum quid non est, ut dicit Damascenus. Ergo non possumus demonstrare Deum esse.*

3. Praeterea si demonstraretur Deum esse, hoc non esset nisi ex effectibus eius. Sed effectus eius non sunt proportionati ei: cum ipse sit infinitus et effectus finiti; finiti autem ad infinitum non est proportio. Cum ergo causa non possit demonstrari per effectum sibi non proportionatur, videtur quod Deum esse non possit demonstrari.

"1. Then that God exists is an article of faith. But what is proper to faith is not demonstrable: because the demonstration makes known, and faith refers to what is not manifiest, as it results evident from the saying of the Apostle *ad Heb. II.* Consequently, that God exists is not demonstrable".

2. Moreover, the minor [premise] of the demonstration is *what something is.* But concerning God we cannot know *what He is,* but only what He is not, as it is said by Damascenus [*De Fide Orth., Lib. I,* cap. 4 (PG 94, 800)]. Consequently, we cannot demonstrate that God exists.

3. "Moreover, if it is demonstrated that God exists, that could only be from His effects. But His effects are not in proportion with Him, since He is infinite and the effects are finite; now, there is no proportion between finite and infinite. Consequently, as the cause cannot be demonstrated by an effect which has not proportion with it, it seems that it cannot be demonstrated that God exists".

In the remaining part of the *Article 2* Saint Thomas refutes the indicated fundaments of the thesis of the indemonstrability of God.

In *Summa Theologiae, Prima Pars, Qu. 1, A. 8, Utrum* [sacra] *doctrina sit argumentativa,* Saint Thomas, without dealing with the problem of the indemonstrability of God, extols the value of faith and gives to argumentation a subordinated fonction:

RESPONDEO *dicendum quod, sicut aliae scientiae non argumentantur ad sua principia probanda, sed ex principiis argumentantur ad ostendendum alia in ipsis scientiis; ita haec* [sacra] *doctrina non argumentatur ad sua principia probanda, quae sunt articuli fidei; sed ex eis procedit ad aliquid aliud ostendendum ...*

AD SECUNDUM *dicendum quod argumentari ex auctoritate est maxime proprium huius doctrinae: eo quod principia huius doctrinae per revelationem habentur, et sic oportet quod credatur auctoritati eorum quibus revelatio facta est ...*

Utitur tamen sacra doctrina etiam ratione humana: non quidem ad probandum fidem, quia per hoc tolleretur meritum fidei; sed ad manifestandum aliqua alia quae traduntur in hac doctrina ...

"I ANSWER that it is necessary to say that, in the same way as the other sciences do not argue in order to prove their principles, but starting from their principles they argue to show other things in the same sciences; so this [divine] doctrine does not argue in order to prove its own principles, which are articles of faith; but starting from them proceeds to show something different.

CONCERNING THE SECOND it must be said that to argue from an authority is the most proper [procedure] of this doctrine, because the principles of this doctrine are got by Revelation, and thus it is convenient to give credit to the authority of those to whom Revelation was granted.

Nevertheless, the divine doctrine also has recourse to human reason: not certainly in order to prove faith, since thereby the merit of faith would be eliminated; but in order to manifest other different things that are transmitted in this doctrine ..."

3. Kant. Finally, it is interesting to point out again Kant's position. Kant in his treatise *Der einzig mögliche Beweisgrund zu einer Demonstration des Daseins Gottes*, p. 738, Suhrkamp ed. = A 205, denies the validity of the ontological proof of the existence of God, considered by him as the ground of all the other possible proofs, and nevertheless he expresses:

Es ist durchaus nötig, dass man sich vom Dasein Gottes überzeuge; es ist aber nicht eben so nötig, dass man es demonstriere.

"It is absolutely necessary that one be convinced of the existence of God; but it is not so necessary that one demonstrates it".

That means: Kant keeps on maintaining the *principium primum,* God, even without the possibility of being demonstrated. The Western "cultural dogma" of God in Western Philosophy just as the "cultural dogmas" of Indian Philosophy subsist although there are no proofs which support them, founded as they are in the faith that has been deposited in them by the successive generations.

V.4 Indian Philosophy as Hindu Philosophy and Western Philosophy as Christian Philosophy, at least up to 17th century

Thus not only Medieval Philosophy but a great part of Western Philosophy – because of being founded on Christian dogmas, because of not daring to go out from the limits that these dogmas impose on it, and because of using these dogmas as a means to get rid of the theorical difficulties that it has to face (as in the case of the English idealistic philosopher Berkeley the use of the notion of God in order to solve a problem of his system) – is nothing else than "Christian Philosophy", in the same way as the majority of the Indian *darśanas* or philosophical systems are tightly linked to some of the great Indian religions, especially to Hinduism, and are for this reason "Hindu Philosophy".

Another reason in favour of the previous assertion of the Christian character of Western Philosophy is the frequent presence in Western philosophers of themes specifically related to religion. For instance the Eucharist Christian doctrine interested many philosophers as Descartes and Leibniz among others, and even some who abandoned or could be accused of abandonning the official interpretation of that doctrine given by the *Council of Trent* (1545-1563) had serious problems. According to Michel Adam, in his work *L'eucharistie chez les penseurs français du dix-septième siècle,* p. 37: "*the Eucharistic dispute was the true detonator of this scandalous process*" [that of Galileo (1564-1642)]. An equally bad destiny – although *post-mortem* - had Marco Antonio de Dominis, "*aristocrat, archbishop, learned theologian of international reputation*

... *dead since more than three months ago*". He was exhumed (in 1624) "*for the event!: He was condemned to the punishment of fire; his portrait, his mortal remains, his books were transported in a cart, and everything was burnt*"[5] – all this because of having maintained on the Eucharist an opinion not in agreement with the Trentine orthodoxy. For de Dominis bread continued being bread although sanctified. On this event see Michel Adam, *ibidem*.

The *Grundriss der Geschichte der Philosophie, Die Philosophie des 17. Jahrhunderts*, in articles by several authors refers to the preoccupation and interest of Western thinkers of the 17th century, presented as belonging to the History of Philosophy, for the Christian religious subjects. That preoccupation and interest did not weaken in the following centuries, as it can be seen by the works of Kant, Hegel, Fichte, etc.

The subordination of Western Philosophy to the Christian beliefs is in part explained by the fact that the teaching of philosophy was in Europe almost completely and at least until the end of 17th century under the control of the Christian Church, whose doctrines, in a great extent inspired by the Aristotelian theories (at that time already 20 centuries old), were transmitted to and imposed on the students. And the severity and even cruelty of the fearsome Inquisition induced the thinkers not to go away from the orthodox Christian ideas that have been taught to them. In fact the subordination of Philosophy to that control meant for it at least a limitation. Cf. in *Grundriss der Geschichte der Philosophie, Die Philosophie des 17. Jahrhunderts*, Band 2, pp. 3-32, the article by Laurence W.B. Brockliss.

This fact of the subordination of Philosophy in the West to the dogmas of Christian religion must not surprise if one thinks that even up to the end of 17th century the teaching of Physics in France did not dare – with few illustrious

[5] On the Inquisition practice of the excommunication *post-mortem* and of the punishment of mutilation and burning of the corpse of the excommunicated person, see H.C. Lea, *Histoire de l'Inquisition au Moyen Age* I, pp. 207-208 and page 219, note 22, for the bibliographical references.

exceptions – to turn away from the teachings of the Holy Scripture or to contradict it, to the extent of giving to God and His angels a direct causal intervention to explain several natural phenomena, of rejecting rationally obtained results if they contradicted any dogma of faith, and of assuming as governing principle that the affirmations of the Bible should be literally understood. Cf. in *Grundriss der Geschichte der Philosophie, Die Philosophie des 17. Jahrhunderts,* Band 2, pp. 29-30, the quoted article of Laurence W.B. Brockliss.

An example of the interest of the thinkers dedicated to the study of the Philosophy of Nature (Physics) for the themes of religious character and of the influence in them of the cultural dogmas of religious inspiration in relation to their physico-philosophical themes they deal with is offered by Max Jammer in his book, *Concepts of Space,* which deserved a preface by Albert Einstein and that we quote from its German translation, *Das Problem des Raumes. Die Entwicklung der Raumtheorien.* In the beginning of Chapter II, dedicated to the Judeo-Christian ideas on the space, it is said:

> *"Since the days of Philo until the times of Newton and even much later Theology manifested itself as an important factor besides Metaphysics and Physics properly said in the constitution of the physical theories of space* (p. 27) ... *Since the 1st century A.D. until the 18th century a religious tradition clearly recognizable and without interruption exerted a powerful influence on the physical theories of space.*
>
> *This influence culminated in the assertion that the space is only an attribute of God or even identical with God. For Newton the absolute space is the percipient apparatus* [das Sensorium] *of Gods, for More, his divine extension"* (p. 28).

The identification of the absolute space with God is expressed by Newton himself in his famous *General Scholium,* with which he closes the Third Book of his *Principia,* and where he gives free course to his religious enthusiasm, p. 545 (of the English translation of his work *Philosophiae Naturalis Principia Mathematica =Mathematical Principles of Natural Philosophy and his System of the World* by Andrew Motte, done in 1729, Volume 2):

> *"He endures forever, and is everywhere present; and by existing always and everywhere, he constitutes duration and space ... God is the same God, always and everywhere. He is omnipresent* not virtually *only, but also* substantially; ... *In him are all things contained and moved; yet neither affects the other: God suffers nothing from the motion of bodies; bodies find no resistance from the omnipresence of God ... Whence also he is all similar, all eye, all ear, all brain, all arm, all power to perceive, to understand, and to act".*

Jammer, in pages 123-124 of his quoted book, deals with the question whether Newton (1642-1727) really affirmed that the space is a *sensorium*, a "sense-organ" of God. He quotes then, in German translation (pages 122 and 123 of his book), two passages of Newton's *Opticks* (p. 403 and p. 370 of the Dover edition, 1952), which we reproduce but in a larger quotation, taken from the Latin translation (authorized by Newton himself, and done by Samuel Clarke) *Optice*, published in Switzerland in 1740.

In the former text (*Lib.* III, *Quaestio* XXVIII, p. 298) Newton expresses that the natural phenomena make evident the existence of God, who perceives all in his sensory constituted by the infinite space, an that although the progress of the Philosophy of Nature does not lead us to the knowledge of God, at least brings us each time nearer to that knowledge, and this is the reason why that progress must be considered most valuable:

> ... annon ex phaenomenis constat, esse Entem incorporeum, viventem, intelligentem, omnipraese-ntem, qui in spatio infinito, tanquam sensorio suo, res ipsas intime cernat, penitusque perspiciat, totasque intra se praesens praesentes complectatur; quarum quidem rerum id quod in nobis sentit et cogitat, imagines tantum ad se per organa sensuum delatas, in sensoriolo suo percipit & contuetur ? [the difference of typography belongs to the original] *Utique si verus omnis in hac philosophia factus progressus, non quidem statim nos ducit ad Causae primae cognitionem; at certe propius propiusque nos ad eam perpetuo adducit, eaque re permagni est aestimandus.*
>
> *"Is it not evident from the phenomena that there exists an incorporeal, living, intelligent, omnipresent Being, who in the infinite space as in his*

> *sensorium* [= sense-organ] *sees things themselves intimately* [in an immediate way], *who perceives them in their innermost being, and who, being present, grasps them, present in himself, in their integrity – while what in us feels and thinks* [= the soul], *that perceives and sees in its limited sensory only the images of these things that are brought to it* [= to the soul] *through the sense-organs? Certainly, if all true progress made in this Philosophy* [of Nature] *does not lead us at once to the knowledge of the First Cause, at least it assuredly brings us always more closely to it* [= to that knowledge] *and for this reason that progress must be considered as most valuable".*

In the latter of the mentioned texts (*Lib.* III *Quaestio* XXXI, p. 328), reiterating and making more explicit the idea expressed in the former text, after referring to the marvels of Creation, which manifest themselves in the planetary system and in the conformation of the living beings, Newton, in the *Quaestio* that closes his *Book* III, which constitutes the final part of his book, concludes that those marvels and that conformation can only be attributed to an intelligent cause, God:

> *... horum sane omnium conformatio prima, nulli rei tribui potest, nisi intelligentiae & sapientiae Entis potentis semperque viventis; qui sit ubique scilicet praesens, possitque voluntate sua corpora omnia in infinito suo uniformi sensorio movere, adeoque cunctas mundi universi partes ad arbitrium suum fingere & refingere, multo magis quam anima nostra voluntate sua ad corporis nostri membra movenda valet.*

> "... the originary creation of all these things indeed cannot be attributed to anything else but to the intelligence and wisdom of a powerful and everlasting Being, who is undoubtedly present everywhere, and who can move by his mere will all the bodies in his infinite, uniform sensorium, and even form and transform at his own discretion all the parts of the universe – with a much greater capacity than that our soul has for moving according to his will the members of our body".

Leibniz, in a letter addressed to the Princess Wilhelmine Charlotte von Anspach, probably in 1715, and given by her to the English thinker Samuel Clarke (in Leibniz, *Die philosophischen Schriften*, ed. C.I. Gerhardt, Vol. 7, p. 352) says:

> *M. Newton dit que l'espace est l'organe dont Dieu se sert pour sentir les choses.*

"M. Newton says that the space is the sensorium God uses in order to feel things".

However Samuel Clarke (1675-1729), friend and follower of Newton, who, as already said, translated Newton's book *Opticks* from English into Latin, in his answer to Leibniz, maintains that the expression ***Sensorium*** is a simple comparison used by Newton, i.e. it has a metaphoric meaning – interpretation this one that seems rather incorrect since it is against what Newton himself affirms.

The theory of the absolute space, the identification of the absolute space with God, and the idea that the absolute space is the ***Sensorium*** of God constitute an amazing association of a physico-philosophical theory as is that of *space* with a theologico-religious notion as is that of *God,* i.e. between Philosophy of Nature and Religion. One example more of what we have been affirming: the identification of Western Philosophy with Christian Philosophy.

It is worthy to point out with relation to this subject that the two most important works of the powerful scientific genius of Newton, *Principia* and *Opticks*; conclude with pages of a clear theological inspiration.

Max Jammer, in the second chapter of his quoted book, considers that the idea of the identification of the space with God and other related ideas, go back to the Judeo-Cabalistic and Neoplatonic-Alexandrian philosophies, interested very much thinkers and philosophers of Renaissance as Pico della Mirandola (1463-1494), Telesio (1509-1588), Campanella (1568-1639), Cornelius Agrippa (1485-1535), English Platonists (of the 16th century), Henry More (1614-1687), etc.

Perhaps one of the reasons why many Western philosophers or persons dedicated to the study of Philosophy in the West are opposed to admit the existence of an "Indian Philosophy" is the idea of religious inspiration that the acceptance on an Indian ***philosophy,*** founded on the principles of the Hindu or Buddhist *religion,* and valid as such, would imply to admit that there exist other possible fundaments for philosophical thinking different from the Christian fundaments. This would mean a threat: that acceptation would introduce an element of relativism in the search of truth, and would deprive Western Philosophy and Christian principles of their allegued universality and uniqueness.

V.5 Forms of irrationality

We also think that in the theories dealt with in *Chapters II, III* and *IV* of this book, can be found numerous manifestations of irrationality in Indian thought as well as in Western thought.

The first source of these manifestetions of irrationality is the mentioned conscious or unconscious constant recourse to the cultural dogmas as starting point of philosophizing, since these are generally founded in faith more than in arguments of reason.

We count as very important instances of irrationality fancy and fiction and the products of the imagination which are not based on facts and are offered as serious explanations of reality: ideas, theories or doctrines, which on being rigorously examined are nothing else than mere fanciful creations of mind.

In India and in the West are found many intellectual products of this kind that are seriously taken as philosophical doctrines. The union of matter (human body) and spirit (soul) was a problem both for Indian and Western thinkers, and both imagined fanciful solutions for it – even extravagant solutions, as we have seen in *Chapter IV*, sections *The relation between Matter and Spirit and its effects* and *Remarks on the previous subject: The problem of the union of the soul and the body in the West.*

The Sāṃkhya philosophical system solved the problem having recourse to a comparison: the union of Matter and Spirit consists in that the spirit reflects itself in matter – let us add: as the light of a lamp on any object. It is nothing else than a comparison, which does not establish anything.

In the West the union of matter and spirit received several solutions.

Descartes thought that the soul moves the pineal gland and this in turn propels the animal spirits towards that part of the body that the soul wants to move by means of them.

Descartes' disciples were not satisfied with this explanation and proposed the system of the "occasional causes", adopted also by Malebranche, according to which it is God himself who moves that part of the body that the soul wishes to move.

Leibniz, who does not accept that system, thinks that it would force God to accomplish "moving" miracles all the time or to count on the assistance of angels to help Him to move all the limbs that are moved in the world. The same Leibniz proposed a new system under the beautiful name of "Pre-established harmony". According to this system God creates two *automates* (Leibniz himself says in French: *automates*; today we would say two *robots*): one is the soul, the other one is the body. These two *automates* (or *robots*) are programmed up to their smallest details in such a way that, when a certain movement is produced in one, another movement occurs in the other which exactly corresponds with the previous one. In the case of the two robots and in that of the two clocks carefully coordinated (another example used by Leibniz), there are physical movements only; in the case of the soul and the body, there is a psychic "movement" in the soul, and a physical "movement" in the body. Really human fancy has no limits even within the realm of the sternest philosophy.

These creations of imagination in Philosophy appear with the same frequency in both Indian and Western philosophical thought.[6]

The presence of evidently irrational elements in the theories and doctrines presented in this book serve to support our **second thesis** according to which, *in the history*

---

[6] Let us remember what Cicero (106-43 B.C.) says in *De divinatione* II, § 119: *Sed nescio quo modo nihil tam absurde dici potest quod non dicatur ab aliquo*

of Greek and European philosophies, we can find what is usually (correctly or incorrectly) called manifestations of irrationality *in many forms (one of which is fanciful mental creation or imagination), and these are as numerous as they are in the history of Indian thought,* not only in the centuries which correspond to the ancient (Greek) and mediaeval (European) periods, but also in the centuries that followed.

Other, similar instances of irrational approaches to the explanation of reality will be included in the results of our research on the other systems of Indian thought compared to Western Philosophy.

V.6 Limitation of intellectual freedom: Tolerance and intolerance

Other important consequences of our study of both forms of philosophical thought, the Indian and the Western ones, concern two other essential attributes of philosophy, usually considered in the West – together with that of rationality – as the most important: intellectual freedom and search of truth for its own sake.

Our opinion is that philosophical thought has generally been subjected to many limitations, both in India and in the West. Only in very few instances have Indian and Western thinkers been able to rid themselves of *beliefs*, i. e. the "cultural dogmas" imposed on them by the *Past*, consciously and freely accepted or unconsciously adopted by inertia or forced upon them by violence or by the power of authority. Thinking must arise in agreement with the "cultural dogmas" and be subordinated to them, and consequently it cannot be considered *free*.

---

philosophorum: "But I do not know why nothing so absurd can be said that has not been said by some of the philosophers" (cf. Pascal, *pensée 363, Article VI*, in *Pensées*), and also what Varro (116-27 B.C.), in *Satura Menippea*, fragment 122, Bücheler ed., says: *Postremo nemo aegrotus quicquam somniat / tam infandum quod non aliquis dicat philosophus*: "Finally no ill person dreams something so unutterable that some philosopher has not said", quoted in note by Arthur Stanley Peace in his edition of *De divinatione*.

V.6.1 Indian tolerance

Nevertheless, we also think that, within the limits imposed by cultural dogmas, intellectual freedom existed to a much greater degree in India than it did in the modern European world. Tolerance was not a specific characteristic of Christian Europe.

We base this assumption in relation to Indian intellectual freedom on facts such as the following ones:

– the acceptance by Hinduism, as orthodox systems of thought, of systems which present large and obvious differences amongst themselves, such as Sāṃkhya Dualism, Vedānta Monism, Nyāya Theism, Mīmāṃsā Atheism;

– the acceptance of different Vedānta schools with great oppositions amongst themselves: Advaita or Non-Dualism of Śaṅkara, Dvaita or Pluralism of Madhva for instance;

– the fact that, although power in India has generally been held by people adhering to the Hinduist *darśana* (philosophical and religious point of view), violence has never been used against adherents of other *darśanas*, or, when used, it was only accidentally and under unwonted conditions and without extreme measures of repression;

– and, finally, the fact that the appearance of the Buddhist *darśana*, which negated the very foundations of Hinduist society, religion and philosophy, did not lead to bloody religious wars or ideological mass persecutions of any kind.

The greater freedom of thought which was enjoyed by Indian philosophers was undoubtedly possible thanks to the spirit of tolerance in regard to ideas that characterized Indian culture. Alfred S. Geden, D.D., who was Professor of Old Testament Languages and Literature and of Comparative Religion in the Wesleyn College, Richmond, Surrey, in his article "Persecution (Indian)", in *Encyclopaedia of Religion and Ethics*, Vol. 9, pp. 762-765, refers to the Indian tolerant tendency, to the introduction of the intolerance in India by Muhammadans, and the conflicts since the arrival of

European missionaries between Christian and Hindus fundamentally due the "*aggressive spirit and action of the new* [Christian] *religion*".

V.6.2 Paul Hacker on Indian tolerance

It is interesting for our purpose to point out some ideas of the great German indologist Paul Hacker whom nobody could accuse of partiality in favor of India owing to his scientific spirit, his objectivity in the study of Indian Culture, and specially if one takes into account his peculiar conception of "Inclusivism" applied to Hindu tolerance.[7]

Paul Hacker, in his article "Religiöse Toleranz und Intoleranz in Hinduismus", throws into relief some facts, which undoubtedly reveal (leaving aside the consideration of the causes or motives that may have produced it) the existence of tolerance in Hinduism regarding religious doctrinaire ideas and questions:

---

[7] According to Hacker, in his posthumous work, "Inklusivismus", in Gerhard Oberhammer's ed., *Inklusivismus. Eine indische Denkform*, Wien: Publications of the De Nobili Research Library, Occasional Papers 2, 1983, p. 12: "*Inclusivism means that one considers that a central conception of a group alien to one's own, with its own religious conception or its own cosmovision, is identical with one or the other central conception of the group to which one belongs. In general Inclusivism implies an explicit or implicit form of affirmation that the alien, which is presented as identical with the own, in some way is subordinated or inferior to it*".

Thus Inclusivism, according to Hacker, in a certain way tries to make disappear the other's identity. In the Introduction of 1977 to his *Kleine Schriften* of 1978 Hacker ratifies the facts that he points out in his article on tolerance in India, but concludes it explaining: "*What for the European seems to be tolerance* [in Indian Culture], *is almost always Inclusivism*". So for Hacker the value of Indian tolerance because of being the same as Inclusivism is at least restricted or diminished.

We consider that it is not possible to identify this notion of Inclusivism with that of tolerance. Inclusivism, understood as Hacker does, may be one of the possible causes of tolerance, as may also be the desire to maintain social peace, the avoidance of violence in any circumstance, the search of the economic benefits which derive from social harmony, or a compassionate attitude towards all living beings, etc. We think that whatever may be its cause tolerance still is, in India or in Europe, a most positive value.

"In regard to the state legal order referring to tolerance the Hindu law treatises prescribe that the king must treat all the religious sects, even those that do not respect the Veda and the brahmanical caste, and that consequently are outside Hinduism, according to their own customs and even more he must take care of the maintenance of those costums. And we know through the scarse sources of the History of India, especially through the inscriptions, that in fact not few princes, behaved in a very friendly way with Buddhists and Jainas, i. e. with religious communities outside Hinduism, and also with the old Christian churches of South India, with parsis, who looked for refuge in India, and with groups of Jew emigrants" (pp. 377-378).

"It can be assumed that the norm of Indian Law, which prescribed the state tolerance of the non-Hindus, although not without exceptions, nevertheless was mostly followed" (p. 378).

"... but such Indians [Buddhists, Jainas and materialists], who did not recognize the authority of the Veda, were not vexed" (p. 381).

Hacker also points out that in some legal texts was prescribed not to have a relationship with the heretics, Buddhists, Jainas and materialists, but that:

"In practice these prescriptions with complete certainty were never followed. Otherwise later Buddhism, for instance, could not have had on Hindu thought the influence that it actually exerted" (p. 381).

"Doctrinaire tolerance is without any doubt the most interesting manifestation of tolerance in Hinduism" (p. 384).

Hacker indicates also that in Indian Middle Ages important metaphysical questions were strongly debated and with all seriousness, but that fact did not involve "*acts of practical intolerance*" (p. 385).

In pp. 378-380 Hacker refers to the great Buddhist Emperor Ashoka, who exerted an all-embracing power on all India, and who manifested towards non-Buddhists the same great tolerance that before and after him Hindu princes showed towards those who did not adhere to their own ideas.

In the West the situation was not the same. Tolerance was not a specific characteristic of Western Culture, and especially of the Christian Europe, as it is made evident by many diverse facts studied by numerous authors.[8]

V.6.3 The beginning of intolerance in the West: Christianism as religion of the Roman State

This destiny of intolerance in Europe began with the conjuction of the Christian Church with the Roman Empire thanks to Constantine (274?-337), who, when he defeated Maxentius the 28 October of the year 312 and Licinius in the year 323, became the exclusive master of the Roman world, taking place in this way the reunification of the Roman Empire that was divided as a result of Diocletian's reforms.[9]

In the year 313 Constantine, after his victory over Maxentius, together with Licinius at that time his co-

[8] Cf. R.I. Moore, *The Formation of a Persecuting Society. Power and deviance in Western Europe 950-1250*: French translation: *La persécution. Sa formation en Europe (Xe-XIIIe)*; René Rémond, *Religion et Société en Europe: Essai sur la secularization des sociétés européennes aux XIXe et XXe siècles (1789-1998)*; John Locke, *Lettre sur la tolérance*. Latin Text and French translation; Voltaire, *Traité sur la tolérance*, Heinrich Schmidinger (Hrsg.), *Wege zur Toleranz. Geschichte einer europäischen Idee in Quellen*; Raúl González Salinero, *El antijudaísmo cristiano occidental (siglo IV y V)*; H. Méchoulan, *Le sang de l'autre ou l'honneur de Dieu*; P. Jurieu [1673-1713], *Des droits des deux souverains en matière de religion* [against tolerance]; Aubert de Versé, *Traité de la liberté de conscience* [in favor of tolerance]; article by G. Schlüter/R. Grötker "Toleranz", in *Historisches Wörterbuch der Philosophie*, Vol. 10, col. 1252-1262; Erna Paris, *El fin de los días. Los judíos en España: una historia de tolerancia y tiranía*; Iogna-Prat, Dominique, *Ordonner et exclure, Cluny et la société chrétienne face à l'hérésie, au judaïsme et à l'islam (1000-1150)*; *Théâtre des cruautés des hérétiques de notre temps de Richard Verstegan*, Texte établi, présenté & annoté par Frank Lestringant, in Annexe *Le martyre des trente-neuf allant au Brésil* de Louis Richeome (on the persecutions against Catholics by Protestants); Claude Postel, *Traité des invectives au temps de la Réforme* (on verbal violence between Protestants and Catholics in France during the 16th century); David Nirenberg, *Violence et minorités au Moyen Âge*; Cohen, Esther, *Le corps du diable. Philosophes et sorcières à la Renaissance*, *Martyres et martyrologes, Textes réunis par Frank Lestringant et Pierre-François Moreau*; Lea, Henri-Charles, *Histoire de l'inquisition au Moyen Age. Origines et procédures de l'inquisition. L'inquisition dans les divers pays de la chrétienté*, Grenoble: Éditions Jérôme Millon, 1997, 2 volumes (I y II).

[9] Cf. Otto Seeck, *Geschichte des Untergangs der antiken Welt*, Volume I.

governor and ally, adopted a policy of tolerance in regard to Christians. A product of this policy were diverse dispositions issued by Constantine and/or Licinius, both of them with the aim of achieving that new tolerant policy.

V.6.4 The Edict of Tolerance

The *Edict of Tolerance* or *Edict of Milan* (part of which we transcribe afterwards), which granted freedom of cult and determined the restitution to Christians of confiscated churches and properties, constitutes one of those dispositions. This new policy of tolerance constituted an act of gratitude on the part of Constantine and Licinius to the God of Christians to whom were attributed their victories, and at the same time a political act inasmuch as they won over the each time more numerous members of the Christian community in the Roman Empire.

The so-called *Edict of Tolerance* or *Edict of Milan* has been traditionally attributed to Constantine and Licinius and it was thought that it had been issued in Milan in the year 313 by the two emperors. At present historians are inclined to favor the hypothesis that this Edict was issued by Licinius in Nicomedia, after defeating Maximin (another pretender to the Roman throne) in the same year 313, adopting of course ideas that he shared with Constantine.[10]

This *Edict of Tolerance* has been preserved in its integrity in its Latin version by Lactantius in his *De mortibus persecutorum*, section XLVIII, Iohannes Pesenti ed., in a letter that Constantine and Licinius send to the governor of Bithynia (?). We transcribe and translate some noble dispositions of this edict, which – whatever the motives that gave rise to them may have been – promoted indeed elevated concepts of coexistence, respect and harmony among the sectors of the Roman society with their different ideas and beliefs, integrating to it especially the Christian sectors, previously

[10] Cf. Eusèbe de Césarée, *Histoire Ecclésiastique*, Books IX and X of Volume III and note 2 of page 104 of Volume III. Eusebius has preserved the Greek text of the *Edict of Tolerance*, pp. 104-107 of Volume III.

object of cruel persecutions and shameful intolerance. It is lamentable that on their turn the Christian sectors which were then favored by the edict did not adopt the same ideas with respect to persons of other creeds when the events of history brought them to a situation of power and hegemony:

> *... haec inter cetera, quae videbamus pluribus hominibus profutura, vel in primis ordinanda esse credidimus, quibus divinitatis reverentia continebatur, ut daremus et christianis et omnibus liberam potestatem sequendi religionem quam quisque voluisset, quo quicquid divinitatis in sede caelesti, nobis atque omnibus, qui sub potestate nostra sunt constituti, placatum ac propitium possit existere. Itaque hoc consilium salubri ac rectissima ratione ineundum esse credidimus, ut nulli omnino facultatem abnegandam putaremus, qui vel observationi christianorum vel ei religioni mentem suam dederet, quam ipse sibi aptissimam esse sentiret; ut possit nobis summa divinitas, cuius religioni liberis mentibus obsequimur, in omnibus solitum favorem suum benivolentiamque praestare. Quare scire dicationem tuam convenit placuisse nobis, ut, amotis omnibus omnino condicionibus, quae prius scriptis ad officium tuum datis super christianorum nomine continebantur, et abrogentur illa, quae plane sinistra et a nostra clementia aliena videbantur, et nunc libere et simpliciter unus quisque eorum, qui eandem observandae religionis christianorum gerunt voluntatem, citra ullam inquietudinem ac molestiam sui id ipsum observare contendant. Quae sollicitudini tuae plenissima significanda esse credidimus, quo scires nos liberam atque absolutam colendae religionis suae facultatem isdem christianis dedisse. Quod cum isdem a nobis indultum esse pervideas, intellegit dicatio tua etiam aliis religionis suae vel observantiae potestatem similiter apertam et liberam pro quiete temporis nostri esse concessam, ut in colendo quod quisque delegerit, habeat liberam facultatem, neque cuiquam honori neque cuiquam religioni aliquid a nobis detrahi videatur.*

"... we thought that, among all the things which we saw would be beneficious for many men, in first place had to be settled those that referred to the veneration of the divinity, in order to give to Christians and to all the free power to follow the religion that each of them wished, whereby any divinity in the celestial abode could become appeased and propitious for us and for everybody who is established under our power. Thus we believed that this decision with sound and most correct reason should be taken – that we thought that to nobody, who adhered to the observances of the religious duties of Christians or to that religion which he felt the most suitable for himself, this faculty should be denied at all, in order that the supreme divinity, whose religion we freely obey, could offer us in every thing his usual favor and benevolence. Because of this it is convenient that Your Loyalty know that it is our pleasure that - putting aside completely all the legal dispositions contained before in the decrees sent into your sense of duty in relation to Christians - all that seemed sinister and far from our clemency be annulled, and also that now anyone of those who have the will to observe the religion of the Christians, without any fear or personal trouble, could endeavour to observe it freely and simply. We thought that what preceeds should be notified to your care, in order that you know that we have given to the Christians the free and absolute right to honor their own religion. When you come to know that that by us has been allowed to them [= to the Christians], your Loyalty will understand that to the other persons has been conceded the faculty similarly open and free of observing their own religion according to the peace of our time, in order that anyone have the free faculty of honoring what anyone has chosen, and that it do not seem that by us something has been taken away either from the integrity of wealth and rights either from any religion".

With the course of time Constantine, the sole master of the Roman Empire since the year 323, in which he defeats and puts to death Licinius, his former ally, gradually comes politically closer to the Christians and moves aways from the Pagans. Constantine himself and the Christian Roman Emperors who followed him, most part of the time with the consent, incitation and/or advise of the Christian clergy, emitted many edicts (*constitutiones*) against *heretics*, against *apostates*, against *Jews*, against *pagans*, that is to say against those who did not adhere to the Christian orthodox ideas as accepted by the Catholic Apostolic Roman Church, inflicting on them severe personal and economic punishments, even the capital punishment by fire or by sword, simply because of their different beliefs, ideas, conducts or activities.

V.6.5 Imperial Edicts inspired by intolerance

These Edicts, which constitute landmarks in the history of intolerance in regard to ideas in the West, are preserved in the *Codex Iustinianus* and are grouped together in sections with titles on their contents, mentioning the emperors who issued them and the year in which that happened. We shall mention some Edicts of *Codex Iustinianus, Liber Primus*, Section V.

Section V in *Liber Primus* of *Codex Iustinianus* contains 22 Edicts against heretics, Manichaeans and Samaritans (*De hereticis et manichaeis et samaritis*).

Edict 5, contained in that section, which was issued in the year 428 and emotted by the Emperors Theodosius and Valentinian, enumerates a long series of "heretics", against which it is directed:

> *Ariani et Macedoniani, Pneumatomachi et Apollinariani et Novatiani sive Sabbatiani, Eunomiani, Tetraditae sive Tessarescaedecatitae, Valentiniani, Papianistae, Montanistae seu Priscillianistae vel Phryges vel Pepuzitae, Marcianistae, Borboriani, Messaliani, Eutychitae sive Enthusiastae, Donatistae, Audiani, Hydroparastatae, Tascodrogitae, Batrachitae, Hermeieciani, Photiniani, Pauliani, Marcelliani, Ophitae, Encratitae, Apotactitae, Saccophori et, qui ad imam usque scelerum nequitiam pervenerant, Manichaei.*

Edict 1 of the year 326 issued by Emperor Constantine expresses:

> *Privilegia, quae contemplatione religionis indulta sunt, catholicae tantum legis observatoribus prodesse oportet. haereticos non solum his privilegiis alienos esse volumus, sed et diversis muneribus contringi et subici.*
>
> "It is convenient that privileges, which have been granted taking religion in consideration, only benefit those who obey Catholic religion. It is our will that heretics not only be outside those privileges, but also be constrained and submitted to diverse taxes".

Edict 2 of the year 379 issued by Emperors Gratian, Valentinian and Theodosius disposes:

omnes vetitae legibus et divinis et imperialibus constitutionibus [?] haereses perpetuo conquiescant et nemo ulterius conetur quae reppererit profana praecepta vel docere vel discere ... haereticorum autem vocabulo continentur et latis adversus eos sanctionibus debent succumbere, qui vel levi argumento iudicio catholicae religionis et tramite detecti fuerint deviare.

"All the heresies forbidden by the divine as well as the imperial laws ... must cease for ever and nobody must attempt teaching or learning the profane teachings that come into his hands ... in the term "heretic" are included, and must yield to the penalties dictated against them, all those who have been discovered, according to the judgement and procedure of the Catholic religion, as being deviated from the correct path even in a minor matter".

Edict 3 of the years 396 emitted by the Emperors Arcadius and Honorius disposes:

cuncti haeretici procul dubio noverint omnia sibi loca adimenda esse, sive sub ecclesiarum nomine teneantur sive diaconica appellantur vel etiam decanica, sive in privatis domibus vel locis huiusmodi coetibus copiam praebere videantur: his aedibus vel locis privatis ecclesiae catholicae vindicandis. Ad hoc interdicatur his omnibus ad litaniam faciendam noctu vel die profanis coire conventibus: statuta videlicet condemnatione centum librarum auri ...

"All the heretics undoubtedly must know that all their places will be taken from them, either if they are kept under the name of churches, or if they are called deaconry [*diaconica*], or also deanery [*decanica*], or are seen to offer in private houses or places the opportunity for this class of meetings: these temples or private buildings are to be expropiated for the Catholic Church. Moreover let it be prohibited to all of them to congregate by night or by day to pray in profane meetings: ... [and in what follows the Edict enumerates the fines for the cases of violation of this Edict]".

Edict 4 of the year 407, emitted by Emperors Arcadius, Honorius and Theodosius, declares:

Manichaeos seu Manichaeas vel Donatistas meritissima severitate persequimur. huic itaque hominum generi nihil ex moribus nihil ex legibus sit commune cum ceteris. Ac primum quidem volumus esse publicum crimen, quia, quod in religione divina comittitur, in omnium fertur iniuriam.

quos bonorum etiam publicatione persequimur: quae tamen cedere iubemus proximis quibusque personis, ita ut ascendentium vel descendentium vel venientium ex latere cognatorum usque ad secundum gradum velut in successionibus ordo servetur. Quibus ita demum ad capiendas facultates esse ius patimur, si non et ipsi pari conscientia polluuntur. Ipsos quoque volumus amoveri ab omni liberalitate et successione quolibet titulo veniente. Praeterea non donandi, non emendi, non vendendi, non postremo contrahendi cuiquam convicto relinquimus facultatem. In mortem quoque inquisitio tendatur. nam si in criminibus maiestatis licet memoriam accusare defuncti, non immerito et hic debet subire iudicium. Ergo et suprema illius scriptura irrita sit, sive testamento sive codicillo sive epistola sive quolibet genere reliquerit voluntatem qui Manichaeus fuisse convincitur: hoc quoque casu eadem illa circa gradus superius comprehensos condicione servata. Sed nec filios heredes existere aut adire permittimus, nisi a paterna pravitate discesserint: delicti enim veniam paenitentibus damus. In eos etiam auctoritatis aculei dirigantur, qui eos domibus suis damnandu provisione defendent. Servos in super extra noxam esse volumus, si dominum sacrilegum evitantes ad ecclesiam catholicam servitio fideliore transierint.

"With the most deserved severity we persecute the Manichaeans or Manicheans or Donatists. Thus this kind of persons must have nothing in common with the others either in customs either in laws. And in first place we want that [to belong to these sects] be a public crime, because whatever crime is committed against divine religion brings harm for everybody. We persecute also [the indicated heretics] with the confiscation of their properties. However we order to transfer them [= the indicated properties] to some close persons, so that the order of relatives ascendents or descendents or colaterals up to the second degree be maintained as it happens in successions. Nevertheless we admit that they have the right to take possession of the properties only if they themselves are not contaminated with the same [heretical] conscience. We want also that they [= the heretics] be deprived of any donation and inheritance coming to them under any title you will. Moreover, we do not leave to anybody who has been convicted [of this heresy] the right to donate, to buy, to sell, and finally to conclude a contract. [We dispose that] the investigation against them be continue after their death, since if in the crimes of *lése majesté* is allowed to accuse the memory of the deceased person, not undeservedly also this [heretic] must be submitted to trial [even after death]. Thus let his last will be invalid, whether he who would have been convicted of being a Manichaean had expressed it by testament or by codicil or by letter or by any other means: also in this case must be kept the same disposition concerning the kinship degrees previously mentioned, but we do not allow that the sons be heirs or enter on the heritance unless they would have gone away from the paternal depravation: to those who repent we give the pardon of the offence. Let also the aculei of the authority be directed against those who give protection to them [= the heretics] in their houses with condemnable concern. Moreover, we want that their slaves be beyond any harm if they, avoiding their sacrilegious master, go over to the Catholic Church with a more faithful servitude".

In the same *Liber Primus,* Section VII contains 6 Edicts directed against the apostates (*De apostatis*).

Section IX of the same First Book has 18 Edicts against Jews and Coelicolists (*De iudaeis et caelicolis*).

Section X has 2 Edicts against heretics, pagans and Jews. All these Edicts present great similarities with the Edict, we have already quoted, against the Manichaeans, in what concerns the attitude of intolerance and the severity of the punishments.

Section XI of *Liber Primus,* which contains 10 Edicts, deals with the pagan sacrifices and temples (*De paganis sacrificiis et templis*), prohibiting them or putting limitations to their use.

Edict 1 of this Section XI of this *Liber Primus,* of the year 354, emitted by Emperor Constantius, disposes:

Placuit omnibus locis atque urbibus universis claudi protinus templa et accessu vetito omnibus licentiam delinquendi perditis abnegari. Volumus etiam cunctos sacrificiis abstinere. Quod si quis aliquid forte huiusmodi perpetraverit gladio ultore sternatur, facultates etiam perempti fisco decernimus vindicari et similiter puniri rectores provinciarum, si facinora vindicare neglexerint.

"It is our will that in all places and in all cities temples be immediately closed and that, by the prohibition of the access the liberty of committing a crime be denied to all those miserable. We want also that all abstain from sacrifices. If somebody by chance perform something of this kind, let him be striken by the vengeful sword; we also dispose that the possessions of the executed person be confiscated for the emperor's purse and that in the same way governors of the provinces be punished if they neglect castigate these crimes".

Edict 7 of the same Section XI of *Liber Primus*, of the year 451, issued by the Emperors Valentinian and Marcian, declares:

Nemo venerantis adorantisque animo delubra, quae olim iam clausa sunt, reseret: absit a saeculo nostro infandis exsecrandisque simulacris honorem pristinum reddi, redimiri sertis templorum impios postes, profanis aris accendi ignes, adoleri in isdem thura, victimas caedi, pateris vina libari et religionis loco existimari sacrilegium. Quisquis autem contra hanc serenitatis nostrae sanctionem et contra interdicta sacratissimarum veterum constitutionum sacrificia exercere temptaverit, apud publicum iudicem reus tanti facinoris legitime accusetur et convictus proscriptionem omnium bonorum suorum et ultimum supplicium subeat. Conscii etiam ac ministri sacrificiorum eandem poenam, quae in illum fuerit inrogata, sustineant, ut hac legis nostrae severitate perterriti metu poenae desinant sacrificia interdicta celebrare.

"Let nobody with the intention of venerating or honoring open the temples, which has formerly been closed: let it be absent from our age to render the old worship to the abominable and execrable images, to wreathe round with garlands the impious door-posts of the temples, to kindle fire in the profane altars, to burn incense in the same, to sacrifice victims, to offer wine to the gods and to consider the sacrilege as religion. Whoever would intend to perform sacrificies against this measure of our Serenity and against the prohibitions of the most sacred old edicts, let him be accused according to the laws before a public judge as a being guilty of such a great crime and, if convicted, let it suffer the confiscation of all his possessions and the capital punishment. Let also the accomplices and the assistants of the sacrifices suffer the same punishment inflicted to him [= the principal guilty of the crime], in order that terrified by the severity of this our law, because of the fear of the punishment, they desist to celebrate the prohibited sacrifices".

Let us mention together with these Edicts the important *Novella* 146 of the same Justinian, of the year 553, which ordered that in the sinagogues the Bible should be read -if somebody thus desired- not only in Hebrew but also in its

Greek translation called *Septuaginta* that the *Novella* extremely praised, in order that those who did not understand Hebrew *could not be deceived by the tendentious and depraved interpretations of the rabbis,* and expressed that *the Hebrews, on reading their sacred books should not hold to their literal meaning,* but aim at their *prophetic sense that already announces the coming of the Saviour of mankind, Jesuchrist,* causing them to abandon in this way their own beliefs and bringing them over to the Christian conceptions.

V.6.6 Other instances of European intolerance

Afterwards, during the Middle Age, and even in modern times, in Christian Europe the intolerant and cruel way of behaving against those that had different ideas or beliefs continued under diverse masters and in diverse kinds of societies.[11]

As another example of this European intolerant attitude, let us point out the famous Spanish book *Las Siete Partidas,* a most important legal monument, composed between 1256 and 1263 by order of the King of Castilla, Alfonso X, the Sage. In the *Partidas* are dictated a series of laws, inspired in a spirit of discrimination and intolerance against Jews, heretics, Moorish, apostates (Christians who abandon Christianity), imposing on them severe punishments, even the capital punishment, in case they violated these laws. See especially the *Seventh Partida, Titles XXIII (Law III), XXIV, XXV, XXVI.* Cf. also the detailed Indices, contained in Volume V of the edition of the *Partidas* by Gregorio López, published in Paris, by the editors Lecointe et Lasserre between the years 1840-1844, *sub* "Apóstata", "Herejes", "Judíos", "Moro", where is found the mention of other passages with dispositions against the Jews, etc.

---

[11] On the intolerant attitude in Europe see the bibliography in note 8 of these *Final remarks* and the Section *Remarks on the previous subject: Dualism outside India* of *Chapter IV* of this book.

Many of these laws of *Las Siete Partidas* concerning Jews are within the Western tradition of intolerance in regard to Jews that is already found in the *Corpus Juris Civilis* of Justinian and in the decrees dictated against them in the Councils of Toledo and by many of the kings who governed Spain. See a brief syntheses of the history of this behaviour in Salvador Minguijón Adrián, *Historia del Derecho Español*, Vol. I, pp. 234-241.

This policy of intolerance, which necessarily had to afect and limit the freedom of ideas and expression, manifested itself also in invectives full of aggressivity, which could be considered the predecessors of the violent actions of the religious civil wars and the persecutions that sadly and sinisterly darkened the history of Europe. Cf. C. Postel, *Traité des invectives*. This policy of intolerance, which limited in Europe, as already said, freedom of ideas and put an obstacle to the free development of philosophical thinking, lasted more than sixteen centuries.[12]

V.7 The gratuity of philosophical thinking

As for the idea that philosophical thinking is a search for "*truth for its own sake*", let us say here that this has been of *very limited* application in the history of Western Philosophy.

If the criterion of "*truth for its own sake*" were applied strictly for determining whether a system of *thought* is or is not *Philosophy*, many schools of philosophy would be eliminated from the History of Philosophy. Examples from Greece would be Stoicism and Epicureism, whose efforts were directed towards finding the correct way of living in

[12] According to H.B. Workman, a Member of the Board of Studies in the Faculty of Theology, London University, and Principal of Westminster Training College, in his article "Constantine", section "IV. Constantine and the Church", sub-section "(b) Constantine and heresy", in *Encyclopaedia of Religion and Ethics*, Vol. 4, p. 80: "*Constantine's whole policy as regards heresy and unity fastened upon the Church for sixteen hundred years a policy of intolerance*". It was thus the union of the political power of the state with the religious power of the Church what brought the abominable consequences of intolerance that are registered by history.

order to enjoy peace and happiness; an example from mediaeval Europe would be Christian Philosophy with its mainly religious preoccupations and its concentration and aspiration fixed on eternal Salvation. We would also reach the same conclusion if we were to analyze the works of many of the great modern European philosophers, whose real aim was often only to demonstrate via their so called *philosophical* reasoning a certain *religious* thesis to which they necessarily adhered in advance.

In relation to the *Meditationes* of Descartes, Alexander Koyre, in *Descartes und die Scholastik*, p. 12, says:

> "*It is the work of a Christian, Catholic philosopher, who fights* [streitet] *for the honor and the glory of God and his Church, and intends to demonstrate against the atheists, the skeptics, and the freethinkers the existence of God and the immortality of the soul – this bold work of mystic apologetics, ... which certainly wants to replace the overcome Metaphysics of the Aristotelian Scholastics but also endeavours to put Christian Philosophy and Theology on immovable bases*".

Descartes himself, in the *Epistola*, Vol. VII, p. 1, which precedes his *Meditationes De Prima Philosophia, in quibus Dei existentia, & animae humanae a corpore distinctio*, points out which is the *aim* of Philosophy: it has to demonstrate its two principal tenets: the existence of God and the immortality of the soul in order to convince the non-Christians. To Philosophy and to philosophers would correspond thus an apologetic and proselytist task directed to make that the "infidels" (*infideles*, p. 2), the "impious" (*impii*, p. 3) and the "atheists" (*athei*, p. 6) – as Descartes also calls them – accept the beliefs of the Christian Religion. This task was imposed on the Christian philosophers in an explicit way by the *Concilium Lateranense*. Descartes, as he himself says in p. 3, of the Latin text, did not hesitate to take on this commitment and composed these *Meditationes:*

> ... *et expresse mandat* [Concilium Lateranense sub Leone 10 habitum, sessione 8] *Christianis Philosophis ut eorum* [infidelium, impiorum, atheorum] *argumenta dissolvant, et veritatem pro viribus probent, hoc etiam aggredi non dubitavi.*

And in p. 5 of the French version by Descartes himself, Vol. IX of his *Oeuvres*:

> *... & qu'il ordonne expressément aux Philosophes Chrestiens de respondre à leurs argumens, & s'employer toutes les forces de leur esprit pour faire connoistre la verité, y'ai bien osé l'entreprendre dans cét escrit.*
>
> "... and [the *Lateran Council* under Leo 10, section 8] expressly orders the Christian Philosophers to destroy the arguments of those [infidels, impious, and atheists], and demonstrate the truth according to their forces – I did not hesitate to undertake also this task".

In turn, Leibniz composed his *Théodicée* with the aim of demonstrating God's justice and goodness, and of showing man the path he must follow. At the beginning of his treatise *Causa Dei* Leibniz clearly indicates his purpose when writing his *Théodicée*:

> Apologetica Causae Dei tractatio *non tantum ad divinam gloriam, sed etiam ad nostram utilitatem pertinet, ut tum magnitudinem ejus, id est potentiam sapientiamque colamus, tum etiam bonitatem et quae ex ea derivantur, justitiam ac sanctitatem amemus, quantumque in nobis est imitemur.*
>
> "*The apologetic treatise of the Cause of God* concerns not only the divine glory, but also our own advantage, in order that we worship His greatness, i.e. His power and wisdom, and also in order that we love His goodness and whatever derives from it, His justice and sanctity, and that we imitate them as much as it is possible to us".

And in the same work *Causa Dei* § 81 Leibniz uses the (of course erroneous) theory of Pre-formation (according to which in the egg, the sperm and the seed exists, in extremely small proportions, provided with all their characteristics, the living being or the plant that will come forth from them) with the aim to demonstrate the thesis, accepted in advance, of the transmission of the original sin of Adam and Eve to all their descendants, mankind, the sad *massa perditionis*.[13]

[13] See Section *Remarks on the previous subject: The notion of evolution in the West* in *Chapter IV* of this book.

It is also amazing how even in the field of Science still linked with Philosophy (Philosophy of Nature), one of the most powerful minds that humanity has had, Isaac Newton, subordinates his magnificent scientific work to a religious necessity. In a letter to Richard Bentley of 10 december 1692, quoted by Florian Cajori in his edition of *Principia Mathematica,* Volume II, p. 669, Newton writes:

> *"When I wrote my treatise about our system, I had an eye on such principles as might work with considering men for the belief of a Deity; and nothing can rejoice me more than to find it useful for that purpose".*

Jammer, in his quoted work p. 120, gives the following German translation of Newton's passage that can serve as an interpretation of Newton's idea: *Als ich meine Abhandlung über mein System schrieb, da dachte ich auf solche Prinzipien, welche die Menschen zum Glauben an eine Gottheit zu führen vermöchten. Nichts kann mir grössere Freude machen, als mein Werk in dieser Hinsicht hilfreich zu finden:* "When I wrote my treatise on my system, I was thinking on such principles which could lead men toward the belief in a Divinity. Nothing can give me greater joy than to find my work helpful in this respect".

In his work *Opticks* 3, q. 31, Newton reaffirms what he has said on the purpose of his treatise but extending it in a more general way to all Philosophy of Nature:

> *"... The main business of natural philosophy is to argue from phaenomena without feigning hypotheses, till we come to the very First cause ... and though every true step made in this philosophy brings us not immediately to the knowledge of the First cause, yet it brings us nearer to it".*

Colin Maclaurin, in his work *Account of Sir Isaac Newton's philosophical discoveries* published by Patrick Murdoch in 1748, in a passage quoted by Max Jammer, pp. 27-28, also affirms in general terms the subordination to Religion of the Philosophy of Nature:

> *Aber die Naturphilosophie dient höherrangigen Zielen. Ihr Werk liegt vor allem darin, dass sie eine sichere Grundlage eines natürlichen Religion und einer Moralphilosophie legt. Und dass sie uns in zufriedenstellender Weise zur Erkenntnis des Schöpfers und Lenkers des Universums leitet. Das*

> *Studium der Natur ist ein Erforschen seines Werkes: Jede neue Entdeckung eröffnet uns einen weiteren Teil seines Planes.*
>
> "But the Philosophy of Nature serves to purposes of higher rank. Its task lies above all in the fact that it establishes a surer fundament for a Natural Religion and a Moral Philosophy, and that it leads in a satisfying way to the knowledge of the Creator and Controller of the Universe. The study of nature is an exploration of His work: Each new discovery reveals us a larger part of His plan".

Western Philosophy did never forget that it has been during many centuries the *ancilla theologiae*, the "female slave of theology", and as such "she" had to serve and obey "her" *domina*, her "mistress", whose severity was known by everybody, and to have always present her interests and preoccupations; the *saṃskāras* (impressions, habits or predispositions) left by that condition survived in her for a length of time much longer than it is usually admitted.[14]

As for Indian philosophers, they were clearly aware that their activity as such had an aim external to that activity: the attainment of the Supreme Good, i.e. Liberation from reincarnations as it is expressly asserted in *Nyāyadarśana* I, 1: *niḥśreyasādhigama.*[15] This did not obstruct them in their rational task. Indian philosophers were more conscious of the links that existed between their philosophical activity and their religion.

In Hindu Philosophy this position is frankly expressed, as we said, in Gautama's *Nyāyadarśana* (Science of Logic) *sūtra* I, 1. Gautama affirms that from "*the knowledge of the true nature*" of the sixteen logical categories, which the *sūtra* enumerates, is produced "*the obtention of the supreme good*":

---

[14] Cf. the articles "Ancilla theologiae" by W. Kluxen and "Philosophie" by H. Görgemanns, in *Historisches Wörterbuch der Philosophie*, Band I, col. 294-295, and Band 7, col. 619, respectively; in *Enzyklopädie Philosophie und Wissenschaftstheorie*, Vol. I, p. 111; and "Ancilla theologiae", in J. Ferrater Mora, *Diccionario de Filosofía*, Vol. I, pp. 108-109; Jean-Luc Solère et Zénon Kaluza (éd.), *La servante et la consolatrice. La philosophie dans ses rapports avec la théologie au Moyen Age*; and P. Hadot, *Qu'est-ce que la philosophie antique.*

[15] Cf. F. Tola, "Budismo y Humanismo", in *Revista de Estudios Budistas* No. 9, México-Buenos Aires, 1995, pp. 64-70.

pramāṇaprameysaṃśayaprayojanadṛṣṭāntasiddhāntāvayavatarkanir-ṇayavādajalpavitaṇḍāhetvābhāsacchalajātinigrahasthānānāṃ tattvajñānān niḥśreyasādhigamaḥ.

According to what the commentators Vātsyāyana, Uddyotakara and Vācaspati Miśra say in relation with this *sūtra* we must understand that the expression "knowledge of the true nature (*tattvajñāna*)" means, in each science, a specific object proper to each science. In the Science of Logic, the object, whose true nature it is necessary to know, is constituted by the 16 logical categories, but it must be taken into account that the *ātman* (individual spiritual principle, the true man) belongs to one of these categories (*prameya*). Moreover, in the Science of Logic, what is obtained through this true knowledge is the *Supreme Good,* which is nothing else than Liberation from reincarnations.

Vātsyāyana's commentary related to this subject affirms:

tad idaṃ tattvajñānaṃ niḥśreyasādhigamārthaṃ yathāvidyaṃ veditavyam. Iha tvadhyātmavidyāyām ātmādijñānaṃ tattvajñānam. Niḥśreyasā-dhigamo 'pavargaprāptiḥ.

"That knowledge of the true nature [of things] with the aim of reaching the Supreme Good [spoken of in the *sūtra*] has to be known according to Science. But here in the Science of the *Ātman* [we are dealing with: Logic-Metaphysics] the knowledge of the true nature is the knowledge of the *Ātman* and the other objects [of cognition]; and the obtention of the Supreme Good is the attainment of Liberation".

The Uddyotakara's *vārttika ad locum* is very explicit and clear:

Sarvāsu vidyāsu tattvajñānam asti niḥśreyasādhigamaśceti. Trayyāṃ tā-vat kiṃ tattvajñānaṃ kaśca niḥśreyasādhigama iti? Tattvajñānaṃ tāvad agnihotrādisādhanānāṃ svāgatādiparijñānaṃ anupahatādi-parijñānaṃ ca. Niḥśreyasādhigamo 'pi svargaprāptiḥ, tathā hyatra svarga' phalaṃ śrūyata iti. Atha vārtāyāṃ kiṃ tattvajñānaṃ kaśca niḥśreyasādhigama iti? Bhūmyādiparijñānaṃ tattvajñānam, bhūmiḥ kaṇṭakādyanupaha-tetyetat tattvajñānam. Kṛṣyādya-dhigamaś ca niḥśreyasam iti, tatpha-latvāt. Daṇḍanītyāṃ kiṃ tattva-jñānaṃ kaśca niḥśreyasādhigama iti? Sāmadānadaṇḍabhedānāṃ yathākālaṃ

> *yathādeśaṃ yathāśakti viniyogas tattvajñānam, niḥśreyasaṃ pṛthivījaya iti.*
>
> "In all the Sciences there is 'knowledge of the true nature' and 'obtention of the supreme good'. What is 'knowledge of the true nature' and 'obtention of the supreme good' in the Triple [Science of the Vedas]? 'Knowledge of the true nature' is the knowledge of the appropriate and the knowledge of the not inadequate implements for the Agnihotra, and other sacrifices. 'Obtention of the supreme good' is the obtention of Heaven, since in the Vedas is said that Heaven is the result [of the rites]. In the Science of Agriculture, what is 'knowledge of the true nature' and 'obtention of the supreme good'? 'Knowledge of the true nature' is the knowledge of earth, etc. – that it be not affected by thorns, etc., that is the knowledge of the true nature. And 'obtention of the supreme good' is the obtention of the harvest. In the Political Science, what is 'knowledge of the true nature' and 'obtention of the supreme good'? 'Knowledge of the true nature' is the use of conciliation, gifts, punishments, dissensions, according to time, according to place, according to power, and 'obtention of the supreme good' is the conquest of the earth".

These texts make it clear that for Hindu thinkers knowledge does not limit to itself, it has a superior aim, a purpose different in each science and which trascends it.

V.8 The proposed Four Theses and the end of the Myth

Finally, as we have tried to show in this book, it can be said that ideas and systems of thought, which appeared in India at least until the end of the 17th century **(fourth thesis)** present numerous points of coincidence with Western ideas and systems of thought currently considered as belonging to Philosophy **(first thesis)** and that, in Indian and Western ideas and systems of thought, we can find instances presenting the same degree of irrationality **(second thesis)**.

To these two facts, we can add that, due to respect for the *Past* (assumed freely or accepted out of fear), Indian and Western thinkers were obviously subject to limitations in the exercise of the free use of reason, and that the submission of philosophical thinking to interests or purposes alien to Philosophy were equally common in India as they were in the West, the idea of a "search of truth for its own sake" evidently being nothing but a desiderate which was as remote from Indians as it was from Westerners.

As a result of the foregoing remarks, it is possible to affirm that *Philosophy* indeed did exist in India (**third thesis**) as it did in the West, with the same expectations, with the same weaknesses – thus the *myth* of the existence of *Philosophy* only in the West, and of only *Thought* in India is eliminated.

V.9 Unity in Diversity

The great emphasis we put in the similarities between Indian Philosophy and Western Philosophy points at the *Unity* of both cultures, unity that must not surprise, since both have – as we have said – a common past: the mysterious Indo-European people in whose culture the West as well as India are rooted, but this unity also must not make us forget the *Diversity* with which both cultures manifested themselves in history, developing each one of them their proper characteristics, their peculiar individuality, their identity. Coexistence of *Unity* in *Diversity* – as when the same blow of air entering into the different pipes of an organ makes them resound in a variety of musical effects.

Bibliography

A. Reference Works :

Codes noirs de l'esclavage aux abolitions. Introduction de Christiane Taubira députée de Guyane, Paris: Éditions Dalloz, 2006.

Codex Iustinianus, see *Corpus Iuris Civilis*, Volume II.

Corpus Hermeticum, tomes I-IV, texte établi par A. D. Nock, et traduit par A. J. Festugière, Paris: Les Belles Lettres, 1954-1960.

Corpus Iuris Civilis, Vols. I (2000), II (1997), III (1993), edd. Paulus Krueger, Theodorus Mommsen, *et alii*, Hildesheim: Weidmann.

Der kleine Pauly Lexicon der Antike, München: Deutscher Taschenbuch Verlag, 1979.

Dictionnaire des philosophes, Denis Huisman et alii (ed.), Deuxième édition, revue et augmentée, Paris: Presses Universitaires de France, 1993.

Doxographi Graeci, H. Diels ed., Berlin: W. de Gruyter, 1965.

Enciclopedia Iberoamericana de Filosofia, Vol. 19, *Filosofias no occidentales*, Miguel Cruz Hernández ed., Madrid: Editorial Trotta / Consejo Superior de Investigaciones Científicas, 1999.

Encyclopaedia of Religion and Ethics, J. Hastings *et alii* edd., Edinburgh: T. & T. Clark, 1964.

Encyclopaedia of Indian Philosophies, Vol. IV, Sāṃkhya. A Dualist Tradition in Indian Philosophy, edited by Gerald James Larson and Ram Shankar Bhattacharya, Delhi: Motilal Banarsidass, 1987.

Enzyclopädie Philosophie und Wissenschaftstheorie, Jürgen Mittelstrass *et alii* edd., Stuttgart-Weimar: Verlag J.B. Metzler, 1995-1996, 4 Volumes.

Esclaves des Îles françaises. Lettre sur les Noirs de Bernardin de Saint-Pierre. Présentée par Jean-Charles Pajou, Paris: Les éditeurs libres, 2006.

Grundriss der Geschichte der Philosophie, Die Philosophie des 17. Jahrhunderts, see Ueberweg, F.

Historisches Wörterbuch der Philosophie, Joachim Ritter *et alii* edd., Darmstadt: Wissenschaftliche Buchgesellschaft, 1971 ff.

La raison corrosive. Études sur la pensée critique de Pierre Bayle. Réunies par Isabelle Delpla et Philippe de Robert, Paris: Honoré Champion, 2003.

L'argomento ontologico, M.M. Olivetti ed., Padova: Cedam, 1990.

Las Siete Partidas, Gregorio López ed., Paris: Lecointe et Lasserre, 1840-1844.

Le Code noir et autres textes des lois sur l'esclavage, Paris: Éditions Sépia, 2006.

Le livre secret des Cathares. Interrogatio Iohannis. Apocryphe d'origine bogomile, edition critique, traduction, commentaire par Edina Bozóky. Préface d'Emile Turdeau, Paris: Beauchesne (CNRS), 1980.

Les Cathares. La croisade albigeoise [by different authors], Paris: Éditions Tallandier, 1999.

Les lapidaires grecs, texte établi et traduit par J. Schamp et R. Halleux, Paris: Les Belles Lettres, 1985.

Mani et le Manichéisme by several authors, in *Connaissance des Pères de l'Église* No. 83, Montrouge: Éditions Nouvelle Cité, septembre 2001.

Paulys Real-Encyclopädie der classischen Altertumswissenschaft, Stuttgart: J.B. Metzler, 1894 ff. See also *Der kleine Pauly Lexicon der Antike.*

Porphyrii Philosophi Platonici Opuscula Selecta, iterum recognovit Augustus Nauck, Hildesheim-New York: Georg Olms Verlag, 1977 (Bibliotheca Teubneriana).

Routledge Encyclopedia of Philosophy, Edward Craig *et alii* edd., London and New York: Routledge, 1998.

Spinoza Opera, Carl Gebhardt ed., Heidelberg: Carl Winter, 1972, 5 volumes.

Taishō = The Taisho Shinshu Daizokyo, J. Takakusu and K. Watanabe edd., Tokyo.

Théâtre des cruautés des hérétiques de notre temps de Richard Verstegan, Texte établi, présenté & annoté par Frank Lestringant, en Annexe *Le martyre des trente-neuf allant au Brésil* de Louis Richeome, Paris: Éditions Chandeigne, 1995.

The Cathars, see Lambert. M.

Tibetan Buddhist Canon, Tanjur and Kanjur, Peking edition, and Sde dge edition.

Tōhoku = A Complete Catalogue of the Tibetan Buddhist Canons, edited by H. Ui *et alii*, Sendai, Japan: Tōhoku Imperial University, 1934.

B. Primary Sanskrit Sources

Bhartṛharis Vākyapadīya, Wilhem Rau ed., Wiesbaden: Franz Steiner, 1977.

Khaṇḍanakhaṇḍakhāḍya of Shri Harṣa, Ganganath Jha ed., Delhi: Sri Satguru Publications, 1986.

Nyāyadarśanam, Calcutta, 1936 (reprint: Rinsen Book Co., Kyoto, 1982).

Nyāyadarśanam, Bhāṣya of Vātsyāyana, Calcutta, 1936 (reprint: Rinsen Book Co., Kyoto, 1982).

Ṛgveda-Samhitā, with the Commentary of Sāyaṇāchārya, Poona: Vaidic Samshodhan Mandal (Vedic Research Institute).

Sāṃkhyakārikās with the commentary of Gauḍapāda: in Les Strophes de Sāṃkhya (Sāṃkhya-kārikā), avec le Commentaire de Gauḍapāda, Texte Sanskrit et traduction annotée par Anne-Marie Esnoul, Paris: Les Belles Lettres, 1964.

Sāṃkhyapravacanabhāṣya of Vijñānabhikṣu, R. Garbe ed., Cambridge Mass.: Harvard Oriental Series, 1943.

Sāṃkhyasūtras in *The Sāṃkhya-pravacana-bhāṣya* of *Vijñānabhikṣu,* edited by Richard Garbe, Cambridge, Mass.: The Harvard University Press (Harvard Oriental Series), 1943.

Tattvakaumudī of Vācaspati Miśra, Srinivasa Ayyar Srinivasan ed., Hamburg: Cram, de Gruyter and Co., 1967.

Vyākaraṇa-Mahābhāṣya of Patañjali, F. Kielhorn ed., Pune [Poona]: Bhandarkar Oriental Research Institute, 1962 (3rd. edition).

Vākyapadīyam of Bhartṛhari, with the commentary of Helārāja, Kāṇḍ III, Part I, Critically edited By K.A. Subramania Iyer, Poona: Deccan College, 1963.

Vyomavatī of Vyomaśiva, in *Praśastapādabhāṣyam,* Varanasi: Chaukhamba, 1983.

The Yogasūtras of Patañjali. On Concentration of Mind, see F. Tola and C. Dragonetti (2005 5th edition).

Yogavārttika of Vijñānabhikṣu, T.S. Rukmani ed., Delhi: Munshiram Manoharlal, 1989.

Yuktidīpika, R. C. Pandeya ed., Delhi: Motilal Banarsidass, 1967.

C. Western Texts and Secondary Sources

Adam, Michel, *L'eucharistie chez les penseurs français du dix-septième siècle,* Hildesheim: Georg Olms Verlag, 2000.

Adelard of Bath, *Traktat De eodem et diverso*, H. Willner ed., Münster: Beiträge zur Geschichte der Philosophie des Mittelalters, 1903.

Agrippa, Cornelius, *De occulta philosophia*, V. Perrone Compagni ed., Leiden: E.J. Brill, 1992.

Apulée, *Opuscules philosophiques. Fragments*, texte établi, traduit et commenté par J. Beaujeu, Paris: Les Belles Lettres, 1973.

_______, *Apologie. Florides*, texte établi et traduit par P. Vallete, Paris: Les Belles Lettres, 1924.

Aristotelis Opera, I. Bekker ed., Darmstadt: Wissenschaftliche Buchgesellschaft, 1960, 2 volumes.

Aristotelis De Melisso, Xenophane, et Gorgia Disputationes cum Eleaticorum Philosophorum Fragmentis, F. G. A. Mullachius ed., Berolini: 1845.

Arnou, R., *Le désir de Dieu dans la philosophie de Plotin*, Paris: F. Alcan, 1921.

Athanase d'Alexandrie, *Contre les païens*, Paris: Les Éditions du Cerf, 1983.

Athenagoras of Athens, *Supplique au sujet des chrétiens et Sur la Résurrection des morts*, Introduction, Texte et Traduction par Bernard Pouderon, Paris: Les Éditions du Cerf, Sources Chrétiennes, 1992.

Atticus, *Fragments*, texte établi et traduit par E. des Places S.J. ed., Paris: Les Belles Lettres, 1977.

Aurelius Augustinus, *De Trinitate*, (Bücher VIII-XI, XIV-XV, Anhang: Buch V), Johann Kreuzer ed., Darmstadt: Wissenschaftliche Buchgesellschaft, 2001.

Bachelard, Gaston, *La formation de l'esprit scientifique. Contribution à une psychanalyse de la connaissance humaine*, Paris: Librairie Philosophique J. Vrin, 1969.

Belloch, Karl J., *Griechische Geschichte*, Berlin: Walter de Gruyter, 1967, 4 volumes.

Benveniste, É., *Le vocabulaire des institutions indo-européennes*, Paris: Les Éditions de Minuit, 1969, 2 volumes.

Bernabé, Albertus, *Poetae epici graeci, Testimonia et Fragmenta, Pars II, Orphicorum et orphicis similium testimonia et fragmenta,* Fasciculus I and II, München und Leipzig: K.G. Saur Verlag, 2004-2005.

Bhaduri, S., *Studies in Nyāya-Vaiśeṣika Metaphysics,* Poona: Bhandarkar Oriental Research Institute, 1975.

Bhattacharya, Ramkrishna, "Cārvāka Fragments: a new collection", in *Journal of Indian Philosophy,* Vol. 30, No. 6, December 2002 (2003), pp. 597-640.

Bloch, R., *Les prodiges dans l'Antiquité Classique,* Paris: Press Universitaires de France, 1963.

Bocheński, J. M., *Formale Logik,* Freiburg/München: Verlag K. Alber, 1996. English translation: *A History of Formal Logic,* Notre Dame (Indiana): University of Notre Dame Press, 1961.

Bonnet, Charles, *Considérations sur les corps organisés,* Paris: A. Fayard, 1985.

Bopp, Franz, *Über das Conjugationssystem der Sanskritsprache in Vergleichung mit jenem der griechischen, lateinischen, persischen und germanischen Sprache,* Frankfurt am Main: Andreäischen Buchhandlung, 1816. Reprint: Hildesheim-New York: Georg Olms Verlag, 1975.

Bordonove, Georges, *La tragédie Cathare,* Paris: Éditions Flammarion, 2004.

Bouché-Leclerq, Auguste, *Histoire de la divination dans l'Antiquité, Divination hellénique et Divination italique,* Grenoble (France): Éditions Jérôme Millon, 2003.

Bouveresse, Renée, *Spinoza et Leibniz. L'idée d'animisme universel,* Paris: Librairie Philosophique J. Vrin, 1992.

Brachtendorf, Johannes (Hrsg.), *Gott und sein Bild - Augustins De Trinitate im Spiegel gegenwärtiger Forschung,* Paderborn-München-Wien-Zürich: Ferdinand Schöningh, 2000.

Bronkhorst, J., "Why is there philosophy in India?", Amsterdam: Royal Netherlands Academy of Arts and Sciences (1998 *Gonda Lecture*), 1999.

Brown, W. Norman, "The Rigvedic equivalent for Hell", in *India and Indology*, Selected Articles, edited by Rosane Rocher, Delhi: Motilal Banarsidass, 1978, pp. 14-20.

________, "The Creation Myth of the Ṛg Veda", in *India and Indology*, Selected Articles, edited by Rosane Rocher, Delhi: Motilal Banarsidass, 1978, pp.20-34.

________, "Theories of Creation in the Ṛg Veda", in *India and Indology*, Selected Articles, edited by Rosane Rocher, Delhi: Motilal Banarsidass, 1978, pp. 42-52.

Giordano Bruno, *Oeuvres Complètes* IV, *Le souper des cendres*, Paris: Les Belles Lettres, 1994. With the Italian text: *La cena de le ceneri.*

________, *Oeuvres Complètes* V, *De l'infini, de l'Univers et des mondes*, Paris: Les Belles Lettres, 1995. With the Italian text: *De l'infinito universo e mondi.*

________, *Oeuvres Complètes* III, *De la causa, du principe et de l'un*, Paris: Les Belles Lettres, 1996. With the Italian text: *De la causa, principio et uno.*

________, *Oeuvres Complètes, Documents*, I. *Le Procès*, Paris: Les Belles Lettres, 2000.

Bulcke, C., S.J., *The Theism of Nyaya-Vaisesika. Its Origin and Early Development*, Delhi: Motilal Banarsidass, 1968.

Bunge, Mario, *La Causalidad. El principio de la causalidad en la ciencia moderna*, Buenos Aires: Editorial Sudamericana, 1997.

________, *Matérialisme et humanisme*, Montreal: Liber, 2004.

________, *Chasing Reality: Strife over Realism*, Toronto-Buffalo-London: University of Toronto Press, 2006.

Burkert, W., "Tragedie grecque et rite sacrificiel", in *Sauvages origines, Mythes et rites sacrificiels èn Grèce ancienne*, Paris: Les Belles Lettres, 1998.

Bury, J. B., *A History of Greece*, New York: The Modern Library, s.d.

Chattopadhyaya, Debiprasad, *Indian Atheism. A Marxist Analysis*, Calcutta: Manisha, 1969.

Chaturvedi, Vibha, "Causality of Kārmic Justice", in *Journal of Indian Council of Philosophical Research*, Delhi, 2001, Vol. XVIII, No. 3, pp. 129-156.

Chenu, M. D., *La théologie au douzième siècle*, Paris: Vrin, 1976.

Cicero, *De Divinatione*, Arthur Stanley Pease ed., Darmstadt: Wissenschaftliche Buchgesellschaft, 1963.

Clemens of Alexandria, *Stromata*, O. Stählin ed., Leipzig, 1905-1909.

_______, *Les Stromates*, Volume V.1 and Volume V.2, Volume VI, and Volume VII, Paris: Éditions du Cerf, Sources Chrétiennes, 1981 (V), 1999 (VI), 1997 (VII).

_______, *Le Protreptique*, Paris: Éditions du Cerf, Sources Chrétiennes, 1949.

Cohen, Esther, *Le corps du diable. Philosophes et sorcières à la Renaissance*, Clamecy (France): Éditions Lignes & Manifestes, 2004. Texte traduit de l'espagnol (Mexique) par Fabienne Bradu, México: Taurus, 2003.

Colebrooke, H.T., *Essays on the Religion and Philosophy of the Hindus*, London-Edinburgh: Williams and Norgate, Paris: B. Duprat, 1858.

Cumont, F., *Les Religions Orientales dans le Paganisme Romain*, Paris: Paul Geuthner, 1929.

_______, *The Mysteries of Mithra*, New York: Dover Publications, 1956.

_______, *Astrology and Religion among the Greeks and Romans*, New York: Dover Publications, 1960.

Damascius, *Traité des premiers principes*, Paris: Les Belles Lettres, 1986-1991, 3 volumes.

Decharme, P., *La critique des traditions religieuses chez les Grecs*, Paris: A. Picard et Fils, 1904.

Denys l' Aréopagite, *La Hiérarchie céleste*, René Roques ed., Paris: Les Éditions du Cerf, 1970.

Denzinger, H., *Enchiridion Symbolorum, Definitionum et declarationum de rebus fidei et morum*, Friburgi Brisgoviae: Herder & Co. Typographi Editores Pontificii, 1937.

Descartes, *Oeuvres de Descartes,* Charles Adam & Paul Tannery ed., Paris: J. Vrin, 1996.

Deussen, Paul, *Sechzig Upanishad's des Veda,* Darmstadt: Wissenschaftliche Buchgesellschaft, 1963.

_______, *The Philosophy of the Upanishads,* New York: Dover Publications, 1966.

de Versé, Aubert, *Traité de la liberté de conscience,* Paris : Fayard, 1998.

d'Holbach, [Paul-Henri], *Système de la nature,* [*ou des loix du monde physique et du monde moral*], Paris: Fayard, Corpus des Oeuvres de Philosophie en Langue Francaise, 1990.

d'Holbach, Paul-Henri Thiry, *Oeuvres Philosophiques,* Tome I Paris: Editions Alive, 1998.

de Labriolle, Pierre, *Histoire de la littérature latine chrétienne,* Paris: Les Belles Lettres, 1924.

de Lubac, Henri, *La rencontre du bouddhisme et de l'Occident,* Paris: Aubier, 1952.

Diels, H. / Kranz, W., *Die Fragmente der Vorsokratiker,* Berlin: Weidmannsche Verlagsbuchhandlung, 1952-1954.

Dodds, E.R., *The Greeks and the Irrational,* Berkeley: University of California Press, 1964.

Dragonetti, C., "Filosofia de la India II. Budismo", in the volume *Filosofias no occidentales de la Enciclopedia Iberoamericana de Filosofia,* Miguel Cruz Hernández ed., Madrid: Editorial Trotta/Consejo Superior de Investigaciones CientÌficas, 1999.

_______, "Los seis Maestros del Error", in *Yoga y Mística de la India,* Buenos Aires: Kier, 1978, pp. 129-153.

Droit, Roger-Pol, *Le culte du néant. Les philosophes et le Bouddha,* Paris: Éditions du Seuil, 1997.

_______, *L'Oubli de l'Inde. Une amnésie philosophique,* Paris: Presses Universitaires de France, 1989.

Ducrey, Pierre, *Le traitement des prisonniers de guerre dans la Gréce antique des origins á la conquéte romaine,* Paris: De Boccard, 1999.

Duhem, P., *Le Systéme du Monde,* Paris: Hermann, 1954 ff., 10 volumes.

Dumézil, G., *Mythe et Èpopée*, I, II, III, Paris: Gallimard, 1995.

_______, *Jupiter Mars Quirinus IV*, Paris : P.U.F., 1948.

Eberhard, W., *Histoire de la Chine*, Paris: Payot, 1952.

Eliade, M., *Yoga, Immortality and Freedom*, New York: Pantheon Books, 1958.

Epicurus, *Epistulae tres et ratae sententiae*, P. von der Mühll ed., Lipsiae (Leipzig): Teubner, 1922.

Eucken, Rudolf, *Geschichte der philosophischen Terminologie*, Hildesheim: G. Olms: 1964.

Eusèbe de Césarée, *Histoire Ecclésiastique*, Paris: Les Éditions du Cerf (Sources Chrétiennes No. 31), Tome I, 2001, Tome II, 1955, Tome III, 1993.

Ferloni, Julia, *Marchands d'esclaves. De la traite à l'abolition. Entretien avec Aimé Césaire par Jean Loiseau*, Paris: Thalassa-Edition de Conti, 2005.

Ferrater Mora, José, *Diccionario de Filosofía*, Barcelona: Editorial Ariel, 1994, 4 volumes.

Festugière, A.J., *La révélation d'Hermès Trismégiste*, Paris: Librairie Lecoffre, J. Gabalda et Cie., 1950-54, 4 volumes.

Feuerstein, G., *The Yoga-Sūtra of Patañjali. An Exercise in the Methodology of Textual Analysis*, New Delhi: Arnold-Heinemann, 1979.

_______, *The Philosophy of Classical Yoga*, Manchester: Manchester University Press, 1980.

Fichant, Michel, *Gottfried Wilhelm LEIBNIZ, De l'horizon de la doctrine humaine (1693). 'Αποκατάστασις πάντων (La Restitution Universelle) (1715)*, Textes inédits, traduits et annotés, Paris: Librairie Philosophique J. Vrin, 1991.

Flacelières, R., *Divins et oracles grecs*, Paris: Presses Universitaires de France, 1961.

Franco, Eli, *Perception, Knowledge and Disbelief. A Study of Jayarāśi's Scepticism*, Stuttgart: Franz Steiner Verlag, 1987.

Frauwallner, Erich, *Geschichte der indischen Philosophie*, Salzburg: Otto Müller Verlag, 1953-1956, 2 volumes.

Frisk, H., *Griechisches etymologisches Wörterbuch*, Heidelberg: Carl Winter Universitätsverlag, 1954-1972, 3 volumes.

Ganganath Jha, *The Khaṇḍanakhaṇḍakhāḍya of Shri Harṣa*, Delhi: Sri Satguru Publications, 1986.

Garbe, Richard, *Die Sāṃkhya-Philosophie. Eine Darstellung des indischen Rationalismus*, Leipzig: Verlag von H. Haessel, 1894.

García Belsunce, Eduardo, *Immanuel Kant. El único argumento posible para una demostración de la existencia de Dios*, Estudio preliminar, traducción y notas, Buenos Aires, Prometeo Libros, 2004.

Garnsey, Peter, *Conceptions de l'esclavage d'Aristote à saint Augustin*, Paris: Les Belles Lettres, 2004.

Garrido-Hory (ed.), Marguerite, *Routes et marchés d'esclaves. 26e colloque du GIREA, Besançon, 27-29 septembre 2001*, Paris: Presses Universitaires Franc-Comtoises (Diffusé par Les Belles Lettres), 2002.

Gaunilo, *Quid ad haec respondeat quidam pro insipiente*, in Saint Anselm, *Proslogion*.

Geldner, Karl F., *Der Rigveda in Auswahl*, Stuttgart: W. Kohlhammer, 1909.

Gerl, Hanna-Barbara, *Einführung in die Philosophie der Renaissance*, Darmstadt: Wissenschaftliche Buchgesellschaft, 1995.

Gilson, É., *Le Thomisme, Introduction au système de Saint Thomas d'Aquin*, Paris: J. Vrin, 1927.

________, *L'Esprit de la philosophie Médiévale*, Paris: J. Vrin, 1998.

Glotz, G.. *La cité grecque*, Paris: Editions Albin Michel, 1953.

González Reimann, Luis, *Tiempo cíclico y eras del mundo en la India*, México: El Colegio de México, 1988.

González Salinero, Raúl, *El antijudaísmo cristiano occidental (siglo IV y V)*, Madrid: Editorial Trotta, 2000.

Gopinath Kaviraj, M.M., "The problem of causality – Sānkhya-Yoga View", in *Selected Writings of M. M. Gopinath Kaviraj*, Varanasi: Centenary celebrations Committee, 1990.

Goudy, Henry, *Trichotomy in Roman law*, Oxford: Clarendon Press, 1910. (Reprint: Aalen: Scientia Verlag, 1980).

Graf, Fritz, *La magie dans l'Antiquité Gréco-Romaine. Idéologie et pratique*, Paris: Les Belles Lettres, 1994.

Grassmann, H., *Wörterbuch zum Rig-Veda*, Wiesbaden: Otto Harrassowitz, 1955.

Graves, R., *The Greek Myths*, Middlesex: Penguin Books, 1957.

Green, Peter, *Alexander to Actium. The Hellenistic Age*, London: Thames and Hudson, 1990.

Gregory, T., *Anima mundi. La filosofia di Guglielmo di Conches e la Scuola di Chartres*, Firenze: G.C. Sansoni, 1955.

Grousset, René, *L'empire des steppes. Attila, Gengis-Khan*, Tamerlan, Paris: Éditions Payot, 1965, (English translation: *The Empire of the Steppes*, New Brunswick N.J., USA: Rutgers, 1988).

Hacker, P., "Religiöse Toleranz und Intoleranz im Hinduismus", in *Kleine Schriften*, Wiesbaden: F. Steiner, 1978.

________, "Inklusivismus", in *Inklusivismus. Eine indische Denkform*, herausgegeben von Gerhard Oberhammer, Wien: Publications of the De Nobili Research Library, 1983,

Hadot, P., *Qu'est-ce que la philosophie antique?*, Paris: Gallimard, 1995.

Halbfass, Wilhelm, "Hegel on the Philosophy of the Hindus", in *German Scholars on India*, Vol. I, Varanasi: Chowkhamba Sanskrit Series Office, 1973,

________, *Indien und Europa. Perspektiven ihrer geistigen Begegnung*, Basel/Stuttgart: Schwabe & Co. Ag -Verlag, 1981 (revised and augmented English translation: *India and Europe. An Essay in Understanding*, New York: Suny Press, 1988).

________, *Karma und Wiedergeburt im indischen Denken*, München: Diederichs, 2000.

Hambly, G. (ed.), *Historia Universal Siglo Ventiuno, Asia Central*, Madrid: Siglo XXI, 1972.

Hamelin, O., *Le systéme de Descartes*, Paris: Librairie Félix Alcan, 1931.

Haussig, Hans Wilhem, *Die Geschichte Zentralasiens und der Seidenstrasse in Vorislamischer Zeit,* Darmstadt: Wissenschaftliche Buchgesellschaft, 1983.

Haribhadrasūri, *Yogabindu,* Ahmedabad: Bharatiya Sanskriti Vidyamandira, 1968.

Hariharānanda Āranya, *Yoga Philosophy of Patañjali,* Calcutta: University of Calcutta, 1963.

Hauer, J.W., *Der Yoga. Ein indischer Weg zum Selbst,* Stuttgart: W. Kohlhammer, 1958.

Hegel, G.W.F., *Werke,* Frankfurt am Main: Suhrkamp Verlag, 20 volumes.

———, *Vorlesungen über die Geschichte der Philosophie,* Hamburg: Felix Meiner Verlag, 1993.

———, *Leçons sur l'histoire de la philosophie,* Paris: Gallimard, 1954. 2 volumes. French translation from German by J. Gibelin.

Hornung, Eric, *Der Eine und die Vielen. Ägyptische Gottesvorstellungen,* Darmstadt: Wissenschaftliche Buchgesellschaft, 1973.

Hulin, Michel, *Hegel et l'Orient,* Paris: Vrin, 1979

———, "Spinoza l'oriental?", in *Cahiers Spinoza* 4, Paris: Éditions Réplique.

———, "Die Seelenwanderung: Indo-griechischer Mythos oder Herausforderung an das zeitgenössische Denken?", in Fritz Graf Erik Hornung Hrsg., *Wanderungen,* Wilhelm Fink Verlag.

———, *Sāṃkhya Literature,* Wiesbaden: Otto Harrassowitz, 1978.

———, "Vertige et lucidité", in *Le dépassement de soi dans la pensée philosophique,* Neuchâtel, France.

Husserl, Edmund, *Ideen zu einer reinen Phänomenologie und phänomenologische Philosophie,* Halle, 1913.

Iamblichus, *De mysteriis,* see Jamblique.

Iogna-Prat, Dominique, *Ordonner et exclure, Cluny et la société chrétienne face à l'hérésie, au judaïsme et à l'islam (1000-1150),* Paris: G.F. Flammarion, 1998.

Isidorus Hispalensis (Isidore de Séville), *Le livre des nombres. Liber numerorum*, édition, traduction et commentaire par Jean-Yves Guillaumin, Paris: Les Belles Lettres, 2005.

Jacobsen, Knut A., *Prakṛti in Sāṃkhya-Yoga*, New York: Peter Lang, 1999.

Jaeger, W., *The Theology of the Early Greek Philosophers*, Oxford: Oxford University Press, 1947.

Jamblique, *Les Mystères d'Égypte*, texte établi et traduit par Édouard des Places, S.J., Paris: Les Belles Lettres, 1996.

Jammer, Max, *Das Problem des Raumes. Die Entwicklung der Raumtheorien*, Darmstadt: Wissenschaftliche Buchgesellschaft, 1960.

Janicaud, D., *Hegel et le destin de la Grèce*, Paris: Vrin, 1975.

Johnston, E.H., *Early Sāṃkhya. An Essay on its Historical Development according to the Texts*, Delhi: Motilal Banarsidass, 1974.

Jurieu, P., *Des droits des deux souverains en matière de religion*, Paris: Fayard, 1997.

Kant, I., *Werkausgabe*, Frankfurt am Main: Suhrkamp Verlag, 12 volumes.

———, *Kritik der reinen Vernunft*, Felix Meiner Verlag: Hamburg, 1998.

———, *Der einzige mögliche Beweisgrund zu einer Demonstration des Daseins Gottes*, in Kant, *Werkausgabe*, Vol. II. See García Belsunce, Eduardo.

Keith, A.B., *The Religion and Philosophy of the Veda and Upanishads*, Cambridge, Mass.: Harvard University Press, 1925 (reprint: Delhi: Motilal Banarsidass, 1989), 2 volumes.

Kern, Otto, *Orphicorum Fragmenta*, Berlin: Weidmann, 1922.

Kirk, G.S. & Raven, J.E., *The Presocratic Philosophers*, Cambridge: University Press, 1962.

Klimke, F., *Institutiones Historiae Philosophiae*, Roma: Università Gregoriana, 1923.

Koyre, Alexander, *Descartes und die Scholastik*, Bonn: Bouvier Verlag Herbert Grundmann, 1971.

Krüger, Manfred, *Ichgeburt, Origenes und die Entstehung der christlichen Idee der Wiederverkörperung in der Denkbewegung von Pythagoras bis Lessing*, Hildesheim-Zürich-New York: Georg Olms, 1996.

Lacoste, Jean-Yves, *Dictionnaire critique de théologie*, Paris: Quadrige / PUF, 1998.

Lambert, M.D., *Medieval Heresy*, London: Edward Arnold, 1977.

_______, *The Cathars*, Oxford: Blackwell Publishers, 1998. German translation *Geschichte der Katharer*, Darmstadt: Wissenschaftliche Buchgesellschaft, 2001.

Lanata, G., *Medicina magica e religione popolare in Grecia*, Roma: Edizione dell' Ateneo, 1967.

Lange, F.A., *Geschichte des Materialismus*, Frankfurt: Suhrkamp, 1974.

Larson, G. J., *Classical Sāṃkhya. An Interpretation of its History and Meaning*, Delhi: Motilal Banarsidass, 1998.

Lea, Henri-Charles, *Histoire de l'inquisition au Moyen Age. Origines et procédures de l'inquisition. L'inquisition dans les divers pays de la chrétienté*, Grenoble: Éditions Jérôme Millon, 1997, 2 volumes.

Leibniz, G.W., *Philosophische Schriften*, Frankfurt am Main: Insel Verlag, 1986-1992, 5 volumes.

_______, *Die philosophischen Schriften*. Heraugegeben von C.I. Gerhardt, Berlin, 1875-90; Hildesheim: Georg Olms Verlag, 1996, 7 volumes.

_______, *Considérations sur la doctrine d'un Esprit Universel Unique [1702]*, in *Die philosophischen Schriften von Gottfried Wilhelm Leibniz*, C.J. Gerhardt ed., Berlin: Weidmannsche Buchhandlung, 1885, Vol. 6, pp. 529-538.

_______, *De l'horizon de la doctrine humaine*, see Fichant, M.

_______, *Opuscules philosophiques choisis*, texte latin et traduction par P. Schrecker, Paris: J. Vrin, 2001.

_______, *Opuscules et fragments inédits. Extraits des manuscripts de la Bibliothèque Royale de Hanovre*, edités par Louis Couturat, Hildesheim Zürich New York: Georg Olms Verlag, 1988.

________, *Catena mirabilium demonstrationum de summa rerum*, in *Philosophische Schriften*, Band I, Frankfurt am Main: Insel Verlag, 1986.

Lentz, Thierry, Branda, Pierre, avec la participation de Chantal Lheureux-Prévot, *Napoléon, l'esclavage et les colonies*, Paris: Fayard, 2006.

Leopardi, G., *Saggio sopra gli errori popolari degli antichi*, Torino: G. Einaudi Editore, 2003 (reprint of the original edition of 1815).

Lévi, Sylvain, *La doctrine du sacrifice dans les Brāhmaṇas*, Paris: Presses Universitaires de France, 1966.

Lévy, Carlos, *Les philosophies hellénistiques*, Paris: Librairie Générale Française, 1997.

Lieu, Samuel N.C., *Manichaeism in Central Asia and China*, Brill: Leiden-Boston-Köln: Brill, 1998.

________, *Manichaeism in Mesopotamia & the Roman East*, Leiden-Boston-Köln: Brill, 1999.

Linforth, I. M., *The Arts of Orpheus*, Berkeley and Los Angeles: University of California Press, 1941.

Locke, John, *Lettre sur la tolérance*. Texte latin et traduction française, Paris: Presses Universitaires de France, 1965.

Lucretius, *De Rerum Natura Libri Sex*, C. Bailey ed., Oxford, 1951.

Lüders, H., *Varuṇa, II Varuṇa und das Ṛita*, Göttingen: Vandenhoeck und Ruprecht, 1959.

Lullus, Raimundus, *Die neue Logik. Logica Nova*, Charles Lohr ed., Vittorio Hösle and Walburga Büchel trans., Darmstadt: Wissenschaftliche Buchgesellschaft, 2002.

Luterbacher, F., *Der Prodigienglaube und Prodigienstil der Römer*, Darmstadt: Wissenschaftliche Buchgesellschaft, 1967.

Macdonell, A.A., *The Vedic Mythology*, Varanasi: Indological Book House, 1963.

Macherey, P., *Introduction à l'Èthique de Spinoza*, Paris: Presses Universitaires de France, 1998.

Malliṣeṇa, *Syādvādamañjarī*, Bombay: Bombay Sanskrit and Prakrit Series, 1933.

Manilius, *Astronomica*, G.P. Goold ed., Leipzig: B.G. Teubner, 1998.

Marbodus Redonensis (Marbode de Rennes), *Liber lapidum. Lapidario*, Texte établi, traduit et commenté par M.E. Herrera (in Spanish), Paris: Les Belles Lettres, 2005.

Masson-Oursel, Paul, *Esquisse d'une Histoire de la Philosophie Indienne*, Paris: Paul Geuthner, 1923.

Māṭhara, *Vṛtti*, Vārāṇasi: Chaukhamba, 1990.

Mathieu, Vittorio, "L'argomento ontologico per dimostrare l'esitenza dell'etere nell' <Opus postumum> di Kant", in *L' argomento ontologico*, a cura di M.M. Olivetti, Padova: Cedam, 1990,

Mauthner, Fritz, *Der Atheismus und seine Geschichte im Abendlande*, Hildesheim-Zürich-New York: Georg Olms Verlag, 1985, 4 volumes.

Mayrhofer, M., *Kurzgefasstes etymologisches Wörterbuch des Altindischen*, Heidelberg: Carl Winter, Universitätsverlag, 1956 ff.

Méchoulan, Henry, *Le sang de l'autre ou l'honneur de Dieu*, Paris: Fayard, 1979.

Melluso, Marco, *La schiavitù nell'età giustinianea, Disciplina giuridica e rilevanza sociale*, Paris: Presses Universitaires Franc-Comtoises, 2000.

Menéndez y Pelayo, Marcelino, *Historia de los heterodoxos españoles*, Buenos Aires: Emecé Editores, 1945, 8 volumes.

Miller, Joseph C., *Slavery and Slaving in World History. A Bibliography*, Millwood, New York: Kraus International Publishers, 1999.

Minguijón Adrián, Salvador, *Historia del Derecho Español*, Vol. I, Barcelona: Editorial Labor, 1927.

Ming-Wood, Liu, "The Doctrine of the Buddha-Nature in the Mahāyāna Mahāparinirvāṇasūtra", in *The Journal of the International Association of Buddhist Studies*, Vol. V, No. 2, 1982, (Spanish version in *Revista de Estudios Budistas*, No. 6, Octubre 1993-Marzo 1994.

_______, "The Problem of the *icchantikas* in the Mahāyāna Mahāparinirvāṇasūtra", in *The Journal of the International Association of Buddhist Studies*, Vol. VII, No. 1, 1984.

Mittal, K.K., *Materialism in Indian Thought*, Delhi: Munshiram Manoharlal Publishers, 1974.

Moltmann, J., "Gedanken zur 'trinitarischen Geschichte Gottes' ", in *Evangelische Theologie* No. 35, 1975.

Mondin, Battista, "L'argomento <ontologico> nella metafisica dell'essere di San Tommaso d'Aquino", in *L'argomento ontologico*, pp. 161-171.

Moore, R.I., *The Formation of a Persecuting Society. Power and deviance in Western Europe 950-1250*, Oxford: Basil Blackwell Ltd., 1987. (French translation: *La persécution. Sa formation en Europe (Xe-XIIIe)*, Paris: Les Belles Lettres, 1991).

_______, *Le Dieu des philosophes (Leibniz, Kant et nous)*, Paris: Librairie Philosophique J. Vrin, 1969.

Moreau, J., *L'âme du monde de Platon aux Stoiciens*, Hildesheim: Olms, 1981.

Müller, Max, *India What can it teach us?*, Delhi: Munshiram Manoharlal, 1961.

Murakami, Shinkan, "What is *caintanya*? – eternal or non-eternal", in *Asiatische Studien* LIII. 3. 1999.

Nasemann, Beate, *Theurgie und Philosophie in Jamblichs de Mysteriis*, Stuttgart: B.G. Teubner, 1991.

Newton, Sir Isaac, *Principia. Mathematical Principles of Natural Philosophy and His System of the World*, translated into English by Andrew Motte in 1729. The translations revised, and supplied with an historical and explanatory appendix, by Florian Cajori, Volume One: *The Motion of Bodies*, Volume Two: *The System of the World*, Berkeley, Los Angeles, London: University of California Press, 1962.

Newton, Isaac, Optics = *Optice : sive de reflexionibus, refractionibus, inflexionibus et coloribus Lucis, Libri tres. Auctore Isaaco Newton*, Latine reddidit Samuel Clarke, Editio Novissima, Lausannae & Genevae, Sumpt. Marci-Michaelis Bousquet & Sociorum, 1740.

Nicolaus of Cusa = Nikolaus von Kues, *De docta ignorantia*, in *Philosophische-theologische Werke*, Band I, Darmstadt: Wissenschaftliche Buchgesellschaft, 2002, 4 volumes.

Niel, Fernand, *Albigeois et Cathares*, Paris: Presses Universitaires de France, 2000.

Ninck, M., *Die Bedeutung des Wassers im Kult und Leben der Alten*, Darmstadt: Wissenschaftliche Buchgesellschaft, 1967.

Nirenberg, David, *Violence et minorités au Moyen Âge*, Paris: Presses Universitaires de France, 2001.

Norden, E., *Agnostos Theos*, Stuttgart und Leipzig: B.G. Teubner, 1996.

Novellae, see *Corpus Iuris Civilis*, Volume III.

Numénius, *Fragments*, texte établi et traduit par Édouard des Places, S.J., Paris: Les Belles Lettres, 1973.

Oberlies, Thomas, *Die Religion des Ṛgveda, Erster Teil – Das Religiöse System des Ṛgveda –*, Wien: Publications of The De Nobili Research Library, 1998-1989.

Oberste, Jörg, *Der "Kreuzzug" gegen die Albigenser. Ketzerei und Machtpolitik im Mittelalter*, Darmstadt: Wissenschaftliche Buchgesellschaft, 2003.

Obolensky, Dmitri, *The Bogomils. A Study in Balkan Neo-Manichaeism*, Twickenham Middlesex: Anthony C. Hall, 1972.

Oeing-Hanhoff, Ludger, "Hegels Trinitätslehre. Zur Aufgabe ihrer Kritik und Rezeption", in *Theologie und Philosophie* No. 52, 1977, pp. 378-407.

O'Flaherty, Wendy Doniger, (ed.), *Karma and Rebirth in Indian Classical Traditions*, Delhi: Motilal Banarsidass, 1983.

Oldenberg, H., *Die Religion des Veda*, Berlin: Verlag von Wilhem Herz, 1894. English translation: *The Religion of the Veda*, Delhi: Motilal Banarsidass, 1988.

________, *Vorwissenschaftliche Wissenschaft, Die Weltanschauung der Brāhmaṇa-Texte*, Göttingen: Vandenhoeck & Ruprecht, 1919.

________, *Vedaforschung* (1905), in *Kleine Schriften III*, Stuttgart: Franz Steiner Verlag, 1993.

________, *Indien und die Religionswissenshaft* (1906), in *Kleine Schriften III*, pp. 1689-1746.

Olivares Guillem, A., "Prisciliano entre la ortodoxia y la heterodoxia. Influencia del ambiente político y religioso en la evolución histórica del priscilianismo (ss. IV-VI d.C.)", in *Ilu, revista de ciencias de las religiones,* Vol. 7, Madrid, 2002 pp. 97-120.

Oracles Chaldaïques, texte établi et traduit par Édouard des Places, Paris: Les Belles Lettres, 1996.

Origen = *Origenes vier Bücher von den Prinzipien,* herausgegeben, übersetzt, mit kritischen und erläuternden Anmerkungen versehhen von Herwig Görgemanns und Heinrich Karpp, Darmstadt: Wissenschaftliche Buchgesellschaft, 1992.

Otto, Walter, *Der Dichter und die alten Götter,* Frankfurt am Main: Vittorio Klostermann, 1942.

________, *Theophania,* Hamburg: Rowohlt, 1956.

________, *Die Götter Griechenlands,* Frankfurt am Main: Verlag Schulte-Bulmke, 1961.

________, *Das Wort der Antike,* Darmstadt: Wissenschaftliche Buchgesellschaft, 1962.

Paris, Erna, *El fin de los días. Los judíos en España: una historia de tolerancia y tiranía,* Buenos Aires: Emecé, 2003.

Pascal, *Pensées,* ed. L. Lafuma, Paris: Éditions du Seuil, 1962.

________, *Pensées,* Texte de l'édition Brunschvicg, Paris: Librairie Garnier Frères, s.d.

Pāthak, Sarvānanda, *Cārvaka Darśana ki Śāstrīya Samīkṣā,* Varanasi: Chaukhamba, 1965.

Pétré-Grenouilleau, Olivier, *Les traits négrières, Essai d'histoire globale,* Paris: Gallimard, 2004.

Philostratus, *The Life of Apollonius of Tyana,* The Loeb Classical Library, 1960.

Piclin, Michel, *Les Philosophies de la Triade ou l' histoire de la structure ternaire,* Paris: Vrin, 1980.

Pincherle, Alberto, *Sant'Agostino,* Bari: Laterza, 1930.

Platon, *Oeuvres complètes,* texte établi et traduit par A. Rivaud et *alii,* Paris: Les Belles Lettres.

Plotin, *Ennéades,* tomes I-VI, texte établi et traduit par Émile Bréhier, Paris: Les Belles Lettres, 1924-1954.

Plutarque, *Oeuvres morales, Tome XII, 2e partie, Opinions des philosophes,* texte établi et traduit par Guy Lachenaud, Paris: Les Belles Lettres, 2003.

(Plutarch), *De placitis philosophorum* in Plutarch, *Moralia,* Vol. IX, The Loeb Classical Library.

Postel, Claude, *Traité des invectives au temps de la Réforme,* Paris: Les Belles Lettres, 2004.

Powell, E.E., *Spinozas Gottesbegrieff,* Hildesheim: G. Olms Verlag, 1980.

Proclus, *The Elements of Theology,* a revised text by E.R. Dodds, Oxford at the Clarendon Press, 1964.

Pring-Mill, R.D.F., "The Trinitarian World Picture of Ramon Lull", in *Romanistisches Jahrbuch* 7 (1955/56), pp. 229-256.

Reitzenstein, R., *Die hellenistischen Mysterienreligionen,* Darmstadt: Wissenschaftliche Buchgesellschaft, 1966.

Rémond, René, *Religion et société en Europe: Essai sur la sécularisation des sociétés européennes aux XIXe et XXe siècles (1789-1998),* Paris: Éditions du Seuil, 1998.

Renou, L., *Les maîtres de la philologie védique,* Paris: Librairie Orientaliste P. Geuthner, 1928.

Revel, J.P., *Descartes inutile et incertain,* Paris: Stock, 1998.

Rikhof, Herwy, "Aquinas and the <<ratio Anselmi>>, in *L'argomento ontologico.*

Ries, Julien, "Bouddhisme et manichéisme. Les etapes d'une recherche", in *Indianisme et Bouddhisme. Mélanges offerts à Mgr Ètienne Lamotte,* Louvain-la-neuve: Institut Orientaliste, 1980.

Riepe, Dale, *The Naturalistic Tradition in Indian Thought,* Delhi: Motilal Banarṣidass, 1964.

Rohde, E., *Psyche, Seelencult und Unsterblichkeitsglaube der Griechen I,* Darmstadt: Wissenschaftliche Buchgesellschaft, 1961.

Roquebert, Michel, *Histoire des Cathares. Hérésie, Croisade, Inquisition du Xe au XIVe siècle,* France: Perrin, 1999 et 2002.

Rossi, Paolo, *La naissance de la science moderne en Europe*, Paris: Éditions du Seuil, 1999 (French translation from the Italian original).

Ruben, Walter, *Die Philosophen der Upanishaden*, Bern: A. Francke Verlag, 1947.

Saint Anselm, *Proslogion*, in *L'Oeuvre d'Anselme de Cantorbéry*, Tome Premier, Paris: Les Éditions du Cerf, 1986.

Saint Augustin, *Oeuvres de Saint Augustin, 17. Six Traités antimanichéens*, Paris: Bibliothèque Augustinienne Desclée de Brouwer, 1960.

________, *Confessions*, Paris: Les Belles Lettres, 1925.

________, *Oeuvres de Saint Augustin. La cite de Dieu. De civitate Dei*, Bourges: Desclée de Brouwer-Institut d'Études Augustiniennes.

________, *De Trinitate*, see Aurelius Augustinus.

Saint Thomas = Thomas von Aquins, *Summa contra gentiles*, T. Schönberger ed., Darmstadt: Wissenschaftliche Buchgesellschaft, 2001.

________, = Sancti Thomae de Aquino, *Summa Theologiae*, Milano: Edizioni Paoline, 1988.

Saloustios, *Des Dieux et du Monde*, texte établi et traduit par Gabriel Rochefort, Paris: Les Belles Lettres, 1960.

San Agustín, *Obras Completas de San Agustín, Escritos antimaniqueos*, Vol. XXX and XXXI, Madrid: Biblioteca de Autores Cristianos.

Scharfe, H., *Grammatical Literature*, Wiesbaden: Otto Harrassowitz, 1977. Vol. V, Fasc. 2, of *A History of Indian Literature* edited by Jan Gonda.

Schelling, F.W.J., *Von der Weltseele*, Hamburg: Friedrich Perthes, first edition 1798, second edition 1806, and third edition 1809.

Schmidinger, Heinrich (Hrsg.), *Wege zur Toleranz. Geschichte einer europäischen Idee in Quellen*, Darmstadt: Wissenschaftliche Buchgesellschaft, 2002.

Schuhl, P.M., *Essai sur la formation de la pensée grecque*, Paris: Presses Universitaires de France, 1949.

________, *Platon el l'art de son temps*, Paris: P.U.F., 1952.

Schultz, J.H., *Das autogene Training*, Leipzig: Thieme, 1932.

Schwenn, F., *Die Menschenopfer bei den Griechen und Römern*, Giessen: Verlag von Alfred Töpelmann, 1915.

Scotus Erigena, *De divisione naturae* in *Joannis Scoti Opera*, Migne, Patrologia Latina (Vol. 122), reprint: Turnhout (Belgium): Brepols, 1999.

Seeck, Otto, *Geschichte des Untergangs der antiken Welt*, Stuttgart: Primus Verlag, 2000, 6 volumes.

Sertillanges, Antoine, R.P., *Les grandes thèses de la philosophie thomiste*, Bloud et Gay, 1928.

Sinha, Jadunath, *A History of Indian Philosophy*, Calcutta: Vol. I, Sinha Publishing House, 1956, and Vol. II, Central Book Agency, 1952.

Solère, Jean-Luc, et Kaluza, Zénon (éd.), *La servante et la consolatrice. La philosophie dans ses rapports avec la théologie au Moyen Age*, Paris: Vrin, 2002.

St. Augustine, see San Agustín = Saint Augustine.

Stein, R.A., "Une mention du manichéisme dans le choix du bouddhisme comme religion d'État par le roi tibetain Khri-sroṅ lde-bcan", in *Indianisme et Bouddhisme. Mélanges offerts à Mgr Étienne Lamotte*, Louvain: Institut Orientaliste, 1980.

St. Thomas = Sancti Thomae de Aquino, *Summa Theologiae*, Milano: Edizione Paoline, 1988.

Suárez de la Torre, E., "Oráculos de Apolo en la Grecia Antigua" (Bibliografía), in *'Ilu, revista de ciencias de las religiones*, N⁰ 4, 1999, pp. 371-386.

Suarez-Nani, Tiziana, *Les anges et la philosophie*, Paris: J. Vrin, 2002.

Synesii Cyrenensis, *De Insomniis* ["On dreams"], in *Opuscula*, N. Terzaghi ed., Roma: Academia Lynceorum, 1944.

Takashi, Iwata, *Sahopalambhaniyama*, Stuttgart: Franz Steiner Verlag, 1991.

Taubira, Christiane, *L'esclavage raconté à ma fille*, Paris: Bibliophane-Daniel Radford, 2002.

Theodoret de Cyr, *Thérapeutique des maladies helléniques*, Texte critique, Introduction, Traduction et Notes par Pierre Canivet, Paris: Les Éditions du Cerf, 2000 (revised and corrected reprint of the first edition).

Thieme, Paul, review of Heinrich Lüders *Varuṇa*, in P. Thieme, *Kleine Schriften*, Wiesbaden: Franz Steiner Verlag, Teil 2, 1971, pp. 777-788.

Tola, F., "Muerte e inmortalidad en el *Rig Veda* y en el *Atharva Veda*", in F. Tola y C. Dragonetti, *Yoga y Mística de la India*, Buenos Aires: Editorial Kier, 1978, pp. 70-90.

_______, "Fundamentals Principles of Indian Philosophy", in *Proceedings of the Fifth World Sanskrit Conference*, New Delhi: Rashtriya Sanskrit Sansthan, 1985, pp. 680-688.

_______, "Tres concepciones del hombre en la Filosofía de la India", in *Pensamiento*, Vol. 42, Madrid, 1986, pp. 29-46.

_______, "Budismo y Humanismo", in *Revista de Estudios Budistas* No. 9, México-Buenos Aires, 1995, pp. 60-87.

_______, "Filosofía de la India I. Vedismo, Brahmanismo, Hinduismo", in the volume *Filosofías no occidentales de la Enciclopedia Iberoamericana de Filosofía*, Miguel Cruz Hernández ed., Madrid: Editorial Trotta/Consejo Superior de Investigaciones Científicas, 1999.

Tola, F. and Dragonetti, C., "Misticismo y Yoga", in *Revista Latinoamericana de Filosofía*, Vol. I, N° 1, March, 1975, pp. 61-63.

_______, *Yoga y Mística de la India*, Buenos Aires: Editorial Kier, 1978.

_______, "Anāditva or beginninglessness in Indian Philosophy", in *Annals of the Bhandarkar Oriental Research Institute*, Poona, 1980, pp. 1-20.

_______, "Saṃsāra y Nirvāṇa", in F. Tola and C. Dragonetti, *Filosofía y Literatura de la India*, Buenos Aires: Editorial Kier, 1983.

_______, Āryabhavasaṃkrāntināmamāhāyanasūtra: The noble sūtra on the passage through existences", in *Buddhist Studies Review*, Vol. 3, No. 1, 1986, pp. 3-18.

_______, "On the Yogasūtras of Patañjali", in *Annals of the Bhandarkar Oriental Research Institute*, Pune (Poona), India, Vols. LXXII and LXXIII, 1991-1992, pp. 437-462.

_______, "Buddhist Conception of Reality", in *Journal of Indian Council of Philosophical Research*, Delhi, 1996, Vol. XIV, No. 1, pp. 35-64 (Spanish version: "La concepción budista de la realidad", in *Anales de la Sociedad Científica Argentina*, Año 1999, Vol. 229, No. 1 pp. 65-88.

_______, "The system of Śaṅkara: Reality, Illusion, Perpectivism", in *Indologica Taurinensia*, Vol. XXVI, 2000, Torino, Italy pp. 161-186.

_______, *The Yogasūtras of Patañjali. On concentration of Mind*, Delhi: Motilal Banarsidass, 2005 (Fifth edition).

_______, "Buddhism and Justification of Violence", in *Hokke Bunka Kenkyu*, Tokyo, No. 27, March, 2001 pp. 63-100.

_______, "Los estudios lingüísticos en la India Antigua I", in *Argos* 25 (Buenos Aires, 2001), pp. 127-150, y "Los estudios lingüísticos en la India Antigua II"(Pāṇini), in *Argos* 26 (Buenos Aires, 2002), pp. 159-185.

_______, "El sistema de Shaṅkara. Realidad, ilusión, perspectivismo", in *'Ilu. Revista de Ciencias de las Religiones*, Vol. 7, Madrid, 2002, pp. 141-169.

_______, *Cinco Sūtras del Mahāyāna*, New Jersey: Primordia, 2002.

_______, "Lo que la filosofía de la India le debe a Hegel", in *Pensamiento*, Vol. 58, núm. 222, Madrid, sept.-dic. 2002, pp. 353-385.

_______, "Rāmānuja. No-dualidad calificada. Realismo, teísmo, panteísmo", in *Boletín de la Asociación Española de Orientalistas*, Vol. XXXVIII, Año 2002, Madrid, pp. 271-288.

_______, "What Indian philosophy owes Hegel", in *Annals of the Bhandarkar Oriental Research Institute*, Poona, India, Vol. LXXXIII, 2003.

_______, "Aportes desde la Filosofía de la India: Multilateralidad, Perspectivismo, Tolerancia, Inclusivismo, rechazo de todo Etnocentrismo", in *América*, Vol. IX. Córdoba, Argentina: Editorial Alejandro Korn, 2003 (Proceedings of the International Congress of Philosophy, held at Cordoba, Argentina, November 2003).

_______, *Being as Consciousness. The Yogācāra Philosophy of Buddhism*, Delhi: Motilal Banarsidass, 2004.

_______, *Filosofía de la India. Del Veda al Vedānta. El sistema Sāṃkhya*, Barcelona: Editorial Kairós, 2010.

Trevelyan, H., *Goethe and the Greeks*, Cambridge: Cambridge University Press, 1942.

Tucci, G., *Minor Buddhist Texts*, Part II, Roma: Istituto Italiano per il Medio ed Estremo Oriente, 1958.

_______, "Linee di una storia del Materialismo indiano", in *Opera Minora*, Roma: Dott. G. Bardi Editore, Vol. 1, 1971, pp. 49-155.

Ueberweg, Friedrich, *Grundriss der Geschichte der Philosophie, Die Philosophie des 17. Jahrhunderts*, Basel: Schwabe & Co. Verlag, 1993.

Uray, G., "Tibet's connections with Nestorianism and Manicheism in the 8th-10th centuries", in *Contributions on Tibetan Language, History and Culture*, edited by Ernst Steinkellner and Helmut Tauscher (*Proceedings of the Csoma De Körös Symposium Held at Velm-Vienna*, Austria, 13-19 September 1981), Vol. I, Delhi: Motilal Banarsidass, 1995.

Vaneigem, Raoul, *Les hérésies*, Paris: Presses Universitaires de France, 1997.

Vergès, Françoise, *La mémoire enchaînée. Questions sur l'esclavage*, Paris: Albin Michel, 2006.

Vogel, Claus, *The Teachings of the Six Heretics*, Wiesbaden: Franz Steiner, 1970.

Vogt, Joseph, *Sklaverei und Humanität im klassischen Griechentum*, Wiesbaden: Verlag der Akademie der Wissenschaften und der Literatur in Mainz in Kommission bei Franz Steiner Verlag GMBH, 1953.

Voltaire, *Traité sur la tolérance*, Paris: GF Flammarion, 1989.

von Arnim, J. (ed.), *Stoicorum veterum fragmenta*, Suttgart: B.G. Teubner, 1979, 4 volumes.

von Gabain, Annemarie, *Einführung in die Zentralasienkunde*, Darmstadt: Wissenschaftliche Buchgesellsschaft, 1979.

von Glasenapp, Helmuth, *Die Philosophie der Inder*, Stuttgart: Alfred Kröner Verlag, 1958.

von Glasenapp, Helmuth, *Das Indienbild deutscher Denker*, Stuttgart: K.F. Koehler Verlag, 1960.

von Harnack, Adolf, *Lehrbuch der Dogmengeschichte*, Tübingen: J.C.B. Mohr (Paul Siebeck), 1990. First edition: 1886.

Waldc, Alois, *Lateinisches etymologisches Wörterbuch*, Heidelberg: Carl Winter's Universitätsbuchhandlung, 1910.

Walli, Koshelya, *Theory of karman in Indian Thought*, Varanasi: Bharata Manisha, 1977.

Wallon, H., *Historie de l'esclavage dans l'antiquité*, Paris: Bouquins, 1988.

Weinreich, Otto, *Antike Heilungswunder. Untersuchungen zum Wunderglauben der Griechen und Römer*, Berlin: Walter de Gruyter & Co., 1969.

Werner, E. und Heinrichs, J. (ed.), *Sklaven und Freigelassene in der Gesellschaft der römischen Kaiserzeit*, Darmstadt: Wissenschaftliche Buchgesellschaft, 1993.

Wilkens, Jens, *Alttürkische Handschriften*. Teil 8. *Manichäisch-türkische Texte der Berliner Turfansammlung*, Stuttgart: Franz Steiner Verlag, 2000.

Willson, A. Leslie, *A Mythical Image: The Ideal of India in German Romanticism*, Durham: Duke University Press N.C., 1964.

Windisch, Ernst, *Geschichte der Sanskrit-Philologie und indischen Altertumskunde*, Strassburg: Verlag von Karl J. Trübner, 1917.

_______, "Ueber den Sitzt der Denkenden Seele, besonders bei den Indern und Griechen", in *Kleine Schriften*, Stuttgart: F. Steiner, 2001,

Winternitz, M., *A History of Indian Literature*, Vol. I, New Delhi: Oriental Books Reprint Corporation, 1972 (English translation from the German original revised by the author).

Wolff, Christian, *Psychologia rationalis [methodo scientifica pertractata]*, Frankfurt und Leipzig, 1740; Hildesheim-Zürich-New York: G. Olms, 1994, critical edition by Jean École.

Woods, J.H., *The Yoga-system of Patañjali. On the Ancient Hindu Doctrine of Concentration of Mind*, Delhi: Motilal Banarsidass, 1966 (Harvard Oriental Series Volume Seventeen).

Yovel, Yirmiyahu, *Spinoza and other Heretics*, Princeton: Princeton University Press, 1992.

Zander, Helmut, *Geschichte der Seelenwanderung in Europa. Alternative religiöse Traditionen von der Antique bis Heute*, Darmstadt: Wissenschaftliche Buchgesellschaft, 1999.

Zeller, E., *Die Philosophie der Griechen in ihrer geschichtlichen Entwicklung*, Hildesheim Zürich, New York: Georg Olms Verlag, 1990, 6 volumes.

Zimmer, H., *Altindisches Leben. Die Cultur der vedischen Arier nach den Saṃhitā dargestellt*, Hildesheim: New York, Georg Olms Verlag, 1973.

Zintzen, Clemens, (ed.), *Der Mittelplatonismus*, Darmstadt: Wissenschaftliche Buchgesellschaft, 1981.

Index

A

D

E

F

G

N

O

T

U